Le Morte Darthur

In sending out this second instalment of Dr. Sommer's Edition of Malory the Publisher begs to thank the Original Subscribers for the patience with which they have waited for it. As will be seen by the Preface, a third instalment has still to be issued. The Publisher trusts that Original Subscribers will appreciate the fact that when they have received this third instalment considerably more will have been supplied to them than was contemplated when the Subscription price was fixed at 21s. The Original Subscribers will easily understand that this price cannot be remunerative, and the Publisher appeals to them with confidence to aid in increasing the sale of this great Edition by mentioning it to their friends. The present Subscription price (valid up to the publication of Part III.) is 30s. for Small Paper Copies, and £5 5s. for the few remaining Large Paper Copies. Even at this advanced price Sommer's Malory is probably the cheapest book of its class ever offered to the public.

PREFACE.

WHEN, two years ago, I resolved upon reproducing the editio princeps of Sir Thomas Malory's "Le Morte Darthur," I determined that, as far as lay within my power, my edition should be a standard work of English literature, and should serve as a worthy token of the gratitude which, in common with all scholars who have worked at the British Museum, I feel towards the English people for the unrivalled organisation of that magnificent institution, and towards the unfailing courtesy and helpfulness of its officials. Bearing this high purpose in my mind, I have done my utmost to test and sift every question relating to this best of all English romances, as Sir Walter Scott so rightly styles it. Whatever shortcomings there may be in my humble work, they are not, I can honestly say, due to lack of zeal and energy. I have hopes that this will be recognised by the world of scholarship to which I offer the result of my labours.

The consequence of this purpose, from which I have never swerved, has been a considerable delay in the issue of my prolegomena to Caxton's reprint. This delay, though chiefly due to ill-health, which necessitated abstention from work during several months, is also partly due to the fact that I was unable at the outset to clearly recognise the magnitude of the task that I had taken upon me. I found, for instance, the investigations into the question of Malory's sources longer and more arduous than I had anticipated from the very scanty remarks in even important works bearing on this subject. To discuss this theme adequately required much more time

and space than I had at first calculated. With the concurrence
of my publisher, I therefore determined, instead of bringing all
the editorial matter into the second volume, to divide it, and to
issue first the critical and philological apparatus, and, independently,
in a third volume the literary discussion.

The second volume now lies before the reader, comprising the
Bibliographical History of Malory's romance, a substantially complete
List of Various Readings between Caxton's and Wynkyn de Worde's
second edition, an exhaustive Index raisonné of Names and Places,
Notes on the Language of Malory's work, etc., and a Glossary.
The third volume, containing my Treatise on the Sources[1] and Mr.
Andrew Lang's Essay on Malory's Prose Style, is being actively
pushed forward, and will be issued as soon as is compatible with
a thorough examination of the complex questions involved. I trust
that original subscribers will feel compensated for the delay by the
greater completeness of what is offered to them. I venture also
to think that those who use this edition will find it a decided
advantage to have the critical and the literary apparatus in distinct
volumes, though those who are not so minded will be able to bind
the two in one if they wish.

It only remains for me to acquit myself of the pleasant duty of
thanking all those who have aided me in my task.

I must again renew my expressions of gratitude to Mrs. Abby E.
Pope, of Brooklyn, N.Y., for her fresh collation of the four pages I sent
for the second time to America, and to His Excellency Herr Dr. von
Gossler for his grant of an additional subsidy from Prussian Government funds. To Sir Edward Strachey, Bart., I am indebted for the
use of his private copy of Southey's edition, containing his collations
with the Althorp and Osterley Park copies of the Caxton. To the
authorities of the British Museum, and in especial to Dr. Richard
Garnett, to Mr. W. Y. Fletcher, and to Mr. E. J. Scott, of the MSS.
Department, I am deeply beholden for the facilities afforded me in

---

[1] Concerning the sources of "Le Morte Darthur," see my letter to *The Academy*
London, January 4th, 1890.

the course of my studies. Mr. Henry Bradley, one of the editors of the great English Dictionary on Historical Principles, assisted me with his kind advice, and placed at my disposal the rich apparatus of texts and books of reference of the Delegates of the Clarendon Press deposited at the British Museum. To my eminent friend Mr. William Blades I owe not only the information derived from his great work on England's first printer, but also generous help spontaneously rendered me at a critical moment. Last, not least, I must thank my friend Mr. Alfred Nutt for advice and assistance of every kind rendered me during the whole period I was engaged on this work. It is to his love for Arthurian romance, to his enthusiasm for scholarly studies, that these volumes owe their existence.

H. OSKAR SOMMER.

EARTHAM HOUSE, CHICHESTER,
March 1890.

CONTENTS.

INTRODUCTION.

SIR THOMAS MALORY AND THE VARIOUS EDITIONS
OF "LE MORTE DARTHUR."

HE cycle of stories of King Arthur and the Knights of the Round Table, known as "Le Morte Darthur," was first presented to us in a volume by England's earliest printer, William Caxton. About the personality of Sir Thomas Malory[1] very little indeed is known, and this little must be gleaned from Caxton's preface and colophon. There we read that Thomas Malory was a knight, that he completed his work in the ninth year of the reign of King Edward IV.—*i.e.*, 1470—twenty-five years before it saw the light *fifteen* of day in print. Caxton further states that Malory "reduced" his work from certain books in French, and that he was the servant of Jesu both day and night, which fact and the general tone of the "Morte Darthur," have sometimes given rise to the hypothesis that he was a priest. The name "Malory" occurs in Leland's time[2] in Yorkshire, and is quoted in the next century in Burton's "Description of Leicestershire,"[3] but no clue can be found to connect the

---

[1] The name "Malory," is also sometimes spelt "Malorye" and "Maleore." See Caxton, p. 861*, line 9; also, W. de Worde, Copland, East and Stansby.

[2] John Leland's "Itinerary," 2nd ed., Oxford, 1744, vol. viii. p. 22: "There be two Lordshipps lyenge not very far from Ripon, that is Norton Conyers and Hutton Coniers. Norton hathe Northeton Coniers, and Malory hathe Hutton Coniers. Thes Lands cam to their Aunciters by two doughtars, Heirs Generall of that Coniers Malory hath another Place caullyd Highe Studly, a litle from Fontaines."

[3] W. Burton, "Description of Leicestershire," 1st ed. 1622, 2nd ed. Lynn, 1777, folio, p. 140, Thomas Malory; p. 262, Sir Thomas Malory, knyght of Winwick, Newbould and Swinford, 19, 27.

author of the "Morte Darthur" with the bearers of his name. The
"Bibliographia Britannica"[1] says that Leland, and others after him,
stated Malory to be a Welshman, but I can find no reference to this
fact in Leland's works.

The "Morte Darthur" has been in all twelve times printed or
edited previously to the present edition: seven times in black letter
and five times in Roman type.

BLACK LETTER.				ROMAN TYPE.		
1. Caxton	.	. . 1485 folio.	viii.	Hazelwood .	. 1816	3 vols. 12mo.
2. W. de Worde	.	. 1498 ,,	ix.	Walker's Class	. 1816	2 vols. 12mo.
3. W. de Worde	.	. 1529 „	x.	R. Southey	. 1817	2 vols. 8vo.
4. W. Copland	.	. 1557 ,,	xi a.	Th. Wright	. 1856	3 vols. 8vo.
5. Th. East	.	about 1585 ,,	b.	Th. Wright	. 1866	,, 2nd ed.
6. Th. East	.	about 1585 4to.	xii a.	Sir E. Strachey	. 1868	Globe ed.
7. W. Stansby .	.	. 1634 b.	b.	„ „	. 1880	„

W. Caxton's impression was finished, according to his own statement, in 1485.[2] He was induced to print the book "by many noble
and dyuers gentylmen of thys royame." This edition was brought out
in folio and printed in black letter. Only two copies of this first and
original edition are known to exist. Of a third copy the second leaf of
the table of contents of the book is alone preserved.[3] One of the two
above-mentioned copies is throughout perfect and in good condition,
and is unanimously considered one of the finest specimens of early
printing. Belonging originally to the Harleian Library, this copy was
sold to the Earl of Jersey for his library at Osterley Park. In 1885
it became the property of Mrs. Abby E. Pope, of Brooklyn, N.Y., in

---

[1] "Bibliographia Britannica," vol. iii. p. 372, "Caxton:" "If this Sir Thomas
Malory was a Welshman, as Leland and others after him assert, he was most likely
a Welsh priest."

[2] (a) W. Blades, "The Life and Typography of William Caxton." London, 1861-3,
folio, vol. ii. p. 178.

(b) "Bibliotheca Spenceriana, or a Descriptive Catalogue of the Books printed in the
Fifteenth Century, in the Library of George John, Earl Spencer, K.G., &c." by T. F.
Dibdin. London, 1815, folio, vol. iv. pp. 403-9.

(c) Dibdin, "Typographical Antiquities, or the History of Printing in England, Scotland, and Ireland." London, 1810-19, 4to, vol. i. pp. 241-85.

(d) Lowndes, "Bibliographer's Manual." London, 1864, 8vo, p. 74.

(e) W. Carew Hazlitt's "Hand-book to the Popular, Poetical, and Dramatic Literature
of Great Britain, from the Invention of Printing to the Restoration." London, 1867, 8vo
p. 13.

[3] Bagford, "Fragments," vol. viii. No. 58.

the United States.[1] The other copy is No. 1194 of the famous library of Earl Spencer, Althorp, Northampton. This copy, too, is in good condition, and not, as some sources say, very much damaged. It wants eleven leaves (not twelve), which are, however, replaced by facsimiles from the Osterley Park copy, due to the skilful hand of Mr. Whittaker: which indeed resemble the original pages so much, that, at first sight, one might easily mistake them for the latter; but on close and careful examination one cannot help noticing many very characteristic, though small, differences in the single letters. Dibdin in his Spencerian Catalogue only mentions that the copy wants eleven leaves, and refers to his "Typographical Antiquities," where he describes the Osterley Park copy. According to a written note by Messrs. Longman[2] attached to the Althorp copy, and to Mr. Blades' account[3] of the book, these leaves were the following: 1. Sig. lj (fol. 98); 2. Sig. r_7 (fol. 152); 3. Sig. r_8 (fol. 153); 4. Sig. T_4 (fol. 357); 5. Sig. T_5 (fol. 358); 6. Sig. ee_2 (fol. 427); 7. Sig. ee_3 (fol. 428); 8. Sig. ee_4 (fol. 429); 9. Sig. ee_5 (fol. 430); and 10. Sig. ee_6 (fol. 431). This statement proved to be not throughout correct, as I discovered when I had done about two-thirds of the text. 1°. There are only nine leaves accounted for. 2°. Sig. ee_2 (fol. 427) is no reproduction, but the original. 3°. Sig. N_2 (fol. 307) and Sig. N_8 (fol. 312) are facsimiles, though not stated as such. The present edition is based on this copy.

---

[1] At the Osterley sale, in May 1885, the British Museum gave a commission of £1800 to their agent, but the copy was sold for £1950. It is very much to be regretted that the English nation lost this splendid specimen of Caxton's printing, containing, as it does, the traditional history of their King Arthur, a national epic.

[2] This note reads thus:—

> Leaves wanting in Caxton's
> Morte d'Arthur left with
> Messrs. Longman & Co. 21 Feb. 1816.
>
> The whole of l;
> Part of r_7
> The whole of r_8
> Part of T_4
> The whole of T_5
> Part of eeij
> A few leaves following to the end of the Work.—LONGMAN & CO.
> Also see Note at Nij.

The parts of the leaves in question alluded to in this note must have been removed. I was unable to discover where the "note at N_2" refers to.

[3] Blades, vol. ii. page 178 : "Imperfect, wanting lj; r, 7 and 8; Tiiij and 5; ee ij. iij, 4, 5 and 6 all of which have been supplied in beautiful facsimiles.

Neither copy has a title.[1]   According to Mr. Blades' treatise on
Caxton's Typography, the type is No. 4*. The volume is 11¾ inches
high and 8 inches broad. The lines are all 4⅝ inches long.   Thirty-
eight lines make generally a full page, but pages occur with a few lines
less, and some with thirty-nine lines.   Neither folios nor catchwords
are given.   Books and chapters commence with woodcut initials, the
former with ornamental ones, five lines high ; the latter with plain
ones, three lines high.[2]   The first leaf of the book is blank.   Caxton's
preface commences on the second recto, with a three-line woodcut
initial.   This preface consists of two paragraphs, and finishes on
signature iiij.   On the verso the table of contents, or " rubrysshe," as
Caxton styles it, begins, and runs without interruption through thirty-
four pages, terminating on the eighteenth verso.   The history itself
commences on signature a, with an ornamental five-line woodcut initial.
The leaves are distinguished by three sets of alphabets, each in
eights, intended merely as a direction to the binders, only half of each
sheet being marked, in the beginning, alternately, one page with a
signature and one without, afterwards four leaves with signatures and
four without, these latter being the halves of the signed sheets.   In
the first alphabet, after z, follows &, also in eights.   The second
alphabet concludes with Z, and then follow aa, bb, &c., to ee, in
eights, but ee has only six leaves, as the book finishes on the verso of
ee₆.   R iij is misprinted for sig. S iij, and S ij for T ij.   The Althorp
copy is beautifully bound in olive morocco by Lewis.

Caxton's helpmate and successor, Wynkyn de Worde,[3] printed the
next two editions of the " Morte Darthur : " the second in 1498, and
the third in 1529, both in folio and black-letter.   Only two copies

---

[1] The title of the present edition is literally repeated from Caxton's colophon (comp.
sig. ee₆, p. 861*, lines 12–18).   " Title-pages," says Mr. Blades (vol. i. p. 33), " are purely
typographical in their origin, the scribes having satisfied themselves with heading their
first page with the *Hic incipit* and name of the treatise.   Caxton followed the manuscript practice in this particular ; for, with one single exception ('The Chastising of God's
Children,' plate Lii. vol. ii.), where the title of the book is printed alone in the centre of
the first page, his books appear without any title-page.   Wynkyn de Worde adopted
title-pages immediately after the death of his master."

[2] Compare the photographic facsimile specimen page, selected because it illustrates
both sorts of initials, as well as some other particulars referred to later on.

[3] The title which W. de Worde is supposed to have given to his editions, for his
copies also want the title-page, runs thus :

"The Booke of Kynge Arthur and of his noble Knyghtes of the
Rounde Table.   Printed at Westmestre 1498 folio.

of his impressions are known to exist, fortunately one of each edition.
That of 1498 is in Earl Spencer's library, No. 907, and that of
1529 in the Grenville Collection of the British Museum. The first
copy, though lacking ten leaves,[1] and having thirteen partly injured by
smaller or greater portions of the text being torn away, is of particular
interest, as an example of the first attempt ever made of illustrating a
text throughout with engravings. These are very coarsely executed
woodcuts. Dibdin, who has reproduced several of them in his
Spencerian Catalogue,[2] says: "They are very little superior to the

---

[1] The first leaf of the table ; signatures a₃; r₂; 𝕰₃; 𝕰₄; 𝕿₃; 𝕻₃; B₁; C₆; D₁; and
E₂. The damaged leaves are those: a₇; i₇; n₃; n₄; o₄; p₃; q₃; r₂; v₃; v₈; 𝕽₆; 𝕾₄
and D₈. Dibdin also mentions r₇ as wanting, but that I found preserved and not
damaged.

[2] (a) Dibdin, "Bibliotheca Spenceriana," vol. vi. 403 ff. Lord Spencer's copy has been
bound in a very elegant manner in dark-red morocco by C. Lewis. On a visit to Lord
Spencer's library on February 1, 1889, at Althorp, I examined this copy and copied as
a specimen the last 26 lines, which run thus :

> For ye tranſlacõn of this
> booke was fynyſſhed . the . ix . yere of the
> reygne of kynge Edwarde the fourth
> by Syr Thomas Maleore knyght / as
> Iheſu helpe hym' for his grete myght .
> as he is the ſeruaunt of Iheſu bothe
> daye and nyghte.
> ¶ Thus endyth this noble & Ioyous
> boke entytled Le morte dathur . Not
> wythſtonding it treateth of the ſayd kynge
> Arthur of his noble knyghtſ of the rounde
> table . theyr merueyllous enqueſtes & ad
> uentures . thachyeuynge of the Sanc-
> greall . And in the ende of the dolorous
> deth . & departynge out of this worlde
> of them al . Whyche boke was reduced
> into Englyſſhe by the well dyſpoſyd
> knyghte afore namyd . And deuyde .
> in to . xxi . bokes chapitred . & enprynt . .
> fyrſt by Wylliam Caxton . on wh . . .
> ſoule god haue mercy . A newel . . .
> prynted . and chapitres of the ſam . . .
> briſſhed at Weſtmeſtre by Wynk . . . .
> Worde yᵉ yere of our lord M.C. . . . . .
> .lxxxx viij. and ended the . xxv . . . . .
> Marche . the ſame yere.

The points denote that the ends of the lines are damaged.

(b) Dibdin, "Typographical Antiquities" (vol. i. pp. 248–52), gives some of the variations from Caxton.

(c) W. C. Hazlitt's "Handbook," &c., p. 13.

clumsiest embellishments which distinguish the volumes of the two
Coplands; yet to the curious antiquary they have a certain degree of
value, and to the bibliographer such a volume, remarkable for the
beauty of its execution, as well as for the rarity of its appearance,
cannot fail to be held in very considerable consideration." The book is
arranged in the following way. Unlike Caxton's, it is printed in
columns. The table of contents consists of eight leaves. The ninth
leaf is upon sig. ij—as in Caxton's impression—and this leaf and a
small portion of the ensuing one—sig. iij—contain a prologue precisely
similar to that in Caxton's own volume. The prologue is followed by
a summary of the contents of each of the twenty-one books. The text
commences on a; the signatures run in three sets: a to v in eights
and sixes alternately, v having eight leaves. Then, in Gothic characters, 𝕬, 𝕭, 𝕮, in sixes, 𝕯, in eights, 𝕰, in six, 𝕱, 𝕲, 𝕳, in
eights, and 𝕵 to 𝖀 inclusively, in sixes; 𝖃 has four, and finally 𝖄 five
leaves, the sixth blank leaf probably torn out. The third set, in Roman
type—A, B, C, D, E, in sixes; E_6 being blank.

The British Museum copy,[1] originally in Archdeacon Wrangham's [2]
library, represents the third edition of 1529. It is complete, with the
exception of seven leaves of the table of contents and the title-page,

---

[1] "Bibliographical Memoranda, an Illustration of Early English Literature," Bristol
1816, 4to, p. 398.
  [2] It contains the following manuscript notes, 1° by Mr. Grenville, 2° by Archdeacon
Wrangham:—1°. "A singular degree of rarity prevails as to the earlier editions of this
romance. It was first printed by Caxton, but the only copy known is wanting twelve
leaves and with others much damaged at Althorp. The 2nd edition, by W. de Worde,
1498, is known only in two copies, one perfect, in Lord Jersey's library, the other
at Althorp." Mr. Grenville evidently mistook Caxton's for W. de Worde's editions.
As far as I could ascertain, there has never been an edition of W. de Worde at Osterley.
Compare also C. Hazlitt's "Handbook," p. 13.   2°. "Ames, in his History of Printing,
p. 57, Herbert's Edition, enumerates among Caxton's Works, 'La Morte de Arthur,' but
Herbert adds:—'I make no question but that Mr. Ames saw the book, but that it is
rather extraordinary that he has not told us in whose possession it was, according to
his usual custom. I have examined Bibl. Harleiana (it stands, however, No. 372 in
Harl. Cat. III. 25), Westiana, Radcliffiana, &c. &c., but have not been fortunate enough
to meet with any copy of this Edition or any intelligence where to find one.' But
although the above Edition of this curious and interesting Romance from the press of
Caxton seems at present unknown, it may be worth stating that it was reprinted by
Wynkyn de Worde in 1498 in folio, and also by William Copland without date in the
same form. The latter Edition had escaped the research of the illustrious Herbert; but
an imperfect copy was purchased by W. Mason at a sale in 1794 for three guineas and a
half. It was reprinted by Thomas East without date in folio, and so late as 1634 in
quarto. (Beloe's Anecd., i. 43, where see, also, a Memorandum of Dr. Lort's on the year
of Caxton's death, 1491.) J. W."

but this defect can easily be supplied, as the contents are repeated before each chapter. The table of contents is printed on signatures aaa$_{1-8}$, only aaa$_8$ existing; then follow bbb$_{1-8}$. The history commences on a, and the signatures run alternately in eights and sixes to v, which has eight leaves. Then follow, in Gothic characters, 𝔄, 𝔅, ℭ, in sixes, 𝔇, 𝔈, 𝔉, 𝔊, 𝔥 in eights, and 𝔍 to 𝔓 in sixes, and finally, Roman characters A to D in sixes, and E with five leaves. On the verso of E$_5$ is the ornamental device of the printer, covering almost the whole of the page. The two editions of Wynkyn de Worde do not exactly correspond to each other as concerns the text.[1]

The next, or fourth, edition was brought out by William Copland, in the year 1557,[2] also in columns and folio. The press-work is superior to what is generally observable in works by the two Coplands. The volume has a title-page, running thus:

"The ftory of the moft noble and worthy Kynge Arthur, the whiche was one of the worthyes chryften, and alfo of his noble and valiaūte knyghtes of the rounde Table. Newly imprynted and corrected. MCCCCClvij. Imprynted at London by Wyllyam Copland."

There are two copies of this edition in the British Museum;[3] the one is perfect, the other wanting several leaves, which are, however, replaced partly by facsimiles, partly by reprints. On the title-page, above the last line, is a woodcut of a knight on horseback, similar to that of St. George and the Dragon. A woodcut also precedes every book; after the colophon may be observed the device of the printer. The title and table of contents occupy fourteen leaves. The signatures

---

[1] The following lines give the beginning of the book as a specimen. The words in brackets are not in the edition of 1498 :—

"Here begynneth the fyrft booke of the [mooft] noble [and worthy prince] kyng . Kyng Arthur fometyme kynge of [grete Brytayne now called] Englonde [whiche treateth] of his noble actes and feates of armes [and] of chyualrye . [of] . his noble knyghtes [of the] & table round and [this volume] is devyded in to . xxi . bookes."

[2] Dibdin, "Typograph. Antiquities," p. 143.

[3] Also one copy in the Huth Library. See Catalogue, vol. i. p. 83. Some of the early cuts, including that of the title, have been illuminated, but the artist fortunately abandoned his task before he had proceeded far

run a to d in eights; e has nine leaves, f to z in eights, and A to O in eights.

Malory's work was then twice printed, once in folio, and once in quarto,[1] by Thomas East, about 1585.[2] I have not seen a copy of the quarto edition. The folio is in the British Museum—a fine copy, complete throughout. It bears the following title:

> "The ftorye of the moft noble and worthy Kynge Arthur, the which was the fyrft of the worthyes Chryften, and alfo of hys noble and valyaunt knyghtes of the rounde Table . Newly imprynted and correéted, betweene Paules wharfe and Baynardes Caftell by Thomas Eaft."[3]

Finally, the "Morte Darthur" was printed for the last time in black letter, in the year 1634, by William Stansby, with the title:

> "The moft ancient and famovs hiftory of the renowned prince Arthur, King of Britaine. Wherein is declared his Life and Death, with all his glorious Battailes againft the Saxons, Saracens, and Pagans, which (for the honour of his Country) he moft worthily atchieued. As alfo, all the

---

[1] There is one copy also in the Huth Library and another in the library of the Earl of Ellesmere in Bridgewater House. *See* Collier's Catalogue, page 11.

[2] Both editions are undated. Thomas East printed, as we know, from about 1560 to 1607. I determined the date 1585 in the following way :—The "Transcript of the Registers of the Company of Stationers of London from 1554 to 1640 A.D." (reprinted privately by E. Arber, 1875) was looked through and the following entry found in vol. ii. fol. 187b :—"Thomas Easte : Receaved of him for his licence to printe these xvj bookes followinge" (then follows a list of sixteen books). Among them is mentioned "King Arthur," and on the same line "Johannes de Vigo." A copy of this latter is in the British Museum, with the genuine date, 1586, attached to it. (Comp. "Catalogue of Books in the British Museum Library to the year 1640," vol. iii. p. 1539.) Thus the book may fairly be dated about 1585, not as the Brit. Mus. Catalogue, vol. i. page 56 states "1560"; this is at least as near as we can get the date.

[3] Comp. J. Payne Collier, "A Bibliographical and Critical Account of the Rarest Books in the English Language," 2 vols., London, 1865, p. 31 :—"A few of the woodcuts of East's edition are considerably older than the datte when he printed; one of them was used by W. de Worde in 1520 before Christopher Goodwyn's poem, 'The Chaunces of a Dolorous Lover.' The block then came into the hands of W. Copland, and having been used by him in his reprint of the 'Morte Darthur' it was subsequently in the possession of East, who applied it to the same purpose in his reprint preceding the 16th book. Thus W. de Worde's 'Dolorous Lover' served the turn, in the hands of Copland and East, to represent a dead man in a white shirt an hundred winters old. At the time the block was employed by East, it had been considerably worn and battered."

Noble Acts, and Heroicke Deeds of his Valiant Knights
of the Rovnd Table. Newly refined[1] and publifhed for
the delight, and profit of the Reader. London, Printed
by William Stanfby for Jacob Bloome. 1634."

The work consists of three parts, each having this title separately.
Title, preface, and frontispiece occupy four leaves, prologue two leaves,
Caxton's prologue one leaf, table of contents five leaves. The first
part has signatures A to Z, and Aa to Ii₄, the second A to Z, and
Aa to Rr₁, and the third part A to Z, and Aa to Pp₄, all in fours.
Caxton's division of the whole, in twenty-one books, is departed from.
In each of the parts the chapters are numbered from one to the end.
The first book contains cli., the second clxxiii., and the third clxxvi.
chapters. There are two copies of this edition in the British Museum.[1]
One is quite complete, the other wants the title-page, the preface to
the reader, and two leaves of the first part.

Almost two hundred years later (<u>186</u> exactly) in 1816, the first _182_
two editions in Roman type appeared independently from each other,
one in two, the other in three volumes 12mo; both being reprints of
the last-mentioned black-letter edition of 1634.

The edition in three volumes (F. Haslewood) has the title :

"La Mort D'Arthur, The moft ancient and famous hif-
torye of the renowned Prince Arthur and the Knights of
the Round Table by Sir T. Malory. London. 1816."

and that in two volumes (Walker's British Classics):

"The History of the renowned Prince Arthur, king of
Britain with his life and death and all his glorious Battles,
likewise the noble acts and heroic deeds of his valiant
knights of the round table. London. 1816."

Though both editions are said to be exact reprints, they contain,
besides an endless number of mistakes and errors of the worst kind,
alterations of the text. In many cases the long "f" has been mistaken
for "f," and the "c" for "r," &c. Wright quotes other strange mistakes.

---

[1] This edition is, as the Catalogue of the Huth Library styles it, "modernised and
ignorantly corrupted." Compare my note, p. 13, with regard to the meaning of "newly
refined." (Catalogue of the Huth Library, vol. i. p. 53.)

In 1817 there appeared, under Southey's illustrious name, an edition, with the following title :

> " The byrth, lyf and actes of kyng Arthur ; of his
> noble knyghtes of the Rounde Table ther merueyllous
> enquestes and aduentures thachyeuyng of the sanc greal,
> and in the end le morte Darthur with the dolorous deth
> and departyng out of this world of them al. With an
> introduction and notes by R. Southey.   Printed from
> Caxton's edition, 1485.   London, 1817.   8°."

It is supposed to be a scrupulously exact reprint from Caxton's copy in Lord Spencer's library ; but such is by no means the case.[1] Southey wrote the introduction, and gave his name to a bookseller's speculation ; he had nothing whatever to do with the text, the passing through the press of which was entrusted to Mr. Upcott, who, I am inclined to believe, left much to the care of the printers, as the text contains no inconsiderable number of mistakes. And, before all, Lord Spencer's copy still wanted twenty-one pages in 1817, as can be seen from a note by Messrs. Longman, given on page 3, and from the minute pencil paging on the left-hand side of the recto of every leaf. The defect was supplied in a very strange way. Sir E. Strachey, who has investigated this matter thoroughly, writes about it in his introduction thus : " The substitutes for them which actually appear in Southey's edition differ widely from the restored, or the original text. Thus, in chap. xii. of the last book, besides the interpolation of the long passage, ' O ye myghty and pompuous lordes,' &c., which is not in Caxton, there are in the first eleven lines thirty-five variations of spelling and punctuation, besides the introduction of the words 'but continually mourned un—' and 'needfully as nature required,' which are not in Caxton, and the change of Caxton's ' on the tombe of kyng Arthur & quene Gueneuer,' into 'on kynge Arthur's & quene Gweneuer's tombe.' And thus throughout the pages in question—seventeen in number [2]—

---

[1] Comp Warton's " History of English Poetry," ed. W. C. Hazlitt. Lond. 1871, vol. ii. p. 189, note 4. Also, Sir Edward Strachey, Introduction, p. xv. London, 1868. 8vo. Globe edition.

[2] The pages (in Southey's edition) are vol. i. p. 167, line 18, to p. 169, line 17 ; p. 275, third line from bottom, to p. 279, line 5 from bottom ; vol. ii. p. 202, line 13, to p. 204, line 14 ; p. 446, line 5, to end of p. 455.

the spelling constantly, and words and even sentences occasionally, differ from the real text of Caxton.[1]

" When at page 113 of volume i. the editor introduces the words 'certayne caufe' to complete the sense, he is careful to call attention, in a foot-note, to the fact that these words are not in the original, but taken from 'the second edition,' by which I presume he means that of 1498. But when he subsequently supplies seventeen pages, which were also not in his original, he gives no hint of the fact; and his reticence has been so successful that for fifty years the interpolations have passed as genuine among learned critics, who have quoted from them passages wholly spurious as Caxton's genuine text. It was only last year that, in collating Earl Spencer's copy with the edition of Southey; I discovered that these passages—to which my attention was directed by Messrs. Longman's note above mentioned—did not correspond with Caxton's text, as represented by Whittaker's restorations; and on afterwards collating them with the Osterley text itself, I found the like result. It remained to trace them to their real sources. This has not been so easy as might be supposed, for though it was evident that Upcott must have had recourse to one or other existing editions, the interpolated passages in fact agree exactly with none of them, but a careful collation of the last four chapters of the book (which include more than half the interpolations, and may be taken as a fair specimen of the whole) with the old texts, leaves no doubt that, with the exception of the first thirty-six lines of chapter x., they were taken, like the two words mentioned above, from the first edition of Wynkyn de Worde (1498) but with spelling occasionally altered, and here and there a small word put in, left out, or changed. These alterations throw an ingenious disguise over the whole ; but if we penetrate through this we find that in these four chapters there are only thirteen words differing from those in Wynkyn de Worde's first edition, and these unimportant; while in his second edition (1529), and in those of Copland and East, the variations from Mr. Upcott's text of the same chapters are respectively fifty-seven, fifty-six, and fifty in number, and many of them important in kind : and if we go to the edition of 1634, we find the differences still greater, except as to those

---

Sir E. Strachey gave an account of these interpolations in the *Athenæum* of Sept. 7 and Dec. 10, 1867, and Feb. 10, 1868.

thirty-six lines supplied from this edition, as they were wanting in the other copy. But the colophon, or concluding paragraph of the book, Mr. Upcott could not take from any of the editions which followed that of Caxton; for though Wynkyn de Worde might, and in fact did, supply at least one or two of the first words, the latter part of his colophon relates to his own edition, and departs widely from that of Caxton, while those in the later editions are still more unlike; and yet Mr. Upcott's colophon is a tolerable, though not an exact, representation of that of Caxton. But his other materials can be ascertained beyond a doubt. They are, the colophon as given by Ames and repeated by Dibdin in a modernised and otherwise inexact form,[1] and that which first appeared in the Catalogue of the Harleian Library,[2] and was thence copied in the article on Caxton in the 'Biographia Britannica,' and also in Herbert's additions to Ames. The colophons of Ames and of the Harleian Catalogue have important variations from each other and from that of Caxton; and as Mr. Upcott adopts some portions of each which are not found either in the other or in Caxton, we see the manner in which the paragraph in question was compounded. Each stone of the ingeniously fitted mosaic may be referred to the place from which it was taken. We cannot indeed choose positively between Ames and Dibdin, or among the Harleian Catalogue, the 'Biographia Britannica' and Herbert; but as the two paragraphs which are required in addition to that of Wynkyn de Worde are both found in Herbert's Ames, it seems most probable that Mr. Upcott had recourse to that work, though another combination would have served the purpose equally well. That the interpolated passages are not taken from the Osterley Caxton itself, even in the roughest and most careless manner, is quite evident."

In 1856[3] follows Thomas Wright's edition, entitled:

" La Mort d'Arthure; The Hiftory of King Arthur and of his Knights of the Round Table compiled by Sir Thomas Malory, Knt. edited from the text of the edition of 1634 with introduction and notes by Th. Wright, etc. London. 1856. 8°."

---

[1] "Typographical Antiquities," by Ames and Herbert, 1785, vol. i. p. 61; *ibid.* enlarged by Dibdin, 1810, vol. i. p. 253. The "Additions" are at the end of vol. iii. of Herbert's edition.

[2] "Catalogue of the Bibliotheca Harleiana, 1744," vol. iii. No. 372.

[3] A second edition came out in 1866, " carefully revised, and a few errors corrected, and the number of glossarial notes somewhat increased."

Of all hitherto mentioned editions this is the best beyond doubt with regard to accuracy of the text, &c., and when the text of the edition of 1634 is desired, it will be found to answer its purpose everywhere. Besides, there is sound criticism displayed in the introduction, and the notes contain a great deal of most valuable information. Wright says with reference to Malory's work : "A knowledge of it is indeed necessary to enable us to understand the later Middle Ages in one of their important points of view; while it possesses an intrinsic interest, as giving us, in a comprehensive form, a good general sketch of a cycle of romances which through many ages exercised an influence upon literature and art. . . . . It has been judged advisable to adopt for the text the latest[1] of the old editions, for it is evident that the choice lay between the last and the first, between this we have selected and that of Caxton; there was no reason why we should not take that of the reprints, which was most readable. This choice was made with less scruples, as no particular philological value is attached to the language of Caxton's edition, which would certainly be repulsive to the modern reader, while all its value as a literary monument is retained in the reprint. On the other hand the orthography and phraseology of the editions of 1634, with the sprinkling of obsolete words, not sufficiently numerous to be embarrassing, preserves a certain clothing of mediæval character, which we think is one of the charms of the book," &c.

Finally, in 1868, Sir Edward Strachey[1] reprinted Caxton in a modernised edition, entitled :

"Morte Darthur, Sir Thomas Malory's Book of King Arthur and of his Noble Knights of the Round Table. The original edition of Caxton revifed for modern ufe with an Introduction. London and New York. 1868. 8°. Globe edition."[2]

---

[1] I think neither the antiquary nor the philologist will share Mr. Wright's opinion on this subject, especially if he reads what the printer of the edition of 1634 says about his words "newly refined" in his

"Preface to the Reader" : "In many places this volume is corrected (not in language but in phrafeology) for here and there king Arthur or fome of his knights were declared in their communication to fwear prophane, and ufe fuperftitious fpeeches, all (or the moft part) of which is either mended or quite left out by the paines and induftry of the compositor and corrector of the preffe; fo that as it is now, it may paffe for a famous piece of antiquity, revived almoft from the gulph of oblivion, and refcued for the pleafure and benefit of the prefent and future times."

[2] Reprinted, in unaltered form, in 1886.

In his introduction, Sir E. Strachey,[1] besides an essay on chivalry, gives a short account of the origin and matter of the book and describes especially the edition of 1817, as I have mentioned above. Among other things he says : " This present edition is intended for ordinary readers, especially for boys, from whom the chief demand for this book will always come ; it is a reprint of the original Caxton with the spelling modernised, and those few words which are unintelligibly obsolete, replaced by others which, though not necessarily unknown to Caxton, are still in use, yet with all old forms retained which do not interfere with this requirement of being readable," &c.[2]

---

[1] In my preface to the first volume I have said the Globe edition is "modernised and abridged." As I have seen from an article on this volume in the *Scots Observer* (May 18, 1889), that this statement has been misunderstood, I consider it my duty to say that I hold the opinion that Sir E. Strachey's work perfectly fulfils its purpose,— in fact, it is of all reprints the best ; but my term "abridged" is justified : it means that here and there words and little passages are omitted which are not fit for boys and girls to read.—On p. xvii. of his Introduction, Sir E. Strachey says : " The Early English Text Society promise us a reprint (1868 !) of the original Caxton, which shall be free from the faults of that of Southey, which meanwhile is, except in the interpolated passages, a very faithful representation of that original for the purposes of the antiquarian and philologist."—I am sorry that I must contradict Sir E. Strachey here. He most likely trusted too much to Southey's authority. I have collated Southey's with the original text of Caxton, and must confess I found no inconsiderable number of errors.

[2] Besides those reprints, Malory's "Morte Darthur" has appeared modernised and abridged under the following titles :—

    1. The Story of King Arthur and his Knights of the Round Table. Compiled and arranged by J[ames] T[homas] K[nowles]. Being an abridgment of "Sir T. Malory's Collection of Legends of King Arthur." With illustrations by G. H. Thomas. London. 1862. 8°.

    2. La Morte Darthur. The History of King Arthur. Compiled by T. Mallory. Abridged and revised by E. Conybeare. London. 1868. 8°.

    3. La Mort d'Arthur. Abridged from the work of Sir Thomas Malory. The old prose stories whence the "Idylls of the King" have been taken by Alfred Tennyson. . . . . ed. with an Introduction by B. M. Ranking. London. 1871. 8°.

    4. The Boy's King Arthur, being Sir T. Malory's History of the Round Table. Edited with an Introduction by S. Lanier. Illustrated by A. Kappes. London. 1880. 8°.

In 1886 (London) appeared, as the first volume of the so-called Camelot Classics, an edition of the "Morte Darthur" by Ernest Rhys, under the title "Malory's History of King Arthur and the Quest of the Holy Grail." The text of this edition, however, is not complete, seven out of the twenty-one books in the original edition being omitted, and the reprinted books are modernised and altered from Thomas Wright's edition.

RELATION OF THE DIFFERENT EDITIONS OF
"LE MORTE DARTHUR" TO EACH OTHER.

SIR THOMAS MALORY[1] finished the manuscript of his book, according to Caxton's statement, in the ninth year of the reign of King Edward IV.—*i.e.*, about 1470—and he printed from it : " a book of the noble hystoryes etc. after a copy vnto me delyuerd." All efforts to trace this manuscript in any of the libraries of the United Kingdom or elsewhere, have hitherto proved fruitless, and I think always will ; for most likely Malory's manuscript, being intended for the press, existed only in one copy, and this, having been greatly spoiled and damaged during the process of printing, was destroyed after

---

[1] (a) An almost certain reference to Malory's " Morte Darthur " is found in a book which appeared in 1506, entitled :—

"Paſtime of Pleaſure, or the Hiſtory of Graunde Amour and La Bell Pycel : conteining the knowledge of the ſeven Sciences, and the courſe of man's life in this worlde. Invented by Stephen Hawes, groome of Kyng Henry VII his chamber, dedicated to the king and finiſhed at the beginning of 1506."

In the passage in question (chap. xliii.) Fame appears and promising that she will enroll his name (*i.e.* Graunde Amour) with those of Hector, Joshua, Caesar, Arthur, etc. says with regard to the latter and his knights that their exploits are recorded " in royal bokes and jeſtes hyſtoryall." Comp. Warton, "History of English Poetry," ed. W. C. Hazlitt, vol. iii. pp. 169–188.

(b) Another interesting reference, containing not a very favourable judgment upon the " Morte Darthur," I found in Roger Aſcham's book " The Schoolemaſter." London. 1570. On p. 81 of The Rev. John E. B. Mayor's reprint of this book (London, 1863) we read :

"In our forefathers tyme, whan Papiſtrie, as a ſtandyng poole, couered and overflowed all England, fewe bookes were read in our tong, ſavyng certaine bookes of Cheualrie, as they ſayd, for paſtime and pleaſure, which, as ſome ſay, were made in Monaſteries by idle Monkes or wanton Chanons ; as one for example, Morte Arthure : the whole pleaſure of whiche booke ſtandeth in two ſpeciall poyntes, in open mans ſlaughter and bold bawdrye : In which booke thoſe be counted the nobleſt Knightes, that do kill moſt men without any quarell, and commit fowleſt aduoulteres by ſutleſt ſhiftes : as Sir Launcelote with the wife of King Arthure his maſter : Syr Triſtram with the wife of Kyng Marke his uncle : Syr Lamerocke with the wife of king Lote, that was his own aunte. This is good ſtuffe for wiſe men to laughe at, or honeſt men to take pleaſure at Yet I know, when God's Bible was baniſſhed the Court, and Morte Arthure received into the Princes chamber," &c.

Comp. also Aſcham's " Toxophilus." London. 1545. 4°. Preface.

the book was ready. Wynkyn de Worde has evidently printed his edition of 1498 from Caxton's edition, though he does not give any statement to this effect. Either from Caxton's, but more likely from his own, he printed in 1529 his second, in fact the third, edition of "Le Morte Darthur." The copy of this last-mentioned edition, fully described on page 7, was the one from which the variations are quoted, simply because, in the first place, the interval between 1485 and 1498 is very small ; and secondly, the copy of 1489 has many deficiencies, while that of 1529 only lacks Caxton's preface, and some passages of the table of contents which can be supplied from the contents preceding the single chapters.

This edition deviates considerably, not only in orthography, from Caxton's, as will be seen from the list of various readings. Words are transposed, now and then added or omitted, and obsolete ones are frequently exchanged for more modern ones.

Whether these variations are introduced by the compositors or by some person who read the proof-sheets must be left undecided, but in some instances the latter seems very probable.

Copland's edition of 1559, the fourth in order, is not, as one would suppose, a reprint from Caxton but from W. de Worde's edition of 1529, which, on collation, was found to agree with it word for word and line for line, but not page for page, owing to the difference in size of the woodcuts which precede each book in the two copies.

About 1585 Thomas East printed his two editions either from W. de Worde or Copland. The similarity of title in Copland's and East's editions inclines me to think that Copland's is the basis.

Finally, the seventh and last black-letter edition, that of Thomas Stansby, 1634, in spite of the different arrangement of the book, some arbitrary alterations and omissions, not to speak of slight differences orthographical and otherwise, is a reprint of East's folio, as the following reasons show: firstly, as already stated by Thomas Wright in his introduction, Stansby's edition wants the contents of one leaf in East's folio edition. (According to Caxton: part of chap. ii., the whole of chap. iii., and almost the whole of chap. iv. of Book XIV.)[1] This leaf bears in East's folio the signature Dd_8,

---

[1] Th. Wright has supplied the deficient leaf from Caxton. The editor of the "Morte Arthur" of 1816, in 2 vols., leaves the passage out without mentioning this fact

E WORDE
9)

LAND
1557

EAST
(1585)

STA:
(1...

Book i. Chap. i. Page 35, lines 1-12.

befell in the days
y^e noble Vtherpen-
ragon whã he was
ynge of Englande &
d so regned / there
as a myghty and
noble duke in Cor-
longe tyme warre
y^e duke was named
ll / & so by meanes
or this duke / char-
ge his wyfe w^t hym
yght fayre lady / &
& Igrayne was her
e duke & his wyfe
ige / by the meanes
were bothe accor-
ed & loued this lady
grete chere out of

Book i. Chap. ii.

And thā Merlin was boūden to come
to the kynge. Whan kynge Vther fawe
hym, he fay[t] y^t he was welcome. Syr
fayde Me..., I knowe all your herte
...o ye wyll be fworne to me
...e kynge enoynted to fulfyl
...re fhall haue your defyre.

as boūden to come
1 kyng Vther fawe
was welcome. Syr
owe all your herte
ll be fworne to m...
en...

T befell in the dayes
thenoble Vtherpen-
gon whan he was kir
ge of Englande &
o reigned, there was a
myghtye and a noble
d duke in Cornewayle,
that helde l... tyme warre agaynfte
hym. And t ; duke was named the duke of Tyntagyl, and fo by meanes king
Vther fente for this duke chargynge
hym to brynge his wyfe with hym for
fhe was ca"d a ryght fayre lady, and
a paffyng yfe, and Igrayne was her
name. So whan the duke & his wyfe
were comen to the kyng, by the meanes
of great lordes they were bothe accorded, & the kyng lyked & loued this lady
well, and made, her great chere out of
meafure, etc.

T befell in the daye of
the noble Vtherper a-
gon whan he was kir of
England and fo raig ed,
there was a mighty nd
a noble Duke in Cornewayle, that 'd
longe time warre agaynft him . l
the Duke was named y^e Duke of t-
tagyl, and fo by meanes kinge \ er
fent for this duke charging him to l ng
his wyfe with him, for fhee was call d a
right faire Lady, and a paffing wife, and
Igrayne was hir name . So whan the
duke and his wyfe were comen to the
king, by the meanes of great Lordes
they were both accorded, and the kinge
lyked & loued this lady well, and t ade
hir great cheere out of meafure, et

Book i. Chap. ii. Page 36, lines 31-35.

And than
Merlyn was boūden to come to ye king.
Whan kinge Vther fawe him, he f id y^t
he was welcome . Syr said Merl I
know al your hart euery dele, fo y
be fworne to me as yee be a true
enoynted to fulfyll my defyre, yet
haue your defyre .

T befell in the
dragon when I
fo reigned, the
ble Duke in
time warre aga
named the D
meanes King Vther fent for thi
his wife with him, for fhee was
a paffing wife, and Igraynewas
and his wife were come to the
Lords they were bothaccorded,
thisLadywell,and made her gr

Merlyn was bounde to come to
faw him, he faid that he was
know all your euery dele...
...true Kinga...

fyr Launceto

lot at the croffe . And on the

S O the queene departed from: the
king, and fente for fyr Bors into
hir chamber .

·3·

For the tranflacyon
of this boke was fynyffhed the . ix . yere
of the reigne of king Edwarde y° fourth
by fyr Thomas Maleore knyghte, as
Iefu helpe hym for his greate myghte,
as he is the feruaunt of Iefu both daye
and nyght .

¶ Thus endeth this noble and ioyous
booke entytuled la mort darthur, notwithftandynge it treateth of the byrthe
lyfe and actes of the fayd kyng Arthur,
and of his noble knyghtes of the round
table, their meruaylous enqueftes and
aduertures, .e achyeuinge of the holy
Sancgreall . And in the ende the dolorous death and departynge out of this
worlde of them all, whiche boke was
reduced in to Englyfhe by the moofte
well dyfr... l knyght afore named .

¶ Finis.

¶ I. .d at Londo in Fleteftrete
.ygne of the Rofe Gar-
.le, by Wyllyam
Copland .

S O the Queene
Bors into hir

For this |
the raigne of K
mas Maleor Kn
might, as hee i:
night.

For the tranflacyon
of this booke was fynyffhed the . ix . yere
of the reigne of king Edward the fourth
by fyr Thomas Maleore knyg... ; as
Iefu helpe me for hys greate .ghte,
as he is the feruaunt of Iefu b.. day
and night .

¶ Thus endeth this noble and ioyous
booke entytuled la mort darthur, not-
withftandinge it treateth of the .yrth,
lyfe and actes, of the faide king Arthur
and of hys noble knyghtes of the .ound
table, their meruaylous enqueftes and
aduentures, the achyeuinge of the holy
Sancgreall . And in the ende the dolorous death and departynge out of thys
worlde of them all, which booke was reduced into Englyfhe by the mofte well
difpofed knight afore named .

Finis

So Imprinted at London by
Thomas Eaft dwelling between:
Paules wharfe and Bay-
nardes Caftell .

Thus endet
La Mort Darth
birth, life, and
his noble Knigt
uailous enquefts
Holy Sancgreall
And in the
out of this world

---

e quene departed from the
: / and fente for fyr Bors in
.mbre .

S O the
kynge, .nd fente for .y. .ors in
to her cham .re .

For the tranflacyon
.ke was fymyffhed the . ix . yere
.ne of kyng Edwarde y° fourth
.homas Maleore knyght / as
: hym for his grete myght /
the feruaut of Iefu bothe daye
t .

endeth this noble and ioyous
.rtled la mort darthur / notwith-
.it treateth of the byrthe / lyfe
: of the fayd kyng Arthur / and
.ble knyghtes of the rounde ta-
.yr meruaylous enqueftes & ad-
/ the achyeuynge of the holy
ll . An in y° ende the dolorous
. departynge out of this world
all / whiche boke was reduced
.glyfhe by the mooft well dyfpo-
.ht afore named . ¶ Impryn-
.ondon in Flete ftrete at y° fygne
/ by Wynkyn de Worde . In the
.ur lord god . M.CCCCC . xxix .
.ij . daye of Nouember .

and has, as well as Dd,, the same catch-word, " but." It begins with
the words : " but by waye of kyndness and for good," and ends : " for
a good horse would befeme you right well but." The coincidence of
the two leaves having the same catch-word easily explains the
printer's oversight, but at the same time it reveals the mechanical
and careless nature of the reprint. Secondly, By the reproduction
of some misprints, *i.e.*, in Book XXI. chapter xiii. East prints :
" as Iefu helpe *me* for hys grete mygte as *he* is the feruaunt of
Iefu both day and night." It ought to run, and so indeed Caxton
prints : " as Iefu helpe *him*," &c. Stansby has faithfully reproduced
this blunder.

As to the five modern editions, three are reprinted from the
edition of 1634—namely, the two 1816 and that of 1856 ; and two
from the original Caxton, that of Southey, 1817, and that of Sir E.
Strachey, 1868.

The table on p. 18 gives graphically an idea of the relation of
the editions to each other :—

On the Plate facing this page I have, for the sake of illustration,
reprinted side by side short passages selected by chance from the
principal editions : they will show better than a description the relation the texts bear to one another.

THE PRESENT EDITION.

HE present edition of Malory's " Le Morte Darthur " follows
the original impression of Caxton in every respect (save
that Roman type has been substituted for Black letter) with
absolute fidelity, word for word, line for line, and page for page, and
with some exceptions, which are stated below, letter for letter. Black
letter has been retained for the chapter headings and at the close of
each book, in order to relieve the monotony of the page, but it has
not been thought necessary to use Caxton's type in this case. As far as
the different type permitted even peculiarities are exactly imitated, *e.g.*,

---

at all (comp. vol. ii. p. 244). In the three-volume reprint the missing part is supplied,
most likely from East's, but with the spelling modernised. The passages in question
(pp. 111, 112, 113, 114 of the third volume) are marked by asterisks, but no note or
remark alludes to the deficiency.

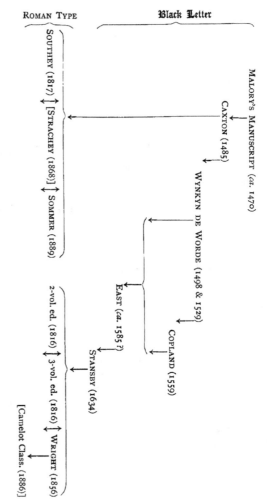

TABLE SHOWING THE RELATION OF THE EDITIONS OF MALORY'S "MORTE DARTHUR" TO ONE ANOTHER.

the spacing between books and chapters and in the various lines, the size and position of the initials in wood, the long " f " in the beginning and in the middle of words (those few cases of course excepted where Caxton himself departs from his custom of using the long " f ").[1] Thus, wherever the reader opens the present volume he will have a faithful impression of the aspect of Caxton's volume. It is superfluous to add that the orthography has been preserved with scrupulous exactness throughout, and that even the misprints occurring in Caxton's text, with some few exceptions mentioned under No. 6, are to be met with in our impression. All these misprints and irregularities of spelling are marked in a list to which one may refer in any doubtful case. This list also registers the few cases where the present and original editions differ in the spelling of words. To understand, however, thoroughly the principle upon which I have based my edition it is necessary to make the following observations :—

1. Caxton's volume commences with a blank leaf, which, as shown by the signatures, is counted. This leaf is also in the present edition, but it is not counted here, for the simple reason that the coincidence of the signatures in Caxton with the marks of the binders in the present edition should be avoided. Thus, on page 65 the fourth sheet begins, and is marked at the bottom by " E," whereas Caxton's fourth sheet only commences on page 67 (c j).

2. There occur in the impression of Caxton three kinds of " w." (Compare the photographic facsimile : firstly, line 20, in the word " was ;" secondly, line 21 in the word " afterward ;" and, thirdly, in the same line in the word " toward.") The first kind of " w," according to Mr. Blades,[2] denotes in type No. 4* the capital " W." Caxton's compositors did not distinguish, as they ought, these " w's " from one another, so that the one denoting " W " frequently occurs in the middle of words and in other places, where it is evidently out of place. I have, therefore, in the present edition, as Roman type does not admit

---

[1] While preparing the Glossary I noticed, to my great regret, that a few cases in which "f" and "f," have been confounded, have escaped my attention as well as that of three readers at the press. Owing to the minute difference between the two characters, and to the fact that the eye is not trained to distinguish them in an ordinary English text, it is extremely difficult to avoid such mistakes, especially before the paper is pressed, which is generally the case with proof sheets. Fortunately no ambiguity arises from any of these oversights.

[2] W. Blades' " Typography of Caxton," vol. ii. p. 35, and Plates xviii. and xix.

of marking the three kinds, rendered it by " W " in all cases where capital
" W " was to be expected, as in the beginning of a sentence and in proper
names, otherwise it is rendered by " w."

3. There are further two styles of " I " used in Caxton's type.
(Compare the photographic facsimile, firstly, line 1, and secondly, line
5.) At first it appeared that a difference was made between "i" and "j,"
but such is not the case ; both kinds are used indiscriminately. I
have therefore, after some consideration, always rendered it by " I."
Moreover, the first kind of " I " occurs more frequently.

4. The character " ȝ " is used in Caxton to express both " z " and
" gh." In words where " z " was to be expected I have rendered " ȝ "
by " z," otherwise I have preserved " ȝ," e.g., " Cezar " and " knyȝt."

5. Caxton has no fixed rules for dividing words at the end of a
line. A word is divided as the space in each special case permits,
and as a rule there is no conjunctive hyphen put—e.g., " horſes "
is not broken " hor- ſes " but " ho rſes." As I found that in
many cases mistakes arose from this deficiency, I have for the convenience of the modern reader always added the hyphen where it was
to be expected.

6. In some cases where Caxton's compositors evidently confounded
" n " with " u," or the reverse, e.g., in " but," I have not reproduced the
error. I have done the same in a few cases where " f " and " ſ " were
confounded, e.g., in " for."

7. In a few cases letters or parts of words are either effaced or
did not come out in printing ; in such cases the missing matter is
supplied in italics, as, for instance, on pages : 203, 25 ; 221, 17 ; 251,
33 ; 258, 34 ; 271, 26 ; 274, 14 ; 304*, 25 ; 312, 8 ; 314, 31 ;
342, 9 ; 349, 31 ; 363, 34 ; 367, 5 ; 367, 30 ; 377, 14 ; 386, 9 ; 406,
7 ; 467, 20 ; 512, 26 ; 634, 34 ; 664, 10 ; 702, 15 ; 707, 6 ; 766,
34 ; 836, 22.

For the convenience of reference the pages and folios, with their
rectos and versos, are marked throughout the book, the former at the
head, the latter at the foot, of each page. The books and chapters
occurring on a page are also indicated at the top ; everything, however,
not found in the text of the original volume is put in brackets, to
preserve, as far as possible, the aspect of Caxton's book. Head-lines
are avoided for the same reason, and the various readings, instead
of being printed at the foot of each page, are given in a list in the

second volume, and referred to by means of figures (5, 10, 15, etc.) down the outer margin of every page.

The twenty-one pages missing in Lord Spencer's copy, but supplied by Mr. Whitaker's facsimiles, are marked by asterisks added to the paging numerals.

LIST OF ERRORS, OMISSIONS, AND ORTHOGRAPHICAL IRREGULARITIES IN CAXTON'S IMPRESSION.[1]

1 18, *for* "kno," *read* know.   2 34, "boookes," bookes. 3 35, "boook," book.   5 8, "boook," book.   6 25, "xvij," xvj. 8 17, "Hrre," Here.   9 2, "lofth ys," loft hys.   11 30, "damofel," *generally* damoyfel ; 37, "fy," fyr.   12 20, "boook," book.   14 36, "hoow," how.   15 20, "triftcum," triftram.   16 21, "lazarootc," lazarcote.   18 5, "fou3ght," fou3t *or* fought.   27 9, "fauggt," faught. 31 15, "lamentacyn," lamentacyon.   37 20, "nyg3," nyght *or* ny3t. 38 4, "lefey," lefay.   52 15, "Cornewallle," Cornewaile.   55 37, "poffyng," paffyng.   56 31, "here," were.   60 20, "the mand," them and ; 36, "ruffched," ruffhed.   61 2, "bloood," blood.   62 33, "dohomage," do homage.   63 10, "Cmyliarde," Camyliarde.   67 31, "af," of.   68 37—69 1, "terme me," ter- me.   74 16, "al one," alone.   75 2, "bnt."   78 7, "af," of ; 29, "mys fenformed," myfen-formed.   81 14, "nat," not.   85 23, "the the," the.   86 1, "on on," on an.   87 30, "werre," werfe ; 34, "knyyt," kny3t.   89 19, "Bafdemagus," Bagdemagus.   96 25, "yew," yow.   99 6, "handeld," handle ; 35, "ouer," euer.   101 6, "Ladegreans," Lodegreans.   110 27, "and one," on one.   118 11, "Pellinre," Pellinore.   123 38, "fenefcha," fenefchal.   132—133, *several words repeated by the compositors.* 134 37, "aduentures," aduenturous.   136 27, "counte ce naun," countenaunce.   141 35, "auentures," auenturous.   145 24, "&," x. 147 29, "ef," of.   152 26, "knyghht," knyght.   153 1, 5, "Pellas,"

---

[1] The first number refers to the page, the second to the line in which the word or words occur. The words marked with inverted commas are such as I found in Caxton, those in ordinary type my corrections, respectively readings. Words marked by asterisks and such in ordinary type with an italic "n" or "u" are such as I have corrected. Those few words marked by a dagger are slips of the press in the present edition.

Pelleas; "Nthurs," Arthurs. 161 26, "counceylleyou," counceylle you; 30, "xy M," xx M. 177 37, "his" *omitted.* 180 17, "wes," was; 31, "rotorned," retorned; 32, "for," for. 183 31, "hxm,"* hym. 186 21, "an," on. 187 10, "caaas," cafe; 31, "laake," lake. 189 21, "goood," good. 190 35, "&," *superfluous.* 194 15, "Turquyne," Launcelot. 197 34, "for," for. 201 30, "feythe," feythe. 206 8, "Ryyght," Ryght. 207 4, "loue," leue; 14, "of of," of. 209 30, "founed," fwouned. 210 16, "three," there; 32, "hrs," his. 211 1, "and," in. 215 30, "whyyfonday," whytfonday. 217 14 and 220 2, "Beumayns," Beaumayns. 233 34, "aftir," after. 235 12, "Noo," Now. 242 20, "te," to. 245, "Cap. xxij," Cap. xxj. 247, *last line a repetition of first line* 248. 248 38—249 1, "ye" *omitted.* 250 27, "knghtes," knyghtes. 251—252, "xxv" *omitted in the numbering of chapters.* 253 33, "Arthurle te," Arthur lete. 254 29, "haue" *omitted before* "the degre." 255 29, "fhal" *omitted before* "haue." 256 15, "Ilelys," Iles *or* Ilys. 258 30, "encountred" *omitted before* "with"; 34, "Launcelot," Lamorak. 261 32, "gym," hym. 265 1, "Thenme," Thenne; 10, "hem," hym. 266, "xxiiij," xxxiiij; 30, "do," done. 269 26, "maryge," maryage. 270 28, "on," an. 271 4, "dukde," duk de. 272 8, "knowm," knowen. 274 5, "gis," his. 282 23, "neuew," eme. 284 20, "fenefcal," fenefchal. 285 10, "arryuayl," arryual. 291 6, "Tcyftram," Tryftram 38, "he þᵗ," þᵗ he. 297—298, "defende" *omitted between* "knyghte" *and* "thyfelf." 305* 26, "racreaunt," recreaunt. 306* 20, "of the beft" *omitted after* "one." 311 19, "my," thy. 312 19, "lady les," ladyles. 314 16, "herborouh," herborough. 316, "xix," xxix. 318 11, "an," on. 320 23, "thr," the; 25, "poffyng," paffyng. 321 28, "flee," flee. 324 1, "ore," fire; 20, "Noo," Now. 330 6, "they"† *omitted before* "coude"; 27, "kay hedyus," kehedyus; 29 "roofe," roofe. 331 21, "Tdeftram," Triftram. 334 23, "he," they. 338 6, "myn," thyn. 347 15, "at euery ftroke" *superfluous.* 349 5, "fupoofed," fuppofed; 10, "Launucelot," Launcelot; 12, "vnto," vntil. 351 22, "nyyhe," nyghe. 357 6, "Ryyght," Ryght; 25, "moder," broder. 358 16, "dn," and. 363 6, "thye," they; 29, "Ifoud, Ifoud. 371 29, "was" *repeated.* 373, "xiij," xxiij; 1, "kyng Mark," fyr Triftram; 2, "nad," and. 374 25, "fperd," fpere. 376 22, "feaufhip," felaufhip. 378 16, "what" *repeated.* 379 35, "gayne," gawayne. 380, "xvij," xxvij. 382 10, "gooldis," goold is. 383, "xix," xxix. 385 10, "Northaglys," Northgalys ; 15, " it a " *omitted before* " fhame." 386 33, "feaufhip," felaufhip. 387 10, " there," theyr ; 31, "theil," their. 390 22, "ye," he. 400 26, "thrnne," thenne. 403 5, "pryny." 409 30, "we" *omitted before* " to fpeke." 410, " xliiij," xliij ; 33, " meruyylled," merueylled. 413 12, "lynyng." 415 9, " is " *repeated;* 10, "bataiylle," bataylle ; 36, "couuceylle." 428 27, "Berlnfe." 430 34, " Dyuadan." 432 11, "was" *or* "hym" *superfluous ;* 24, "rateynge," raceynge. 437 24, " Tdeftram," Triftram. 438 24, "grane." 439 17, "t" *omitted in* "lygh- ly." 441 2, "adone," adoo. 443 17, "done," do. 449 34 " boook," book. 450 30, " man," may. 454 7, " adnenture." 456 25, "Queneuer," Gueneuer. 458 2, " by " *omitted before* "kynge." 462 23, "your," our. 464 3, "blod," blood ; 12, "aud." 464 24, "Elyas," Elyot. 470 20, " & " *omitted after* "Malgryn." 471 17, "kny3," kny3t. 473 2, "he" *repeated.* 475 9, "kuyghtes." 476 13, "pilggrym," pilgrym. 477 8, "deperted," departed. 478 27, " faid " *omitted before* "the queen." 483 28, " Bleoberys," Blamore ; 32, " the " *omitted before* " nofe " ; 33, " therecam," there cam. 484 8, " Bagdemagns." 486 33, " Elyfe," Elyfes. 487 36, " conenable," couenable. 489 9, "dyuer." 490, " xlv, xlvj, xlvij " *omitted in the numbering ;* 8, " to " *omitted before* "the felde." 491 7, " Kyuge." 492 15, " one " *repeated.* 494 37, "kyny,"* kyng. 497 16, " Percyuole," Percyuale ; 27, "Dyanas,"† Dynas ; 33, "pntte." 500 20, " to " *repeated.* 503 4, " Brufe," Breufe ; 16, " ener." 504 2, "for," with ; 32, "wyhle," whyle. 506 36, " do do," to do. 511 10, "knyeght," knyght ; 36, "wherr," where. 515 19, *after* " fuche " " chere " *is evidently omitted.* 516 13, " v,"* a. 518 12, " Palomyders," Palomydes. 521 16, " an " *omitted before* " houre "; 24, " Arthnrs " ; 26, "knygyte," knyghte ; 29, "Lamorck," Lamorak. 529 16, "af," of. 531 20, "we" *superfluous.* 534 4, "Bleberys," Bleoberys. 535, "lxxij," lxx ; 1, "as" *omitted before* " I maye"; 4, " I " *omitted before* "fhalle." 536 4, "make," made. 538 5, " Palomydes," Launcelot. 541 23, " Palmydes," Palomydes ; 35, " parfon," perfon. 543 2 *and* 31, "Dorkeney," Orkeney. 545 12, " cammaundement," commaundement. 548 33, "yours," your ; 34, "nename" (?). 553 13, "pnlled "; 33, " knygthode," knyghthode. 554 3, " Launceloot," Launcelot ; 33, "Trifram," Triftram. 555 7, "do," done ; 13, "doune "; 15, "kyuge." 556 33, "Blebeorys," Bleoberys. 558 15, "tabble," table.   559, "lxviij," lxxxiij ;   33, " Helynor," Helyor. 561 30, "Epyʀogrys."   563 33, "knyytes," knyʒtes.   564 12, "Thenye," Thenne.   566 9, "vppn," vppon.   568 5, "payd" *super-fluous;*   25, "retornod," retorned.   569 1, "launcelot," palomydes ; 9, "ententente," entente.   572 11, "word," world.   574 8, " Queneuer," Gueneuer ;   19, "kʀewe";   22, "man ere," manere ;   31, "Elaye," Elayne.   575 12, "f ſhehalle," ſhe ſhalle ;   18, "teld," told.   576 28, "Theʀne";   29, "meruelle," merueylle.   577 15, "aduentures," aduenturous.   579 23, "owne," one.   580 24, "rebellioʀs";   29, "wile," wille.   581 24, "counteʀaunce."   582 10, "laʀncelot."   585 19, " their," her.   587 26, "brodr," broder.   589 38, *after* "vp-" "*on*" *omitted.*   590—591, "of" *omitted before* "yow."   591 10, " renne " or " mette " *omitted.*   592 1, "n lyuote" not lyue.   593, "boooke," booke.   596 30, "tho," go.   598 37, "hoʀre."   599 34, "kʀowe."   600 32, " be " *omitted after* "ye."   604 8, "fyten," † fyften.   608 2, "aʀd";   36, " ſhat," ſhalt.   609 27, " ſenſhip," ſhenſhip.   614* 6, " thenʀe ";   28, "marhel," marbel.   616 8, " Abarimathye," Arimathye ;   32, " is " *omitted before* "he" ;   33, " but he " *repeated.* 618 21, "aduenturrs," aduentures.   620 11, "an other," on other. 623* 6, "perceyʀe."   624 17, "left," beſt ;   22, "beynge," brynge. 625 16, " good," god ;   33, " greto," grete.   626 21, "meeueyll," merueyll ;   28, "Ioheph,"* Ioſeph.   628 24, "loʀed."   629 34, "faʀe." 632 5, "thy," the.   633 9, "kayes," keyes.   639 3, " ornot,"* or not. 640 11, "morr," more.   641 7, "hard" *probably omitted after* " more."   642, "whiches," whiche is ;   15, "reecluſe," recluſe ;   18, " commauʀded."   647 8, " came " *repeated.*   649 16, "be," † he. 650 34, "flay," ſlay.   651 31, " a " † *omitted.*   658 3, " loetryd," * entryd ;   4, " nt," * not.   659 34, "et," † at.   660 24, " knygthode," knyghthode.   664 19, " his " *repeated.*   666 26, " douʀe";   27, " of " † *omitted before* "full."   667 36, "thotherr," thother.   669 1, *some words omitted;*   25, " Thenʀe."   670 27, "aduenturr," aduenture. 673 16, " fyghto," * fyghte ;   25, " goʀerne."   677 24, " knyʒght," knyght *or* knyʒt.   679 14, " lauʀcelot."   680 10, " abone," aboue ; 31, " Aʀd."   682 38, " floʀre."   685 19, " one " *superfluous.*   687 11, " ſheltes," ſheldes.   689 28, " Thʀs."   691 37, " he " *omitted after* " Certes."   693 26, "werfor," wherfor ;   34, "ſhypthat," that ſhyp.   694 33, " aad myghde," and myghte.   695 1, "we," the ; 10, "bʀt."   696 1, " hym " *superfluous ;*   16, " brauʀche ";   27, " Caym,"

Cayn. 703 29, "k*u*owe." 705 13, "haue" *omitted after* "we."
710 16, "harme," arme ; 20, "fay u," ? faire. 711 38—712 1, *a
repetition.* 719 1, "his" *omitted before* "other." 723 16, "me,"
probably omitted after "refembled." 725 15, "hie," his. 733 28,
"doth," do. 733 35, "wynchefter," Weftmeftre. 736 31, "quene,"
kyng. 737 20, "knytes," knyghtes. 739 4, "launcolot," launcelot.
741 14, "theire," there. 742 2, "kymge,"* kynge. 743 33, "fkynne,"
(?) kynne. 744 35, "A*u*d" ; 37, "e*n*er." 747 21, "feruauytes,"
feruauntes. 751 22, "yf," of. 752 21, "me," (?) hym. 754 8,
"Tlerfor,"* Therfor. 759 20, "goood," good. 762 29, "launcelat,"
launcelot. 764 27, "thy," the. 765, "xx," xxij. 766, "xxij," xxiij ;
7, "I*n*ge." 768 13, "Arthr," Arthur. 769 6, "is" *after* "where," *or*
7, "haue been" *omitted after* "blood." 776 26, "were" (?). 777
10, "tabbe,"* table. 778 2, "Melliagaunce," Melliagraunce ; 30,
"ȝere" (?) ("ere," W. de Worde). 782 34, "r*u*moure." 788 25, "b*u*t."
790 15, "fo,"* of. 790—791, *a repetition.* 792 13, "Triftram,"
Gawayn ; 23, "tre*u*chaunt." 798 26, "Agrauayye," Agrauayne.
799 26, "dyd," hyd (?). 802 8, "raffyng," (?) raffhyng. 803 38,
"wan," than. 804 32, "a a," a. 805 15, "theyir," theyr. 806 37,
"Arthue,"* Arthur ; 38, "be" *repeated.* 811 6, "myhapped,"
myfhapped. 813 30, "your," you. 820 31, "o*u*." 823, "xiiij,"
xv ; 7, "a" *omitted before* "bold." 828 38, "fpap," fpak. 830,
11, "Neroneus" (?) ; 19, "S*n*rlat." 837 33, "Gawyns," Gawayns,
838 14, "nerre," nere. 840 18, "Launcelot," Gawayn. 842 24,
"a" *superfluous after* "For." 843 34, "that" *omitted before* "loued."
845 1, "vaynquyffhe," vanyffhe. 846 19, "ly*n*e." 848 6, "fowned,"
fwouned ; 24, "fad," fayd ; 28, "fef,"* felf. 850 3, "tho*n*" ; 9,
"af," of ; 17, "demyyng," demyng ; 35, "ne*n*er" ; 35, "boookes,"
bookes. 851 5, "Nynyue," *generally* "Nymue." 853 31, "yo*n*r" ;
35, "fewe,"* fewe. 854 38, "fofaken," forfaken. 858* 12, "b*n*t."
861* 1, "book" *repeated.*

RESULT OF THE COLLATION OF WHITTAKER'S FACSIMILES WITH THE ORIGINAL PAGES.[1]

HE following table shows how far Whittaker succeeded in reproducing the original in his facsimile pages. In the first column are quoted the readings of Lord Spencer's copy as I have reproduced them in my text; the second column shows the readings of the only perfect copy, once at Osterley, now in America.

Leaf l₁ [pages 195* and 196*]

	FACSIMILES.	ORIGINALS.
recto : 5	doe	doo
8	roffhynge	raffhynge
13	befpeckled	befperkled
25	leue	lene
29	myȝteſt	myȝtyeſt
35	fore	fayre
—	manayr	manoyr
verso : 12	manore	manoir
23	fays	fayd

Leaf r₇ [pages 303* and 304*]

recto : 28	palfray	palfroy
34	corne	torne
—	xxj	xxij
verso : 8	faunte	faunce
11	reyentyd	repentyd
25	fal wed	falewed
29	fyonas	lyonas

Leaf r₈ [page 305]

recto : 26	racreaunt	recreaunt
30	worlde	world

---

[1] Leaves : r₈ verso [page 306*]; N₂ recto [613*]; N₈ recto [623*]; ee₂ recto [855]; ee₄ verso [857*] and ee₆ recto [861*] are faultless.

Leaf N_2 [page 614*]

FACSIMILES.			ORIGINALS.
verso :	8	faith	faid
	28	marhel	marbel

Leaf N_8 [page 624*]

verso :	22	beynge	brynge
	29	fheef	fhoef

Leaf T_4 [pages 713* and 714*]

recto :	10	enchere	encheue
	24	bere	bare
verso :	8	ye	yo
	22	twelue	a twelue
	33	efcared	efcaped

Leaf T_5 [pages 715* and 716*]

recto :	2	Gatahad	Galahad
verso :	5	departede	departed

Leaf ee_3 [page 856*]

verso :	13	Bleoheris	Bleoberis
	—	Clarras	Clarrus
	14	Gohaleaniyne	Gahalantyne
	16	laft	luft
	18	preefthod	preefthode
	21	bodoly	lowly
	29	then	thou
	30	parouey	puruey
	37	fore	fote

Leaf ee_4 [page 858*]

verso :	17	wekye	wekyes
	24	houe	haue

FACSIMILES.		ORIGINALS.
verso : 25	So	Se
29	hamborow	bamborow
36	bedd	bedde

Leaf ee₅ [pages 859* and 860*]

recto : 10	proue	preue
18	togydere	togyders
20	bernnyng	brennyng
verso : 12	breſte	reeſte
25	Wyllats de balyaunt	Wyllars de valyaunt
—	Clartus	Clarrus
29	countreys	countreyes

Previous to the first issue of his Globe edition in 1867 Sir Edward Strachey collated his text of the Southey edition (of course only the doubtful pages), not only with Whittaker's facsimiles, but also with the originals then still at Osterley. He kindly sent me his volumes to London, and thus enabled me to check the American collation. According to Sir E. Strachey, we have to read : Page 305* 33, "hit," *for* it ; 855* 6, "erthyly," erthly ; 858* 20, "cryſten," chryſten ; 35, "that," then ; 859* 14, "&," and ; 860* 29, "cuntreyes," countreyes ; 39, "hoole," booke.

NOTES ON THE LANGUAGE OF "LE MORTE DARTHUR."

THE language in which Sir Thomas Malory's "Le Morte Darthur" has come down to us in Caxton's imprint offers many peculiar features, and cannot fail to be of interest and value to the philologist. It would be a useful and meritorious task to treat the whole of Caxton's numerous volumes with regard to their linguistic peculiarities ; in short, to write a Caxton-grammar similar to those of the language of Chaucer[1] and Shakspere.[2] This

---

[1] B. ten Brink, "Chaucer's Sprache und Verskunst." Leipzig, 1884, 8vo.
[2] E. A. Abbot, "A Shakspearian Grammar : an Attempt to illustrate some of the Differences between Elizabethan and Modern English." London, 1870, 8vo.

suggestion can, of course, only be realized when trustworthy editions of all the works issued from the press of the first English printer are within the reach of every scholar.[1] Time and space only allow me to note in brief the most characteristic examples of Caxton's orthography, phraseology, and syntax which attracted my attention during the compilation of the Index and Glossary.

If we adopt the common division into three periods of the English language—viz., Old English till 1250, Middle English till 1485, and from thence onward Modern English—our text belongs (taking in consideration that it was in manuscript in 1474, eleven years before it saw the light of day) either to the close of Middle English or to the opening of Modern English. And, indeed, whilst resembling in many respects the familiar language of Chaucer's poetry, it has also a marked modern colouring, and is akin to the language of Shakspere and his predecessors. Being thus the product of a period of transition and change, it is not surprising to find on every page, in every line, the strife of ancient and modern forms. No uniform orthography existed at that time, and the art of printing, still in its infancy, was incapable of effecting such an innovation.

Just as the first printed books closely resemble the manuscripts they were intended to replace, so their language is like that of the manuscripts, the orthography is that of the individual scribe, and here and there abbreviations and contractions occur, though not to the same extent as in the manuscripts.

Caxton's orthography, as I prefer to call it, instead of Malory's, believing that Malory's text underwent a considerable change while passing through the press, is, to say the least of it, most remarkable; what it is like can be best seen from some examples.

The Modern English word *means* occurs in the following different spellings:—1. "menes" (394 35); 2. "meane" (11 30); 3. "moyne" (16 11); 4. "moyan" (10 23); 5. "moyane" (6 4).

Realm is spelled: 1. "reame" (39 34); 2. "royame" (11 2);

---

[1] Dr. L. Kellner, in his forthcoming edition of Caxton's "Blanchardyn & Eglantyne" (Early-English Text Society), of which he kindly submitted to me some proof-sheets of the opening pages of the Introduction, has devoted himself to the study of Caxton's syntax. He quotes not only from his text, but also from the "Foure Sonnes of Aymon," ed. by Miss O. Richardson (E.-E. T. S.), 1885, and from my edition of "Le Morte Darthur." To judge from what I have seen of it, his work will be a most valuable contribution to the study of the English tongue.

3. "reaume" (45 8); 4. "royalme" (4 11); 5. "realme" (67 5);
6. "royaume" (160 15).

Thorough: 1. "thorugh" (1 12); 2. "thorowe" (37 16); 3. "thorou" (235 16); 4. "thurgh" (59 12).

Hair: 1. "hayre" (657 16); 2. "hayr" (27 27); 3. "heyre" (362 19); 4. "here" (83 22).

Whither: 1. "whyder" (378 10); 2. "whydder" (702 28); 3. "whyther" (384 15); 4. "whether" (219 15); 5. "wheder" (297 21).

The Glossary will disclose many more examples of a similar character.

Many words which in Modern English differ in meaning and orthography are spelled alike in Caxton: *e.g.*, "here" (*to hear*); "here" (*the hair*), "here" (*here*); "hede" (*the head*), "hede" (*heed*); "herte" (*heart*), "herte" (*hart*); "mete" (*meat*), "mete" (*meet, fitting*), "mete" (*to meet*); etc.

Compounds of different particles which generally form one word nowadays are written in two: *e.g.*, "to gyder"; "by nethe"; "by caufe"; likewise all pronouns with "felf," as "her felf"; "hym felf." In Caxton "felf" has no plural, or rather the plural *selves* is always spelt like the singular (comp. 389 6; 198 12). The same is the case with "other," which is also plural and singular (305 12; 361 12; 446 13).

The termination "er" occurs both in the Saxon and in the Norman form: "hongre," "honger."

The final mute "e" is more frequently used than in Modern English: "fent*e*"; "gren*e*"; "hand*e*"; "own*e*"; "red*e*"; "non*e*."

Words are not divided according to syllables or roots and terminations, but according to the space. The conjunctive-hyphen is rarely employed.

The prefixes "be-" ("bi-" or "by-"), "for-," "to-," and "male" often occur where unused nowadays, and are mostly separated from the verb.

"*be-*": "bebled" (294 12); "bybledeft" (176 33); "beclofed" (601 2); "bedaffhed" (773 31); "befalle" (420 34), etc.; for others see the Glossary.

"*for-*": "forbled" (350 26); "fordone" (334 32); "fordyd" (99 3); "forfende" (727 8); "forfendyd" (727 13); "forfoughten" (87

25) ; "foriufted" (421 30) ; "forthynketh" (82 2) ; "forwounded" (350 26).

"*male*" : "male engyne" (733 16) ; "male eafe" (338 2) ; "male fortune" (392 21).

"*to-*" : "to braft" (204 20) ; "to cratched" (583 14) ; "to-forne" (247 20) ; "to hewe" (338 9) ; "to rofe" (330 29) ; "to fheuered" (481 12).

The prefixes "dis-" and "es-" occur once each in a short form : "fcomfyte" (146 38) for "difcomfyte" ; "fcape" (92 33) for "efcape."

Two cases are noticeable in which the prefix has been separated from the verb and placed at the end of the sentence.

"for ye haue the water to paffe ouer" (632 22).

"and wold haue ronne fir Triftram thurgh" (526 4).

Something very similar takes place with the preposition *toward*: It is separated, *to* preceding, and *ward* following the noun or pronoun : "to the death ward" (70 27) ; "to yᵉ Iuftes warde" (41 12) ; "comyng to hym warde" (27 17) ; but at the same time we find examples like the use in Modern English : "toward the caftel" (379 2).

The following contractions are used :—

1. The article "the" with the initial vowel or even "h" of its noun : "themperour" ; "tharchbyffhop" ; "thabite" ; etc.

2. The preposition "to" with the initial vowel of the verb : "tenprynte" ; "tefcape" ; etc.

3. The preposition "at" with the article is contracted in "atte" ; "atte requefte" ; "atte turnement" ; sometimes, however, the form "atte," or "att," and the article occur : *e.g.*, "att the caftel" (408 9) ; and with the indefinite article : "att a pryuy pofterne" (403 9).

4. The negative "not" with the present tense of to be : "nys"= "is not" (127 6 ; 219 35 ; 538 4 ; 748 20).

5. The negative with the present and imperfect tenses of to will : "nyll"="wyll not" (297 32 ; 506 2) ; "nylt"="wylt not" (641 17) ; "nold"="wold not" (705 31).

6. The negative with the present tense of "weten" (to know) : "nyft"="he wyft not" (729 12 ; 677 3).

The old prefix of the past participle, "y," only occurs four times : "y fonde" (699 35) ; "y barryd" (780 27) ; "y fette" (822 32) ; "y fought" (754 1).

Finally I must mention a number of words which are either adopted

from the French originals in their proper form or disfigured.   Such are:
"peramour," "paramour"; "per-" or "parauenture"; "maulgre,"
"malgre," "maugre"; "per de," "per di," "par dieu"; "roche";
"lesses les aler" (*herald's cry*); "pounte."

The epithets of many proper names: "le breune"; "faunce pyte";
"de les yles"; "les auoultres"; "le fyfe de roye"; "le" or "la
blaunche maynys"; "le" or "la beale"; "le fyfe vayffhoure";
"maledyfaunt"; "bien penfaunt, beau viuante"; "le fyfe de dieu,"
once corrupted "le fyfe dene"; "le" or "la cote male tayle"; and
finally, "le morte darthur," etc.   It is remarkable that the definite
article of the masculine and feminine genders is constantly misapplied.

Some cases may also be mentioned where the French and the Saxon
form of the same word are placed in a pleonastic way beside one
another, the first forming a sort of adverb for the second: "oute
excepte" (102 11); "enuyronne aboute" (628 12); and "vnmefur-
ably oute of mefure" (640 22).

Whilst the orthography of common names is thus often perplexing,
this is still more the case with personal names.   The name of the
same person occurs in such different spellings that it is often difficult
to identify its bearers, and in many cases it can only be guessed at
from the context.   Some examples will speak best:

"Mellegaunt" (479); "Malegeaunt" (480); "Melyagaunt" (482),
"Melyagaunce" (356); "Melyaganus" (257); "Mellyagraunce" (780);
are all names of the same man.

"Berlufes" (436); "Berlyfes" (*ibid.*); "Berfules" (423); and
"Berlufe" (427).

The lady or "damoyfel" of the lake is called "Nymue" (115), and
"Nyneue" (118).

Another knight, "Gromere Gumorfon" (258), *i.e., son of Gumor*, is
called elsewhere "Grumore gummurfum" (256), and very likely the
form "Gromore fomyr Ioure" (799) is another corruption, as it
only occurs once.   Indeed, the names offer many difficulties, and I
was not surprised to find that Sir Edward Strachey, the only one of
the previous editors of "Le Morte Darthur" who ever attempted to
compile an Index of Names and a Glossary, has made many mistakes
in his Index.   He speaks of three "Gromeres," whereas they are all
one and the same person.   He mentions two "Vryens," whereas there
is only one: "King Vryence," or "Vriens of the land of Gore,"

husband of " Morgan le fay." The same error occurs with " Gracian,"
"Grastian," and " Gratian "; " Epinegris," " Epynogrys"; " Gillemere "
and " Gilmere " ; " Lamerake of Wales" and " Lomarake of Galis " ;
" Melyot de Logres " and " Melyot de Logurs "; " Neroneus " and
" Nerouens "; " Pertilope " and " Pertolepe "; and some others.

The numerous epithets are most puzzling : " the valyaunt," " the
son of," " the aduenturous," and the like. Persons often have epithets
characteristic of others, and the same person has different epithets ;
of course this caused much confusion. There are, for instance, two
" Galahads," " Galahalts," or " Galahaults," one the son of " Launcelot "
and "Elayne doughter of King Pelles "; the other, son of "Sir Breunor
of Surlufe." Both are surnamed "the haute prynce." In "Vwayne's"
case the reverse takes place ; he has three different epithets. In the
first two hundred pages he figures without any epithet, later on he is
once "Vwayne les auoutres," once " le fyfe de roy Vreyne " (comp.
Index of Names, etc.), " les aduenturous," " le " or " la blaunche
maynys," etc.[1] In the " table or rubryffhe " and once in the text
(page 38) his name is spelled " Ewayne le blaunche maynys." Sir
Edward Strachey in his Index has three different persons.

Names of places afford still more difficulty. Not to speak of the
poor geographical and chronological knowledge of those days that
identifies " Camelot " with " Winchefter," or that speaks of a *Westminster
Bridge* in the fifth century, the spelling of the names of cities, countries,
etc., is so bad, and the original names are so much disfigured, that in
many cases it is, despite the greatest efforts, absolutely impossible to
identify them. Compare, for instance, on page 163 the enumeration of
the different parts of the Roman Empire : " Arrage "; " Ambage ";
" Cayer "; " Ertayne "; " Pounce "; " Cateland "; etc. etc.

After these general remarks I proceed to enumerate a few of my
observations, which must not be supposed to exhaust the subject.

I. The personal pronoun of the second person of the plural is
rendered in Caxton by " ye " and " yow," the former representing
the nominative, the latter the accusative ; if there should be met
anywhere " ye " for the accusative it is most probably a mistake

---

[1] Compare text, page 667, lines 32 and 33 : " Vwayne les auoultres that fometyme was
fone of kynge Vryens"; and page 401, 5-6: "V. le fyfe de roy Vreyne / and fomme
callid hym le blaunche maynys."

due to the compositors, who misinterpreted the abbreviation in the manuscript.

My is invariably rendered by "myn": "myn ende" (755 32); "myn vnhappynes" (753 22).

It is generally spelt "hyt" or "hit" (61 5; 148 6); *them* is replaced by "hem" (85 21; 631 26); and *their* is written "her" (643 25; 816 11).

Hym felf stands for he: "and the noble name that hym felf had" (567 5); and *he* stands for hym felf: "he weneth no knyght fo good as he" (202 11).

These, the plural of *this*, occurs in the form "this": "this thre yere" (61 21); "this feuen yere" (207 16).

Which is both a relative and an interrogative pronoun, and refers to persons as well as things: "whiche was fomtyme the rycheft woman of the world" (652 31).

Who, or *he who*, is mostly rendered by "the whiche": "Ban thy fader the which was" (660 17).

That what is rendered by "that that": "for now I fee that that hath ben my defyre" (723 8).

In many cases the relative pronoun is entirely omitted, an infrequent usage in Modern English; some examples will best illustrate the practice.

"There is no maker can reherce the tenthe parte" (562 32); "fende hym a gyfte fhalle pleafe hym" (101 2); "a knyght wold fyghte for hym" (127 8); "found one was fair and ryche" (84 5); "for here ar no moo wille haue adoo with me" (443 5); "for there is no tonge can telle the Ioye" (708 34); "there was a monke broughte him vnto a tomb" (627 31).

What is sometimes used for *some* or *any*: "what by land what by water" (556 19); "delyuer hym to what poure man ye mete" (39 7).

Each other or *one another* occurs in the following forms:—1. "*other*": "they fmote other in the fheldes" (97 8); 2. "*eche other*," either separated or together: "eche falewed other" (659 28); "eche of hem dreffid to other" (109 37); "how ij bretheren flewe eche other" (98 27); 3. "*eueryche other*": "wounded eueryche other dolefully" (97 21); 4. "*eyther other*": "wounded eyther other" (142 32); finally, 5. "*to gyder*": "they loued to gyder" (707 25); "they kyffed to gyder" (725 19).

Both, written "*bothe*," is mostly placed at the end of the sentence: "vnto my grete dommage and his bothe" (134 10); "I am fo hurte and he bothe" (134 11); "bothe his hors and he" (accusative!) (112 30); "conferue me and you bothe" (709 35).

Al, alle (= altogether) is used adverbially in order to give more stress; it has the sense of *entirely :* "al only" (832 16; 573 26); "al dede" (715* 33); "tale al hole" (855* 26); "al to long" (133 2); "alle to hewe hym" (513 9); "braft it vpon hym alle to fheuers" (554 14); "were foughten wyth al" (29 14)

The imperative is frequently followed by the pronoun.

II. The Saxon or possessive genitive is used more frequently than to-day, and with regard to things as well as to persons. There are different ways in which it occurs. 1. *s* is added to the nominative, the use of the apostrophe being entirely unknown, the *s* being considered as a remainder of the old genitive: "Lots wyf" (425 12); "Bryfens wytte" (573 34); "mans herte" (670 21); names terminating in *s* remain unchanged: "Pelles doughter" (612 11). 2. *es* is added to the nominative[1]: "Mordredes wylle" (839 15); "Cadores fone" (860* 17); "mennes bodyes" (52 22). 3. *ys* (*is*) is added to the nominative: "childis" (37 3); "Markys party" (463 30); "Tyrreis fhelde" (749 15); "Percyualis fyfter" (91 28). In the plural no *s* is added: "lyftes ende" (734 33); "feuen kynges Realmes" (814 14); "knyghtes names" (101 31).

A few instances occur where the *s* is omitted in the singular: "atte brydge foote" (589 17); "at the raunge ende" (573 34); and "fir Patryfe dethe" (733 13).

The plural of nouns is formed by the addition of "s," "es," and frequently "ys" or "is." Such plurals are: "handys" (61 29); "fallys" (477 5); "gatys" (459 37); "dedys" (888 13); "membrys" (649 34); "ornementys" (711 16); "complayntys" (562 31); "meanys" (840 14); "buryellys" (851 11); "lordis" (829 23); and many others.

Many abstract nouns only used in Modern English in the singular occur in the plural, such as: "valyaunces, proweffes, appertyces" (173 14); "aduyfes" (308 14); "wronges" (373 12); "ententes"

---

[1] Cases like the following : "fowles helthe" (705 25); "worldes ende" (649 35); "woodes fyde" (745 24), cannot be enumerated here, as the *e* occurs already in the singular.

(247 26) ; "refcowes" (502 10) ; "buryels" (466 23) ; "myrthes" (500 1 ; 562 21) ; "lyfers" (474 35).

In other places we find the singular employed where we should expect the plural : "two *myle* hens" (267 36) ; "a thoufand *pound*" (785 32) ; "fourty *pounde* a pees" (853 19) ; "*a* thre myle Englyffhe" (437 8) ; "*a* thyrtty *couple* of houndes" (434 12). The addition of the indefinite article in the last two examples is as remarkable as in the following : "*a* large amendys" (plural !) (438 4) ; "*a* ten dayes afore" (396 13) ; and "fewe *a* felaufhip" (53 33).

Often the article, as well the definite as the indefinite, is omitted : "I put caas" (600 30 ; 608 17) ; "neuer fpak word" (451 33) ; "wythin fhort tyme" (78 19) ; "in fhort tyme" (707 24) ; "for fone" (8 25) ; "at auauntage" (560 35) ; "yeue anfuer" (38 12) ; "in deferte" (708 17) ; "As worldes fhame" (785 16) ; "I caft me neuer to be wedded man" (758 22).

The substantive "*heuen*" is used both with and without the article : "under heuen" (804 9) ; "toward —" (723 7) ; "from —" (699 1) ; "fader of —" (710 35) ; "lady of —" (273 33) ; on the other hand : "under *the* heuen" (87 14) ; "to *the* —" (681 11) ; "toward *the* —" (659 1) ; "up to *the* —" (659 3).

The substantive "*loue*" is treated as a masculine noun : "loue is free in hym felfe / and neuer wille be bounden / for where *he* is bounden," etc. (762 22).

Not unfrequently substantives are treated as adjectives : "quenes *forcereffes*" (187 27) ; "*traitour* knyght" (289 34) ; an example of the independent genitive occasionally occurs : "take that hors *of his yefte*" (841 24).

The substantive "*maner*" is used in connection with other nouns with or without "*of*" : "maner *of* wyfe" (811 28) ; "— *of* difportes" (800 21) ; "— *of* knoulechynge" (733 13) ; "— *of* nobleffe" (770 36) ; and in other places : "ony manere knyghte" (762 18) ; "in ony maner wyfe" (680 21) ; "in this — wyfe" (74 22) ; "alle — aduentures daungerous" (803 18).

III. The adjective precedes or follows the noun, the former more frequently than the latter : "feeft Royal" (401 4) ; "leges englyffhe" (428 35) ; "knyghtes aduenturous" (410 9) ; fege perillous" (452 4) ; "table round" (429 22).

The use of two or more adjectives with a noun differs greatly from that of Modern English. One generally precedes the noun, whereas the other follows as a sort of apposition joined by "*and*," with or without the article: "a grete wounde and a peryllous" (412 26; 442 21); "a pyteous complaynte and a dolorous" (435 7); "a horryble lybard and an old" (579 5); "a good *old* man and an *auncyent*" (616 1); "to a ftrong towre and an hyhe" (672 37); "a ryche kynge and a myghty" (621 1); "a *moche* man and a large" (802 16); without the article: "wylde beeftes foule and horryble" (844 6); "grete botes and fmal" (841 12); "the mooft merueillous man of the world and mooft aduenturous" (663 2); "in the beft maner and freffheft" (773 32).

In a few cases the adjective takes an *s* in the plural, but only in words of French origin: "moft valyaunt*s* men" (83 31); "the mefcreaunt*s* Sarafyns" (135 30).

Sometimes the adjective is treated as a substantive: "he fhalle haue many his better" (579 32).

The comparison of adjectives is very peculiar; all, whether *monosyllabic*, or *bi-syllabic* with the accent on the second, or terminating in -*le* with preceding consonant, or ending in *y*, indicate comparison not only by adding *er* to the comparative and *est* to the superlative, but also by putting *more* or *most* before them. Some superlatives may be found without *most*, and some comparatives without *more*: "more gladder" (218 23); "— leuer" (269 11); "— reufullyr" (425 26); "— wrother" (405 2); "— rychelyer" (580 33); "— heuyer" (749 26); "— nobler" (842 24); "— hotter" (725 19); "— largelyer" (754 10); "— blacker" (651 30); etc. etc.; "mooft curteyft" (394 29); "— worfhipfulleft" (361 35); "— mefchyeuouft" (413 32); "— profytelyeft" (733 32); "— nobleft" (747 15); quite exceptionally: "moofte noble" (367 21); "mooft orgulift" (840 6); etc. etc. Without *more* or *most*: "valyaunter" (447 17); "falflyer" (520 10); "traitourlyer" (520 11); "oftyner" (566 3); "fyerfer" (181 31); "horrybleft" (296 3); "valyaunteft" (454 21); "famofeft" (278 25); "merueillouft" (278 23); "freyffheyft" (763 23); etc. etc.

Most is used like an adjective with nouns: "*mooft* coward" (502 12); "*mooft* kyng" (840 29); "*mooft* vylayn" (414 35). The same is the case with *moche*: "a moche man" (802 16).

The negative before a comparative is *not* or *no*: "not lenger" (723 9); "noo lenger" (735 14).

Instead of the adverb *very*, adjectives and adverbs are preceded by "full," "right," "paſſyng," "paſſyngly": "ful bolde" (841 14); "ryghte parfyte" (695 34); "paſſynge wyſe" (35 8); "paſſyngly wel" (763 8).

IV. Here and there occur irregular or obsolete forms of preterites, infinitives, and past participles; these are registered in their respective places in the Glossary. Present and preterite have often the same form, *e.g.,* "*come,*" which is both present and preterite: "By than come in to the field" (57 34); "Sone come merlyn" (38 26).

The past participles generally end in *en* or *n,* as "abyden," "ryden," "comen," "holpen," etc.; some participles are, however, to be found where the final *n* is dropped: "undertake" (340 34); "ryde" (82 16); "founde" (434 34); "befalle" (420 34); "be" (147 10); [comp. "*ben*" (203 22)]; "take" (715* 32); "diſcomfyte" (766 26); "benome" (674 23); "bete" (667 8). There occur also some shortened participles; *e.g.,* "fond" (590 18) for "founden" (246 36).

The plural of the present tense is formed in "*-eth,*" but many forms of the Midland plural "*-en*" occur: "ſaiden" (140 29); "pleaſen" (101 17); "vſen" (128 14); "ſpeken" (425 27); "comen" (280 12); "bryngen" (771 4); "floryſſhen" (771 4); "defyen" (632 24); "defenden" (632 25); "ſygnefyen" (682 36); "repayren" (643 22); "putten" (149 10); "ben" (101 91; 1 12; 801 3; 445 1); etc. etc.

The second person of the singular has often no inflexion: "thow goo" (107 7); "thow doo" (593 30); "thow took" (111 15); "thow were" (66 15); but: "ſaweſt thou" (66 15).

The auxiliary *to be* has the form *be* for all persons singular and plural in the present tense: "god be not thy friend" (70 28); "it be taken" (78 12); "we be not yet come therto" (704 29); "why be ye" (94 28); "ye be welcome" (89 32); "volumes be made" (3 8).

The auxiliary *to do* is not used in negative and interrogative sentences: "knew not" (100 3; 97 6); "gate ye" (41 32); "come ye" (86 12). But *to do* is used in connection with other verbs in order to increase the emphasis: "do made" (1 7); "dyd do ranſake" (174 11); "made do crye" (92 9); "dyd do calle" (180 34); "dyd do cere" (174 22).

Once "*done*" occurs as second person plural: "conſyderyng the grete dedes of armes I haue ſene you *done*" (444 33).

Many verbs are treated as reflexive which are no longer such nowadays. The reflexive pronoun is not *myself, thyself, himself, themselves,* but "*me,*" "*the,*" "*hym,*" and "*hem*" (*them*). Only very rarely forms with *self* are to be met. Such is, *e.g.*, the case: "hydeſt thow thy ſelf" (834 1); "ſhe rofe her ſelf" (82 28); whereas: "he roofe *hym*" (95 35); some examples are subjoined: "I aſſente me" (71 12); "I compte me" (342 12); "I ſhalle remembre me" (381 17); "I wylle repoſe me" (417 1); "I complayne me" (650 2); "I drede me" (745 29; 767 24). Other verbs used as reflexives are: "to rcſt" (131 3; 183 19); "excuſe" (367 30); "bethink" (239 31); "arme" (137 23; 90 33); "defende" (404 1); "drawe" (385 3); "torne" (39 35); "retorne" (46 11); "byhaue" (24 18); and many others.

Many verbs are used impersonally: "me oughte to doo" (214 16); "me ſemeth" (127 28); "me lyketh" (74 13); "me lyſt" (90 27); "hit lyketh the" (222 10); "how lyketh yow" (215 26); "it myſfortuned me" (418 17; 557 12); "hit fore forthynketh me" (643 12); "as it telleth" (64 31); "as it reherceth afore" (105 11); "hit fortuned" (364 21); etc. etc.

The active voice is frequently used instead of the passive: "for to nouriſſhe" (37 1); "herde a grete horne blowe" (529 11).

In phrases expressing a wish the pronoun generally precedes the verb: "god yow ſaue" (541 5); "fayre knyght god the bleſſe" (745 13); "god yow blyſſe" (753 21); "god me forbede" (207 8).

Many verbs are conjugated with to *be* instead of with to *have:* "were mette" (561 22); "was become" (366 15); "is become" (68 16); "was ryden" (151 7); "was arryued" (367 15); "I am come to the dethe" (706 4); etc.

The short dative is not strictly necessary after some verbs: "ſente to me" (3 13); "tolde to Lucius" (11 12); "graunte to hym" (12 27); "gyuen to hym" (15 2); "tolde hym" (15 29); "graunte hem me" (213 17); etc.

Make in the sense of *to bid, to order,* is generally constructed with *to:* "made to yelde" (13 22); "made alle lordes to come in" (44 4).

V. The use of the prepositions differs greatly from that of the present day, and is arbitrary in many respects. To enumerate all the differences would take too much space, but I subjoin a few of the most noticeable examples:

By: "*by* my dayes" (842 11); "now do *by* me what ye lyft" (371 31).

Of: "defyred *of*" (29 18); "receyued thys fhelde *of*" (26 16); "fyr L. was rebuked *of* the quene" (24 15); "reuenge hym *of* his enemyes" (63 15); "praid the king *of* accord" (37 27); "prayd hym *of* his knyghthode" (767 23); "made hem clene *of* her lyf" (plural!) (40 15); "lyberal *of* his expenfe" (518 20); "haue pyte *of* hem" (181 31).

Til, vntil: "*til* a tree" (380 10; 389 18; 630 3); "*til* a frende" (385 28); "*vntyl* hym" (752 9).

With: "affayled *with* xij knyghtes" (18 19); "eten *with* lyons" (107 3); "came *with* kyng Arthur," *i.e.,* to his court (99 26); "many queftions *with* her" (37 9); "afhamed *with* hym felfe" (654 33).

At: "afk counceil *at* hem" (47 10); "come *at* the caftel" (37 12); "oute *att* wyndowes" (236 31).

For: "that they be content *for*" (134 24); "complaynyng *for*" (19 31).

On: "thynke *on* me" (627 12; 708 6); "troweft thow more *on* thy harneis than *in* thy maker" (710 18); "compleyned *on*" (10 12), comp. "for"; "kneled *on his knee*" (489 21); "*vpon* his *owne knee*" (524 9).

In: "come *in* the courte" (68 22); "put hem bothe *in* the erthe" (84 6).

Further, some phrases conftructed with different prepositions: "leyd fyege *vnto* hym" (64 14); "*on* the caftel" (64 8); "*aboute* the toure of London" (852 7); "*aboute* fir L." (852 7); "blewe *the* felde" (490 10)[1]; "blewe *vnto* lodgynge" (549 14); "blewe *to* the felde" (766 8); etc.

In two passages the prepofition *with* seems at first sight to be omitted, as it is generally used under similar circumstances, but such is not the case; the examples denote a sort of instrumental case: "I fhold flee the myn owne handes" (556 11); "I fhall flee the myn owne handes" (849 12).

VI. Many conjunctions have a pleonastic *that* after them, which in a few cases is used in Modern English: "after that" (23 5; 19 4);

---

[1] Another example where a verb governs the accusative is: "I difcharge the *this* Courte" (727 7).

"how —" (25 5 ; 434 31) ; "wherfore —" (1 6) ; "but —" (3 5) ; "by caufe —" (84 27) ; "why —" (114 9) ; "fauf —" (171 1) ; "though —" (77 27) ; "or —" (451 27) ; "tylle —" (690 26).

To with the infinitive is, with very few exceptions (33 4), generally preceded by "*for*": see 30 22 ; 38 32 ; 567 2 ; 657 9 ; etc. etc.

Unless is rendered by "*but yf*": 417 15 ; 514 14 ; 52 2 ; 91 18 ; sometimes by "*but and*": as 61 11.

And replaces *if:* "and kyng Lot had ben" (87 16) ; "and he lyue" (92 35) ; "and I wold" (70 26) ; occasionally "*and yf*" occurs : "and yf I myght lyue" (98 8).

As is constantly used for *as if:* "as he hadde ben dede" (393 28) ; sometimes "*as though*": "as though he had ben dede" (393 31) ; "as though he myght not haue gone" (253 6).

Where and *lyke* are often followed by "*as*": "lyke as god wil" (395 22 ; 555 24) ; "where as came" (14 4).

Without stands for *unless:* "without ye doo me homage" (75 3) ; "without ye haue my counceyll" (85 14).

Ne is often used for *nor* or *neither*, and at the same time is part of the negation (compare below, No. VII.) : "whos vyrgynyte ne was peryffhed ne hurte" (703 10) ; "I care not ne doubte hem not" (221 5) ; "ne none of myn elders" (74 35).

For occurs sometimes in the sense of *because* or *as:* "but *for* tho aduentures were with wylde beeftes / and not in the queft of the Sancgreal / therfor the tale," etc.

VII. In this paragraph I bring together a few syntactical remarks :—

The negative is usually double, much as in French, sometimes even threefold : "It may not be by no reafon" (214 35) ; "there nys none other boote" (209 6) ; "myght not abyde no lenger" (130 38) ; "but in no wyfe he coude not" (377 5) ; "*neuer* erst *ne* myghte *no* knyghte knewe the truthe" (703 28) ; "neuer had I foo grete nede of no knyghtes helpe" (305 4) ; "ne lete me not be fhamed" (654 16) ; "but of that fhame ne reke I noughte" (684 14) ; "for thy pyte ne haue me not in dyfpyte" (711 4). There occur a few cases where only "*ne*" is used : "that I ne lay ten tymes where" (717 11) ; "ne had your tydynges ben" (699 36).

Inversion is often used ; regularly after *therefore* and *thenne:* "therfor cam I hydder" (735 13) ; "therfor fhalle I neuer loue the no more" (727 6); "thenne was he not a lytel fory" (714* 31); "thenne wote I" (571 14). In many cases, it appears, inversion is used to emphasize certain words: *e.g.*, "an holer man in his lyf was he neuer" (207 38); "as for my ladyes name that fhall not ye knowe for me as at this tyme" (216 5); "and cryftend wylle I be" (490 2); "and vnto the dethe he is Iuged" (753 31). A number of such examples are to be found throughout the work.

The subject is often changed and the verb omitted: "and fo fhe yede to the knyght that fhe loued / and he her ageyne" (404 25).

Occasionally the subject is entirely omitted in the second part of the sentence: "for they bare no harneis ageynft the / nor none wold bare" (825 5); "Marke euer haft thou ben a traytour / and euer wylle be" (496 11).

Direct and indirect speech occur in the same sentence: "But for her loue that gaf me this whyte fhelde I fhalle were the" (141 30); "ij ladyes to take the child bound in a cloth of gold / & that you delyuer hym" (39 5); "G. fente to kyng Arthur for focour and that he hye hym for I am fore wounded" (170 32); "and thenne the kynge commaunded his knyghtes to take that naked man with fayrenes / and brynge hym to my caftel" (370 15–18).

Not is occasionally used elliptically: "and there he thoughte to affaye his armour and his fpere for his hurte *or not*" (755 18).

The use of the infinitive of the perfect tense is further remarkable in sentences such as the following:—"he rode to haue foughten" (18 12); "wolde haue had Arthur to haue cryed hym mercy" (131 27); "he wende he fhold haue dyed" (392 29); "for ye haue fene me thys day haue had grete traueylle" (412 15); "for ye neded not to haue doubted no knyght" (402 15).

In conclusion I shall quote some sentences which are most peculiar in their construction: "and he that was vpon hym the whiche was the nobleft hors in the world ftrayned hym myghtely and ftably" (755 24); "There is in this Caftel a gentylwoman whiche we and this caftel is hers and many other" (705 13); "yf ye wold afke how he lyued / he that fedde the peple of Ifrael with manna in deferte / foo was he fedde" (708 18); "and not foo hardy in Gawayns hede" (487 27).

LIST OF THE VARIOUS READINGS BETWEEN
CAXTON'S AND WYNKYN DE WORDE'S EDITIONS.

THERE exist differences between Caxton's text and Wynkyn de Worde's editions of 1498 and 1529. I have decided upon giving the various readings from the third edition (1529): firstly, because the lapse of time between the first and second edition is too short to allow of manifest change in the language ; secondly, on account of the imperfect condition of the only known copy of the second edition; lastly and chiefly, because all later Black Letter editions, and all modern reprints, with the sole exception of Southey's and Sir E. Strachey's, can be traced back to Wynkyn de Worde's edition of 1529.

Concerning the variations between the first and third edition of Malory's " Le Morte Darthur," I may state, that they consist of alterations as well as of omissions and additions. Whether Caxton's text was purposely revised previous to the third edition being sent to press, or whether the changes were made by Wynkyn de Worde's compositors during printing,[1] it is obvious that the alterations were made with the intention of modernising and of rendering the text more readable, although this intention has not always been strictly carried into effect. Sometimes only the position of words in a sentence is altered ; now and then a whole sentence is either entirely omitted or replaced by another one ; and in many cases obsolete or difficult words are replaced by more modern ones. Sentences begin with capital letters, as do all names of persons and places. Full-stops and commas are distinguished; " þ " is throughout rendered by " y," whereas " gh " is never rendered by " ʒ," nor " them " by " hem " or " their " by " her," &c. Occasionally I observed that some of Caxton's terms were misunderstood and wrongly rendered, but on the whole, W. de Worde's text is superior to Caxton's, both in exactness and correctness : I can hardly call to mind a misprint. If we take

---

[1] Observing that the variants are periodically more or less in number leads me to conclude that at least two different hands dealt with the text. In the whole 861 pages of Caxton's volume only one page (105) corresponds absolutely to Wynkyn de Worde's text.

into consideration that in those days philology did not exist, and that no one cared to reproduce a text with scrupulous exactness, the variations are rather improvements upon Caxton's text, for many errors are corrected, words, and even whole passages, often added, which, to conclude from the sense, Caxton's compositors evidently omitted. From the point of view of the modern critic it is, however, apparent that owing to these changes Caxton's text had already in 1529 lost its most characteristic peculiarities.[1]

The difference of orthography in both texts is so considerable, that to quote all variations in this respect would be almost equal to reproducing the whole of W. de Worde's second edition. But as W. de Worde's orthography is consistent, and all passages quoted are rendered exactly, one can easily form an opinion about his spelling.

The following list contains only the various readings of "Le Morte Darthur" itself, as the Preface òf Caxton is wanting, and the Table of Contents is not complete in the Grenville copy; The Clarendon figures refer to the pages, the ordinary Roman ones to the lines. All words included in brackets are those omitted by W. de Worde. As W. de Worde prints throughout "Kyng Arthur," whereas Caxton frequently simply puts "Arthur," I have not thought it necessary to register each single case.

Book i.

35. ¶ Here begynneth the fyrſt boke of the mooſt noble and worthy prince kyng Arthur ſometyme kyng of grete Brytayne / now called Englande whiche treateth of his noble aĉtes and feates of armes & chyualrye / and of his noble knyghtes of the table roūde and this volume is devyded in to . xxi . bokes; 2, of Englonde; 3, regned there; myghty and a noble; 4, longe tyme warre; 5, named; 7, a ryght fayre; 8, and Igrayne was her name; 9, to the; 10, bothe accorded; 11, her grete; 12, lyke as; 20, As foone; 21, wonders; 26, at your commaundement; for than haue ye; 30, wonders; 33, he had; 36, & that other hyght.

---

[1] Compare what is said, p. 13, about Mr. Wright's characterisation of Thomas Stansby's edition. The number of variants which I quote here amounts to nearly ten thousand; I estimate that about double the amount of variants exists between Caxton's and Stansby's editions.

36. 2, and he put hym felfe ; 7, Igrayne kynge ; Than ; 8, to kyng ; 13, gete yow ; 27, vnto kynge ; 29, tary lōge ; 31, bounden ; 32, he faid y^t he ; 34, to me.

37. 1, whan that is ; 3, as moche as ; 5, this nyght ye ; 10, But be ware ye make ; 12, So as they had deuyfed it was done ; 19, and begate on her Arthur the fame nyght ; 20, & or day ; 27, betwene ; 34, were accorded.

38. 10, vnto ; 11, Than was fhe ; 12, Fere ye not ; 22, fere ; 26, came ; 27, wylt ; 36, vnto me ; As.

39. 1, As Merlyn had deuyfed ; 4, the quene ; 6, in ryche cloth of golde & delyuer hym ; 11, owne breftes ; 15, in ; 23, moche ; 25, to L. ; And within a whyle he was paffyng ; 27, there is none ; 29, loke that ye ; 30, before hym to morowe ; 34, appertenaunces ; 38, yelded.

40. 1, belonged vnto ; wherefore I. the quene ; 8, fhold come to L. afore Xmas ; 9, that as Iefu was ; 16, to god ; 18, lyke to ; 23, a fote of heyght ; 24, and letters of golde ; 26, of E. ; 23, cōmaūde you ; 30, all the ; 31, all the ftates ; went for to ; 35, to be knowen.

41. 7, to the field ; 10, Kay ; 12, toward the I. / fyr Kay had ; 14, Arthur to ; I wyll with a good wyll ; 20, Arthur alyghted ; he went ; 23, he pulled ; 30, to fwere.

42. 2, fir Ector ; 7, Therwith fyr ; 9, affay you ; to ; 12, With a good wyll ; 14, Kay alfo and my brother ; 16, ne of ; 18, hym to ; 21, fyr E. ; 29, foftred ; 31, done fyr ; 32, whyle that ; 34, And vpon the . xij. daye ; 35, for to affay ; 37, but onely A. ; many grete l.

43. 2, be gouerned ; 5, both day ; 7, And at C. ; 8, but none of them ; 13, And yet ; 14, theyr kynge ; 16, purueye of the ; 17, that myght be gotten ; 18, as Kynge V. ; 20, and fyr B. ; 31, kneled doune all at ones ; 32, forgaue it ; 33, offred it vp to ; 34, and was made.

44. 1, to the lordes ; 6, vnto kynge A. ; 9, for to be ; 15, tyme as for the ; enemy vnto the kyng ; 18, a parte of Wales ; 19, and all through ; 21, Than the kyng ; 23, Coronacyon ; 25, vnto this ; 26, Gore whiche brought with hȳ ; 27, to this feeft there came ; & with hym ; 34, Than was kyng A. glad ; 37, and fente vnto.

45. 2. receyue gyftes ; 4, And that ; 5, betwene ; 8, the rule ; 10, this anfwere vnto kyng Arthur ; And for this caufe ; 11, men of armes ; 13, afore ; 15, Merlyns comynge ; 16, berdles boye ; 18, begoten ; 19, vpon ; wyfe of Cornewayle ; 22, Vtherpendragon ; 23, who fo euer ; 24, and or that ; 26, many moo realmes ; 31, for to come fafe and to go fafe ; 32, affurance was ; he fholde not fere ; 6, wyll not.

46. 2, vndernethe ; maylle whiche was good and fure ; 4, Kay the Seneffhall ; 6, mette togyder ; but lytel mekenes / for there was ; 11, returned to ; 18, vnto ; 20, that ye had ; 21, to yᵉ worfte ; 31, king ; 33, vnder hym ; 7, them backe.

47. 1, all the knyghtes ; 6, to London ; 9, be auenged on hym ; 10, of them al ; 17, and was fayre ; 18, I fhal tel you fyrs ; 21, vnto ; 22, duke alfo / and but yf ; 23, make hym felfe ; 25, this cafe ; 28, the one ; 34, worfte ; 35, that our kynge fende vnto the two.

48. 1, to ; 4, vpon ; 6, in mooft pleafaunt ; 15, our prifoners ; 18, grete ftrengthe ; 19, and the other two ; 20, vnto ; 23, at the thyrde ; 25, but that he ; 32, Than they ; 38, delyuered them ftreyght.

49. 1, better ; 4, taryed ; 5, & had as good chere as ; 8, Ha ha fayd kynge B. & B. ; our ; 13, to kyng ; hafte they ; 24, the Seneffhall ; 28, had waffhed & were ryfen.

50. 1, couched ; 2, yᵗ was called Ladynas ; 7, And whan ; he quyckly horfed ; 11, downe hors and man ; 12, none that ; 13, came in fyerfly ; 20, wonders wroth ; 22, to waxe ; 27, to Syre G. ; 28, to counfeyle ; 30, to bedde ; 31, morowe ;—and after went to.

51. 3, fared ; 6, on horfbacke and on fote ; 17, vnto kyng A. ; 20, told them that ; 26-27, where the kynges enemyes ; 34, that the fyxe.

52. 3, armes whiche ; 6, that he wold ; 10, Than kyng Lot fwore ; 13, Ewayns ; 29, And foo by ; 35, wonderfull.

53. 9, that they made ; 11, fayre felde ; 22, for than they wyll ; you haue but : 25, and the barons ; paffynge ; 26, done anone ; morow ; 34, fyerfly agayn ; 35, well and meruayloufly.

54. 2, whan ; 4, to ; 13, to ; 14, to ; 21, and fmote doune ; 23, to ; 32, In the meane ; 34, whiche ; 35, yᵉ hors fete ; 36, Cradelmont.

55. 2, an hors ; 4, wonder therof ; Cradelmont ; 7, to ; 11, kerued ; 15, yᵗ hyght ; 16, fmote down ; 20, vpon ; 24, bothe fholder ; into yᵉ felde ; 25, fyr G. ; fuche refcowe ; 29, fyr G. ; 34 and 36, fyr L.

56. 4, trembled ; 6, a ftronge ; 8, Vryence ; 11, kynge A. ; 16, fyr G. ; 17, And than ; 19, Cradelmans ; 26, Cambenet ; wyll ; 27, aparte ; 31, So anone they as they had ; 35, the uaunt warde ; two kynges.

57. 2, Cambenet ; 3, on them with ; 6, put backe ; 7, as the men of Inde ; 12, world is ioyned to ; 16, by yᵉ aduyfe of ; a knyght ; 17, if ; 18, whan it is nede ; 19, may for you ; 20, tyll they ; 21, as a bowe fhotte ; 23, whiche ; 25, theyr armes ; 28, bothe the partyes ; 32, knyght / & was but ; 34, as a fyers ; 35, ha ha ; 36, now fhall we be dyfcomfyted.

58. 5, and forowe ; 8, to hurtle togyder ; 9, with theyr ; flewe

downe ryght ; pyte to ; 10, and a grete multytude fledde ; 11, wyth
the hondred ; 13, dedes of ; 14, wyth ; 16, fmote hym a myghty
ftroke vpon ; 17, whiche aftonyed ; Than was king ; 18, fet vpon
hym ; whan that other fawe that he ; 22, cut in twayne ; hors alfo ;
23, with ; 26, Ban with grete dylygence voyded the hors / and came
and fmote at the other fo egrely vpon the helme ; 30, By that tyme ;
31, that founde ; 35, no man myght ; 38, therwith he.

59. 1, helme with fuche force ; 2, cutte hym in two peces / that
the one halfe fell on the one fyde / & the other on ye other fyde /
& kyng A.; hors & ledde; 5, grete nede; 7, myn hurte; 11, a newe;
17, in the felde ; 18, & theyr knyghtes affembled ; 19, all dyfcomfyted ; 22, grete dedes ; 23, not ; vnder heuen ; 30, knowe ; 35, ye
muft take ; 37, vpon.

60. 2, almooft ; For kyng A.; 3, therfore they ; 5, loke that ;
fuche an ; 7, for to flee ; 9, we be ; vnto me ; 15, And they fwore
that ; the one vnto the other ; 16, who that ; 17, Than anone ; 29,
whiche ; valyaunt ; 32, of Gorre ; 33, with grete ; 34, as faft as ;
theyr horfes ; 35, good knyghtes ; 37, thyckeft.

61. 3, kyng A.'s vifage ; 6, vpon ; 7, to ; haue ye ; 8, thoufand
ye haue ; 10, you ; ye wyll ; 11, yf ye tary on ; 12, and theyrs ;
13, to ; 14, rewarde well ; 15, ryght well ; 16, for there may ; 18,
this daye ; 21, thefe thre yeres ; hurte ; ne greue you ; 23, to kyng
A.; 24, in hande ; 27, thefe thre yeres ; 28, y^t ye haue goten ; 29,
kynges that be here ; 32, at a nede ; able ynough ; 36, gyuen them ;
38, go fe ; whiche.

62. 4, told hym ; 8, the werfte ; 8, caufed Bleyfe his mayfter
to wryte them ; 10, caufed hym ; 13, ftode ; 15, all furred ; 21,
thou chorle ; 22, the whiche ; 23, place where as ; 26, fmyled at
hym ; 29, fporte ; 36, begate vpon her ; and his ; 37, rounde t. ;
38, ftronge warre vpon.

63. 1, Leodegraunce ; 2, bycaufe ; 3, the ordynaunce ; 4, they all ;
7, Than Kyng A.; 16, doughter vnto ; [Camylyard] ; 17, and after ;
18, as it fhall be fhewed here after ; 19, thefe two kynges took ; 20, on
bothe theyr ; 21, kynge A.; 22, do in thefe ; 25, many good ;
malyce of ; 29, not nede fayd ; 31, for or . xij . monethes be paft ;
32, he fhall ; 33, haue reuenged ; 34, one day ; 35, as it fhall be
fhewed here after ; 36, whiche ; 37, as ony be now ; vnto.

64. 1, whiche ; to ; [the] ; 2, Vryence lande ; 5, that there was ;
6, lawleffe ; 19, on the water and the lande ; 23, of Scotlande ;
26, lordes and gentylmen ; Northwales / whiche ; 28, man of
good men alfo ; 30, ordynaunce that belongeth to warre for to ;
31, reherceth ; 33, Than after that k. B. and k. B. were departed.

65. 3, keft ; 5, mothers ; 6, fhe departed ; Than on a tyme y^e ;

7, ryght fore; 10, land many; 13, domage; 14, awoke; ryght penfyfe of; 15, for to put aweye all thefe; 19, his hors; longe after; 25, fate there alone; 26, nombre; 30, whyle that; 34, a fote to; 36, Arthur vnto the knyght; 37, that beeft; 38, haue kylled.

66. 3, that hors; 4, thefe . xij . monethes; eyther; 6, Kynge P.; 10, to kyng A.; 11, thy defyre is in; 12, to; 13, is myn; 16, I wolde be cōtent; 17, paffed forth; 14, grete ftudy; 19, came M.; 21, penfyf & heuy; 22, for here euen now; mooft merualyeft; 26, and alfo who; and alfo one whome; 32, M. departed; 34, was gladde; a ryght wyfe man; 36, kynge A.; dyuers; 38, that olde.

67. 3, late wherfore; 4, lyen; 12, moche fhameful deth as; into; all quycke; 13, As they thus; 14, horfes; 17, hym that; 18, kynge A. faid vnto M.; 25, & all that were there myght here; 26, Beware Vlfius; 29, fyr Vlfius; for to; 30, that fayth; 31, caufe; grete warre that ye haue had; 34, ye fholde neuer haue had; halfe; whiche; 35, your grete lordes / barons and gentylmen.

68. 1, god and you; 2, vpon; 11, to; 13, than fyr V.; 15, that I bare; 18, kyng V.; 19, bothe his; 21, whiche; 33, hym there; 26, Myles; 27, fome good; 32, done to; 36, were pyte; 37, he cometh to aege.

69. 2, he fhall be in; 6, muft graūte; 7, will my lorde; 8, body that; 10, that in the fame maner; 11, withoute any queftyon or; 12, fir G.; 18, ende of his; 21, it were; dyd; 25, but of whens; 26, they ran; 27, fyr G.; 29, his fpere; 33, gaue hym; 34, vpon; [and gate him wynde]; 37, where as; moone.

70. 2, his lyfe faued; 6, may ye; or; 8, wyll I hold; vpon; 10, fhall be within thefe fewe dayes; 12, as wrothe as they; 14, And by and by; 16, belonged to; that it be; 17, in the mornynge afore daye; 21, whiche chafed M.; 22, them a good pace; & cryed to; 24, fled away; you; 25, crafte; 26, yf I; 27, thy deth; towarde thy d.; 29, pauylyon by it; 30, knyght fate all; 37, defende it.

71. 1, [anone]; 2, drewe; 3, [faid the knyght]; 6, fperes ynough; 7, two good; loke one; 8, theyr myght; 9, kynge A.; 11, [ones]; good; 16, yᵉ myddes; 17, fore angred; drewe; 22, thought it was; 23, fuche a vauntage; 24, & fo alyght; dreffed hȳ to kyng A.; 26, where they; 27, was all bloody; 28, to batayle; 29, two wylde bores; eyther of them; 33, to the kynge; 36, But as to.

72. 2, a paffynge; 8, reame in; 25, & faue one; 26, the one fhall be named P. & that other L.; 27, & they fhalle telle; 28, begoten fon; 30, vnto an heremytage; where as was; 33, & the kynge ; 34, And ſo Merlyn & he departed ; 37, lake whiche ; 38, a brode.

73. 2, the hande ; Merlyn to the kyng ; the ſwerd ; 4, ſayd yᵉ kynge ; 8, therwith came ; 9, to kyng A. ; 10, the kynge ; 11, whiche yᵉ arme holdeth yonder ; 12, Syr kynge ; damoyſell of the lake ; 14, king A. ; 15, ony gyſte that ; 16, vnto ; 19, barge ; 22, to the lande ; 23, Than kynge A. ; 25, for he is not ; 27, gyder a grete whyle ; 28, hym to ; 29, It is well ; 30, quod kynge A. ; 34, my counſeyle is ; 37, to wyfe ; 38, aduyſe me.

74. 1, kynge A. ; vpon ; 3, king A. ; 6, no bloode ; 7, on to ; 9, king A. ; 10, and ſo ; 11, the kyng ; 19, The meane ; haſtely from ; 20, And he was ; 28, lacked for ; 30, thy ; kynge A. ; 32, to a ; 33, for to ; 35, longe he.

75. 1, I ſe well ; 3, homage vnto me ; 6, hym well ; 9, hym / and that ſhall he fynde ; 13, on Maye daye ; 23, by cauſe that ; 25, what for loue.

❡ Here endyth the fyrſt boke of kynge Arthur.

Book ii.

❡ Here after foloweth the ſeconde boke of the noble and worthy prynce kynge Arthur.

75. 31, ſone whiche ; 33, kynges at yᵗ tyme ; 35, vpon.

76. 4, that ; 7, Than king A. let ; 9, caſtel thus was ; 12, as them ; came a damoyſell whiche ; 14, told hym ; 16, and ſhe ; 22, a good knyght / and ; 24, [and withoute treaſon] ; 26, ſwerd of the ſcawberd ; 27, for it ; and it be ; 35, ſcawberd.

77. 4, ſtreme ; 6, but none myght ; 9, kyng ; 11, I am gretely ; 12, It ſo happened that ; 15, knyghte / whiche ; to ; This knyght was named ; 20, his herte reyſed ; 21, for by cauſe ; 24, was there ; 25, [ſo departyng] ; 27, to ſuffre ; 28, be poorely ; 29, other lordes ; 31, but by cauſe of ; araye ; 33, to ; it is no nede ; 34, ony more ; beſemeth ; 36, not all onely ; rayment.

78. 2, rayment and clothynge ; trouth ; 4, ſcawberde ; 5, vpon ; 7, & many ; 8, Truly ; 9, beſt man ; 11, aſcheue ; ſayd the damoyſel / gyue ; 13, by force ; 15, in this ; 17, to me ; 22–23, as grete pite as euer I knewe ; 23–24, yᵉ greteſt ſorowe yᵗ myght be ; 27, I byleue ; 29, myſſe enformed ; 31, courte with my good knyghtes ; 32, that ye ſhal ; 33, for youre ; 34, but as now at ; 37, that ye wyll not ; 38, all my ; all that is amyſſe and that.

79. 1, [grete] ; 9, had promyſed ; 11, whiche ye ; 14 ; yf it ; 16, & though I haue bothe theyr hedes I force not ; 22, thyng of you ; 23, Lake there / by whofe meanes was flayne his owne moder ; 25, demaunded ; 28, in the prefence ; 30, I was moche ; 31, vnto ; 32, My lord ; 33, this lady ; 34, & wytchecrafte.

80. 3, ye hafte ye ; 21, full rychely buryed her ; 22, was in king A.'s courte a knyght that ; 24, & he was a proude ; 25, beft knightes ; 27, acounted of more proweffe than he was ; 29, kynge A.; 30, wroth with ; 33, to kynge A.'s courte ; 34, it was ; 35, to you.

81. 7, her brother ; 9, whiche ; 10, drawe ; fcawberd ; yf he were ; 11, hardy ; 14, ye do / fayd Merlyn / wolde to god ; neuer ; 17, wherfore it fhalle ; 18, for there is not lyuynge ; 19, lord kyng A. ; 20, pyte it is for ; 21, and as for ; 25, as faft as his hors coude renne ; 27, cryed to hym and fayd ; 28, wyll not ; 29, helpe you ; that noyfe ; 32, am I come ; 36, am comen ; 37, that ye haue done.

82. 2, whiche ; 3, of his knyghtes ; fymple to me ; 7, to me ; for one of vs ; 8, fperes in all hafte they myght ; 9, the kynges fone of Irlande ; 10, that his fpere wente alle to fheuers ; 11, fmote hym with fuche a myght ; 12, and Balyn ; 17, rydyng myght galop ; 18, than fhe ; 25, to ; 26, faft / that in no wyfe he myghte take the fwerde ; handes ; 27, but he ; 28, And whan ; 30, grete loue / fhe had vnto fyr Launceor ; 34, them ; a foreft ; 35, afpyed the ; 38, fayd B.

83. 1, wende lytell ; 3, pryfonynge ; 6, And anone B. ; vnto his ; 7, all his ; 8, how that ; 10, full fore ; 11, vnto yow ; 12, heuy of mynde ; kynge A. ; 14, the erthe ; 15, for kynge ; atte the ; 18, do fo & ; 19, Brother fayd B. let ; 21, as faft as ; 24, [it] ; 26, defence ; 29, loue and fauour ; 31, thou wel ; B. that ; 36, rydynge whiche was named ; 38, by one of the.

84. 1, kynge M.; 7, bothe theyr ; [How] ; 12, in doyng ; [in] ; 13, vnto ; 14, this place ; 27, dyd not faue ; 29, coude not nor myght ; 35, in many.

85. 9, for to telle ; as at this ; 10, fyll euyll ; 11, the two ; 12, but I ; 34, yf he had not ; 35, the kynge thus.

86. 5–6, what they be ; 10, in the fpryngynge ; [thenne] ; 16, vnto ; 20, euer was of ; 22, beholden ; full euyll ; 24, knowe or it be longe ; 26, vpon ; afore dyner ; myghty hooft ; 30, myghty ; for he ; mocke ; So Nero hymfelfe ; 35, he had therof worfhip.

87. 4, had grete meruayle therof ; 5, that they ; 10, that whyle ; 11, through my ; 12, is flayne many ; yf we ; 14, to matche vs ; 16, yf kyng L. ; 17, and all his people fholde haue ben deftroyed and flayne ; 18, knewe well that ; 22, is it better ; 23, the mooft party ; 24, vpon kynge A. ; 25, for he and his men ; wery of fyghtynge ; 30, worft ; 31, dyd grete ; 33, abode & withftode ; not euer; 34, was fhold; 36, had wedded; 37, by caufe; [the whiche was Arthur's fyfter].

88. 3, [called]; 5, with his; 8, to; 10, many a; 24, and his tombe ftode by it felfe aparte; 26, made them to be ouergylte with fyne; fygne and token; euery ymage helde a; 28, them all; 31, fayd to kynge A.; 32, the . xij . tapers; 33, of the holy; 34, fhall alfo be afcheued; tolde vnto kynge A.; 37, fyr P.

89. 1, brother Balan; 2, Now by; 4, ferre of ony; for I am; 5, to god; 7, for as I tolde you ye; as longe as; 9, afterward; 12, flayne; 14, a knyght named; 25, pauylyons dore; 26, grete forowe; 28, amende it; 33, forowe; 35, and gentylnes; that ye wylle; 37, fo rode.

90. 1, my lorde; the caufe of; 4, nedes go; 8, the good knyght B.; 9, there the damoyfell; [euen]; 13, and garde; 14, traytour knyght; the whiche; 15, where as; 16, may beft; therof I; 17, to you by my; 19, vpon; 20, & alfo how ye trechery was done by y^e; 29, for I am; 32, as longe as my; 36, good knyght.

91. 2, to me; 8, to haue gone; 10, came many men; 11, And whan; 12, by caufe he; And than; 13, vp vpon the walles and lepte ouer into; 15, fayd that; 19, fyluer dyffhe; 20, that there; 21, but that; 23, her lyfe; 26, all that nyght; 29, fhe dyed; 33, herd one.

92. 7, defpyte that; 15, and had; 20, to a; 22, wyll I not; 26, to the; 29, faid y^e.

93. 10, to hym; for to; 11, arofe vp; 23, folowed hym; 36, kyng P.

94. 13, for that ftroke turned hym to; 15, neuer mete more; 34, you; 36, to.

95. 11, the two; 30, this entent y^t it fhold afwage; 32, that ladyes loue.

96. 1, he dreffed hym from thens; that he had; 10, And therwith he; 20, [not].

97. 3, in reed; 4, And whan; 7, it fholde not be he; 8, and fmote eyther other; 11, fore bryfed; 16, brake his helme; 21, eche other greuoufly; 22, to; 25, reed of theyr blode; 25, fmytten eyther other; 26, the world; 33, to; 36, went; 38, bebledde.

98. 7, to the deftruccion of vs bothe; 9, the ylle; 20, that place; 21, wepynge chere and fayd; 23, the facrament and blyffed body; 29, And anone; 32, by the handes of his owne broder; 34, morowe; 35, vpon; [that].

99. 2, alfo a bedde; lye in; 6, Than M.; to handle; 12, this world; 21, and crafte; 33, meruayllouft; 35, euer; 36, as they were.
❡ Here endeth the feconde boke of kynge Arthur.

Book iij.

❡ Here foloweth the thyrde boke of the noble and worthy prynce kynge Arthur.

100. 1, after yᵗ; 6, but kynge A. full well; 8, moche ruled; 14, ony fayre lady; 16, Leodegraunce; Camelyarde; whiche L. holdeth; 18, gentylleſt and; 25, pryuely; 32, to; 35, and of; 36, that it.

101. 5, but I lacke fyfty; 6, kynge L.; 12, he made grete ioye for theyr comynge; [and that ryche preſente]; 15, to; 16, pleaſaunt; 17, Than in; 19, honourableſt; 22, Merlyn made the beſt ſpede he myght and founde . xxviij . good knyghtes; coude he fynde; 24 archebyſſhop; ſente for 25 ſyeges of this table rounde; 27, to; 30, in the ſyeges; 36, to; 37, muſt ſo do.

102. 11, [oute]; 25, bothe daye and nyght; that he myght be made; 33, Aryes the.

103. 22, to; 26, to; 27, morowe; 31, kynge P.; 33, the fyrſt that.

104. 4, ye be; 5, had; 6, & ſayd; vnto; 8, ſyr G.; 9, whiche; not do ſo; 14, ſyr G.; 18, wente vnto; 30, to kyng A.; 35, with hym by force; 36, mone; bycauſe.

106. 3, of the whyte harte; 4, ſyr G.; 9, wolde haue folowed; 10, on the other; 22, helme ſo harde; 25, ſyr G.; 27, chaced; 28, harte that; 30, [drawe].

107. 5, yᵉ dombe beeſtes; 24, to the; 27, Me repenteth it fore; 28, to haue ſtryken at the; 32, But for drede; 33, vpon; 34, behynde hym alſo.

108. 4, well thynke; 5, here aboute; 7, ſayd thus; 9, Thou haſt alſo; whiche is vnto the grete ſhame for euermore; 12, ſuche a; that he had nygh felled; 15, one of them; 17, wonders; bothe flayne; 21, ſyr G.; moone; 24, On the morowe erly came; 25, whiche; 28, whiche wyll; 31, or that; 32, kyng Lots ſone of O.; 34, ſpede for; 38, the heed of the whyte herte.

109. 3, Her heed; 4, mane of his hors; And in this maner he rode forth towarde C.; 5, to yᵉ courte; 6, & ſo he was . And ſhewed how he ſlewe; 8, to; 9, vylaynouſly ſlayne; 12, hym euer; 19, [Amen]; 20, and he; 21, forth his waye a good pace after; 22, whiche; 23, more than his ſpere; 24, In what entent doſt thou ſmyte my hors; 25, way ſaid the dwarfe; but that thou ſhalte fyrſt iuſte with yonder knightes that abyde in yonder pauelions that thou feeſt; 26, 32 & 33, ſyr T.; 30, [alle]; 33, yelded.

110. 2, yᵉ myddes; 3, lowe that it went thorough the ſyde;

9, to ; that we ; 13, Langdok ; 15, to ; 16, you to gyue ; 19, hors anone ; & come on & ryde with me ; 22, through a foreſt ; 24, re- newed ; 25, his ſpere ; 26, foo came ; 27, lye therin on a payllet ; And than he ; 28, [therin] ; 29, And ther ; 30, anone the lady awoke & went ; 32, What wyll ye do ; Wyll ye take away ; 34, to this place ; 36, mette withal or it be longe / and alſo euyll handled ; abyde it.

111. 2, forth on ; 4, fyr T. ; 5, ſuche lodgynge ; 14, and ſayd ; 16, and ſawe he ; 17, and armed ; 19, and ſmote eche other y^t bothe hors and men fel to the erth ; 20, they lyghtly ; 23, & alſo they brake ; 25, grounde ; and they had bothe ; 28, & made hym fall to the groūde ; 33, brachet & the / or els ſlee the.

112. 3, fyr T. ; 4, this fals ; 6, I am ryght ſory and lothe ; whiche I haue graunted you ; 7, make you ; that whiche ; 8, agaynſt you . He can not make amendes ſayd the damoyſell ; hath ſlayne ; 9, [afore myn owne eyen] ; whiche was ; 10, than euer he was ; no mercy vpon hym ; in ſo moche that I ; 11, whiche ; 13, as knyghtes auenturous do ; and for all that I coude do or ſaye / he ſmote of my brothers heed ; 20, for whan ; 30, fyr T. and his hors ; 32, them ; ſayd he ; 33, late was ; 36, gentyll ; yf.

113. 3, gladde ; 4, but that his father ; 11, made grete ; 14, full of good ; 15, do outrage ; 22, bytwene ; 24, ſake . Kynge P. wold not ; 28, And as ; [there] ; 29, laye there ; 30, with her loues ſwerde ; So as ; 31, labouryng man ; 32, kyng P. ; 33, poore man ; 34, moone.

114. 2, nere coſyn ; 5, her frendes ; 6, ye ryde ; 7, them yet ; lady is in the keepyng ; 9, tyll that ; 11, rode he ; 12, ſayd to her ; court of ; 14, be two ; 16, owne pleaſure ; 17, them in ſonder ; 18, why they ; 25, quod kynge P. ; in there all ſodeynly as ; 28, you alſo ; 30, vnto hym ; 31, more for her ; yow bothe ; 33, knyght ; 37, [are] ; ſawe ; 38, he was wroth and fyerſly and lyghtly lepte.

115. 1, and in grete haſte drewe out ; 5, and therwith he ; 7, had ſeen ; buffet y^t the other had ; 12, with a ; 13, kyng P. ; 15, I lacke ; kyng P. ; [but] ; 22, morowe ; and after ; 26, P. kynge of ; 28, man as ye be ; 29, What is now ; kynge P. ; 30, Syr ſayd he ; 31, that is in that ; 35, vpon.

116. 1, 3, 4, kyng P. ; 4, gretely welcome there ; 5, alſo gretely ; 8, [and there] ; 9, wherwith ; 10, and anguyſſhe ; of ioynt ; 12, where as ; 17, kyng P. ; 22, frō ; 26, that they ; 35, hath receyued ; 38, towarde Camelot.

117. 2, where ; 4, moone ; 5, I myghte ; 8, kyng P. ; of this lady ; 12, vnto kynge A.'s courte ; 14, and that ; 16, labour and ; 18, where ; 19, with fair ; 20, vpon ; 22, kynge A. ; glad ; 24, all the; 25, from the begynnynge vnto the endynge; the quene; 27, kyng P.; 28, fauynge your honour; 38, very cowarde.

118. 7, may well; 8, all deftenyes; 9, that fyr G.; 10, fone vnto; 14, gaue them landes that; outrage; 21, worldly; ❡ Here endeth the thyrde boke of kynge Arthur and of his weddynge.

𝔅ook iv.

❡ Here foloweth the fourth boke of the noble and worthy prynce kyng Arthur.

118. 24, Than after; 25, and of; befelle; 27, courte with hym; 28, whiche; hyght Nymue; 30, her in euery place; 33, vpon; vnto kynge; 34, & that for.

119. 2, fwerde Excalybur; 9, And than; from kynge A.; 11, fo euer; 21, no; 22, [fame]; 29, peryll; 30, And than; 31, waye as they wente; 36, put hym awaye.

120. 1, whiche; [grete]; 2, crafte &; 6, And than; and there made; 13, to kynge A.; flewe all that they founde afore them; 14, grete pyte; 19, who wylle; 29, hardyer; 31, fo euer; 35, tydynges came; to the.

121. 9, or it be day; 10, fhall fo flee of; not one; 12, the; 15, he and his knyghtes beynge in; 17, the quene; Kay; 21, we are all; 22, cryed he than; 23, to kyng A. & fayd to hym; 31, than for to; 32, to be; 34, [euen]; 38, vndertake two.

122. 2, therwith fyr K.; 4, fadom depe; 6, [all]; 8, fell downe; 9, that he brake his necke; 11, vpon; to the fholders; 14, as longe as I; [all]; 15, in Humber; 16, noble dedes; 22, kynge A. founde; 24, let we hold vs; [and]; 25, hooft efpye; 26, forowe; not be able to helpe; 28, forowe; 29, downe fro; [all]; [but]; 30, on the right hande and on the lefte; 33, full mekely; 34, and fhe came anone; 35, for the vyctory of that daungerous batayle.

123. 3, and fayd; 4, haue knowledge; 7, kyng A.; 8, not paft; 9, rounde table; 10, buylde; 12, call it; 15, forowe; And whan; 18, to; 20, good knyghtes of the table roūde; 22, beft that; 24, bothe olde; 26, the other half; 32, kyng P.; 34, [beft]; 37, wel worthy fyr Kay the Seneffhall.

124. 5, all the dayes of; 6, Now fayd; 14, & that knowe I full well; 15, and he; 16, but he doth; 20, And whan; 22, as afore is reherced; 23, wonders; 24, was fo; 25, Courte of kynge A.; 26, he alyght; 29, agayne to; 33, tyll men; 35, and by.

125. 3, moone; 4, to; 6, that he; 10, courte of kynge A.; And fo; 12, kyng A.; 25, harte there; 26, kyng A.; aboute hym;

28, cam ftrayght ; 29, kyng A. ; 33, by that tyme ; 34, on all ; 35, and gaue ; [all].

126. 3, [ryght] ; 6, belonged ; 7, they were ; 9, [as] ; 12, [fuche] ; 14, ryche ; 15, ryght eafely ; 16, all that ; 19, was aboute a two ; 20, And alfo ; 23, Than fayd kyng A. / what ; 27, The lord ; is named ; 32, But that ; 33, his proweffe ; 35, people & comynalte.

127. 1, very coward ; 4, do nothynge ; or elles ; 6, is no ; 7, that wyll ; fyr Damas ; 8, that wold ; 9, in a wayte ; to take ; 11, in to ; 16, fyr D. ; 20, [alle] ; 21, not tell ; 22, quod fhe ; 23, or elles ye fhall neuer efcape wᵗ your lyfe ; 25, yf I may be delyuered with this and alle.

128. 1, kynge A. ; 2, this batayle ; 5, fyr A. ; 9, And whan ; 15, And with ; 18, ftronge of herte ; to morowe ; 21, defyreth ; 22, haue ; 24, that ; 25, a ryche quene for euer ; 29, Quene Morgan ; 30, done as ; or elles ; 35, hym to.

129. 10, moone ; but for all ; 11, in hande ; 12, fyr A. ; 13, fyr O. ; 15, fcawberde ; 16, morowe ; 17, in hande ; 18, hertely ; 19, [al] ; 20, to his ; 22, morowe ; kyng A. ; 23, go to ; 24, [and fo Arthur herd a maffe] ; on ; 28, of the ; 31, was vp on ; 36, [&].

130. 3, theyr fheldes ; [hede] ; 4, grounde ; 5, drewe ; And in yᵉ ; 6, thus fyghtynge ; 7, had put ; 11, to do theyr ; 12, fyr A. ; 13, fo that for ; 14, fore that he ; 15, faft frō ; 18, was fore adrad ; 20, fyr A. ; 21, to ; 24, grounde ; 27, bothe wroth ; 29, that he ; 31, a droppe of ; 37, as dyd kyng A.

131. 8, fyr Accolon ; brake ; 10, [fure] ; 13, began to faye thus ; 19, my lyfe lafteth ; 22, leuer fo often dye than to yelde me to the / for though I lacke wepen & am wepenles yet fhall I ; 24, to thy ; 31, and worthyneffe ; 34, be fo ; 37, [alle] ; 38, and quykly gate.

132. 1, [al] ; he aperceyued clerely ; his good ; 4, by fyr Accolons fyde ; 8, to ; 11, and have loft ; 12, vpon ; 15, nofe and mouth ; 24, quod ; 26, for than ; 33, fyr A. ; 35, And quene M.

133. 2, man whiche fhe mooft hateth in this ; 3, the mooft ; 4, as her ; 6, with her ; 9, fyr A. ; 11, for to haue ; 12, fyr A. ; 13, the trouthe ; that you wyll ; 14, 16, fyr A. ; 17, O my gracyous lorde ; 18, you not ; 22, blame the ; 24, foo be auenged ; 27, [alle] ; 30, [are] ; 31, to vs bothe ; 35, that there were ; 37, [the] ; full fore.

134. 1, that in all yᵉ worlde lyueth ; our mooft fouerayne lyege lorde and kynge ; 2, grete myfhappe and grete myfauenture ; 3, agaynft my kynge and ; 8, one of my owne knyghtes ; 9, to ; 10, haue ; 14, a very proude ; 15, no thynge worth of ; 17, this maner of fourme ; 20, than on ; 21, no erraūt knyghtes ; 23, kepte in pryſon ; 24, that thou content them ; 28–29, I wylle that in all goodly haſte ye come ; to me and to my ; 31, auaunce ; 33, as dooth your ; you of your ; 34, grete goodnes ſayd ſyr O. and I promyſe you that from hens forth I ſhall be at ; 37, whiche ; ryght ſore.

135. 1, Wolde god ; 5, for to ; 7, fals engyn & treaſon and ; 8, [euer] ; 10, youre perſone ; 11, ſhort ſpace ; 14, my ſelfe ; 16, So than ; 17, on ; 19, ſurgyens and leches ; 20, dayes after ; 22, So whan ; 23, on horſbacke ; to ; 25, that I ; 27, that kynge ; 29, how he lay ; 30, damoyſell.

136. 1, Ewayne ; 2, wakened ; 5, her his ; 6, the ſwerde vnto M. ; 7, & ſhe ; drewe ; 10, for to ; 15, ſayd Morgan haue ; 20, therto I ; 21, ſyr A. ; 22, to ; 24, ſyr A. ; 27, countenaunce outwarde ; 28, and yf ſhe ; 29, ſaue her lyfe ; 34, quene G.

137. 2, the mooſte ; 4, Arthur laye ; that he ; 5, anſwered her and ſayd that he had layde hym downe ; 8, tyll I awake hym my ſelfe ; fro her ; 17, wonders wroth ; and he ; 22, hors that ; 25, And as they rode they ; 27, lady late ; 30, faſt after ; 31, of her ; 32, And whan ; 37, ſo heuy.

138. 2, nedes be ; 3, So anone [with al] ; 9, that he came ; [So] ; 11, wyll ⁄ for my brother A. is gone ; 12, my brother ſyr A. ; 16, you well ; 17, with a ; 19, that knyght ; what he wolde do ; 21, ſayd ſhe ; 25, of me ; 35, Tell hym not that . . . . but for the loue of ; 37, hym that.

139. 6, kynge A. ; to ; 11, to the ; 14, morowe ; 16, in that ; 17, one by another ; 27, vpon ; 32, ſayd ſhe ; 34, man.

140. 2, wonders ; 7, ſyr A. ; 11, Ewayne was charged ; 13, coſyn Ewayne ; 18, ſyr Gaherys ; 20, tyll they ; 23, vpon two grete horſes ; 26, vpon it ; 35, & alſo ; ſomme cauſe.

141. 5, Ewayne ; 6, is lyuynge ; 7, Iuſtynge ; 15, vpon ; 21, ſyr M. ; 22, [and the hors back] ; 24, ſyr M. ; 30, myn here in yᵉ ſtede ; 31, And than ; 34, ſeke ; a knyght auenturous.

142. 2, to ; 4, in this worlde ; vs two ; ſholde matche ; 6, yf he were ; 8, more weyker ; ye are ; 18, two ſheldes that ; 20, aroſe vpon ; 21, drewe ; 22, drewe ; 26, not accordynge for ; 29, to ; 38, euenſonge tyme ; febled ſore.

143. 2, waxed than ; 6, I perceyue ; 8, wordes ; 12, Marhaus place ; 13, I merueylle ; 15, nor gentylwomen ; 16, [tho] ; it is the ; 19, wytches and enchaũtereſſes ; the mooſt parte of them ; 20, ony man ; 24, And as yᵉ frenſſhe book reherſeth ; 26, as ſyr L. ; 27, Bors de Gaule ; [ſyr Pellias] ; 28, fyue knyghtes ; 29, [lytel] ; 30, [the] ; 32, had [all thre] there.

144. 6, So longe they rode tyll they ; 7, and aboue ; 20, [be] ;

[one] ; 24, god fpare ; 27, fhall we chofe eueryche ; 31, Than fayd ; 33, Than fayd.

145. 1, them to ; 3, monethes ; [and] ; 4, eche knyght ; 9, where as ; 12, morowe ; 16, moone ; 18, to god ; 20, to you ; 22, to that one ; 24, G. fawe x knyghtes ; 25, made ; 30, & fmote them downe bothe ; 31, And whan.

146. 4, veryly fayd ; and yf that he ; 6, that hit ; and honour to ; 8, wolde be gladde to ; 10, me femeth ; Ryght thus ; 11, that other ; 12, on that ; of the launde ther ; 14, dwarfe whan he came nyghe to the knyght fayd ; 19, put it to his iudgemēt ; 20, euen fo be it ; And than ; 21, they two ; 22, in to my handes ; ye fyr ; 24, bytwene ; 25, And fo whan the damoyfell was ; 33, vnto.

147. 1, go our way ; 3, they were bothe accorded ; 5 demaūded ; 7, bothe hand and ; 10, euen now more ; 11, he is named ; 15, and alfo the ; 18, at thofe ; 21, but y^t he ; 22, the thre ; 25, was there ; 31, by caufe ; 38, to the worfte.

148. 4, fomtyme ; 6, alle this ; [hyt] ; 11, nyghte in the mornynge ; goo feke ; 12, that I can ; 23, that grete ; 27, moone ; and ; 31, A my good frende ; 32, that ye wyll tell me ; 34, and am.

149. 2, therfor I praye the ; 5, vnto ; 6, do fuffre ; for to take ; 8, afore this tyme ; I neuer one fayre worde ; 10, that euer fhe may ; her knyghtes take me and ; 12, for to be ; but fo ; 13, not take me ; 18, to her ; 20, haue her loue ; 21, [all] ; 22, Whan they . . . . ye one to the other / they chaunged ; 27, [in] ; Than fyr G. ; 31, [foo] ; 32, to alyght ; 33, [her] ; 34, fyr G. told ; that his ; 35, fyfters.

150. 2, for that ye ; 3, [to] ; may ; 16, And than it was ; 18, bedde made ; 23, agaynft ye faythfull promeffe that he made to fyr P. ; 24, had not ; 31, theyr beddes ; 33, went ; 34, in a ; 36, herte almooft ; 38, lenger abyde.

151. 2, [fafte] ; 4, thus to ; 5, not flee ; 6, and left them flepyng ; 9, ony man ; might make ; 10, to ; 11, ftreyght to ; where as they ; 12, grete fhame for hym ; 13, and than he ; 14, forth his ; 17, and faythfull feruyce that ; 19, I be ; 20, [oute] ; 21, vnto her ; 23, to his ; 24, the greteft forowe that euer man herde ; 25, And than ; the lady E. ; wakened out of ; 27, that it was ; 28, fyr P. alfo ; 29, me y^t ; 36, [his] ; 37, moone ; caufe of his forowe ; 38, Than the ; how that.

152. 2, wolde ; he were ; 3, [fayd fhe] ; that he ; 5, euyl a ; is now or ; 6, prefumptuous lady ; 7, his lorde and mayfter ; 8, fo lyenge ; 9, had neuer feen ; 10, And in the meane whyle ; 11, to ; that no ; 15, [for] ; fhe keft ; 16, hym out of meafure ; 18, [vnto] ; now loue ; 19, whiche I tofore mooft hated of all men lyuynge ;

This is ; 21, the lady E. ; 23, Go thy waye hens thou ; no more ; 32, fente fuche ; 34, lorde god.

153. 5, theyr lyues ; 6, returne ; 11, vnto a ; demaunded ; 12, not herborowe ; treatynge ; 17, fo euer ; 18, and my ; 22, and forth-with he fhewed to ; 24, come in ; happen that they ; 25, here in this caftell ; 30, how he hyght ; 31, with what man ; 32, faid he ; 33, I am borne ; 34, to.

154. 1, of all thy ; 2, for to morrow ; 3, with the ; none other ; 6, encountre ; 7, neuer noo ; 9, wolde reuenge the deth of my . vij . fones ; 10, Syr I requyre you fayd fyr M. ; 11, ye ; 14, and vnto ; 17, the ; to thy chambre where thou ; 23, where they ; 30, fones of the duke ; 31, dyd not touche them.

155. 3, fayd fyr M. ; 4, Than whan ; 6, vnto fyr ; 7, vnto fyr M. ; 8, [vp] ; 9, by a comyn ; 10, Pentecoft ; 11, he to come ; his fyxe ; 16, renomed to haue fmytten downe ; 19, dayes ; 20, whofe name was called F. ; whiche ; 22, comen to ; 28, fayd fyr M. / vfeth he to ; 30, bere hym he is fo grete ; 33, was ware of hym ; holy tree ; 36, clubbe of yren [in his hande] & came agaynft fyr M. as faft as he myght dryue ; 37, al to peces & lyght on a ftone & al to fruffhed it in to y⁰ erth & there.

156. 3, [in] ; 4, coude not ; 5, [hym] ; 6, he gaue ; many a ; 7, to fall ; in y⁰ ; 10, [grete] ; 11, all the ; 12, man after ; 13, gretely thanked ; 19, Ofanna ; 24, whiche ; 28, wherfore ; the pryce was ; 29, and the pryce was a Ierfawcon ; 31, that went with hym ; 32, to a ; [the] ; 33, a full curteys lady.

157. 3, fyr Ewayne was ; 4, vnto ; 15, the lady ; foo many ; 16, to ; neyther vpon ; nor ; 17, [no] ; to fpeke ; 21, vpon your bodyes ; wronge and extorcyon vnto this lady ; the two bretherne ; 24, affygne vs ; playne batayle ; 26, morow ; 28, bothe the ; 32, and after rode ; 34, Than rode they.

158. 2, horfe tayle ; and yet brake not his fpere ; 6, auoyded fodeynly ; 8, grete ftrokes ; 9, paffynge fore ; 10, that he ; fought they ; 11, enraged and without reafon ; 15, And whan fyr H. fawe that ; 16, vnto ; 19, and fyr H. made grete moone ; 20, vnto her landes ; 24, And than whan it ; 25, [fyr Marhaus and fyre Vwayne] ; 30, And ryght at ; 32, Gawayn had with hym.

159. 2, whiche had ; 4, yf that ; 7, vnto kynge A.'s courte ; 9, were all they of the ; 14, than lyuynge ; 22, had ben flayne in thofe . xij . monethes ; 24, fyr P. ; 25, but that ; 27, fo it is ; Frenffhe boke ; 30, and fire T. was fore ; 35, where as ; 36, to be ; 37, on fyr L.'s fyde . ❡ Thus endeth the fourth boke of this prefent volume.

Book v.

¶ Here foloweth the fyfth boke of the noble and worthy prynce kynge Arthur.

160. 1, had refted a whyle after; 11, vnto; 13, vnto the; 16, as it is; 17, as a; 22, and thy; 30, fet vpon; them for; 31, vnto.

161. 9, them for to; 25, in all chriftendom.

162. 3, Yder; [promyfed to brynge]; 8, yᵗ they fholde here theyr; his noble; 13, creature nor prynce; 18, to; 30, tofore ye; 35, fo to do; 36, we do you to wyte; 37, his chere and; that ye haue.

163. 1, an other maner man; 4, his grete; 5, fawe in our dayes; 9, and he; 12, wayes in the; 15, of his; Geneweys; 24, to Turkye; 27, Than all; 31, And alfo he; 35, mountaynes of Sauoye.

164. 9, concluded that . . . . fhold be arefted; 20, la beale.

165. 2, in to; 3, drowned; 13, was; 15, to the bore; 20, a might; 25, hym to; 28, your realmes; whiche ye haue; 32, ye are; 33, right horryble.

166. 1, ye; 2, cõquerour cõfort; foone after; 3, Bireflete; 20, the whiche was full nygh of your blode; 21, ye; 22, a valyaunt; 28, ye fe; 29, there fhall ye not fayle to; 30, as I; the realme of F.; kynge A.; 32, and called vnto; 34, and for.

167. 1, them; 2, them; theyr; 4, [euer]; vnto the forlonge; 6, and fayd he wold; [in]; 7, vp the mounte; 11, vnto whome; 16, deed [the]; 17, vnto; 18, [duc]; 20, from the grete; 22, fayd the wydowe; nought by; 25, hath ouer comen &.

168. 4, [murthred]; 6, handes; Than anone; 11, with grete anguyffhe threwe; clubbe of yren; 12, thre damoyfels; 13, vnto our lorde Ihefu Chryft; of the noble kynge A.; 14, was one; 15, whyle aboue; 17, [euer]; fo tombeled & weltred; 18, vnto; 19, yᵗ kepte; 27, and alfo the grete; take it to you; 28, fo that I haue his; 33, vnto.

169. 1, vpon; 2, morowe after the noble kynge A.; grete hooft; 3, countye of; [and]; 4, pauylyons; 7, parte therof; 8, made a; 11, kynge A.; 13, to L. the Emperour; [ye]; 17, on horfbacke; 18, pyght in a medowe many; 20, towarde whiche pauylyon; 25, or elles; 27, [ye]; 28, fore an angred; 34, was fyr G.

170. 1, drewe; 2, And anone; 6, & than; 8, ftarke dede on the grounde; came there; 12, grounde; 15, came vnto; 16, vnto; downe right; 25, drewe; 30, paffyng grete; & oure; 31, vnto; 32, and hurte; 34, vnto.

171. 6, fame nyghte; 7, morowe; 8, Launcelot and fyr Cador /

with ; 13, thre fcore thoufande ; 15, fyr L. ; 23, goodly araye ; 24, manfully ; detrenched ; 26, [of the party] ; farafyns partye ; 29, where fo euer ; 30, & his myght ; 33, flyght that ; 34, apparayled ; 35, how his knyghtes.

172. 3, [fauf my felf] ; 4, knyghtes as I haue ; fyr C. ; 7, this daye ; 14, fyr L. ; 16, of the noble kynge A. and of ; 18, Senatoure that ; 20, [for] ; 24, [for] ; 26, Than anone ; 27, afore ; 28, haftely folowe ; Than was kynge A. pryuely warned ; 30, kynge A. ; 34, the noble.

173. 1, Soyffons ; 2, baners ; 3, and fawe that he was befette ; 5, to ; 9, And he therwith commaūded ; 13, men were ; 14, [apper-tyces] feates of warre ; 17, in all efpecyall of them ; in to ; 18, he hymfelfe ; 19, as it ; 20, his good ; [as] ; 23, there he ; 24, meruay-lous quantite ; 27, heed / & the body flewe . vj . farafyns in the fallynge downe ; 28, [fo dyd] ; 29, table dyd full nobly ; batayle endured long ; 31, that ; 32, oftentymes ; 33, longe fo ; 34, and at the ; [themperour] ; 37, ouerthwart.

174. 2, his helme ; 3, he his ; 4, Than whan ; 8, vnto the noble conquerour ; 9, [& the trumphe] ; 13, thofe that ; caufed ; 14, to ferche ; all theyr ; 18, & the kyng of Ethyope ; 19, dyuers other ; 20, thre fcore ; 21, noble kynge A. ; 22, aromatyke gommes ; he dyd ; thre fcore folde ; 23, & than ; 25, bodyes were fette ; 27, that were ; vnto ; 33, of me ony ; that you ; 34, vnto ; 35, vnto.

175. 1, fhold fuffyfe ; 4, nor afke of me ne of my landes ony trybute ; 7, Lucius lyenge ; 14, [no] ; 16, feynge ; 18, to ; 20, Brabande ; 11, hye Almayn ; 23, maner wyfe ; 24, the noble ; full longe ; 27, tolde hym ; 31, Wycharde ; 32, and alfo ; 33, ye may gete there.

176. 3, on the nexte morowe ; 4, aduentures ; 5, knight armed ; 6, vnto ; 7, faue onely ; 11, vnto ; from whens [that] ; 23, drewe ; 25, fmote hym ; 28, Than that ; 31, bled faft ; 32, thy blode ; 34, all the leches.

177. 1, fyr G. ; 5, I wyll ; 9, fyr G. ; 16, Alexandrye ; 17, the lord ; 24, arte / & of thy beinge ; fyr G. ; 25, pryce kynge ; 26, for to ; 27, At Chryftmaffe ; 33, knyght or knaue ; [thou] ; 34, tell the trouth ; 35, noble courte ; 37, his owne ; 38, fortuned & comen.

178. 2, than yf ; 3, prouynce of Parys ; 4, fholde haue ; 7, and hath ; of armes of all D. ; 9, to the nombre of thre fcore thoufande ; men of warre ; 10, flee & hye vs faft fro hens ; wyll do ; to vs ; 11, he blowe no ; 12, here faft ; 13, vpon ; the ones ; 14, nor ; 15, hymfelfe ; 16, after hym ; fo they ; 17, that ; where as ; 20, who it was that had fo hurte & wounded hym ; fyr G. ; 26, hote blood ranne downe ; 32, [vnto] ; 34, many a thoufand ; 35, fayd fyr.

179. 9, with them; 14, lepynge; 15, wherfore he; 20, vpon the colde; 23, grete; 27, toward them; 30, many a; 34, fyerfly with.

180. 1, And than; 3, gyue backe & flee; 4, well my; 6, a gyaunt named I.; 14, quytte them fo well; 15, [and ward]; 16, flayne of fyr G.; 23, hym theyr; and tolde to hym; 26, [noble]; 28, fyr G.; 30, he ben; 34, by his; 36, do make.

181. 3, the kynge [Arthur] and requyryng; 7, ne none of your damoyfelles; 13, [for]; 19, [there] a; femed it was mooft beft; 22, fo wanne; & after they wanne; 23, kynge A.; 24, vpon; by the; 25, wonne & goten; fent a cōmaundement; 27, through & came to the; and there; 28, in heuyneffe; a knyght of his owne countree to be capytayne; 29, the forefayd; 30, vnto kyng A.; 31, vpon them; 32, his true; 33, and of Pauye; 34, Than king A. rode; 35, there he wanne; 36, all that he foūde; wolde; as fo went to; 38, of Rome; for to.

182. 1, lord & chefe gouernour or not; vpon; 3, whiche at that tyme; within the Cite of; 4, and they all; largely goodes; 5, they all; 6, Baronny of the R.; 7, hym as; holy creme; to fuche an hygh and noble eftate; 8, vnto you fayd kyng A.; 10, there as; 11, crownacyon; 12, the Romayns tell; there he was; 13, folempnyte; 14, certayne tyme; 15, vnto F.; he gaue; 16, deferuynge; 17, none of them; neyther ryche nor; 18, vnto; 19, that he; and be his true fubgecte al the; 20, that he made; and cōftytued his men vnto grete rycheffe and honour; 21, and all the grete men of eftate; togyder afore the tryumphaunt conquerour kynge A.; 22, Noble Emperour blyffed be the eternall god; mortal warre; is all; 23, conqueft is; 24, make ony; 25, and hertely praye your noble grace; and alfo we praye you to gyue; for to; 26, a longe feafon; 27, for to; with grete; 28, kyng A. vnto them; 30, was there; 31, of other baggage & had; 32, kyng A. returned; 33, [not]; [ne take] by the waye neyther take vytayle ne none; 34, truly paye; 36, [his wyf]; with hym.

❡ Thus endeth the fyfth boke of the conqueft that kynge Arthur had agaynft Lucius the Emperour of Rome ❡ And here foloweth the fyxth boke whiche fpeketh of fyr Launcelot du lake.

𝔅ook vi.

❡ Here foloweth the fyxth boke of the noble and worthy prynce kyng Arthur.

183. 1, Anone; the noble and worthy; 2, [thenne]; 4, [but];

good knyghtes; 10, [other]; 13, wherfore he is; 14, after that;
16, certaynly; 17, ladyes and; all the dayes of his lyfe; 18, grete;
19, a longe whyle; 21, his brother fyr L.; 22, [for]; 23, vpon; all
poyntes; 24, a grete playne; 28, vs &; 29, for of all this feuen
yere; 30, there &; 32, layde his.

184. 1, flepte; 4, after thofe thre; 5, behelde; that he had
neuer feen; 7, at all poyntes; 8, thefe thre knyghtes that fledde;
[he]; 9, downe to; groūde; 10, fuche a ftroke; hors and man; 11,
vnto the erthe; than he rode; vnto; 12, more than the length of a
fpere; 13, and reyned; 15, And whan; 17, [for]; his brother fyr;
And fo; 18, and had ouertakē; [&]; 20, and than he; [doun]; 23,
he vnarmed them; 29, that was; 31, which; 32, [by]; 36, hangeth;
that belōged; vnto.

185. 1, ende of; 3, ony knyght had; 4, and fo he; 8, and there
he; 9, brother fyr L.; And anone; bete vpon; 11, Anon there;
13, & fewtred his; 17, and caught; 18, and fo; [owne]; 23, all
yᵉ dayes of; 26, he toke; [garte to] vnarmed hym; fharpe thornes;
27, and after; in to; 31, a flepe; 32, whan I went frō; 35,
fyr T.

186. 3, heet of yᵉ fonne; 6, canape of; 9, and than; 12, [for]
to; eche of them fayd fhe; 13, vnto; 23, colde chambre; 28, fayd
the damoyfell; 31, [fayre damoyfel]; 33, ony perfone.

187. 1, that ye are; 2, that is now; 6, is alfo; 8, ye one; ye
wyll; 9, vnto your; yf ye wyll not do thus / here fhall ye abyde;
10, tyll that ye dye; 13, be ye; 14, haue none; 16, vpon; 17,
lyuyng vnto; 21, [the]; to; that brought hym his; 23, in all; 24,
fayd fhe; 27, am aferde; quenes wytches; 30, that your; 31, of
all the; that ben lyuynge; 33, me for to.

188. 1, laft paft; 3, yf ye; vpon; 4, morowe; 7, 11, fayd the
damoyfell; 14, [be fhe that fhall]; 15, and there; to abyde me;
20, and arayed; 21, vnto his; 24, & in no wyfe; 25, ony hyghe;
29, and fo; 30, and founde there; 31, [fadly]; 32, [there]; 33,
belonged the.

189. 2, lyghtly out; 3, lepte after; 6, flade; 7, And fyr L. toke
hym to his mercy; 10, my loue & lady; 12, fyr L.; was fore; 13,
lately; 17, [al]; whiche; 18, fyr B.; 19, fo fore; 20, moone; 21,
fyr B.; a very; 23, he goodly; and toke me to his mercy; 25,
you; are; 28, often tymes; 30, fyr B.; 36, all my; yf ye; or
myghty of; 37, than ye; 38, ftode thus talkynge; daye appered.

190. 2, fhewed hym; towarde the; 4, As foone; 5, kynge B.
doughter; 6, than fhe; wente; 7, that it was fyr L.; 8, haftely;
[from hym]; [lete]; 10, there he; 11, fyr L.; 12, that was; 16,
fro his hors; he wente; 22, wyft; whether; 23, wherfore fhall

whyle ; 24, frendes & kynrede ; 25, now on ; 26, vnto my ; 30, that foule fared with ; 32, [here] ; 34, truft beft ; 35, payntynge.

191. 2, fo I fhall ; 7, and [to] ; 21, with that falle ; 23, A.'s courte ; 26, out of ioynte ; fyr M. ; 29, his fpere ; 31, helme pyght ; 34, [grete] ; fyr L. ; all y^e ; 35, all to brake.

192. 1, drewe out ; 2, gaue eche other ; 4, nofe and his mouth ; on bledynge ; and his eeres alfo ; 5, [therwith] his hors ; 10, he was hytte ; 14, [there] ; 18, they promyfed ; 20, kynge B. ; goo feke ; 24, knowlege therof ; 27, with a ; 30, fayd the ; 32, as for ; 33, fayd the damoyfell ; a ryght ; 35, as the beft knyght is ; 36, name is ; and of what courte and.

193. 2, that I ; 6, done this ; 8, and [to] ; [dayly] ; 9, and defyre damoyfel ; 10, to ; 12, and vnto ; wheron the bacyn henge ; 14, ende of ; and with fuche a myght that he made the bottom fall out ; 16, well nygh ; 21, fyr G.'s ; 26, the better in his ; 31, from the ; 32, and than ; ftrength togyder ; 33, and fhewed me ; 35, the now fhortly ; fyr T.

194. 1, in theyr ; 2, as it was poffyble for them to ren ; 3, in the ; 4, wherof y^e ; 8, grete ftrokes ; 9, holde theyr dyntes ; 12, [Thenne] ; were bothe ; 15, Saye on fayd fyr Launcelot ; 16, art fayd fir T. ; 17, one a ; 18, fo y^t thou be not he ; 21, neuer [to] ; [that] ; 24, Truly ; 26, whiche was ; 27, than lyuynge ; 28, for and ; 29, of an other ; to that I ; 31, haue vtterly ; after myght ; 33, I haue.

195*. 1, [that] ; be bytwene ; 4, [very] ; table round ; [and] ; 6, was ony ; 7, And than hurtled ; 13, befperpled ; 15, [a] ; full lowe ; 16, That foone ; 17, as a lyon ; & fo he ; 18, and than he ; afonder ; 20, than he went ; 22, take ye . . . . fayd the damoyfell ; ye this ; 23, to go & delyuer ; 24, And fo ; fyr G. ; 25, lende ; 26, fyr G. ; 30, excepte your felfe ; 34, [owne] ; [that].

196*. 1, fyr Kays ; 6, fay to them that ; 8, [that] ; 9, hygh feeft ; I thynke to be ; 11, went ; 12, [ther] ; 13, And forthwith ; porter agaynft ; 14, that his eyen ftarte out of his heed ; [haftely he] ; 15, [dore] ; 16, eueryche ; 18, bycaufe he was wounded that he had flayne fyr Turquyne ; fyr G. ; fyr L. ; 20, well all ; 22, fyr E. ; 28, [euer] belonged ; 29, [fatte] ; 31, one good ; 34, for to.

197. 7, to his ; 8, yourfelfe alone before ; 11, damoyfell ; 13, [oute] ; 22, longe haft ; 24, as T. ; 27, du foreft ; 29, fayd fhe ; 30, go or ryde ; 32, But fyr ; that ye.

198. 1, this countree ; 3, what fo euer ; But to be ; 4, neuer to be / for yf I were than fhold I be boūde to tary w^t my wyfe ; 9, in ye warres ; 10, Or els ; 14, rode he ; 15, in to ; 16, grete longe ;

21, a myghty; 22, full of pynnes of yren; 23, vnto the nauyll; 25, [men and wymmen]; 28, wente ſtrayght.

199. 6, of that; ſtroke; 7, ſyr L.; ran after; as faſt as he myght; 8, to the foundement; 14, [knyȝte]; 15, thou were; dede of worſhip; 16, ony knyght dyd; and therof; 19, ſayd he; [ſyr] 20, [al]; 21, no knyght; 23, theyr lyues / & alſo many; 27, in to; 29, is the; 30, as his ryght and appertenaunce; 32, & after V.

200. 2, it happened hym; 4, with a; 5, he & his hors were well chered; 12, that came; 13, vpon; with theyr; 14, hymſelfe; 16, I ſholde be; 25, and therfore; 27, [for]; 35, were we; 38, ſyr L.

201. 1, or els not; 2, ſayd they / than; 3, as ye; 4, vpon; 7, for to be; 9, knyght ſwore vpon theyr; 12, ſo in; 15, chambre wyndowe for to; 16, in the; 19, ſayd he; haue done; that I; [for]; 21, [ſhall ye repoſe yow]; ye take your reſt; 22, and anone there; brought hym; 24, morowe; 31, kynge A.'s courte.

202. 1, had longe; 13, whoſe name; 14, [that]; 23, on the; one to another; 29, ynough ado to; 30, [euer]; 32, Anone they; 37, my herte ryſeth.

203. 3, myght; 7, whiche ful; 11, at the; 19, ſo that we; 20, well ye; 25, and the thre.

204. 2, [bothe]; 3, ſayd ſyr Ector; 11, [al]; 14, [that he was aſtonyed] that of a grete whyle; 15, I wel ſe; 16, and ſo he; 19, horſes ren as faſt as; 20, theyr ſheldes; brake; 27, [al]; 30, of grete; my lyfe; 34, Now let vs ſpeke of.

205. 9, in to yᵉ myddes; 21, [called]; 25, that knewe; 26, wᵗ a loude voyce; 27, you of your; to helpe; 29, fought he; 32, tyl that.

206. 1, logres; 4, [euen]; 6, hyther; yf you; 10, to a lytell; 14, ſawe ſtande by hȳ. xxx .; 16, grynned; 17, them ſore; 18, redy to do; 21, through them; 25, couerd wᵗ; 28, wherof he was aferde; 30, As ſoone as he was; 35, Therwith; [out].

207. 3, I wyll not leue it; 4, ye dyd leue; 6, ſyr L.; 8, [me]; 10, ſayd ſhe; 13, whiche there lyeth; 14, ſyr G. the baſtardes lyſte hand; 15, that I; 18, body alyue; 19, haue had; I wolde; 24, [ſoo]; 27, Nigramus; 30, to; 31, ſyr M. laye; [And]; 32, [paſ-ſynge]; [the]; 35, went vnto; 38, a holer; was there.

208. 3, to kynge A.'s courte; 7, [And]; 10, two lytell; 11, yᵗ came; 13, [aboute]; 14, as ſhe wold; henge faſt; 16, In the meane; 18, of yᵉ worlde; 20, flypte awaye; 21, knowe it; 23, to yᵉ; 24, [wel]; lady ſayd ſyr L.; 26, that I may; 32, clymmed; 33, rotten braūche; doune with the braūche; 34, with her.

209. 1, [and]; 2, ſyr L.; 3, wolde haue the; 5, [but] as I

commaunded her fayd fyr Phelot; 7, [vnto the]; that an armed
. . . . fhold; 11, other wyfe; 15, the therfro; 16, euer ony; 17,
loked aboue; 18, [ther with]; 19, body of yᵉ tree; 25, Than fyr
L.; 32, coude; 33, [foo]; 34, And as foone as; 35, thens &
thanked; oure lord god.

210. 1, [out]; 2, many other wayes; 8, why wylte; to; 11,
[two]; 16, tofore god; there; 18, named; 19, to kepe me; 21,
fyr L.; 23, & the lady; 24, other fyde; but that yᵉ; 25, [fyre];
26, rydyng after vs; [foo]; 28, ftroke; 30, [he fayd and]; 32, from
his; drewe; 33, [al]; caught fyr L.; 36, wyll not; 38, fyr L.

211. 1, in my; 3, neuer doo; 6, vnto; 7, fyr L.; 8, me thy
name; 9, fyr L.; 13, a fore; for fyr L.; 14, [many]; 21, and as
the freuffhe boke fayth; 22, to; 28, full glad of; 30, fyr K.; 33,
now and than; 34, had taken.

212. 6, whan he was in daūger to haue ben flayne; 11, Than
anone; [ther] came; 16, they vnderftode; Than fyr M.; 18, all
the; 20, by yᵉ doughter of; 22, [for]; 24, Gahalatyne tolde; 25,
they thre; [fame]; 26, [that]; 30, bothe of. ❡ Thus endeth the,
etc. ❡ Here after foloweth the ftory; whiche was called, etc.

ℬook vij.

❡ Here foloweth the feuenth boke of the noble and worthy
prynce kyng Arthur.

213. 1, plenare; 3, folempne & hygh; 6, had euer; 7, all other
hygh; 9, fome grete aduenture or; 11, before; 17, at [the]; 19,
faue thofe; 20, an encountre; 22, accompliffhed; 25, [al]; 29,
fcylence & roume; 30, went; 31, bygge yonge; drewe; 32, to
kynge; 33, blyffe you; 35, for to; [and requyre you]; 37, to me.

214. 1, ne loffe; And as for the fyrft gyfte; 2, this fame; 3,
that ye; 4, your petycyon; 5, fayd he ∕ this; 6, to me; thefe; 11,
conceyte; 12, fayd he ∕ as for that be it may be; 15, nor my; I
wolde fayne knowe; 16, That haue I meruayle of; 17, thy owne;
one of the; 18, [one]; noble kyng A.; vnto the ftewarde fyr K.;
21, haue; 24, had ben comen; 25, and harneys; [fo] he hath
afked; 27, that is to faye; 30, men that had brought hym; 37,
fyr B.

215. 3, [& brothe vpon]; 4, brought vp & foftred; 15, nerer;
16, [as] fyr L.; 18, euery nyght; 19, alle thofe; 21, knewe of ony;
24, where as were; 25, yᵉ barre ne; 27, Pentecoft; 29, yerely he;
30, on; 31, had herde of; And than came; 34, came in; 35, [in
to the halle].

216. 1, that here in your courte ; 3, What call ye ; 5, fayd fhe ; not be knowen ; 16, that bē here ; 18, Than with thefe ; 26, fyr L. ; 34, that his hors.

217. 2, [as] ; 3, of fyr ; 4, hym that ; [al] openly ; 9, of the kechyn ; for to ; 11, fayd ꝑ yet ; 14, what fyr B. ; 15, that it ; 19, to hym ; 21, the fpere ; 28, [they] ; 30, to auoyde his ; 31, put his.

218. 9, the vttermeft ; 13, [fo] ; 19, I fhal tell you ; 21, fayd he ; 23, fir L. ; now more ; 25, nor drynke ; 27, go on his iourney ; 31, alfo fyr L. ; that it ; 32, what kynne ; 33, vnto.

219. 1, haft goten in ; 3, haft flayne ; 6, waffher of dyffhes ; 7, fyr B. ; ye lyft ; 9, of kynge ; [fo] ; 10, or I fhal ; 14, So as they thus ; 15, [euer] ; 20, as the knyghte was bounden ; 21, vnto the theues one at the fyrft ftroke ; 25, & than ; 29, fyr B. ; 30, of the ; 35, done is but.

220. 2, tofore ; 3, for to ; 5, of her ; 9, morowe ; 18, [vpon other] ; 19, eche at other egrely ; 21, in to ; [he] ; 22, vnto the lande ; 30, knightes hors ; 32, and myght ; 33, fhamefully.

221. 4, fayre language ; 7, for yf thou ; 10, that ye ; 11, So thus ; 12, the chode ; 16, by it ; 18, Whan the damoyfell fawe ; the blacke knyght ; 20, the valey ; I thanke you ; 22, came to the damoyfell and fayd ; 25, has ben fedde ; 26, Wherfore cometh he in ; 29, wold god that ye wold ; or elles ; yf ; 31, to daye ; for I ; 34, the whiche is ; 35, Syr they ; 36, [for] ; [that].

222. 1, well be ; 2, neuertheleffe how ; [as] ; he is ; 5, his fete ; 6, his harneys ; 14, fro the lyghtly ; not a ; 16, thou arte ; 17, vpon ; 19, fyr B. ; 21, ftacke ; 23, fyr B. ; 25, in a ; 26, dyed forthwith ; And whan fyr B. ; 27, [thenne] ; 29, nyghe her ; to hym . Awaye ; 30, go oute ; 32, as thou haft flayne ; 33, through thyn ; is a knyght that ; 34, flee backe ; 35, fyr B. ; 36, awey for hym ; 37, wyll flee me.

223. 2, than thus to rebuke me aldaye ; 3, I fele ; 4, or truly ; 7, dryuynge ; 9, of her ; 10, fayd fhe ; 14, [that] ; 17, fyr B. ; 20, notes ; 21, that lightly ; 24, anone they ; out their ; 26, fyr B.'s hors ; 28, groūde ; lightly auoyded ; 29, his fete ; fyr B. ; 30, [al] ; 31, champyons ; bledde fore ; 33, why ftāde ; 35, for to fe ; fuche a ftynkyng boye [fo] ; a valyaunt.

224. 1, [the wede ouer grewe the corne] ; The grene knyght herynge thefe wordes was afhamed ꝑ & incōtynent he gaue fyr B. a myghty ftroke ; 3, through out ; fyr B. ; 4, of the damoyfels language ; 6, fyr B. threwe hym downe ; 7, And incontynent ; 8, fyr B. mercy ; 9, graunte hym his lyfe ; 10, fyr B. ; 11, whiche is comen ; 12, haue flayne ; [falfe] ; 13, thou kechyn page ; 15, fyr B. ; 17, my lyfe ; O fayre ; 23, [the] not ; 26, for yf ; 35, grete nede ; I am fore adradde ; 37, morowe.

225. 1, vnto; 2, alwayes the damoyfell; 3, [as]; 4, and fet hym at a; Me thynketh meruayle; 5, why that; 16, went vnto theyr reft; 18, fyr B.; 19, morowe; 24, commaũdemēt; 25, and where fo euer; 26, fyr B.; and whan I; 27, [that]; 31, Than departed; 34, the yet / and flee away.

226. 5, thou fhalte; thou; 12, in pauylons & vpon fkaffoldes; 13, at that caftell; 14, and there he fawe; a page and; 17, fo anone he armed hym / and toke his hors haftely; 18, whiche was all reed; 19, belonged vnto hym; 20, [that]; nyghe fyr B.; 22, here is; 23, not your brother; whiche has ben; 26, vnhappy knaue; flayne your; 27, and [this]; 28, fawe hym ouercome; 29, with his owne; 30, I can not be; 31, And with this; bothe the; 34, to other; 35, as now here; and; 37, the damoyfell cryed out.

227. 4, fyr B.; wonders fore fo; 5, and grete meruayle it was to beholde; 8, vnto the; 9, [with me]; 17, thanke ye now; 18, all that; 19, And fo; [thenne]; 21, fyr B.; 24, morowe; 25, [dyned] brake theyr fafte; fyr B.; 28, fyr B.; 32, fyr B. and the damoyfel departed.

228. 1, fyr B.; 8, you to wyte; 9, yf I; 11, mete with the; 12, man of mooft; in yᵉ; 13, it well; 14, it be; 15, within a whyle they; before; a fayre cite; 18, goodly to; 19, is fuche / that whan; 20, he lyeth; for to; 21, and all gentylmen; 23, or thynke; fyr B.; 26, there he; 27, [there]; 28, bothe men; 34, fyr B.; 36, for yf.

229. 1, fayle hym; 3, fayd fir B.; 8, I well; 11, myle hens; 13, or domage; 15, that this; nor of; 16, hath layde; 18, this good; 19, it were grete fhame to me yf I withdrewe me now; 24, I haue meruayle; of man; 26, for more fouler nor more; 27, rule nor rebuke; 34, batayles; 37, [it].

230. 3, you or; 4, fayd fhe; 6, fayd fyr B.; 7, as ye ought to; 8, fyr B.; fpeke thus; 9, fayre to me; gretely myne herte; 13, to knowe whether; 14, vnto; fyr B.; 17, wel fayd he / than; 18, vttermeft; 19, And whan fyr B.; 20, all the myght that; [euer]; brake; 24, gaue eche other; 25, they fo; fell bothe; 27, many places; 31, [though hym lothe were] fyr B. [aboue]; ouerthwarte vpon hym; 33, for to.

231. 1, knowe well; knyghte my broder; 6, thefe knyghtes; 34, morowe.

232. 1, On the morowe; 3, fyr P.; awaye; 4, fayd fhe; 5, fyr P.; 6, laundes; 9, fyr B.; 12, lady is; 20, And for this caufe he taryeth; 25, fyr B.; 31, fyr L.

233. 3, fyr B., haue a good; [and]; 4 cam of; 8 [thenne]; 9, fyr G.; 13, knoweth not; 15, and brought a; 17, lady dame Lyones; 20, the lady; 23, du lake was; 26, fayd he; 27, fhold do; 28, fayd the lady; were ftronge; 29, de brewfe & that; 30 was called.

234. 1, [to fore]; 2, erth; 6, here befyde; and thyder; 11, & whan thou haft thus done / go to; 13, [to] drynke; 17, & good courage; 19, none other thynge; 25, waye; betoke; 26, vnto; 34, [but]; 36, and fyr G.

235. 6, in fcorne; 7, not for hym; reed knight; 8, and yf fo be that I; 12, we of; 13, fyr B.; 14, on the; there a maffe; 16, vnto a; 17, as were; 23, henge fhamefully nyghe; [ful]; 27, vnto this; 32, fyr B.; 33, I thus.

236. 1, [for]; for in; 5, fyr B.; 9, vnto the; 10, ftronge walles; 12, bette vpon; 18, vnto hym; 19, batayle with hym; 21, whiche as; 25, wyll I worfhipfully wynne; 26, vnto; 27, fo egrely; 28, knyghtes lepte there out; 30, that were.

237. 2, mery and; 5, fyr B; 7, fayd he; [for]; 9, glad chere; 11, grounde; her; 15, fyr B.; 17, it is a grete; 18, for yf; 21, company; 23, els dye in the quarell; 25, yonder grete elmes; Fye fye for; fyr B.; 26, and fuche fhamefulnes; 27, & the ordre of; 28, thy deteftable; 30, me and make me agaft; 32, And yf; thou be; 33, all the myght they had.

238. 1, in the; 3, bothe to the groūde; with the reynes; 7, that the; 10, they lyghtly; 13, reled bothe; 18, wolde not; 19, bothe wynde; ftakerynge; pantyng; 20, fo that; 21, and whā; 22, went; 23, [at]; 24, two wylde; [fometyme]; 25, grounde grouelynge; at; 26, of theyr owne; 28, lykelyeft; 29, fore hewen; 33, but full fore he bought or efpyed; 35, eche other; a whyle.

239. 4, for them to; it on; 6, vnto the; 8, and ioyfull; 9, he fterte vp fodeynly and badde; [of the reed laundes]; redy to doo; 11, the reed; 12, fyerfly; 16, on; fell downe; 18, damoyfel; 20, fo that; And whan; 21, arofe vp; 23, caught; 24, togyder a newe; 26, out of the reed knyghtes; 28, groūde; 29, for to; and than the reed; 32, hanged fo; 34, fo many; 35, [ful]; 36, ye your.

240. 2, [els]; that as; 4, vnto the tyme that I had; 8, alle this; 13, prayed fyr B.; 14, [to your]; 16, all fayd; better to take homage; 18, [for]; for by; 20, al y^t be here; 22, fyr B.; 24, as al; 25, [that he] &; 28, that he; 31, he afke; 32, that he hath had; 35, And than whan.

241. 2, damoyfel L.; vnto; 5, and fo; 9, in the lady Lyones grace; 16, to the; 18, a full noble; 29, whiche; 32, hym at al poyntes.

242. 2, entre in; 6, in armes worffhipfully; 9, this / that ye;

[and]; 10, haue had; 11, and kyndnes; that I haue; 18, and honour; and alfo; 19, be / foone gone; you me; 20, vnto you; fhall neuer; 21, vnto; 23, moone & forowe; 24, whether he rode; 27, coude haue no; 28, fo on the; 29, and his armure and rode tyll it was noone; 30, vnto a; 34, fyr B.; 37, haue hym in a wayte.

243. 2, haue your watche; wyfe ye; 3, from hym; [ye]; 5, that the dwarfe; 6, name is; 8, this dwarf; 9, to your; 10, [that]; 11, name is; or els I fhall; 13, as ye haue defyred; 14, departed and rode bothe daye and; 15, flepynge by a water fyde; and had layde; 16, [for to flepe]; fawe y^t; 18, toke hym; 20, armure and alle that to hym belonged; was; 22, of helpe; 23, therwithall; fyr B. awoke; 24, fyr G.; 31, nexte waye.

244. 2, and a; 3, the poore; paffed by me; a knyght that is called; 5, but I coūfeyle you that ye folowe hym not; 7, within thefe two; & therfore; after hym; 8, to hym; Leue we now to fpeke of; 10, of the; 12, was borne; 13, thàt he was; [yf]; me the trouth; 14, for euer; 17, vnto; 18, vnto the; [of]; 19, [and] now; 20, now I praye; agayne vnto; 21, tyll he; 23, or [that]; you moche; 29, in hym; 30, a curteis and mylde man / the; 31, well faye; 33, as I haue reuyled hym; 35, fyr B.; [in]; 37, fayeng thou.

245. 10, not he; 15, aboue all other knyghtes; 16, wold I; 19, [ryght]; 21, agaynft your perfone; owne will; 23, here in this; I than; 28, down from his hors; 29, many euyll; 31, and there was fyr G.'s wyfe.

246. 1, there came forth in to the hall; 5, tyme thought in hymfelfe . Ihefu wolde to god; 6, fhe is; 7, bothe of; 9, his vnder-ftandynge; 10, went to; 12, fyr G. efpyed; [thenne]; 15, that he; 17, to hym; ye be; 18, beftowed; 28, fholde not lyue; 29, to my; 34, my lorde kyng A.; 36, be gretely; 38, vnto [the].

247. 2, faythfully to; neuer none; 3, And than; 6, how that; 10, damoyfel L. whiche; 12, plyght theyr trouth vnto; 19, was knowen; 22, in that thynge / as that; 26, entent; the one with the other; tyll; 27, [At]; 29, to his; fayd he; 35, And anone he; 36, [there he]; 37, comynge towarde hym; a grete lyght.

248. 3, a grymme; 5, fwerde in his; went; 8, the fame; 9, [al]; 11, to the erth; fyr G. lepte; 12, and quyckly; [fro the body]; 13, ftande on his fete; [foo]; 15, And than; 16, Than came he; fawe that; 18, dyfhonoured; 19, vnto his fyfter dame Lyones; 20, fo fore; fayd dame L.; 22, [my]; 23, I am not afhamed; 25, [it]; fyr G. alfo; 26, ne by my; 27, is done; And than anone; 29, with [al]; 30, heed of the deed knight; 32, heed ftode; 33, it was;

it was afore; 34, the fame knyght; [vp]; 35, ledde hym; with her.

249. 2, the damoyfell L.; 3, and alfo to; 7, that at the; 8, [that]; 11, fhe hadde; 15, armed anone; and than; 17, to the; 18, ftrayned fo hymfelf; [foo]; 19, brafte out; 24, and whan he had thus done; 25, And whan he was; 27, fo loude; 28, herd her; 30, but the grete; 31, [there] no tongue may; 32, as though fhe; 33, the damoyfel; 34, gobbettes.

250. 1, whiche ye; 2, fayd the damoyfell L.; done; auowe it; 3, for your; 4, for vs; 5, man on lyue; 7, Now leue; 11, and they all yelded; And after; 14, vnto the other two; 15, & they all; [and]; 16, fyr P.; 24, [Soo]; kynge A.; 27, [with hym]; 29, What is your wyll; 30, fayd he; I am called; 32, ye fhall wyte; 33, whiche is; 35, [that euer had the better of me]; 36, and he charged and; vnto your grace and wyll.

251. 3, as moche as lyeth; 6, [And as to the]; 8, [And]; 9, rounde table; 11, [more]; a cuftome; 12, I haue; it at; 15, that I had; them that; 16, [al]; [of] fyr; 17, ye may; 18, vnto; 20, of the euyll wyll & enmyte that he had cōmyfed agaynft them bothe; 24, for all; 25, [one]; 33, euer ben; 35, kyng A.

252. 3, Perearde; 4, kyng A.; 5, in kynge A.'s courte; 7, table round; fyr P.; 8, vnto; 11, two manly; 16, to theyr; 17, at theyr; 18, with a grete nombre of; 21, in the fpace of . xv . yeres; 25, is a grete; 28, me now fore.

253. 2, feke a; 4, yf I; 10, monethes after; 15, & therfore; 17, vnto her brother Kynge A.; 19, of his; grete plente for to; 20, well be; 24, had all; we all; 25, of grete; 26, that he; 29, mocke &; 36, is to me grete ioye.

254. 2, go feke; 7, & I doubte not but that fhe; 8, as ye; 9, quod kynge A.; 10, & in all hafte a meffenger was; that rode bothe nyghte; 14, the meffenger to ryde; 15, yᵉ hafte poffyble; 19, fhall I rule myfelfe; 21, maner wyfe; 23, as I wote; 24, my lord the; 29, yf it; 31, valure; 32, Than dame; vnto; 38, be thus.

255. 4, fro thens; for that; 6, where as; 7, & than fhe; 9, fo fore; 11, as a knyghte fholde do; well hole; 17, commaūde; 24, than anfwered; 26, at kynge A.'s courte; with fyr; 35, as we; 36; quod fyr P.; 37, in all E.

256. 4, [ther]; 10, on the fyde; 15, yles; grūmurfum; 18, Gaunter; 20, [this] fyr T.; 21, tyme was not; 26, knyghtes dyd; 28, fyr G. & his two bretherne fyr A. & fyr G.; 35, and alfo fyr S.

257. 1, [al]; 7, many other; 9, and fyr G.; 10, the noble; many moo / whiche were to longe to reherfe; 11, to fpeke of; 20,

his dukes / his erles / his barons / & all his ; 21, and fyr Ironfyde ;
22, of ynde ; 23, maner of wyfe ; [not] ; 25, neyther of ; 26, nor of ;
nor at the ; 30, of it felf ; 31, And this is ; 32, turne it vnto ; in to
the lykenes of.

258. 6, vnto ; 8, and al maner of mynftralfye ; 10, on the daye
of y^e ; 11, was done ; 12, vnto ; 13, anone there ; 17, fyr G. ; 24,
fyr A. ; 34, fyr Lamoracke ; whiche.

259. 1, eyther of them ; 2, & fyr L. ; 3, [and alle] ; 5, Gaunter ;
7, vnto ; 13, fyr Ewayne ; 16, fyr P. and his ; [and man] ; 17, came
in ; out of the ; 20, of noble ; them ; 22, reed ; whiche ; 27, them
two ; 28, eche other ; 30, Bleoberis ; 31, that grete ; Bleoberis ;
groūde ; 33, vnto the.

260. 3, [redy] ; 4, nor knowlege of ; kynge A. of Irlande ; 9,
there came ; kynge B. ; 10, groūde ; 11, and kyng B. ; 15, herde
that ; [and] ; gate hym ; 20, [fame] ; 23, fyr L. ; [for] ; 25, [vpon] ;
33, yet I wolde not do it ; 35, [thenne] ; a grete.

261. 3, was a ; 4, fyr B. ; [there] ; 5, mette to gyder ; 6, worft ;
8, hym ageyn ; 9, came there ; 12, [And thenne came in fyr G. ;
and knewe that it was fir L.] du lake that ; 16, L. du lake ; whiche
demed ; 21, worfte ; 26, vnto ; 28, whiche ; 29, fyr T. ; 32, loueth
hym agayne ryght hertely ; 38, vnto.

262. 2, fayd they ; 3, mocke y^e ; 9, [that] ye ; put on ; 13, all
the people fawe ; 21, maner of ; afked of ; 22, on ; 23, as nygh fyr
G. ; 25, [helme] is ; 27, wherby all ; 28, of king A.'s partye ; for
hym / and ; they preced ; 31, began to double ; 34, fyr G. herde ;
35, and than he.

263. 7, of his beft ; 9, That is well ; 12, tell her ; and that I ;
13, vnto her ; 14, ye haue ; 16, lorde fyr ; 19, to reft hym ; 21,
haue gone ; 22, as well his hors as hymfelfe ; [So this] ; 24, that
wonder it was to fe ; 26, wayters ; 27, ftreight vnto ; 29, anfwered
hym ; 30, fayd he fay ; 32, A.'s loue ; 34, that wolde ; 37, And
than the ducheffe went vp ; 38, fawe the.

264. 5, the ducheffe ; 10, this maner & forme ; by ftrete or by
way ; 11, vnto ; 14, that in ; 15, [vnto hym and] ; fo that ; 16, I
maye knowe ; yf I may ; 17, than wyll I ; 18, with my ; ryght
well ; 23, lyghtly redy ; 24, to his ; 26, fome of them ; 27, fawe
neuer ; 28, chere al ; 32, of her ; 33, fayd he ; 35, and than fir ;
36, vp vnto a.

265. 3, vnto ; 4, wolde fayne ; 5, vnto ; 6, & than ; and his ;
9, but onely ; 10, all brake ; 11, lyke a noble ; 14, [in] ; 15, full
harde ; 16, [dyd] recouered after ; 18, and than ; 19, which was ;
25, whiche ; 30, where as ; knyght came ; 31, is he comynge ;
36, reft hym there.

266. 4, all but; 6, moone and; 10, your commaūdement; 12, whiche fayd; 17, the fame proude; 19, with the; 23, he alyghted; [they]; a grete; 24, that lafted more; 27, vnto my lord kyng A.

267. 1, on; 5, on euery fyde; 8, amelynge; 12, and after; 15, fyr G.; 18, eche other; 20, was many; 21, a kynde; them bothe; 22, I ought; 24, [me]; hym moo; 27, rode longe tyme with; 28, [dyd]; ftaunched; 30, knowledge; 31, bere you; 34, befallen to me here; 35, fhe; vnto.

268. 1, Than was there; 10, vnto fyr G.; 12, and as; 13, hyr fone fyr G.; 16, fuche a; 19, [ryght], his neuewe; was it; 30, Than go; 32, to be done; 34, make; redy fhe dyd; 36, [fo].

269. 1, [And] amonge; 3, many goodly lokes; 5, quene G.; 10, vnto ·her what; 12, [that is]; 23, dyftreffe [hit]; [And] alfo; 26, was there; 28, [nexte] folowynge; 29, is a; [the]; 31, meffengers vnto; 32, at the day of his; 36, payre of bedes of.

270. 3, in the waye; 4, [Lord]; of Orkeney; L. du lake; 6, du lake; 10, and vnmercyable; and treafon; 15, the guydynge of; 16, on; 17, archebyffhop; 19, fyr G.; 24, vnto; 31, [this].

271. 2, euermore; than he; 3, chefe fewer; 4, came in; 8, at the; 9, moche better; 12, to fyr G.; 19, had delyuerd; 24, was all; 25, reuelles and; 28, [as]; 29, none of them; 31, and he; 34, vnto; 35, fyr T.; 36, and he dyd; 37, made fir; 38, vnto.

272. 4, had grete wonder of his noble dedes; 10, a ful noble; the hyftory; the noble kyng A.

Book viij.

❡ Here begynneth the eyght boke of the noble and worthy prynce kynge Arthur.

273. 1, There was; 3, this kynge M.; was as; lykely a man; 6, and fhe was a ryght fayre lady and good; 7, all hole; 8, Wales and Irlande / and alfo of Scotlande; 14, And fo; 17, a certayne time; 21, no maner meanes; coude neuer; 22, a day fhe let; ordeyne for hym as he rode on; 23, hunter; 27, wyfe myffed; 28, [alfo as]; 29, ftreyght vnto the; for to; 30, ferre within; 31, faft to; trauayle; 32, and her; 35, [the]; that the depe; none other bote.

274. 1, there was; 2, that; moone and forowe; [here]; 8, good frende vnto; me fe I praye you my; 14, befeche; 15, whan my fone fhall be chryftened / let hym be named; 16, as [a]; therwithall; 17, vp her; in the fame place . Than; 18, the fhadowe of; 19, fo forthwithall; 27, grete barons & lordes; 28, and grete

moone ; [Thenne] ; 29, the meane ; 30, morowe ; 33, no tong can
telle it ; 34, bury ; her full ; 35, he let the chylde be chriftened.

275. 3, the yonge T. was well ; 4, vpon a tyme ; 9, to be put ;
in to a ; 11, to the ; 16, [al] ; & dyed ; 17, [Melyodas] ; 18, paffynge heuy ; kyng M. ; 22, yᵉ wyne ; where as the ; was in ; 23,
was mooſt ; therof ; 29, thus fayd ; 34, that ſhe ; 35, the land ; [the].

276. 1, downe ; his father ; 2, [ageyne] ; 4, fayd his father
kynge M. ; 11, I praye ; 13, [thenne faid the kynge] and ; 15, So
yonge T. ; 18, and at ; 20, T. his fone ; 23, his fone yonge T. ; 26,
coude well ; 34, that we neuer rede of no.

277. 1, that fo vfed hȳfelfe therin ; 2, [beeſtes of] ; 9, ſhalle vfe
vnto the worldes ende ; 11, that is of gentyll blode ; 13, yonge T.
continued in ; 15, M. his father ; 17, [fyre] ; 18, ſhe neuer hated ;
19, [Tryſtram] hym ; and euery ; 20, fomeuer he ; 22, to ; 23,
whiche ; wynters afore tyme ; 26, this anfwere and fayd ; 28,
that we.

278. 2, round table ; 3, fyr M. ; 4, vnto hym ; 6, we of ; 9, fyr
M. ; 10, the rounde ; 11, dedes ben ; 13, to this ; 17, fo whan ; 18,
that there was ; Irland the noble knyght fyr M. ; 19, [kynge Marke]
he ; moone & forowe ; *line* 20 *omitted;* 21, he knewe ; 22, that
feafon ; 24, ſtyll in his ſhyppe on ; 25, whiche ; 29, many cryes ;
31, foo be ; [terme] as longe as he lyued ; 32, of Cornewayle fayd ;
33, vnto ; 34, at that ; 35, called the ; of alle the ; 37, it were
labour loſt.

279. 7, [that] ; 8, the caſtel of T. ; 9, [of] this ; 12, fyr T. ;
14, the coūtree of C. ; 18, my fone ; 20, the rounde ; 25, fyr T. ;
to gyue ; vnto ; 29, And than ; and fo ; 31, from the doughter of ;
whiche ; 33, & in the lettres.

280. 2, doughter of the kynge of Fraunce ; 4, for pure ; 6, here
after in yᵉ hyſtory ; 7, vncle ; 9, And fo Tryſtrā went vnto ; 11, to
the vttermeſt with ; M. of Irlande ; 12, come ye ; 14, & wyte ye
well that ; 16, made of body and ; 18, are ye ; [ageyne] ; 20, [yf] ;
22, [fyr] T. ; 23, [But] And ; And forthwith whan he ; 25, whiche ;
thus ; 26, [for] ; vnto the ; 27, tell vnto ; 28, that I ; but yf ; 30,
or els of a ; 33, fyr T. fayd ; [that] ; 34, knowe ; bothe of ; and of ;
35, [fyre] ; 38, ryght hertely welcome.

281. 1, vnto me ; And than ; 5, that his name was ; 9, [of] fyr ;
11, yonge fyr T. ; 12, lytell veffell ; he and his ; vnto hym ; 13, fo
that fyr T. ; 14, maner of thynge ; 16, wyte ye well there ; 17, for
to ; and to ; 20, For to make ſhorte ; that whan ; 26, for to ; 27,
[thenne] ; 31, his feruaunt G. ; 32, ſhadowe ; vpon ; 34, [the noble
knyghte] ; 35, And than he.

282. 1, [ageyne] ; 2, vncle ; 3, bury my ; 4, that I ; for no ;

10, And fo; 13, thus vnto hym; 16, handes; 18, thy fhyppe; [And]; 22, haue I; 23, at my vncles; 24, & to; 25, [And]; ye; 26, that ye; for to; 27, with you / for ye; of the beft; 29, ye haue it wyll doo me good to haue adoo; 30, fyth y^t I was borne of my mother was I; and alfo fyth; 31, I haue taken the hygh ordre; ryght wel; 32, as ye are; 33, ye well; M. of Irlande; 34, to wynne; 36, for to; Cornewayle for euer.

283. 1, And whan the good knyght fyr M.; 2, hym lyft; than fayd he thus; 3, the for to; 4, that no worfhyp; [none]; 5, that for; 7, the rounde; And than; 9, all to the erthe; 11, drewe; anone and keft theyr; 13, as it had ben two wylde bores that ben couragyous; 14, a longe whyle; 15, of theyr ftrokes; breftes; 16, fawe it myght; 17, lyke two; 18, and were bothe fore; 19, [freffhly] on euery fyde; 26, [euer]; 27, vpon his; and the; fyr T.; 28, abode ftyll in; arofe vp & threwe his; 30, vnto; 31, euer ftyll his owne; 33, dooft thou withdrawe y^e; 37, fayd no; went.

284. 4, Than anone; and wente towarde; 5, vnto; 16, his feruaunt; 18, to the; 21, were his woundes; 22, wepte right; 25, [euer he]; 26, to haue dyed of the; had gyuen hȳ fyrft; 27, with his; 28, hole therof; 31, So the kynge; 34, warraunt hym his; whiche was a full; 35, and vnto; vnto alle.

285. 1, in to the; 3, [Thus faid the lady vnto the Kynge]; 4, had well herde what the lady fayd; forthwith he let; 5, and well; 8, in to; 9, quene were; 10, arryuynge; 11, had they neuer herde in I.; 14, wounde; he afked; 15, [then]; 16, fyr T.; have ben thus; 19, [here]; that in; I haue had; 21, fyr M.; [ful]; 22, the round; 28, fo whan; his wounde [hym]; 29, that there was; 30, And within a; 32, [mayde and]; fyr T.; 33, a grete; 34, vnto· fir T.; 35, was wel; bothe of the.

286. 1, this fyr; 2, many grete; 3, ryght well fyr T.; 5, well that; 6, fyr T.; fyr P.; 8, fyr T.; 12, y^t fholde wynne her / fholde wedde; 22, wyll be; [to]; fyr T·; 23, [for]; 24, fyr T.; 34, [faid la beale I.].

287. 3, Gunret; 8, vnto fyr T.; 9, fayd he; 16, Hebes; 19, that countree; 20, fayd he; 21, that of; 22, on me; morowe; 24, fyr T.; 31, all in whyte both; 33, as whyte as it; 35, and fyr T. to hym ageyne.

288. 4, that la·; 7, And than was there none that wold; with fyr Triftram; 8, forfoke fyr T.; 9, Hebes; 11, and fo after; 14, and anone; 20, And then fyr T.; 22, And whan; 23, fore his; hym all; 24, fir T. vnto hym; 26, and alfo; [not] vnto; 28, nor in lyke wyfe; 29, fyr P.; now am I; 30, And than; 32, threwe it; 33, vnto the; Ifoud was; 35, whiche; garde fo.

289. 2, or not; 3, world that; 4, fyr L. du lake; 9, that fhe had neuer feen; 10, [thenne]; 13, where la beale I. kepte hym; 14, full good; 18, and fet by more; 23, her doughter la beale I.; 29, [there]; 33, [thenne]; 35, vncle.

290. 1, for fhe loued fyr T.; 2, ryght well; 3, [alle]; in all the hafte that fhe myghte; 4, and than fhe fought in her cofre that fhe had; founde and toke; 5, was taken; her brothers heed fyr M.; 6, And than anone; 7, vnto fyr T.'s fwerde whiche; [fo]; 8, the fame pyece; vnto the fame fwerd; 9, than as mete as euer; was firft; And fo forthwith; 10, caught that; 11, vnto T.; 14, [Thenne]; to [the]; 16, fell on her knees tofore hym / fayenge; & hufbande; 20, hath heled; 21, [the] kynge A.; 25, that than was; 28, to mounte on; 29, [the] agaynft; 30, wyll I; 32, [for]; 33, fo that thou; 35, my broder fyr M.

291. 1, fhall I; 2, [fir]; 11, fyr T.; 17, as a good; 18, fhold do; 19, fholde do; 21, fyr T.; 22, your goodnes; 23, that my; 24, [fo]; 27, the goodnes of your lordfhip; 33, and [at].

292. 3, of your; neuer yet; 4, vnto; 9, there agaynft I; [feythfully]; 11, [to]; 14, full grete moone; 17, all he fayd; 20, let hym; or [that euer]; from hens; 22, whiche; 26, whiche; 32, wherof; was paffyng; 37, So than by.

293. 8, well fir T.; Whan kynge M.; 9, he was anone ftryken with iealoufy; 11, badde hym faye that as; 12, nexte nyght; and charge hym that he come not to me but yf he be; 15, & fayd; 16, y^t I; at the tyme fhe; 18, had ben with; 19, on; from fyr S.; than fent; 22, to fyr T.; 26, the tyme was; 29, [vpon] fir; 30, on his; 31, fodeynly kynge M.; 34, vpon the; 36, fuche a ftroke; hym fore that; 37, was longe; [euer].

294. 2, bothe to; [cold]; 3, [alle]; 4, lady fore; 6, fhe full fayre welcomed; 7, armes fwetely; 9, they lyghtly; 10, pleafure; 12, nether fhete; 15, and forthwith he; 16, fyr S.; 19, fawe he; 20, fayd he than; 21, [alle]; drewe out his; 22, fhalt thou; 24, [alle]; fyr S.; Tell me; 25, [to me]; 26, towarde me; 27, fyr S.; 28, fayd fhe; 29, fyr S.; 33, Than anone fyr T.; 34, [al]; fyr S.; 35, to brake in peces.

295. 1, drewe; [faft]; 2, full fore ftrokes; Syr; 5, fyr S.; 6, fpurred his; 7, ryght fyerfly; 13, and whan they fawe hym lye fo / they toke hym vp and brought; 14, vpon; or [that] he was; 15, Marke alfo; 17, wyft not that it had ben kynge M. that had; 20, neuer after loued; 21, moche fayre; yet loue; 22, paft on; 24, no more haue; 26, flyppe ouer; 29, fyr B.; vnto fyr B.; 31, And this fyr B.; vnto kynge Markes courte; 33, [that]; 34, And whan; faye fo.

296. 3, to kyng M.; 4, the whiche me; 6, And than fyr B. chofe; 7–8, and anone he fet her vpon horfbacke behynde his fquyer / and fo he toke his hors & rode forth on his way . Whan; 11, than anone he; 12, his wyfe; fyr B.; 13, were wroth; was thus gone; 16, And than; 17, a domoyfell that; in ye mooft fouleft maner; 19, [be]; 21, herte longe tyme; 22, her in this wyfe; 23, here prefent; [And]; 26, that fir S.; than it; 27, [good]; [euer]; 28, out of this; Soo within; 30, fore beten; and in poynte of; for as he; 32, hath fore; [heuy]; 33, courte ryght heuy therof; And whan; 36, his fpere; [faft]; 37, the whiche; 38, [forth]; [euer].

297. 1, through y^e; 4, it was; me than now; 6, the one; 10, of whome the one; 11, fyr S.; fyr D.; 13, [hem]; 14, the two; 15, not to; 20, And anone; [alle]; 23, fayd to hym agayne; 25, [hit]; is but; 27, your; 29, on the; 30, hanfell; 31, [fo]; [that]; 32, wyll or not.

298. 6, than he; [he]; 8, as [the]; 9, a grete buffet; 12, Are there; kynge A.'s courte; 13, grete fhame; fay dyfhonour; 15, you bothe; It is fo fayd; and that; 16, you; 17, vnto; 22, glad that; 23, fyr T.; 26, fir D.; So fyr T.; 27, [on ward]; 28, B. rode with; 29, wyfe; 31, tyll [that]; 32, ouertaken fir B.; 33, [he faid] fyr knyght; 34, [doo neyther] not; fir B.

299. 2, [fame]; 3, myle two knyghtes; 4, [euer]; 5, fyr B.; 6, The one told; that he hyght; 7, that other told me he hyght fyr D.; 9, good men; 10, [grete]; 11, but for all that it be fo that; 12, or that ye; 13, [Thenne]; you than; 16, myghtyly with theyr; 20, [de ganys]; 21, vnto fyr T.; 22, vs two; Saye on [what ye wille]; 23, I fhall anfwere you agayn; 24, 28, fir B.; 29, fyr M.; 30, good knyght; 33, Now fo god; 35, [that]; 38, ben fyfters; whiche is called.

300. 4, that I haue vnto; 5, fyr B.; 9, and vnto; [that]; 10, fyr T.; 12, fyr B.; 15, thou were; 17, other ladyes; 18, no femblaunt to; 22, [alle]; 32, me agayne; fayd fhe; 33, ye were; 35, [euer].

301. 1, where my; 2, fyr B.; 7, to her; 9, her fake I fhall; 10, [a] lady; 13, [fythen] fhe hath refufed me / and as; 14, knowe her; 15, and departed one from an other; And [foo] fir; 22, And thefe; 23, of alle the; 33, that fyr T. fholde be flayne.

302. 13, and that other was; 19, them fore; 24, for grete; 26, fyr B. de Ganys and; 27, his brother; 31, [by].

303*. 4, fyr B.; 8, fommonynge; or [that]; 10, had herde; 11, but for; 12, and yf ony; 13, murther or treafon; 15, was in thofe; And whan; 17, knewe well that; [that he]; 18, and was alfo comen of; Than was; 21, and wente vnto; 22, going by fir T.'s pauylyon; moone; 24, [that]; 28, [my]; 31, therwith fyr T.; 34, turne.

304*. 2, with his; 3, downe to the groūde; 4, [thenne] Come on thy; 7, And he fayd; 8, faūce; 10, And than fyr; 11, repented; enemye; 14, [that]; 15, come there; and how; 16, of Irlande was; 23, charge the to brynge me; 24, And fo G.; 27, whiche; 29, Lyones; 30, that ye; he wyll; 31, on good; 32, [anone]; 33, but a lytell company; 35, kynge A.; 36, But anone; 38, that ye fhewed.

305*. 2, do you feruyce; 3, A worfhypfull knyght; 4, for neuer; 6, kynge A.; 9, or elles to; 10, wote well; 11, that all thefe; 12, [for]; 13, in fyght or batayle; 14, grete goodnes that ye; to me; 16, in hande for; 17, [that] ye; is this that; 18, be fworne vnto me; 25, were redy; 26, rather dye; 31, fyr B.; 32, vnto; 34, fyr B.; 35, yf he were.

306*. 2, and wente vnto; and other; 4, And than; 5, T. de Lyones; 6, theyr charge; And fo; 7, whiche behelde; 8, had flayne; 9, and alfo; he had; the noble knyght fir P.; 11, for to; 12, vnto his; [dere]; 13, that we are; maner a man that fyr L. du lake is; 15, kynrede; 16, in ony; for to be; 17, fyr B.; 20, one of the beft of; 21, but well may it; hym to; 23, me vnto hym; fyr B.; 25, and that knowe I ryght well for; 26, be my spede; fyr B.; 30, his grete; 31, And anone; 32, drewe; and put his.

307. 1, lyke two wylde; 6, [there]; 11, out of hande; erth; 16, And whan; 19, on that other; 22, whiche; 25 [my]; 27, may well here that; 29, I do this batayle; 31, this good; 32, to fyr T.

308. 2, in to theyr; than the; whiche; 4, fyr B.; 5, well faye; 6, [and]; 8, fyr B.; 9, oute of hande; 10, his aduerfe partye; 11, fyr B.; 17, eche other and; 18, eche other; the two bretherne made; 19, of them fyghte; 22, euermore; 27, And than; 28, all the eftates that; as moche of hym as euer they myghte make; 32, on a.

309. 2, of you that; 4, vnto his; 5, [that]; 6, that ye; Syre fayd fyr T. / yf I dyd fo than were I; 7, and fholde be falfe of; 8, and therfore; 9, ye haue; let me haue la; 10, for to; 11, vnto myne vncle; 13, fomeuer it fhall; [for]; 14, were me; 15, that may be in; 16, So for to; a fhorte; 18, And than; 19, la beale I.'s mother; [to her and] vnto; 23, drynke vnto; 25, to G. and to dame B.; 26, fyr T. and la beale I. toke; 31, So fyr T.; 33, whiche; 34, And than they.

310. 1, eche other; loue neuer; 2, wele nor woo; [it]; 4, And fo longe; 6, [by]; reft; 10, lorde of that caftell whiche; 11, yf fo

[it] were ; yᵗ the fame fyr B. ; 12, yᵉ ftraūge knyght and his lady
to be put to ; 13, fo euer ; 15, lady dye [bothe] ; 18, that a ; to
them ; 19, cheryffhe ; haue grete ; fyr T. ; 20, that the lord ; 21,
here in ; 24, ben theyr geftes / it is a full euyll cuftome ; 25, whan
ony ; 26, lord of this caftell ; the weykeft ; 28, with hȳ be ; 29,
lady is ; 30, Now fo ; 31, a ryght foule and.

311. 2, in a ; 4, for to tell ; morowe ; 5, to batayle ; 6 fayd
the ; 9, lacke ; 10, belongeth ; 11, vnto ; 12, and put hym & ;
out of pryfon ; 13, whiche was ; 15, there all ; 16, holdyng ; 17,
by the hande all muffled ; 18, lady was ; 20, than thyn ; 21, yf
that ; 22, Syr knight fayd fyr T. ; 23, horryble cuftome ; 24, to
lefe myne owne heed ; 28, ryghtfull ; 30, with myne owne handes ;
31, vpon his ; 32, therwithall ; 33, drawen in ; 34, he turned his
lady aboute in ; 36, neuer fawe ; 37, fmytten of.

312. 4, that thou and thy lady ; 6, and for ; 8, trouthe ; 9, all
the ; for of ; 10, neuer none ; yf thou ; 14, vnto ; yf fhe ; 15, of
thyne ; fyr T. ; 17, [clene] ; 19, fyth I haue loft my ; 21, as faft as
theyr horfes myght renne ; 22, [clene] ; 24, reled here ; 25, the erth ;
27, nymble ; [euer] ; 28, coude ; 30, full myghtyly ; 34, hurtlyng.

313. 1, woūded other full fore ; 3, as than fyr T. was ; 4, and
the byggeft ; 13, that was ; 19, they wente to horfbacke with grete ;
20, [Thenne] ; 21, fo myghtyly ; 22, groūde ; lyghtly as ; 26, &
thus ; 32, fawe fo many ; 34, vnto fyr G. le ; 35, vnto me.

314. 1, a very grete ; 2, G. vnto fyr T. ; there is but ; 3, vnto
me ; dye . I wyll rather ; 4, fayd fyr T. ; 5, than for the myght of
your owne ; 7, in to ; And there ; [alle] ; 8, and there he began
hard ; 11, vnto you a grete ; 13, gretely blame hym ; 20, for afkynge
of his ; 22, with the hondred knyghtes ; 25, were the good knyght ;
28, [fir] T. de ; 32, Than fayd fyr G. vnto ; 36, by the fayth of my
body ; 37, be more ; as there.

315. 5, mooft his ; 8, in the ; came word ; 9, vnto ; 10, whiche ;
11, had fought wᵗ ; 13, faft to ; 15, kynge C. ; 17, behynde hym ;
20, [outher] ; 30, drewe out theyr ; 32, it wente through ; 35,
fmote of.

316. 2, and vnto ; 5, tyll I ; 9, nobleffe ; 11, there made ;
many grete ; 13, dured longe ; and whan ; 16, whiche was ; 17,
and gentylwoman ; 19, handes & fete vnto ; 22, [for] ; And whan ;
23, her gentylwoman dame B. ; ful heuy ; 25, by caufe fhe ; 26, for
to put ; 28, fyr P. ; 29, vnto her ; 31, vnto you ; 33, fyr P. ; 34,
but half ; 35, vnto ; here fayd the quene I.

317. 1, Than fir P. ; vnto the ; 6, quene I. ; 7, fyr P. ; thynke
vpon ; 9, defyre is ; 10, none yll ; 18, me the ; 20, fyr P. ; 23, or ;
29, fir P.

318. 1, not longe enioye her ; 2, for to ; 8, So the ; 9, fo rode ; 10, kyng M. ; [no wyfe] ; not be ; 12, [to] hunte ; 13, am I ; 14, [owne] ; 16, & than this knyght fayd to hym ; 23, fyr P. ; 24, fyr T. ; fayd he I ; 25, 27, fyr L. ; 33, wyſt not ; 35, fayre well.

319. 1, ledde her vnto ; 2, caſtel therby ; hym lyghtly ; 3, fyr P. ; 4, vntyll ; 11, And than ; 12, out at ; 13, all the gates ; 15, bothe his ; 16, lyke as it had ben a man that had bē ; 17, whiche recked not of ; 18, to ſir T. ; 19, wyſte that ; 21, this day am I ; 23, I knowe fyr ; 24, that I am not in ; 27, fyr L. ; 28, vnto deth ; 31, & he had not ben.

320. 2, your grete ; to the ; 6, to hym and sayd ; 9, that he ; 12, enemy ; 13, ende of ; make you ; 15, your mortall enemy ; 16, ony worde fpekynge ; 19, fyr T. ; 20, So lyghtly ; 22, a ſtronge ; 27, for [dole and] ; 29, that other ; 31, & by caufe ; 33, [alle] ; 35, I knowe well.

321. 1, And than fhe ; 2, thy ; 3, to your ; 4, that is right fore ; 15, And than anone ; fetche home ; 18, the whiche was ; 24, fmytten hym ; 26, pulled it ; 27, kynge M. ; 28, traytour knyght ; 29, [that] ; 31, at the kynge ; 34, vpon the ; his nofe ; 35, forthwith fyr T. wente.

322. 1, [he] ; in to the ; 5, vpon his ; 6, whan the ; 7, there afore ; 16, no where fo ; 20, by all ; 24, vnto the ; 26, quene and ſir T. went ; 29, tentes to be pyght in the ; 31, for to ; 35, yᵉ twenty.

323. 2, gretely fayd ; 4, [wel] ; 6, fayd kynge M. ; 7, [other] ; 8, me thynketh ; 10, and therfore ; 14, for the noble knyght fyr L. ; 23, at a ; 26, with hym ; 29, And fo anone.

324. 2, thou arte ; 5, thy ; 6, the ; 12, & ye haue a caufe why to faye ; 13, hymfelfe ; 14, fmyte ; 23, all garnyſſhed wᵗ gold ; 28, L. du lake ; 30, horne . And thā fayd fyr L. vnto that knyght ; 31, that horne ; 34, vnto.

325. 1, yf that ; vnto ; 3, tolde hym ; 6, la beale I. ; his quene ; ladyes moo ; 8, and fo fwore ; 9, that the quene ; ladyes alfo ; 12, as ony ; 14, vnto ; 20, And than alwayes ; 21, for to ; 25, And than ; 28, I. the quene ; 32, whiche ; 33, and bounde ; 35, other remedy ; that nedes he ; he vnto them all.

326. 1, [for] ; 2, [to take] ; 3, ye are ; good & ; 4, vnto ; for to ; 5, well faye ; yet met ; 6, that I ; or fomwhat better than he ; 7, thy vauntynge ; 8, that thou makeſt yet fhalte thou ; 9, my beſt frende ; 17, and toke ; 18, and than he ; 19, flayne ; And than ; 21, to ſir ; 23, that he ; & fhette ; 29, whiche ; 32, towelles ; 34, Ifoud was ; ledde awaye ; fyr A.

327. 3, And than anone fyr T. toke ; where as ; 4, I was ;

9, wente ; that he fell ; 10, And it fortuned there ; 11, [hand] ; 12,
And therwith fyr T. ; 13, flewe ; 14, told to ; 15, in ye forefayd ;
[euer] ; 16, haue flayne ; 17, he was gone ; than he ; 18, fo ftrayte ;
19, neuer wyte ; fyr T. ; 20, Than whan ; 22, thought well that ;
23, and was fore dyfpleafed / & endured ; 25, fhe toke a ; 26, vnto ;
28, for y^e ; 29, in all ye hafte to go ; 31, helpe you ; 33, ryght
glad ; 34, fayd fyr T. ; 35, that may helpe.

328. 1, whiche ; 2, vpon kyng H. ; 6, vnto ; 8, for to ; 9, went ;
10, for to ; 13, he coude ; dyd there ; 16, and he flewe more ; 17,
fame daye ; was than ryght ; 20, vnto you ; it fayd ; 21, beholdynge ;
22, [grete] ; 23, his fone fyr Kay hedius ; 24, I. le blaunche mayns ;
26, that fir ; 27, he had almooft ; 29, fo at ; 31, abedde togyder /
than ; 32, hymfelfe ; his firft ; 33, fo fodeynly ; all abaffhed & ; 34,
he made her ; 35, fleffhely coniūccion ; neuer had.

329. 1, that there ; 3, whyle ; fyr S. ; 5, vnto the ; there he ; 7,
And than ; 9, falfe vnto ; 10, faye [ye] to hym [this] ; 14, [that] ;
to be his ; 16, for to go agayne in to ; 23, fyr T. ; 26, ladyes
fake ; [in].

330. 5, & thofe fyffhers ; 6, that they ; 7, whiche was a ; 13,
vnto a ryght ; 15, me fore ; 18, [euer] ; 20, fyr L. ; 21, on the ; 22,
A.'s courte ; 24, we agayne ; 28, that drofe ; 29, L. was ; to roue ;
31, 33, fyr S. ; 34, hate in the world.

331. 2, fyr S. ; 4, your man vnto ; 7, vnto a ; 20, nothynge
[by] ; 24, erly they ; 27, fayre knyght ; 31, vpon [a] ; 32, [that is]
fo that ; 37, to me.

332. 1, had fayd ; 3, ye gaue ; 7, put many ; 12, in kyng A.'s ;
[y] lyke ; 15, hath not ; hurte me ; 28, for to ; 29, be there for.

333. 1, that there ; 6, vpon one ; 10, wente ; 17, And whan ;
20, in to ; and take the beft ; 27, flee euery ; 28, hors ; go playe ;
31, for to ; 34, [mooft].

334. 1, for here ; 5, none [haue] therof ; 8, fyr S. ; 9, vnto fyr
S. ; 11, he ruled it ; 20, So fyr L. toke his leue & rode toward ;
21, fir T. & his wyf & ; 24, he meruayled ; to fir L. ; 26, vnto an ;
28, fayd he [the heremyte] ; I gretely ; 31, euyll ; 35, fraūchyfe.

335. 8, [And] ; 9, fpeke alfo ; fir L. ; 11, wordes ; 15, [they
faide] ; 16, thy lyf ; 17, behynde one than ; 20, your parte ; 23,
flewe ; 25, demaūded [hym] ; Syr knyght fayd he ; 28, that came
rydynge ; fyr F. ; 29, lately ; fro my hors & ; 30, [doo foo] ; 33,
myne owne ; By my fayth fayd ; 34, to medle no more ; 36, the
roūde ; 37, fpare hym ; cryed on hym.

336. 1, [whyte] ; 2, [to Iufte with the] ; 13, fyr L. ; 14, fayd he ;
16, you well ; 29, to ; 30, or elles ; 35, fay dyfhonour.

337. 3, And fo they ; 5, deed to the groūde ; 8, & fo armed hym

& mounted on horſbacke ; 12, thou were ; 14, eche other & dreſſed ; 16, as two ; [preued] ; two houres longe ; [So] ; 19, hate in the worlde ; 20, where as ; 24, hath done ; 25, [alle] ; 31, for yᵉ hygh ordre of ; 32, to you ; 33, they dreſſed them agayne to ; 34, other fore ; 35, where as ; ſyr B.

338. 2, your diſeaſe ; A [knyght] ; 4, ſuche a auauntage ; as you had me ; 6, thyn euyll ; 11, ſyr B. ; 12, more that one agaynſt that other. ❡ And thus endeth the . viij . booke. ❡ Here after foloweth, etc.

Book ix.

❡ Here begynneth the . ix . boke of the noble and worthy prynce kynge Arthur.

338. 15, There came in to the ; 16, & a bygge made ; 18, of kyng A. ; 19, was good & ; 20, ſayd the yonge man ; 22, am comen ; 27, Syre ſayd he ; 28, and vpon a daye as.

339. 5, noble ; 9, good and a myghty knyght ; 12, he is ; 13, that is in ; 16, kynge A. ; 22, that this lyon ; 32, claue it in ; 33, and ſo the lyon fell down deed ; 34, [by ſcorne] ; 35, kynge A. ; 36, of my lyfe.

340. 1, [al] ; 4, moche as ; 5, me ſo ; & ſo ; 6, [me] ; 7, Than on the ; 8, kynges courte ; 12, ſayd the damoyſell ; 13, this black ; and many ; vnto ; 14, And he that oughte this ; was a ryght good ; 15, to aſcheue a ; 16, hym that ; 19, on euen ; whiche ; 20, there was none ; 21, vnto ; 24, vnto this ; 26, this blacke ; ſpeke a ; 29, that well is.

341. 1, go ye ; 2, ye wyll ; 5, [pon me] ; that I maye knowe ; 6, ſhold be ; 8, knyghte ; 9, he ſyr ; may ye ; 11, blacke ſhelde ; 15, therwith ; [all] ; 16, a grete ; 24, And than ; 25, after ſyr ; ſo there ; 26, in all haſte made ; 28, ſawe ſyr ; 29, to hym & ; 31, mocked ſyr ; 34, longe chydynge hym.

342. 1, with ſyr ; 5, done the ; 6, ſyr B. ; 9, ſayd he ; 15, ſyr B. had done ; 16, [hand] ; 18, hym a ; 20, ſyr B. ; 21, ſyr P. ; do batayle with ; 23, fro theyr ; 25, company of ; 26, [thenne] ; 31, and the ; 32, anone ſyr ; 33, other knyght ; 34, grounde ; And than ; 35, others hors ; 36, than ſyr ; 38, woūded that knyght.

343. 1, hors to the erth as ; And than ; 2, had mette ; and that knyght toke ; 4, [Orgulous] ; there ſyr ; purſewed hym ſoo nygh / that he claue his heed downe to the ſholders / & ſo fell downe deed to the erth ; 5, ſo anone ; 6, that his ; 9, them all ; to a ; 13, chambre was ; 18, And ſo ; 22, to yonder ; 26, toke his ; 27, [fayre] ; and hurled through the thyckeſt of them ; 29, knyghtes redy ; 34, vnto.

344. 1, vnto ; [alle] ; 5, Ye may preue it fayd fyr ; 8, that fyr ;
14, [and maulgre oure hedes] ; 15, agayne vnto ; 16, all togyder
how that ; 17, And than fhe let falle downe ; 18, but lytel ; 21, not
[yet] ; 23, vnto the ; 26, full wyly ; 29, fyght on ; 32, worfe on ; 35,
to many ; 38, rode away [fure].

345. 1, And whan ; 2, he herde ; fyr la cote ; 5, me helpe ; 7,
all you ; 8, fuche an ; 9, fayd the noble knyghte fyr ; [that] ; 12,
fyr T. ; 13, to her agayne ; 19, ouertook fyr ; 21, [thenne] ; 22, al
the ; 23, the damoyfel Maledyfaunte rebuked fyr la cote male tayle
full vncurteyfly ; 24, lefte of fyr La cote male tayle ; 25, whyle ;
26, in excufynge ; 27, of the fayre damoyfell I. ; 29, le blaunche ;
30, alwaye.

346. 1, yf fo were ; 5, and for to ; 8, vnto ; there they fawe
ftandynge before them ; 10, with fyr ; there fyr ; 11, And after that ;
16, after fyr ; 19, that profered ; 25, hym goodly ; 27, [thenne] ;
33, [al] he felle.

347. 3, In good fayth ; 5, [alle] ; forth vntyll he ; 8, at the ;
11, hym in ; 12, through out the body and through the hors arfon ;
14, and full egrely they ; 15, ftroke that ; beftowed they were
ftryken in fondry wyfe / fo they auoyded ; 17, [paffynge] ; [alle] ;
18, in to the caftel ; 19, called [the] ; 20, and was a grete ; 21, on ;
22, fell to ; 25, in a lytell ; 26, and at the ; [to] ; 27, and therwith ;
lepte vnto hym ; 29, than he ; 30, vnto his mercy and grace ; 32,
kynge A.'s courte ; 34, [thenne] ; And whan fyr.

348. 3, for to ; he had ; 4, they that were ; 7, for he is the
beft knyghte in the world that dyd ; 10, a noble ; 11, and fyr ; 13,
than fhe ; 14, heuy and forowfull ; 17, & gretely they thanked hym ;
19, & fayd ; all true & loyall ; 20, [euen] ; 22, and you fir ; 25,
handes ; whiche fyr ; 26, awaye from ; 33, a ryght good ; 34, but he.

349. 5, vnto hym ; [that] he ; 13, vnto the ; 14, a full fayre ;
16, many gentylmen & yeman that fayd ; 23, entre fyrft ; 25,
am taken pryfoner ; 26, for to ; 30, that one ; 33, fyr P. ; foone
after ; 34, fyr P. ; 35, fyr la ; 37, began full harde to affayle fyr.

350. 4, on bothe ; but [he] ; 5, he gate ; And fo than ; 6,
[thenne] ; 10, them two ; 14, they two ; 22, [euen] ; 23, [forth with
all] ; grete meruayl ; 26, for what ; 29, yf ye had ; 31, dedes and
valyauntnes ; 32, [to] you grete ; euer I ; 33, [al].

351. 5, I was ; fyr P. ; 6, ye truly ; 8, fyr P. ; me at this tyme ;
fyr la ; 13, fyr P. ; 14, grete ; as the hurle wynde had borne hȳ
towarde ; 18, drewe ; 25, handes ; pryfoners ; 30, hym down ; 35,
fyr P. ; 36, on.

352. 6, fo that he ; 10, fo that he wyll ; 11, his fyue ; 14, fyr
P. ; 16, ruled by kyng A. / yf ye be foo pleafed ; 18, refted ; tyme ;

22, there came ; 24, [thēne] ; 25, frō all ; 27, by caufe ; 29, gaue vnto ; 32, rode vnto ; 33, [holy].

353. 2, fyr Brewnor le noyre ; 4, [after] ; called fyr ; 5, and a myghty ; 14, was maryed ; 15, vnto hym ; 16, yf it ; 21, hym & fayd he was.

354. 1, knyght and a well made man all ; 2, a clere foūtayne or welle ; 3, nere vnto hym ; to a grete oke ; 5, that was by yᵉ welle ; 17, thou haft well ; to me ; 18, an other grete fpere ; 21, gaue hym a ; 23, afore hym ; drewe out ; 26, on ; 27, out his ; 31, yf thou.

355. 17, I knowe well ; 18, [my] ; 19, [alle] ; 20, fayenge ; 21, as vnto ; 26, [nor] for ; 28, This meane ; 36, [it].

356. 1, And to make fhorte tale fyr P. ; 5, with them on ; 6, may men ; 7, at euery tyme ; 8, by euyll ; 9, vnto a ; 13, And than the ; 14, at a ; 16, fay vnto hym ; 17, there as ; 19, and rode fondry wayes ; 21, hors to ; 25, vnto ; 26, a lamētable ; 28, [with] ; 29, fhadowe of the wode ; 35, fayd they ; L. du lake.

357. 2, fayd they we ; 4, yet dayes of my lyfe of ; 11, And fo eyther ; 15, it is pyte and ; 22, preue it ; make it ; 25, vnto ; 26, now bereth [the] ; 29, And than ; 30, came rennynge ; 31, fo myghtily ; 32, vnto yᵉ ; 34, as it had ben two.

358. 1, fyr M. ; 2, knyght and man ; to harde and to ; 4, won-ders fore ; fo as ; 5, there came ; 6, anone fyr L. ; them bothe ; 7, for ye ; 8, A.'s courte ; 9, fyr M. ; 12, that quene ; 14, for to ; 15, vnder her ; 16, & we ; 22, not therfore ; 23, be the ; 24, is yᵉ ; 27, yf ye ; 31, [you] but ; 32, [that] fhe.

359. 13, be it [that] ; 15, T. de Lyones ; 17, was comen ; Syr T. anfwered ; 18, Kay the Seneffhall neuer in no place that ; 19, ony good ; 20, T. de L. yf it ; 21, my right name ; 24, lyuynge in the world ; 28, tyl that one ; 29, fall fro his hors ; 33, fo as ; at theyr.

360. 2, [he] fayd but ; 4, In yᵉ mornynge ; 6, and fo ; 7, And than ; du vaffher ; 9, downe from his hors ; 11, fayne knowe ; 12, name is ; on your way with me ; 13, for to ; 14, where as ; 15, at that ; 18, not to that ; 19, you of your ; 20, for to ; 26, whiche ; 27, defyreth mooft to haue youre ; 30, [yet] ; 31, for to be ; 32, man now ; 33, excepte it be ; 37, hym ony.

361. 2, caufe was ; 11, after hym ; & whan ; 12, fir B. ; 20, flayne hym ; 21, vnto ; 24, feke [after] ; 25, [fame] ; 30, fayd fhe ; 33, for as this [fame].

362. 5, [lytel] ; 7, his fete ; 9, and the one ; 12, with his fwerde drawen in his hande ; 13, forthwith all fyr T. ; 14, down deed to the erth ; 15, to yᵗ other knyght ; and with the pomell of his fwerde he fmote hym fo harde that he fell fro his hors & brake his ; 16, vnto ; 17, that vntrue ; 21, his waye forth ; damoyfell ; 22, So whan that ; 23, he full ; 24, hym to tell hym his ; tell it hym ; 26, his owne ; 30, downe from ; fo done ; 31, kynge A. ; your owne ; 33, whiche I. ; vnto ; 35, knowe.

363. 4, where as ; 5, [holy] ; 6, by the ; 7, a good & a trufty ; 9, to kynge M.'s courte ; 13, I may ; 15, to a ; 16, affygned them ; 18, pen can ; 21, myght neuer . . . . the very pure loue ; 23, how fyr K. ; 26, grete pyte ; 34, he [had] foūde ; 35, to fyr K.

364. 1, came to ; 6, me [the] ; 9, whiche fhe dyd ; 11, virgyn ; wel fayd he vnto ; 12, to me ; 13, [alle] ; 15, vnto ; 17, Marke fat ; 27, hym vnto ; 28, for to ; 32, whiche was ; 34, fpere in the ; agaynft.

365. 2, fadel to the erth ; 3, And than ; 4, rode forth ; 5, than anone ; 6, vnto hym ; 11, fore & made forowfull ; And than ; 17, wyte what tydynges there was ; 19, fe how ; 21, place fhall ye fynde hȳ ; 22, And than ; 23, that ony woman myght make ; 27, his waye from ; 29, none take ; 34, euer ony ; 35, wente ; 36, lady of the.

366. 2, me to playe ; 3, & the damoyfel ; 4, So vpon ; 6, armure & went in to yᵉ wyldernes & brake ; 12, the harpe ; And fo wolde ; vnto ; 13, the melodyous fowne therof ; 18, [fomme] ; 22, fyr D. ; 24, by a fayre ; 27, to ; 30, fo brought ; 31, as weet as ; to lepe ; 32, on theyr ; 35, [fhe] went.

367. 3, be [foo] ; 4, yf I ; 9, vnto other ; 16, alone from his ; 18, pyte that ; 20, that mooft ; 23, bothe armed ; 29, our lorde god ; fory and dyfpleafaunte ; 31, hymfelfe ; good frendes ; 32, to ; 35, on ; 37, at hym.

368. 3, [to the erthe] ; 5, vnto one ; 10, Beware ye ; that ye ; 11, naked foole ; 19, whiche ; 20, or that ; 26, T. his neuewe ; 27, the quene ; 29, full nyghe ; 30, for to.

369. 2, of my loue fyr T. ; 6, ftronge toure ; 11, the fwerd ; 12, [a] ten ; 16, go out at ; 17, this fyr T. ; 19, And than fyr T. ; 20, it happened ; 25, to the ; 26, to reft hym ; 27, fyr T. ; 28, [and toke the hors] ; 29, drewe ; 30, on his ; 34, where it ; [foo] ; 35, fmote ; wente.

370. 9, madde man ; 11, on the ; vnto the ; 12, to the welle ; 13, the kynge ; 17, foftly ; 21, nor wyft not fro whens he came ; 22, happened ; 25, And than ; 28, and afked ; man was ; 30, & refteth hym ; 33, [here] afore this tyme ; 35, And la beale I. had ; 36, had gyuen.

371. 1, Ifoud was ; 3, loue fhe had vnto hym ; 5, than fhe ; 13, that as ; 14, fhall knowe ; 18, whan ye may ; 19, and as ye ; 22,

moche anger ; 24, la beale I. departed ; 26, brayed ; [al] ; 28, that
it is he ; So the kyng ; 31, now ye may do w^t me ; 33, So many ;
36, of Cornewayle.

372. 3, were his foes ; 5, fyr D. ; [for] ; 7, vnto ; 9, you ; 11,
& than they ; 14, [thenne] ; 16, in the fhyppe he fayd thus ; 17,
tell them ; 20, [Quene] ; 23, [Pluere] ; 32, am I ; 35, my waryfon ;
tell ye ; 36, the rounde ; 37, I am.

373. 2, And therwith he ; 4, nexte lodgynge ; 7, all on an hepe
to ye groūde ; 9, with his good wyll iufte with ; 17, from them &
rode ; 20, And fo there was ordeyned for fyr L. ; 23, for to ; 24, of
this ; 26, where as ; 28, Bors / fyr Bleoberys / fyr E. and ; 29,
they all ; 31, that they fet ; 32, as well as we.

374. 1, as for to ; or two or ; 7, [by your fheldes] ; 10, me for
to ; 12, that thy ; 13, loke on ; 14, [to] do ; wolde to god ; had
neuer ; 17, eyther fawe other ; 18, yf caufe were ; 22, [by] fir D. ;
29, had iufted ; 31, to ; 33, vnto theyr ; 37, forth on ; 38, and [to
the] heerdmen.

375. 2, there aboute ; 3, nygh here ; 4, cuftome there is ; be
lodged ; he fyrft ; 6, be within ; 7, So there is an euyll lodgynge ;
9, be ye not ; 10, forfake your ; 11, and yf ye ; 13, lodged ; ben
two noble ; 14, be lodged ; 19, had thought ; to haue taken theyr
reft ; 20, gate ; 22, [aray] ; 27, And fo therwith ; 28, and there fyr
G. ; 30, and fyr P. gaue fyr D. a fall ; [thenne was hit fall for
fall] ; 31, And than muft ; and that ; 32, [fo] ; & hurte ; 33, had
gyuen hym ; 36, to do batayle ; 38, whiche wolde.

376. 2, fuche two ; 8, them bothe ; 9, you bothe ; And than ;
13, he badde fyr G. ; 14, had no luft ; 15, And than ; a longe whyle ;
17, thre grete ; 23, defyred ; 24, of the ; 26, vnto ; 33, But as
foone as.

377. 4, fyr P. ; to knowe ; 5, 8, And than ; 9, than wyll I
rather ryde ; 13, to iufte with hym ; 14, foo paft ; 17, of a ; 20, for
the good knyghtes ; 21, lete feke ; 22, for fyr T. ; 24, at thofe
iuftes & turneyment ; 28, at the grete ; 29, to kepe hym and ; 30,
called and cryed ; 31, and ouercomen ; 32, he incontynent ; towarde
hȳ for to iufte ; And whan fyr K. fawe hym come / than he refufed
hym / and ; 33, fayd fyr ; 34, fo fhall I ; with an ; 35, rode on his
waye ; 38, keft downe.

378. 3, whiche ; 5, for to ; 6, with hym ; 12, doth lede ; 14,
drewe ; 17, [ryght] ; 18, fayd the damoyfell ; [and] ; 19, fhall tell
you all as it is ; 20, fayd fhe ; my lady quene ; 21, kynge A.'s
fyfter hath ; [a] ; and efpye ; 23, [fyrft] ; with ony ; with theyr
wyles to Morgan ; 26, for to.

379. 7, whiche ye ; 11, fayd fyr G. ; 21, whiche ; 22, hym well ; 25, paffynge gladde ; 32, for yf he ; 34, B. faunce pyte ; 36, and fo there.

380. 5, fo well ; 9, for to reft ; vnto a ; 16, forgoten the ; 19, this damoyfell B. ; 22, And than ; 23, longe & ferre ; 24, And than ; 26, fayd fir T. ; 27, tyll the ; 32, whiche was.

381. 7, [ynough] ; 11, and knewe that ; 12, a knyght of C. ; I was ones ; 13, by fortune it ; 17, may fe my ; 26, a myghty black.

382. 2, to fyr P. ; 7, where as ; 9, vnto yonder ; 10, of gold ; 11, ye vnto hym ; 13, and fo ; 15, And than ; 16, that anone ; which ; 17, at a vaūtage ; 22, G. his fquyer ; hym ones agayne ; 25, reuenge hym to morowe ; 26, he fhall fe me ; 30, he may be ; 32, be reuenged vpon hym ; 36, to.

383. 3, [with hym] ; I wyll do that I may fayd fyr B. And there fyr L. ; 5, and had a grete ; 10, And than ; 12, that other ; 16, forth on his waye ; By my fayth ; So than ; 19, haftely vnto ; 22, and the caufe why ; 25, [hym] ; 30, hym to iufte ; 31, telle me what is thy lordes name / and whiche is he ; vnto fyr L. ; 32, [the good knyght] ; In goddes name ; 33, For by my knyghthode / there ; in the worlde that I ; 34, wolde rather ; with fyr P.

384. 1, And than eyther of the ; grete & huge ; 2, And than fayd fyr D. ; 3, [foo] ; 5, I can not byleue ; 7, and there fyr ; 9, myghtely ; made hym to auoyde the fadell ; 10, he had not ; 14, to reft ; 15, hym where ; 16, that on ; 17, of this ; [that] ; 18, came fodeynly ; 23, and on the ; 26, full fore [alle that dyd abyde] ; 27, and than he rode forth on ; 28, vnto a ; & there ; 34, to fir T. ; 35, for to.

385. 3, vnto kynge ; 4, of the ; 6, a grete ; 8, they fared ; 9, And than there ; 15, gretely what thought it a fhame ; 16, hym a ; 17, vnto ; 20, fyr T. there ; 28, than ye ; 29, you my fayth ; 30, you more ; of yours ; 31, more on my ; 33, caught hym ; [fo fore] ; and pulled ; 34, [hors] ; 35, And fyr T. ; 36, And than fyr P.

386. 2, nothynge fay ; 6, Syr P. on the nexte morowe returned from the partye of ; 12, and alfo ; 13, his ryght ; 14, [as] ; 17, the [ouer] euenyng afore ; 18, on yᵉ ; 23, that fyr P. ; 25, wolde I be on my lorde kynge A.'s fyde but for his fake ; 26, party / there was rēnynge and fmytynge vpon helmes ; iufted agaynft ; 30, And than came in fyr T. ; 32, that myght ; 33, haunted amonge ; 35, with a grete meyny of.

387. 2, alle the ; 5, ben his good frende ; 6, awaye with the ; 8, were as good as a ; 9, was theyr ; 10, And than ; 12, So fyr ; 14, [fore] ; 21, kyng A. ; 23, [And] ; 24, I fholde fhame myfelfe ; [al] ; 26, vpon [the] ; 27, and thofe . xx. ; 28, alwaye togyder ; & [fo] ; 30, noble dedes ; 31, leuer to ; than to ; 34, to his ; 37, it fhame.

388. 1, And than ; to the ; 2, fayd to hym ; Syr I praye you ; 3, ye fhall ; 4, to many ; to fewe ; 5, [chere and] ; 10, the knyght with ; 13, lyke and femblable ; 19, on theyr ; 22, on his ; 25, that [with] the wynde therof myght.

389. 3, morowe ; wyll I ; 10, fayd fhe ; but for ; and fo fhe ; 15, crye of a man ; And than ; 16, in to the ; 17, founde he ; 18, vnto a ; ben out of his mynde ; 22, And the fquyer toke ; as faft as ; 23, agayn and tolde ; 24, So fhe rode ; 32, fayd he ; 35, and than ; 37, ouer.his nauell.

390. 1, So fyr T. ; 2, hym faft ; 3, fyr P. ; am fayd fyr T. ; 6, and yf ; 8, there and ; Than fayd fyr ; 11, yf ye ; fyr T. here ; 13, for to ; 18, fayd to fyr P. ; 19, that he ; vnto his ; 22, that he ; 26, fyr T. was ; went ; 30, to fyr ; 31, where as ; 32, on the.

391. 10, With that ; 17, were remounted ; So kyng A. ; 18, [he] gate ; 20, on fote ; 23, And than ; 30, And than ; 33, at fyr T. ; 34, with his fpere ; 35, So fyr.

392. 1, So fyr T. ; 3, [thenne] ; 5, [alle] ; 8, affayled kynge A. ; 9, dyd grete feates ; 14, fo grete ; 15, gate he ; 17, And than ; cryed on hygh ; [the] ; 18, for to ; 19, put down ; 24, [he] ; 26, [there] ; ftouped lowe his heed ; 30, And fyr L.

393. 1, fyr D. ; 3, the grace of ; 4, fyr P. ; 5, for to ; 9, [to hym] ; 11, or in to ; 15, [thenne] ; 17, And whan ; made a ; 25, his vttermeft ; 26, & mette ; 27, & had a ; 38, for to go in to.

394. 4, than he ; 7, Northgales in conclusyon ; 8, with the ; 14, contrarye that crye ; 18, worfhyp of ; 21, than yf he ; 25, and [foo] ; [alle] ; 26, vnto ; 29, [mooft] ; 31, [whanne] as he ; his helme ; 33, fayd thryes ; 34, And than.

395. 16, [the] dayes ; 18, all thefe ; 26, for yf I ; 28, knyght dyd ; 31, promyfe you ; 34, And than ; 35, them that ; [And] ; 38, nere hand ; & oute.

396. 7, he put of his ; 9, there came ; 14, & yf it ; 20, What thynge bare ; 22, the good knyght fyr P. ; 24, now lyuyng ; 26, [owne] ; 32, to fyr D.

397. 3, whyle ye hadde ; 4, And than ; 6, [old] caftel ; 10, fyr L. ; 11, caufer of ; 17, Than fir L. ; to brynge ; 18, here ben . x . ; 20, tyl we ; 22, that yf I ; 23, with me vnto this ; 25, Fyrft [was] ; 26, fyr Bleoberys [and] ; 27, fyr Lucas the butler ; 28, fyr L. and fyr G. ; 30, all to gyder ; 31, that ftode bytwene foure hye wayes ; 32, in foure partyes for to ; 33, with the damoyfell dame ; the whiche was ; 34, for to ; 35, myght renne.

398. 1, And whan ; to hym ; 2, [faunce pyte] ; thou fals ; 9, B. faûce pyte ; 12, Lucas ; whiche ; 13, where fyr T. was ;

14, for none ; 15, but for to ; So the ; 19, yᵉ whiche was ; vnto ; 20, tel hym ; 30, fyr L. ; fyr D. ; 35, [foo].

399. 5, du roy ; 8, And whan ; bote / he ; 15, vnto the ; 19, and tolde vnto fyr D. ; 24, So came there ; 25, So fyr ; 26, went ; the chambre of ; 28, And withoute ; 32, wolde euery day ; hate that was ; 33, And alwaye ; but lytel ; 36, [alle] ; 38, owne.

400. 1, it / and kepte them ; 2, had ynough ; 5, of [his] ; 8, may faye ; 9, hath he ; 10, taken hym ; [for] ; 11, that almooft he dyed ; 12, [fpeke and] ; 14, in many ; 15, wente ; 18, owne meafe ; And than afked kyng M. of ; 19, were of hym ; 22, turneyment and iuftes ; 29, were bothe ; 30, Thā it was ; 32, gete [hym].

401. 4, vnto that ; 5, fome folke called ; 10, wente ; 11, And fo ; 19, iufte with hym ; 21, man / and had a grete fall on the erthe ; 22, fayd he ; For [fyre] ; 32, not fo moche as one here.

402. 3, hym lyenge on the groūde ; 7, or [that] ; 8, was there ; for to ; 11, it was not I that dyd hurte hym ; 12, vnto ; 13, vpon you ; for al ye ; 14, be nought ; Ewayne to be caryed ; 15, heled of his woūdes ; 23, fayd kynge M. ; 25, [is] an ; 27, [al].

403. 1, to a lake ; 3, fhadowe ; 5, were all ; 13, and hyt ; 14, as fayre as the ; 15, hors was ; 17, full wrothe ; And than ; fyr knyght ; 18, felowe yf I can ; 19, [fo] ; with an ; 23, quyte & clene a fpere length / fo that ; had nygh ; 24, [al] ; 25, fet fyr K. agayne vpon his hors ; fyr G. & fyr K. went ; to kyng M. & fyr A. ; 26, them for to ; tell them ; or els they ; 27, And than ; 28, This knyght that fmote downe fyr Kay / is ; and therfore beware ; 29, vpon you.

404. 2, [all] ; 13, kynge Marke / fythen ; 14, for to gyue ; 15, [alle] ; 16, rode forth ; 17, [Soo] ; 18, there they refted ; 20, whiche had ; 21, for to ; 22, afked them ; was in ; 24, they had not ; 33, went.

405. 1, he myffed ; 2, he [the] ; 4, for to ; 5, one of his legges and an arme ; 6, fo than ; and his ; vnto fyr D. ; 8, Nay nay ; ones hath ; 11, Now leue we hym & turne we ; 14, & fyr P. & fyr D. ; 25, how ye can fhifte ; [it with] ; 27, [thenne] ; 31, they pleafed ; 32, And with that ; be glad & make good chere ; 33, herde I ; 35, to haue ben put to dethe ; [foone after this] ; 36, he thought 38, [bothe].

406. 2, to fyr D. ; 4, whan ony ; 6, vnto ; 7, bothe his ; anone whan ; 8, I me repent ; 14, thou fhalt ; & all your ; & your ; 15, where fomeuer it pleafe you ; 16, fyr knyght fhalte ; vnto two of my ; 18, fhewe & tell ; 19, and kynge Meliodas was my father ; 20, I am neuewe ; 25, [and] that all ; 27, knyght fyr T. ; for to be ; 31, And than ; 32, hole and ; 33, toke his hors ; 34, vnto a.

407. 1, And fo ; 2, grete moone ; 8, for to ; but wyll be ; 9, of y^e ; 11, B. faūce pyte ; 12, and fayd to fyr D. Syr knyght ; 16, And than ; 17, vnto a ; where fhe ; 21, fro this ; [he] ; 24, on ; 26, defende me ; 27, late ago prifoner ; 28, I knowe ; 31, [Quene] M. le fay ; 34, So the quene.

408. 1, the to ; y^u wylte ; 4, as foone ; 6, fheelde vpon the ; 7, hath ; 9, [for me] ; 12, So the ; 15, quenes heed ; 18, vpon ; 22, not knowe ; 27, as paramour ; 29, to the.

409. 2, And than ; 3, fay as paramour ; and his ; for to folowe after ; My fayr ; for certaynly ; 6, vpon hym ; 9, fayd M. le fay ; 12, And for your ; 13, or els bete hym well ; 14 my ; quene M. le fay ; 15, with that ; 19, vnto fyr T. ; 25, And than ; for to ; 28, vnto a ; 30, leue we ; 31, and than ; 32, his mayfter ; 34, very lytell ; 35, than holde ; 36, for the ; 37, may no lenger ; 38, or euer that I.

410. 1, And with full grete ; 2, vnto ; 3, And whan ; 4, fhe let ; 6, to be put ; 12, It is not ; 28, of Scotlande ; 31, [there] ; 34, [gretely] ; 35, And than was.

411. 3, to kyng ; 5, and to ; 7, And than ; 11, vnto hym ; 15, fuche dedes ; 18, lytell Brytayne ; 23, euer kyng ; eyen were ; 24, But euer ; that it was grete wonder to ; bothe on the ryght ; 27, of Scotlande ; 29, that the ; 31, les blaūche ; 34, fayd he.

❡ Thus endeth the fyrft booke of fyr T. de L. ❡ Here after foloweth the feconde booke of fyr T.

Book x.

❡ Here begynneth the feconde booke of fyr T. and the . x . booke of this prefent volume. ❡ How fyr T. iufted and fmote downe kynge A. & fyr Vwayne & wolde not tell them his name.

412. 1, Than fayd kynge A. / yf ye ; ye be ; 2, thofe armes ; 4, vndefyred ; 5, And as ; 10, Syr fayd fyr T. ; 13, [and] that ; 15, that I had ; [And therfore ye are a vylaynous knyght to afke bataille of me confyderynge my grete traueylle] ; 18, you not ; 21, and than ; 22, [al to pyeces] ; 24, groūde.

413. 5, that he fell down to the ; 6, hym aboute ; for to ; 9, our pryde ; 11, Vwayne by the holy rode ; 16, moone and ; 21, one knyght ; 25, in to the ; 26, [foo] ; vpon that ; 29, to them ; 31, whofe name ; 32, [called] ; 33, & thus he fayd ; 34, medle with vs ; yf ye ; 36, from vs.

414. 1, from his ; 3, he dreffid ; 6, they had felte his ftrokes / they ; 14, [my] ; 15, Syr fayd he ; 17, whiche I ; 24, am fore ; 25, [thenne] ; 26, ony fayle ; 29, thofe ; 30, on myn ; 31, where as.

415. 2, vpon ; 3, for to bury ; 6, or that ; this knyght fyr ; 11, maner of wyfe ; let it not be out of your ; remembraunce the ; 14, affayle you ; [that] ; 16, in to that ; 18, haue I a luft ; 19, fro theyr ; 23, By god ; 25, ende of ; 27, on his ; 33, vnto the grounde ; 38, after this.

416. 1, reft ; 2, fyr P. ; 5, ye are ; 7, for to ; 9, yf that ; it fhall be an ; 11, departed afonder ; [their] dyuers wayes ; 13, where as ; 15, fayd fhe ; 18, thofe ; 19, whiche ; 22, out the body ; 24, grete woo / but I requyre you tell me your lordes name ; 25, is fir G. ; 27, and had good lodgynge ; 32, couered.

417. 3, and he fayd that he fayd it ; 6, he keft me down ; 9, he mette with me and with hym ; 10, was called fyr P. ; 12, full fore ; 16, haue foûde hym ; 17, And he anfwered and fayd / my ; T. de Lyones ; 19, forth on his ; 21, you fayre knyghtes ; 22, None that are very good ; 27, that fame ; 28, that we ; 29, of the kynge grete vylany ; of quene G. ; 34, wold in no wyfe ; 35, and gone ; requyred them to tell hym theyr ; 36, [foo].

418. 1, he refted ; 4, there befyde ; 6, not ben ; 8, of the ; on horfbacke ; 9, in the mornynge ; 12, [and] they queftyoned ; 18, fyr S. ; 24, Than he came ferther with his hors ; vnto ; 27, grounde ; 30, as faft as they ; coude ; 33, vnto them ; fythen that ; you downe ; groûde ; 36, fayd bothe.

419. 1, that ye ; 3, me to do it ; 7, the very caufe ; why that ; 10, [and yf I be hurte I fhalle not be able to doo bataille with hym] ; 11, fyr S. and fyr Dodynas ; 12, [alle] ; Fayre knyghtes fayd fyr Tryftram ; 17, lyghtly efcape from vs ; But gentyll ; 19, fyr S. ; 21, forth on ; 25, in ye fame ; 26, the fayr ; ye whiche ; 32, trueft louers ; 33, fyr L.

420. 3, nyghe vnto ; 6, and theyr ; the myghte ; that theyr horfes coude renne ; 7, [their] horfes ; 8, Than as foone as ; 9, they auoyded ; 10, lyke men ; 12, [out] ; 13, [neuer] neyther of them ; vnto other ; 15, I haue greate meruayle ; 16, vnto ; 22, moone ; 23, ye blode ; 25, therforé I requyre you yf it ; 29, Syr fayd he ; 32, mooft loue ; Now fayre ; 34, therwithall ; 36, [And there with alle fir T. kneled adoune / and yelded hym vp his fuerd] ; 38, [all].

421. 3, toke vp ; ftreight vnto ; [they] ; 4, and [with] ; whiche ; 5, vnto ; 9, fayd vnto ; 10, are ryght hertely ; 12, this countree ; 13, [had] ; 15, that I here not ; 16, dyd mete ; 17, that fyr T. was there ; 20, vnto this ; 21, and how ; 23, moone ; 26, fyr B. ; 30, where as ; 32, vs bothe wonders fore ; 33, that fame ; 35, than / what.

422. 1, maner of knyght ; hym not ; 3, yf ye knowe not than

do I / for I enfure you that it was fyr L. du lake; all togyder at
ones loked; 10, and ledde hym vnto the rounde; 12, all with one;
17, the begynner; 20, are ryght hertely; vnto; 22, fyr T.; 24, I
am lothe; to do in; 29, [letters]; 32, nobleſſe; 33, afore by; 34,
full well.

423. 8, on fyr T. for his; 9, [that]; 10, [bothe]; went out;
14, [men]; 17, [had]; 18, were the noble knyght; 19, & the quene
la beale I. was paſſynge gladde; 22, [for]; 23, fyr B.; 24, fyr A.;
demaunded a; 26, aſked the; 28, ſayd the; 29, now lyueth.

424. 2, vnto the; 3, and hath made; 6, heuy and fory; 9, vnto;
11, he euer; 12, what thynge; 13, ſhamefully dyſpoſed; 15, now
lyuyng; 16, for to; 18, A falſe; 20, fyr A.; 23, thou wel; 25,
fyr A.

425. 2, repoſed; 3, vnto; or not; 5, vpon; 6, vnto a tree;
8, and moone; pytefulleſt; 12, mother vnto; and vnto; 13, for
your; 14, nere to; 15, [Fayr]; made a; 16, it is well; 19, [a]
ſheelde; 23, are of; [there]; 24, that lyueth; 27, that lyueth; of
hym ſpeketh; 28, ialoufye; 29, [ony] ſuche a; 32, of hym ſhame;
33, as ony; 35, Well than ſayd.

426. 4, make it; 6, and he; 10, egged; 11, anone ſmote; 12,
fore on his ſheelde; hors croupe; 17, after and; 19, ſayd he; 20,
your ſpere; 21, [with ſwerdes] forbare hym longe; 22, ſmote hym
many; 23, Whan; that he; he waxed; 25, fore vpon; 26, vnto; 27,
chere with you / me thynketh; 30, leue for to; as ye; Syr gramercy;
31, are not; with kyng; 32, ſayd to hym; for to; 35, vnto a; 36,
for to; the whiche he; 37, for to.

427. 2, that ye; 3, was there; 6, vnto a; 7, ende of that
brydge; 10, one is called fyr; 11, that other is called fyr; 12, fyr D.;
13, alwayes ye are layde to the groūde; Than was; 15, and ranne
agaynſt fyr T.; and there; 16, ſente to; 17, for to; wolde he; 18,
iuſte agayne; in to the; 19, and they prayed; 21, that hyght; 25,
fyr B.; 27, [owne]; And alſo ye wolde haue; yf I had; 34, none
euylle; And it is.

428. 2, are & euer haue ben; 3, and go aboute / is but; 7,
went vnto theyr; 10, and the; 14, the to leue; for he gooth
vnto; 16, vnto my; [with hym]; 17, I haue not his; 18, fyr D.;
20, vnto; 23, out of his; 24, fyr D.; 27, 29, fyr B.; 32, And ſo;
34, had rydden [forth] aboute a four myle [englyſſhe]; 35, [tyl
that]; vnto a; where as.

429. 3, quod kynge; 4, this iuſtynge; knewe well that the
knyght was; 6, he wolde rather that; 7, wold [not] iuſte with
hym; 12, for to do; 16, on that; 20, on theyr waye; 21, for to;
ſayd to hym; 22, rounde table; not in; 25, for to; 27, maner of

wyfe ; 28, ye not ; 29, fore hated ; vnto you ; 30, yourfelfe foo ; y^t
ye ; 31, a grete ; 35, ye are.

430. 1, vnto a ; 2, where as ; he prayd ; 3, refted ; 6, thofe
knyghtes that were of ; 7, of his ; 8, demaunde you ; not yet ; 9,
fyth that I iufted with hym / & he gaue me ; 10, ye ought to haue
no ; 13, thought euer ; fo as ; 14, towarde them ; 15, A.'s courte ;
19, le cueur hardy ; 28, were tyed ; 29, yonder I fe ; 31, we are ;
34, rode from ; 37, the fheelde ; 38, rounde table.

431. 3, [thenne] ; 4, fyr L. or fyr T. ; 11, had refted them ; 13,
all arraūt knyghtes ; 15, he was ; 16, [alle] ; 17, anfwered he ; 26,
kyng Marke ; 30, That am I lothe ; 33, rode forth [on] ; 35,
where as.

432. 1, quod fyr G. ; 8, and [my] ; 10, by the fayth that I owe
to god ; 11, fyr D. was armed ; 13, fyr D. ; 15, vnto a ; 16, on as
faft as his hors ; 18, nyghe vnto ; 22, [all] ; faft as he ; 25, And
whan ; 26, fyr D. ; chace fo ; 27, as they had ben ; 28, for to fe ;
29, were hurte ; 30, with his ; 31, he made kyng A. laugh ; 35, in
that way.

433. 1, come ; 4, paffe by the ; 8, faye foo ; 10, agaynft fyr
D. ; 11, nerehande ; 14, [Knyght] ; 19, fir V. anone ; 21, vnto ;
22, knyght arraunt ; 26, that I ; 29, to them / and reherfed vnto
them ; [of hym] ; 36, but onely ; behynde the other company ; 37,
for he was ; [and D. had his harneis].

434. 1, and alwayes ; 2, hym moche ; 3, to the wordes that
kyng M. fayd ; 5, a page / and fayd to hym ; 6, Ryde lyghtly vnto ;
maner that ftandeth fo fayre ; vnto ; 7, of that maner / and ; for to ;
me fome ; 9, knyght that I am ; 10, is to faye in ; 11, he went ; 12,
as yf that it ; aboute a ; 13, page ; [his way] ; as he was bydden ;
14, he told ; 15, whiche ; 16, [lord] ; 17, fyr P. ; 21, And than ;
26, therwith [alle] ; 32, [that] ; he was as heuy as they ; fyr V. ;
fyr D. ; 34, that I.

435. 9, whiche ; 12, haue ye not mette ; that had a ; 13, hedes
therin ; 15, wente ; Syr I thanke you ; 17, late in the euenynge ;
20, from his ; fyr D. was ; 26, other ladyes ; 27, loue you ; blame
you ; 29, [the] I ; 30, you ; 38, that it was.

436. 2, where as he had ; for to ; 3, to fyr A. ; 4, there redy ;
5, kynge A. ; 6, togyder / and by ; fyr A. ; 7, in the ryghtwyfe ; 11,
whiche ; 14, vnto hym ; 16, fayd he ; [ye] ; 20, I am ; 21, ryghtwyfe ; 22, that noble ; 24, whiche ; 25, thynges hyd and vnknowen ;
27, ryghtwyfe ; it fprange vnto ; 28, vnto ; 34, [the loffe of] ; &
[of].

437. 1, that fyr T. wepte ; 2, vnto ; 3, [to] yonder ; knyght
kynge M. vnto your prefence agayne ; 4, requyre yow ; ageyne to

me ; 6, all the ; 14, fo whan ; the noble knyght fyr L. ; 16, vnto
the ; knyght fyr L. ; 21, the kynge [Marke] ; 22, [that] ; 27, A.'s
courte ; the fame ; 29, flat vnto ; erth before ; 33, your heed ; 34,
or elles had I ; 35, by his ; 36, [to] as.

438. 5, and a fals diffymuler ; 6, them two ; 10, euer he ; 11,
be ye ; 12, ye are ; 14, and yf ; 16, yf that ; 17, are ye rydynge ;
19, ye not of ; 24, fet by ; 26, coude not ; 29, not for fere or ; 31,
[fame] ; mette togyder.

439. 1, than foure ; 2, bothe fo moche ; 14, and alfo fyr P. ;
15, the one ye other ; 22, Syr fayd fyr Dinadan ; 24, ye fhall ;
[now] ; grete and noble ; 28, fyr D. ; 29, fo that ; 30, Sir knight ;
y^t my ; 31, brother vnto fyr S. ; [and noble] ; 32, [I we] ben ; 34,
hertely for ; of that ; 35, name and what ye be ; & here I ; fayth
that I owe to god ; 36, but moche more rather [be] auaunced vnto
grete honour and worfhip ; 38, vpon my.

440. 8, well knowe ; 20, yf [that] ; 21, fayd fyr P. ; 23, owne
brother ; whiche ; 26, knowe it that fhe ; 27, yf that ; 30, as they
fate ; 31, rydynge with a ; 32, And than he ; 33, vnto.

441. 1, that thou ; vnto the ordre ; 2, that thou ; 3, [for] ; 5,
befeche the ; deale with it ; 6, fyr P. ; 7, beholde your dedes ;
there came ; 9, And anone ; 11, vnto the ; 13, [alle] ; 14, vnto the
grounde ; 18, And vpon the walles . . . . there were ; whiche ; 22,
the fadels ; of theyr ; 31, [euer was] ; what fo euer knyght he be ;
33, [alle].

442. 2, [thorou the bented fhelde and] ; 5, to reft you ; 8, you
afore ; 10, and that ye ; 12, fyr P. ; that I wold ; 13, in hand ; 15,
that ye wyll iufte ; 18; thofe two ; 21, [alle] ; 24, for all ; he lefte ;
25, This feynge fyr D. ; 26, knyght with the reed fheelde ; But
the knyght ; 27, bare hym clene ouer his hors tayle ; 28, But the
knyght wolde not fuffre ; 29, with theyr horfes ; [and] ; arraunte
knyghtes.

443. 8, and locked ; 11, vnto fyr D. ; of no ; 14, vpon hym ;
15, fyr D. ; 17, haue had ; 18, fyr P. ; 22, pages ; 24, he alyghted
to reft ; 25, at the fountayne ; 27, [ye] of ; 29, fayd he ; 31, fyr P. ;
33, [all] ; 34, made hym redy for.

444. 1, fyr P. ; 3, and [to] ; 4, fyr P. ; 8, [foo he] ; 10, or that
[euer] ; 13, cutte infonder ; 16, ouercouered ; full fore ; Somtyme ;
17, foyned ; fomtyme ; 19, with a ftroke of a fpere ; 20, fyr P. ;
23, vnto fyr P. ; am I lothe ; 31, hym mercy ; 33, that I ; 34,
batayle with me ; 36, bothe his ; 37, Syr P. ; 38, [fore].

445. 1, haue fought ; [not] ; 3, that no force / for I fhal ; 4, but
that you ; 5, you the better all the ; 6, I excepte the fame ; 7, [ex-
cepte] of my ; 9, [bothe] ; and ftaunched ; 10, in a ; them well and

eafely all that ; 12, fyr Ewayne and ; 13, vnto A.'s courte ; 14, [the kynge] ; 15, [thurgh the foreſt] ; 16, hyt them ; 17, and fporte at ; 18, and [at] ; all they ; 19, that had ; 20, yf [that] ; 23, vnto a ; where that ; mother is ; 24, made a ; 25, vnto my ; 26, why wylte ; not ones ; 27, that his ; the noble ; 29, let vs turne ; 30, and fyr D. ; 32, whiche ; vpon a ; 33, fyr G. ; whiche was ; 35, well at eaſe.

446. 1, towarde the ; of my lorde kynge ; 4, reſt ; me a whyle ; 6, not to longe ; I wyll ; 8, By my fayth ; fyr D. ; 9, talent vnto fyr T. ; 10, fyr D. ; 12, to you ; 20, and fayd / wyte ; 29, for a ryght ; 31, bytwene vs fayd fyr D. ; 32, that fame ; 33, A. laye ; 38, excepte.

447. 1, fyr D. ; 2, and [of] ; 7, he ſlewe four ; [how] ; 8, quod kynge A. ; 9, [very] ; 10, more better ; 11, all the ; 14, endured ; fyr P. had ben there ; 16, My lorde fayd fyr T. ; 17, in all ; 18, to you ; 21, that dyd ; 22, the kyng [Arthur] ; that that knyght ; vnto ; 23, fyr D. ; 24, fyr P. alſo ; 25, fere me ; fyr P. ; 29, fyr T. fyr L. nor fyr D. ; 31, for to wynne.

448. 3, the whiche came ; 6, he had ſmyten ; 8, all the other ; 10, [noyſe &] ; 16, his fadell ; 19, fyr D. ; 27, gyuen to hym ; 33, Than fayd kyng A. ; 34, And whan ; 36, downe from ; 37, vnto hym for to.

449. 2, of eche other ; 3, and in lyke wyſe was ; 5, [at hym] ; 6, bycauſe he had put them vnto ; 7, fyr G. ; 8, vnto them ; 14, kynge P. ; 19, ouer this mater ; of fyr G. & his bretherne ; 20, ſpeke we ; vpon a ; fayd to ; 21, requyre you & praye you for to gyue me a ; 29, vnto god & vnto ; 32, wyll ſwere that ; 34, [there] ſwore.

450. 1, hard faſtned ; 2, ſhall be well ; afterwarde ; 4, for to ; 5, for to ; 8, wyſt that ; 16, them to be accorded ; 17, or elles ; 18, and the [mooſt] ; 21, the noble knyght ; 23, or ſlee that ; 24, vnto our lorde Ieſu Chryſt and vnto the hyghe ; 31, can byleue ; is full well ; 35, was to the.

451. 3, on Aryes ; 5, all theſe ; 6, alſo in ; 12, vnto ; 13, for to ; that yonge ; 18, hym a ; 20, fyr A. ; 22, loue of his father ; 26, all his ; 33, had neuer ſpoken.

452. 3, hym vnto ; 5, vnto the ; 6, And whan ; 9, whiche was moche ; 10, prayſed there ; 11, for theyr ; 12, was to the ; 16, appoynted ; 17, [there] he ; 18, tofore that ; 20, And than ; 25, vnto theyr ; 27, the hote blode ; 28, ye may ryght well wyte that ; 29, [al] ; 30, a man ; 31, to hym thus ; 32, a grete ; 33, whiche.

453. 1, fyr G. ; 2, yet thou ; 4, it is ; 12, that I ; 13, and therfore ; 19, kynge A. ; 23, was fyr Launcelot ; other of the rounde table ; 27, & I am ſure ye ; 28, [the] whiche ; yf ſir ; 30, than all ; 31, [the noble] ; 32, for than were gone two ; 34, that ye.

454. 4, a fleynge ; 9, [alle] ; 10, for to ; 11, 13, fyr M. ; 14, fyr A. ; 17, 18, fyr D. ; 24, [alle] ; 25, Fayre knightes fayd he / ye fhall knowe that my name is fyr D. ; 27, 29, 32, 35, fyr D. ; 28, out of all ; 32, euer ; 33, fyr B. ; 34, was fyr ; 36, his owne ; 37, fayd fyr D. ; all he.

455. 1, for to make fhorte tale ; 2, from his ; 5, fyr D. ; 10, fyr D. ; 18, [out] ; 19, whofe name ; and a ; 20, 25, kynge A. ; 25, [of the] quene ; 32, & the quene and fyr L.

456. 1, and [the] ; 2, L. du lake ; anfwered and fayd [and to make fhort tale] ; 7, fyr T. de Lyones ; 9, fyr L. ; 13, for to ; 14, kynge M. ; to morowe fayd ; 17, Than fyr T. and la beale I. fayd / we pray you ; 18, ye wyll ; 23, [as] at ; 27, than as ; 33, [of] his.

457. 2, vpon many ; vpon his ; 4, L. du lake ; in his mynde ; 5, And than ; 6, his mooft enemy ; 8, And than ; 11, on fyr T. ; 12, had redde ; 23, fyr D. ; 25, feruaunt to ; 27, yet I loue ; 29, fyr D. ; 31, by all thefe thretenynges ; 32, neuer no man ; gete ought of hym.

458. 2, made by kynge M. [the] whiche ; 3, inftrument ; 5, and [to] ; 7, that he ; fore wounded ; 9, reft ; 11, the Senefchall ; 12, with a ; 13, nyghe vnto ; 14, fyr E. ; 15, y^t his ; 17, he wolde ; 19, [thenne] ; 20, thus . Syr ; 22, that ye ; 24, than fayd ; 25, for to ; 27, Whan fyr T. vnderftode ; 28, the kynge ; 29, fofte hackeney ; 35, may I.

459. 1, yet all guaryffhed and hole ; 3, reft you ; 5, kynge M. ; for to go to T. ; 6, to reft ; 9, Markes blode ; 10, grete and myghty ; 13, And the good knyght fyr D. ; 14, with his ; 15, was grete brekynge ; 16, fmytyng of good knyghtes . And euer ; 17, of all ; 21, folowed them fafte ; 23, portcoleys ; 25, fyr T. fent ; 26, he wold come ; he were hole ; for no fooner coude he do hym god ; 28, fyr E. ; kynge M. yelde ; 29, may [not] ; 34, to the caftell of T. ; 35, [wonder] ; 37, vnto.

460. 4, ryght glad ; 11, vnderftode hym ; 12, hym [his] ; 13, hym an ; 14, Than fayd ; [thus] vnto ; 18, [alle] ; 19, fyr E. ; 20, to kynge ; 21, for to ; 23, [that] it ; 27, fyr E. wyft it ; 30, dyf-comforte you not for one ; 31, of ye world.

461. 7, Elyas y^e ; 10, vp agayne on ; 11, [alle] ; mette [with] fyr E. the capytayne ; 14, euery party ; 17, they of without ; 20, ony more ; eyther partye ; 21, fyr E. ; 23, go vnto ; than was he ; 24, this fyr E. the capytayne fente ; defpyte & angre whether ; 28, flee myn ; euer here after ; 29, And than ; 30, lord & capytayn fyr E. ; for to ; 33, all his ; 34, was beft to do.

462. 2, Notwithftandynge all this fayd no knyght coude be founde that wold fyght with hȳ ; 5, fyr E. ; 6, without that ; 8, fayd they al ; in hand ; 10, for to reft ; 11, yf I ; 13, and told hym where he ; 18, was with ; 19, fyr E. ; 21, may not demaūde ; 28, playne feelde ; 29, to me his ; 31, [a] feuen dayes here ; 32, with hȳ to morowe ; 33, meffenger was ; 34, Herken vnto my wordes felowe fayd ; 35, to make ; 36, vpon his ; 38, rounde table.

463. 3, vttermeft ; 4, [all] ; 6, [alle] ; 8, the ende ; 12, that one from that other / and they ; 14, went vnto ; 17, as there had ben a ; 29, there grete ; on the ; 31, kynge Marke ; all fhamed ; [all] for ; 32, the frenffhe ; 37, whiche afore.

464. 1, fyr E. ; 3, vnto the ; 10, he dyed ; to kyng M. ; 11, fyr E. ; 12, for to ; 13, harmes and domages ; 20, let vs ouer paffe this ; 22, [at] ; 23, ioye of the vyɛtory whiche he had / bycaufe the Seffoynes were fo put ; 24, Elyot ; 26, T. de Lyones ; of the lay ; fyr D. ; 28, that fyr D. ; 29, Elyot ; 30, vpon my ; 31, Than as kyng M. was at meet Elyot the harper came in ; 33, fyr D. ; 36, wrothe with hym.

465. 2, Eliot ; *line 7 wholly omitted ;* 10, And than ; 11, deuyfe vnto fyr L. and vnto ; 12, But for ; 14, made & ordeyned by ; 17, whiche befell ; 19, fyr B. whiche ; 20, vpon a ; 21, after that the ; 22, prynce fyr ; 23, of them he ; 24, was day ; 28, the other ; 29, fyr B. ; 30, fet vpon ; 33, that this ; 34, & alfo yᵗ fyr B.

466. 1, beynge out ; and lackynge naturall reafon ; [he] ; for the noble prynce fyr B. ; 2, & cōmaūded them to ; 4, as yᵉ father ; 6, fyr B. ; 10, fayd to hym [thus] ; 13, I myght haue had ; 14, fyr B. ; that yf ; 17, for to ; 20, A. his wyfe ; 22, but that ; 28, to ; 30, Lorfelyn ; 31, chylde Alyfaunder ; 32, rode her waye.

467. 2, fynde A. ; 3, fyr S. ; 4, vpon payne ; 8, fayd fhe ; 10, 11, fyr S. ; 11, fone A. ; 15, [euer] ; 19, [al] ; fyr S. ; 25, refted herfelfe ; vnto the ; 26, that was ; 30, cofyn to her ; 31, and the [that fame] ; told dame ; 33, dame A. ; tyl that her fone A.

468. 1, fyr B. ; vnto dame A. ; 3, made a ; 4, fayd Anglydes ; 6, fyr B. ; 9, I am content that it be ; dame A. ; 10, for to make ; conftable came ; 12, God be ; 13, euer were tolde to me ; conftable fyr B. ; 15, all be ; 18, dame A. ; 19, fayd vnto hym thefe wordes ; [fwete] ; 20, and vpon the ; of knighthode ; 24, And whan ; 28, that for ; 30, tofore my face in my prefence ; the which I ; 31, to you now.

469. 3, [all] ; fyr A. ; vnto ; 6, [that] I may ; 7, vnto god and vnto ; 9, fyr A. ; and well armed ; 11, [a] ; 12, none of them ; 13, for to go to ; 14, fyr A. ; 15, [tyme] ; 16, falfe traytour ; 21, drawen ; M. thou come ; nere me ; 24, & traytourfly ; 25, praye god fende fyr A. ; 27, fyr A. ; 34, nor yet fyr D. ; 36, for to ; 37, and alfo fyr S. ; faued his lyfe.

470. 2, [alle]; 3, vnto; 4, of the noble; he fholde; in the gouernaunce of fyr L.; 6, And fo; to fyr A.; 8, and counfeyle; the knyght whiche had; 9, fyr A.; cōmaunded hym for to; 10, nedes muſt I do fo; 13, [euer]; in thyne owne countree; 15, Wherwith kyng M. was wonders; 16, and vnto; 18, in a; 19, fuche as were; 20, and Breufe; 21, but that; 23, the yonge knyght fyr A.; 26, and that alwayes he bare; 27, dyenge daye; for to; vpon; 28, fyr A. was; for to; 29, vnto; 31, degree; whiche turneymente kynge C.; 33, whiche was.

471. 2, for to; 4, quod M.; 9, was fyr; And yᵉ other; 11, the one; fyr G.; fyr Garaunt; 12, tolde quene; 13, by a; 14, damoyfel of; 20, vnto the; 21, fyr A.; 22, vnto her; [thus]; 23, with a knyght of this; 24, the whiche is; 25, vnto me; and his name is called fyr M.; 28, fyr A.; 29, body I wyll; 30, Than forthwith [all]; 33, full egrely; fyr A.; 34, and fyr; 35, fyr M.

472. 1, yet fhalt thow; 2, quod fyr A.; 4, wylde bores; and fmote vpon theyr; 7, came quene; 8, this fyr; 10, daungerouſt; 12, fyr A.; fo he; 13, on his fete; 14, for fyr; 17, rāmes or bores; fell bothe; 19, fyr M.; 21, fyr A.; 23, fyr M.; for the; 24, [good]; 25, pryde; 26, fayd fyr; 29, to me; 30, for I promyfe the faythfully as I am . . . . flee thee; 33, Than agayne; laſt fyr; 34, fmote fyr; he raffhed; 35, and lyghtly; 36, thus done; 37, vnto hym; 38, mounted but he fell downe flatte on the erth for feblenes.

473. 1, The damoyfel of the caftell feynge that / layde fyr A. in a; 2, neyther fete nor myght; 3, the grounde; 6, & gaue hym; 7, mornynge after; 9, was he; 13, wente to; 14, bad hym; 18, fayd fhe; 20, vnto a; 21, fayd fyr; 23, them to; 24, and to wedde togyder; 25, in a; 27, not but; vnto her; 28, whiche at; 29, quene M.; to fyr; 30, fayd fyr A.; 31, fayd quene.

474. 2, fyr A.; 3, bycaufe he; 5, to quene; 8, fyr A. laye; 10, yf ye; 12, fyr A.; 13, fayd fhe; 15, [Quene]; 17, fayd fyr; 18, rather than; 19, a pleafure; So god helpe me; 21, fayd fyr; 23, for to be; 24, that is a; for he is; 26, he wyll; 29, ye fhall; 31, fyr A.; 33, fayd fyr; 35, fent to.

475. 2, longe afore that; 4, that vpon; 6, fyr A.; 12, ftyll in the; 14, [a]; and a daye; 16, that there; 19, for to goo on; 21, whiche was; 23, vnto kyng A.; 24, that may; 25, the knyght; 28, grete landes; 29, vpon her; as fyr A.; 31, [the] erth; 32, but that there; 33, with fyr; 34, fyr S.

476. 3, ryght well; fayd fyr A.; And than; 4, And whan; than fhe; 5, none other; 7, whan fyr A.; 10, [the] lyfe; 11, Fayre lady fayd he / my name is fyr A.; 12, fayre damoyfel fayd he /

tell me ; 14, eche other ; 16, talked togyder ; 17, fyr H. ; and he
afked ; 21, And there ; 22, And fyr ; 24, fyr A. ; 27, for to ; [and
repofe hym] ; 28, had holpen ; 29, dame Alys ; 30, [her] ; 32, vnto
this damoyfell ; 35, vnto the noble knyght fyr L. Truly fayre lady ;
36, fyr A.

477. 1, to fyr T. ; [Thēne] ; 3, that other ; de les ; 6, on fote ;
7, [a] ; 9, he was ; 10, he was ; 12, fawe that ; on his ; 14, thought
to haue ; 15, had holpen ; 17, on her ; forthwith ; 19, vnto fyr A. ;
21, fyr A. ; 22, out his ; fhe fawe ; 23, & Mordred alfo in to ; 24,
fyr A. ; 26, paffyng wroth ; 27, had fo ; 28, dame Alys ; 33, reherce
them all ; within thofe ; 34, or [with].

478. 2, frenffhe booke ; 3, tyll that ; 4, whiche hyght ; [good] ;
7, & fyr A. lorfelyn ; 8, that fyr ; 9, vnto ; 10, vnto fyr L. ; 11,
that he ; 12, forowe was ; 13, vnto ; 18, came vnto ; all his ; 19,
let doo crye ; 21, for to ; wyll well ; 22, wyte you wel that I may ;
24, of your goodnes to gyue me lycence for to ; with a ; 25, fo that
fyr ; 26, take you vnto his ; fyr G. ; 27, than fayd quene G. ; take
fuche knyghtes wᵗ me as pleafeth ; 29, anone the quene ; for to ;
32, G. the haute prynce.

479. 2, [and] prynces ; 3, many noble ; 4, at the fyrft ; 7, the
range ; 8, was all ; 11, of them gate ; grete fpere ; 16, vpon his ;
19, fyr B. ; 20, he was wonders wroth ; 26, bothe [the] ; 27, partyes ;
34, And whan.

480. 2, this fyr Melyagaunt ; 3, with a ; 4, a fpere ; fame tyme ;
his father met ; 5, vnto whome ; 6, fone fyr ; 7, that he ; 9, And
fo ; fyr M. ; 11, fote togyder ; there fyr ; 12, [there] ; fyr Galahalt
the ; 15, vnto the ; 16, the whiche ; from her ; 17, And that fame
knyght ; 21, go to fuche ; 24, take it vpon hym & graūte to you ;
28, and [to] ; 29, And than the ; 32, And than they drewe [out] ;
35, loued fyr ; 37, fyr P. ; [felf].

481. 2, in doubte ; 18, vnto fyr ; 19, nothynge myght byte ;
20, And whan ; 21, [wyft and] ; downe to the ; 22, was ryght fore ;
23, fyr P. ; 25, fayd fir ; 28, another ryght foone ; 29, vnto you ;
A fyr fayd fyr P. ; 30, are at ; 32, fo there came fyr ; 33, G. the
haute prynce ; fo harde with ; 34, But fyr.

482. 1, whan fyr ; 2, that he ; 4, not fyr ; 6, was fyr ; the
haute ; 9, fyr G. ; 10, fyr D. ; 12, fyr M. ; 13, not fallen ; 16,
vnto the worfte ; 18, fyr S. ; 19, Than [the] ; 20, to lodgynge ; 22,
fyr P. ; 23, And anone ; 25, fyr A. ; 26, to fyr G. ; fyr P. ; 27, fyr
A. ; 29, fayd fyr ; 30, Whan the Haute prȳce ; 33, were bothe ;
36, fyr A.

483. 1, fyr P. ; 4, wente to ; 5, fyr M. ; bycaufe that ; 15, Than
there came in ; 18, fyr A. ; 21, a grete ; 22, vnder yᵉ horfes ; 23,

began fyrſt; 24, Syr G. ſir Gawaynes; 26, & ſmote downe ſyr; man to the erth; 27, And than; 28, ſyr Blamore de ganys ſyr B.'s; 29, and there eyther of them; with theyr ſperes; [theyre]; 32, his noſe / mouth and eeres; 33, by yᵉ helpe of.

484. 1, [there]; 2, whiche; ſyr Elias le; 6, well as he; 7 ſo that; 8, vnto; 10, there came ſyr; 12, was a grete bourder / and; 15, ſyr P.; [thus]; Syr here; here by; 18, 20, ſyr P.; 20, So [the]; 21, [they] were; 24, vnto; 25, therwith [alle]; [in his hand]; 32, ſyr G. the Haute; 33, than they two; 35, ſyr P. [alle]; 36, vnto.

485. 8, Now begynneth; 11, ſyr S.; 13, mother / and how he appeled an erle before kynge A. / for he made; 14, on our; 26, So whan duke; 27, ſyr L.; 29, vpon payne; none of them ſholde touche hym; 34, lefte hande.

486. 2, neuer no; 3, ſyr L. vnto; 5, where on horſback; vnto; 6, whiche; 7, full myghtely agayne; 10, ouerthrewe many good; And there; 11, on the ryght hande and on; 12, drewe abacke; 13, And therwith [all] the Haute prӯce let; vnto; 14, the degree; 15, ſyr P. and ſyr B. de ganys . And ſyr S. and ſyr E. fought on fote; 17, were they; 19, vnto the; 20, in bothe her; 22, And in lykewyſe dyd ſyr D.; 23, no man there; 25, morowe after ſyr G. the; 27, came in the meane feaſon; 31, croupe / ſo that he fell to yᵉ erth; 32, vnto ſyr; 33, ſyr E.; So whan.

487. 2, ſyr P.; 3, [a] ſhorte; 4, [for]; 5, ſyr A.; 6, thus ſmyte; 7, [alle]; 10, ſyr P.; 11, iuſte ony; ſayd ſyr; 14, of them gate; in theyr hande; 15, that ſyr P.; brake; 16, [alle]; 20, vnto; 22, ſyr L.; 25, O ſyr; 27, ſyr G.'s; 29, to me; kyng A.; 30, [the] whiche; 36, couenable.

488. 2, vnto; where as; 4, whiche was; vnto; 5, knyght farafyn whiche; ſyr C.; 7, this ſyr; 8, letted; 10, that ſyr; 14, vnto her; to ſyr C.; 17, ſyr P.; 18, ſyr C.; 19, rode to; 20, ſyr G. the; 21, redy [the]; 22, afore ſyr; 23, [at]; 25, ſyr D.; 26, and ſyr D. ſmote; 28, was a ieſter & a; 33, ſawe ſyr; 35, [that] ye; and [the noble].

489. 6, and to the; ſyr D.; 9, at ſyr; 10, [the] dyner; 11, let blowe; and ſyr C.; 14, downe to the; 15, drewe theyr; 17, 18, ſyr C.; 18, ſyr P.; 20, gaue vnto ſyr; 21, made hym to knele vpon one of his knees; 22, ſyr P.; aroſe vp lyghtely and gaue hym ſuche a buffet vpon; 23, [ryȝt]; 24, [Corſabryn]; 25, ſyr C.; 26, worſte that thou canſt; 27, a ſtenche; ſo that; 30, ſyr P.; 32, vnto ſyr L.; 34, ſyr C.; 38. ſyr P.

490. 3, a vowe; tyll that; 7, And ſo dyd bothe; 10, to the; 12, there; 14, other / [and]; 15, caſt from theyr horſes downe to the grounde; 17, whiche were; 19, grounde; 21, toke a; 22, [alle];

23, drewe out; 25, many knyghtes; 27, there were many knyghtes that fledde; 28, fayd to them; fo frõ; 30, all yᵉ; 33, fayre bretheren; vpon your; 34, Durynge thefe wordes there came.

491. 4, fyr B.; 5, vpon the duke C. of Claraũce; 6, erle [of]; 8, he at hym; 9, vnto; 11, fyr D.; and he; 15, And whan; 16, he fawe; 17, [and that he gatte betwixe two dyffhes]; he ferued; 18, fayd vnto hym thus; 21, [wel]; fyr D. vnto fyr L.; 23, [fir D. faid L.] And I enfure; 24, neuer mete the no more / nor alfo with thy; 25, meteth with me; 26, be fo; buyftous fpere; 27, fyr L.; make euer; 29, Quene G.

492. 5, holpe; 8, they began; 13, [there]; to make; 15, two; 16, ye may beholde; 18, that we; 23, the raungell; 26, fyr G.; 27, where as; 28, all armed; 29, fyr D.; 31, vpon hym; 32, with grete fcornes they; 34, fo they; 35, And than they; 36, vnarmed hym; them all; 38, fo brought in.

493. 1, were there; 2, fyr D. vnto fyr L.; 3, affent of them all; 16, that I fhall; 19, fo euer; 20, vnto my; that I was; 21, [that] whan; 31, fyr L.

494. 1, And than; 9, there fet; 13, fyr T. had he; 14, brufed many knyghtes; 18, yᵉ other were; 19, nothynge fo fore behated; 20, in the; 21, Syr neuewe; am full; 22, God thanke you my; 23, And than; for to be; in to an; 24, hors lytter; fygne of grete; neuewe; 27, for to ete; 29, for to be; in to; 31, for to; 32, and his; 34, Whan the quene la; how fyr T.; fhe fent; 35, fyr T. was; 36, fyr S.; wyfte that; [&] anone he had knowlege that; 38, fyr S.

495. 2, [as] by; 5, [there]; 6, and [there]; 8, fyr S.; 9, & gaue an other a grete woũde; but fyr; 10, on his; 13, tyll [that]; 18, he had fayd; 19, and by; 23, Returne we vnto; 26, were able to bere; 28, let bury; 29, within a; 31, vnto warre; 34, do make.

496. 1, [dyd] made; 6, forthwith; 14, lyke a traytour; that I; 19, other lettres; 21, vpon the farafyns; 22, vnto fyr.

497. 5, fyr P.; 7, ftreyghte to; 9, how he had; 12, ye well; mooft noble; 13, yf that; 17, no more fo; 20, for to; 21, that fhe is; 23, And fo; 24, yᵗ kyng; 26, And than anone; 29, for to; the farafyns; 31, Dynas the Seneffhall; 32, farafyns; than he anone in all the hafte he myght put; 38, Whan la beale I.

498. 8, to that purpofe; 9, and vnto fyr S.; 14, to her worde; 15, had deuyfed; 18, with thofe; 21, this countree; 22, countree foure; 23, whiche; 27, and for to; 29, And whan; how all thefe; [thus]; 30, were ouerthrowen; vnto fyr; 31, how that; 34, fyr T. was there; 35, ryght glad.

499. 1, that fyr T. rode; and than he rode after hym; 2,

ryght grete ; 4, the whiche ; 5, put yᵗ caftell in to theyr gouernaunce
as theyr owne ; 6, was ryght well ; 7, [Royall] ; 14, vnto her lorde
kynge ; 21, of his ; 26, on this ; 27, were not glad ; 28, by this
crye whiche ; 30, at vs ; 37, & [to] la.

500. 1, [in] ; 2, [goo] ; 11, rechace ; 15, vpon a ; 16, me
gretely ; 17, that ye ; 18, alfo well ; 19, for to ; and [to] ; 26, for
to ; 27, drynke of that welle ; 28, vnto ; efpyed that ; 29, helme
vpon his heed ; 33, fyr B. ; fo forthwith [alle] ; 34, to them ; the
good ; 35, that one to that other.

501. 1, fayd fyr Breufe faunce pyte ; 2, well fayd he ; 4,
bycaufe kyng ; 7, the quene ; 8, in this ; 10, fyr P. ; haftely fhall ;
15, vpon a ; 18, and a ; 19, that wyll ; 21, A.'s courte ; 25, fyr B. ;
26, fyr P. ; 30, hors and man ; 31, [thus] ; 33, vttermeft ; 34, for
all ; whiche ; 37, [euer] ; 38, was fore.

502. 1, after hym ; and [thorugh] ; 2, B. faunce pyte ; fledde
thus ; 3, [euen] ; 4, the one ; that other ; 5, and that other hyghte
fyr Harry le ; 6, fyr P. de Galys ; 7, [of his tyme] ; 8, fyr B. ; thefe
thre ; 9, cryed aloude ; 13, is fyr B. ; yf that ; 14, ony mercy ; here
with ; 18, And whan ; 19, hymfelfe alone ; 22, And fo than ; 25,
euer he ; 28, on yᵉ erth [thenne] ; vnto hymfelfe that fyr B. faunce
pite was neuer ; 36, grounde ; 37, dedes & actes ; 38, vpon.

503. 1, put vnto ; 2, B. faunce pite ; 3, And whan ; 4, vnhappy
wyll ; 5, And than ; 7, vnto the ; as though he wolde ; And whan ;
9, fhame of thyfelfe ; 11, bothe hors ; 19, 23, fyr B. ; 23, he is of
all cowardes the ; [knyghte] ; 27, fyr E. ; 28, had mette ; 29, 32, fir
B. ; 30, and forowe ; 33, fyr P.

504. 2, with hym ; 3, all redy ; fyr B. ; 5, 6, fyr P. ; 7, fyr E. ;
8, nor no ; 12, fyr P. ; 14, fyr P. ; 23, And whan ; 24, fyr L. was
dede ; 26, arofe vp ; 28, mete togyder ; [wyde] ; man myght ; 32,
A.'s courte.

505. 3, for to ; 7, to daye ; 8, had flepte ; grēnynge ; 9, [and
his hors ftode by hym] ; 11, vpon ; 12, fayd quod ; 13, quod fyr ;
17, [And] as ; knowe ; 18, fyr D. ; 19, tell me ; 21, fyght but yf ;
22, for to ; 23, ftyll houed ; 24, come ; 25, that wyll ; 26, It is
the ; 29, whofe ; 30, fyr E. ; 31, [ful] ; 35, fyr D. ; 37, all arraunt ;
38, one for to ; another ; fyr E.

506. 1, whether he wyll or not ; 2, Than fayd fyr D. ; 3, [al] ;
4, fyr E. ; 5, how is it with you now ; 6, Me thynketh that ; ryght
well ; vpon ; 7, ony good ; now reuenge my fhame ; 9, from hens ;
13, fyr D. ; 14, moche the ; 16, And foo fyr T. rode ; 18, what
meaneth ; 22, than was ; but a ; 23, [for] ; by caufe he fayd well ;
24, is but a ; vnto vs ; 25, yf fyr L. ; 26, vpon thofe ; 27, incontynent he ; 28, a lytell ; 32, hors croupe ; 34, as he ferued the

fyrſt knyght / ſoo he ſerued hym ; 35, gate them vpon theyr fete as
well ; 36, and theyr ; to do ; vnto the vttermeſt.

507. 3, vs not ; 5, ſyr G. ; brother vnto ; 6, vnto the noble ; 8,
is grete ; 9, ye that ben ; 11, in all ; 12, but late agone (as I herde
ſaye) that ; 13, whiche ; 17, waye as he dyd ; 18, [ther] than had
it ben nede to haue ben many moo knyghtes than ; 19, [all] ; them
and rode ; 20, And ſo ; 21, ſayd the one to ; 25, ſayd quod ; drewe ;
26, myghty buffet ; 27, from his ; and [he] ; 28, And than ſyr T.
turned hym vnto ſyr G. / and he ; 31, rode ſtreyght ; 33, before ;
34, [ſyr] ſhe ſayd.

508. 1, is of all men the ; 2, and is alſo a good knyght ; 6, for
to ; 7, that he hath ; 9, And euen ſo ; 17, reſt ; 18, [there] ; 22,
[that] he ; 23, ſyr D. ; A.'s courte ; 24, rounde table ; 26, the noble
knyght ſyr T. ; 27, ſayd ſyr D. ; 31, vnto you ; 32, but yf that ye ;
33, ſyr D. ; 36, whiche.

509. 1, good and noble ; 8, ſay vnto ; ye are ; 10, that I ; 11,
la beale I. ; 20, whiche ; 22, tyll he ; 24, [he] ; 26, whiche ; 29,
hym wylfully ; brake his ; 30, ſyr D. began ; 31, to drawe out his
ſwerde ; 33, ſyr D.

510. 9, a knyght arraunt ; dreſſynge ; 10, for to ; 12, ſyr T. ;
22, A ſyr D. ; 24, grete ioye ; this ſyr ; 27, how he was ; 29, there
came ; 36, ſyr G.

511. 2, and perceyue full well ; 6, demed in hymſelfe ; Than the ;
7, dreſſed his ſheelde and drewe out ; for to ; 21, praye you ſyr T. ;
26, and ye owe me euyll wyll ye may ; 29, cōmaūde me ; [ryght] ;
31, ſyr D. ; 36, well ynough ; 37, of Ioyous garde.

512. 1, caſtell of ; 5, ſyr P. ; 9, ſyr D. ; ſyr G. ; 10, [there]
laſted ; 15, [but he wanne the degree] ; that he ; 17, that he ; 26,
to ſyr G. ; 28, ſyr A. ; ſyr G. ; ſyr M. ; 32, ſyr G. ; 36, Truly ſayd ;
[& ſoo] I wold I had ; 38, [or] on fote.

513. 2, [in] all the dayes of my lyf ; 3, And whā the degree
was ; 4, ſyr A. ; ſyr G. ; 11, doth it ; 12, ſyr G. ; 13, drawe me
to ; 14, ſayd ſyr ; 15, ſyr D. ; 22, kynrede ; 23, 25, ſyr P. ; 28,
[ſaid ſir T.] ; 29, be he neuer ; [nor ſoo] ; 30, and byge ; 31,
[knyghtes] full ofte ; 32, is nought ; 33, ſaid ſir T. ; 34, [owne] ;
35, [Soo] ; 36, herde a dolefull crye ; 37, veſſell couered.

514. 2, and his company alyghted ; [And] ; 3, [and entred] ;
[And] ; 6, [was] ; [the] ; 8, Than he was ware of ; 10, ſayd he what ;
13, [ſire ſaid the maronners that] ; 17, [that ſomme of vs] we may ;
[as wel as other] ; 18, [ſoo] as ; [maronners] ; it ſhall be ; 21, to ;
22, recōmendacyon / and vnto ; 29, that this ; a ryght ; 31, maner
of ; 37, worſhypfull eſtates ; [be] ; 38, for to.

515. 6, ſeuen dayes ; 9, ſyr G. ; 18, as ye are ; 20, to his ; 27, moche the worfe ; 29, that I ; [euer] ; 30, am not ; 35, forth on ; a lytell ; 36, rydynge all armed.

516. 4, that knyght ; 5, kepe hym well ; 7, hym to the groūde . And that knyght ; 9, full hard ; 10, to leue ; 14, he tombled vp fo ; 15, and there he ; 16, to haue dyed ; 17, fore of ; 18, they departed and rode ; 19, comyng agaynft ; 21, fyr B. ; 23, that other ; 25, whiche at ; 26, [the] whiche ; 29, vnto la ; 30, it vnto ; fyr B. ; 31, ye therwith ; 33, kepe the ; 34, all the myght that theyr horfes coude renne ; 35, And fo the kyng.

517. 4, or that be ; 5, redy to iufte with me ; to fyr T. ; 8, agayn lyghtly ; 9, fadde ftrokes ; 11, fayd fyr D. ; 14, fyr S. ; 15, to fyr D. ; 16, 18, fyr D. ; 17, fyr T. ; 18, fyr G. ; 20, fyr G. / that hors and man fell to ; 21, to fyr D. ; 26, in to the ; 28, fyr D. ; 29, bare the helme of ; 31, there good ; and fporte ; 32, to do to kepe them from laughynge ; 35, vnto.

518. 3, was faft on flepe ; 4, in to the whiche ye ; [in to] ; me therto ; 6, the whiche ; 7, they that were ; 11, was well ; 12, And than ; 14, fuche [a] ; wolde I ; 15, So there ; 19, our lord ; 25, fhall do ; 26, by our kynge ; 30, fyr E. ; 31, fyr P. ; 33, of two chyldren ; 34, had in fo grete fauour ; 35, his blode fo well ; 37, hym and his ; 38, for to haue.

519. 1, ony rule ; 3, hym as them lyft . And ; 7, as it is euer ; 8, he wyll not therwith be fuffyfed ; 12, be well ware ; 15, thefe falfe ; 16, all armed ; 19, two falfe ; the one that ; 22, vnto ; 23, vnto the deth ; 27, that I ; 28, vnto ; 33, as I haue.

520. 1, and tenemētes that ; poffeffed in all ; 2, fyr E. ; 3, his maker ; 6, and that I ; 7, came to ; 9, vpon me / and reuenge ; 10, [nor lord] ; 11, This was ; 13, our kynge ; 14, on his ; 15, ye poffeffe ; 20, of the worlde ; 21, am comen ; 24, at my hertes eafe tyll that ; 27, we that ben ; 30, two falfe ; kepe it ; 33, that ye ; me for to ; 38, nygh vnto.

521. 1, vpon ; 3, here in this countre ; 4, [euer] ; 5, fyr P. ; 9, of kynge H. ; 12, and he that ; 13, in hande ; 14, drewe ; 15, many a ; 16, And thus they fought more ; 18, bothe his ; 20, was curteys ; 21, fyr knyght ; 22, ye be better ; 24, fyr P. ; 25, that hyther am comen ; 26, vnto fyr ; 27, ben now lyuynge ; 28, the feconde fyr T. ; 29, & the thyrde ; 31, It is well fayd quod ; 32, vnto ; 33, vnto my.

522. 6, was not there / whiche is the beft ; 7, fyr H. ; 10, [that was] ; 12, of the courte of ; 15, for moche ; 17, they let ; to the two ; 18, comen a ; 20, in a caftel ; 22, He is ryghte ; 28, the whiche is not yet chriftened ; 29, and yf he ; 30, for to ; 31, vnto ; 36, faythfull ; 37, alfo well.

523. 1, [the] whiche; 2, [full]; 6, fyr H.; 7, that other hyght fyr; 11, [that]; 14, vnto the; 15, thus he fayd; fir H. and fyr; 17, [that]; for to; 19, whiche; 29, as euer; 31, fyr H.; 33, pryde & prefūpcyon; 34, on the grounde.

524. 3, two or thre tymes; 4, Wherof fyr P.; 5, [al]; 6, grounde; 8, a myghty ftroke; made him to fall vpon one of his; 9, they bothe; 11, two wylde; 12, on the erth; 13, reftynge; two large; brethed them; 17, a forowfull doole; 21, had endured well an; 22, vpon his; as well as; 24, vnto; wherfore hāgeft; 28, fell vnto; 29, groūde; And than he ftarte lyghtly to hym and raffhed of; 32, hym vnto; 35, for to; [alle]; 36, [as]; 37, all the.

525. 1, So than were; 3, [as] at; 5, than he; 6, they that were in; knewe; 11, So fyr T.; 12, within [the]; 15, goodly knyght; 19, fyr D.; 24, for to; 26, for to reft; And fo; 30, fpake vnto; afked hym where were thofe; 32, are ye; 33, that ye are.

526. 3, withall; 4, through fyr T.; 5, thwarte the myddes; 6, grounde; therwithall; drewe; 8, for to; 10, [that] he; 11, hors by the brydell; 12, than he turned; 16, he fmote his; 21, fyr E.; 22, now bereth lyfe; 23, tell me yf ye; 24, fyr T.; 26, fyr E.; 28, is fyr; 31, fyr E.; rode vnto; 34, fyr P. talked vnto fyr T.; 36, fo well.

527. 1, for to; 3, quod fyr D.; 8, fawe quene; 9, was fo; yᵗ vnnethes he; 10, vnto theyr; but fyr; 12, morowe; 14, bothe la beale I. & they; 18, 19, fyr G.; 20, full fayre; 22, of fyr; 23, So came a fquyer to fyr; 25, elles [to]; 26, that I bydde; come with; 27, fayd fyr; 31, fhall encoūtre; 32, Than the; told fyr G. his anfwere; 34, fmote fyr.

528. 1, a grete; there came; 5, there came; of fyr; 9, [ryghte]; 10, [euer]; 14, fyr G.; vnto fyr G.; 15, this fyr; hathe ben; 19, thyrde was; 20, fyr D.; 21, that they [four kny3tes]; 23, as longe as; 27, [all]; 29, hors and man; 30, fyr V.; fyr S.; 34, fyr G.; 37, fayd fyr; 38, fyr G.

529. 1, he yᵗ is; 3, la beale I.; 4, tyll [that]; 9, here; 11, a [grete]; 12, by that horne; 18, vnto a; 19, fholde be; 20, vnto; 23, vnto our; 27, his naturall; 29, And whan; 32, wente vnto; 33, that the.

530. 4, not knowe; than fyr T.; 5, I [haue]; meruayle me moche; 7, fyr G.; 8, vs two; 9, vnto hym; [for] to; 14, tyll they; 15, caufe that; 18, I can not tell you yet; 19, be vnto I; 25, fyr G.; 31, 32, fyr S.; [thenne]; 35, tyl that; 36, holpe fyr; 37, holpe vp fyr; 38, to theyr; they vnlaced his.

531. 2, hym ayled; 3, gaue hym; 4, an other as good agayne; fyr P.; 7, nedes; 8, that ye; 10, fyr S.; 13, fyr G.; 15, fayd fir;

16, [alle]; fyr P.; 20, fhall we; 25, was in; 28, I. where fhe; 31, Scotlande; 32, them do; 33, thofe; fyr L.; 34, not fhewe you no certaynte; 35, of a certeynte it ben they.

532. 2, [lyghtely]; 3, roūde table; 4, Kay went; 10, cofyns to; 11, and that; 19, fo that; 24, & fo bothe his hors & he fell to ye grounde; 26, fayd kyng; 27, hath iufted full; 32, my two; 33, feuen of my; 36, whiche were.

533. 1, whiche rydeth vpon; [myghtely and]; 3, made to be set on horfback; thofe two; 4, whiche fyr E.; fyr S.; 6, out his; 9, all other; 11, not to doo his parte on the; 13, wonder of hym; And there; 14, whiche rode at that tyme vpon a; lyke vnto; And he; 15, that rode vpon a; And he lykened fyr G.; 16, two egre; 28, thofe.

534. 3, fyr L.; 5, [foo]; 6, 12, kynge A.; 7, fyr L.; 14, let euery; 15, forth togyder; 16, foo that; 18, groūde; 22, tombled to the groūde; 23, from his; 24, And than [the noble]; 26, how that; 38, [that] thou.

535. 4, quyte it; 14, in this; 22, fhe began to wepe; 25, with a grete fpere / fo that fyr T.; 26, euer that; 29, for to reft hym; 30, foo whan; 33, meruaylous dedes of armes; [none of]; wyft.

536. 3, knewe that; was agayne vpon his hors; 4, made; 7, in hymfelfe that he; 10, that hym; that yf bothe; 17, of his dedes; 20, [hym]; 24, [euer]; fyr D.; 31, [outher] and; 35, there came.

537. 6, to fyr L.; 7, of his; 8, vnto the; 9, groūde; 11, Ryght fo were; 14, but yf it; 15, body for body; 16, And whan; 20, whiche was; 21, and clene from; 22, [naked]; [& fo]; 23, ryghte fyerfly; well that; 24, [worfhypful]; 26, vnto thy felfe; 27, fyr P.; 28, for to; 29, knowe that I neuer dyd; 30, in all; 31, [at]; 32, that I fhall; whyle my lyfe lafteth; And yf; 33, from the gretteft worfhyp that euer I had or.

538. 1, the trouth; 4, yf that; 5, Launcelot ye; haue borne; 6, that your; 9, [this day]; 11, [all]; 14, meruaylous dedes of armes; 18, Lyftynoyfe; 22, there were; 28, and fo well; kynge and the knyghtes had grete; 29, of hym . And than; 30, that fyr P.; 31, to reft hym; 32, bothe on fote and on; 34, degree; 37, fyr D.

539. 1, and vpon; 2, ryght gladde; 6, all other knyghtes; the degree; all the; 10, refted; 13, a ferre; well be; 16, [the] deuyll; 19, thou wereft; 20, fyr D.; 21, of none; in all my; 24, yf fyr L.; 25, good quarell; is [to]; 30, for to be; 32, on the morowe.

540. 5, had I; 6, fyr P.; whyle I lyue; 17, morowe; 18, Triftram & la beale I. were redy with fyr P.; 22, that the kynge &

fyr L. ; 23, [ryde] and la beale I. ; fyr L. ; 25, kyng A. ; 26, whiche ; 27, all poyntes ; 31, fyr L. ; 34, wyll [be].

541. 2, fyr L. ; 5, rode & came vnto her ; gracyoufly falewed her ; faue you fayr lady ; 7, to ; 8, Thou vncurteis ; 10, Kyng A. ; 11, but alway ; 14, his fpere ; fawe the ; 24, full ftrongly ; 27, fuche a falle ; fayd vnto ; 28, muft nedes ; 33, though I haue ; 37, it had ben.

542. 4, vnto fyr ; 8, and thou ; 9, before my ; 10, that thou ; 11, the kynge ; 13, [that] he ; 14, knewe ; 16, one of them ; that he wolde ; 20, tell it hym ; 21, [fomeuer] ; 22, vttermeft ; [ony] ; but that fyr L. ; 24, fayd fyr P. ; 26, not yet ; 28, [faid fire Triftram] ; 29, [And] ; 30, fyr P. ; 32, made vnto ; 33, that they.

543. 2, Lucan the Butler ; 3, there at ; 4, of Scotlande ; 6, bothe fo fyers ; 7, they fell bothe ; grounde ; 9, there in ; 11, And in lyke wyfe fir G. ; 12, kynge A. ; 13, L. du lake ; 14, fyr L. ; 15, hym doo ; meruaylous dedes of armes ; 18, fayd vnto fyr ; 20, fyr P. ; 23, Syr fayd fyr P. ; 24, I haue done ; 25, fyr P. ; to deceyue ; 26, I muft ; 27, befeche you ; And yf nede be ; 29, [thenne] ; 34, he had grete meruayle of hym ; 37, meruaylled gretely.

544. 2, vnto you ; 3, none euyll ; 6, vnto fyr T. ; 7, for to ; 11, whiche now ; 14, all the people there ; double the dedes of armes that ; 22, thofe of ; 24, how he doth ; 26, 28, fyr L. ; 28, it nedes muft ; 34, that he.

545. 1, came there ; 4, the noble knyght fyr L. ; 10, grete wonder ; 13, forbore ; kyng A. ; 15, T. de Lyones ; fe how ; 17, in this ; 20, fyr L. ; 22, that fyr ; 24, Triftram is of ; 26, As kynge A. ; 29, let theyr eyen go frō fyr T. ; 32, haue done ; 34, for to ryde ; 36, vpon his.

546. 4, for ony ; 7, that we ; 8, plucked vp now ; 10, fayd fyr D. ; 12, T. fmyled ; vnto fyr D. ; 18, So than whan ; vnto a ; 21, whiche ; 22, that ye wyll lende.

547. 1, and brake them vnto theyr ; 2, dreffed them togyder ; 3, full egrely ; meruayled moche ; 4, with hym fo ; 8, ftrokes that one to that other ; 12, for fhe ; 19, that fayd vnto hym ; 21, whiche was ; 24, fayd vnto ; 26, to reft you ; 27, by caufe that ; 32, full well apayde ; 33, not that he was fyr T. ; 34, well that he was ; 35, fought they ; 38, fyr L, ; whiche muft.

548. 3, rather than ; 4, fhold be ; 5, for to ; 7, was all ; 8, a grete ; 9, groūde ; 10, & to ; 11, haue ye fmytten ; 14, And than ; 16, that fyr ; 17, hym downe ; 22, hym comynge ; 23, [that] ; 24, for he ; 29, and fyr D. ; 34, 35, fyr L.

549. 4, gaue vnto ; 5, fyr L. ; you all ; 16, wonders wrothe ; had feen ; 17, vnto the ; 18, nor fyr ; 22, fyr G. and fyr D. ; 23, vnto

theyr; And alwaye; 27, that fame; that here is; 28, none of vs;
ony nede; 31, yᵗ from; I not; 35, [A]; 36, [longe].

550. 4, ouermoche for me; 8, fyr P.; 12, whofe name; 13,
that good; 15, neuer he yelded hym to me; 18, it you; vnto theyr;
20, and fo fet them at theyr table and wente to meet; 21, And
whan la beale I.; 22, [thenne] her colour; 25, my dere lorde; 28,
vnto your; 32, for alway; 33, [al]; 38, [fore] fyr L.

551. 2, [fo] ye; 4, holde you excufed; 6, [at that tyme]; 7,
came in to theyr; 10, vpon vs; 27, fyr L.; 30, foo fayre; 32, that
I do knowe; 34, [the noble knyȝt]; 35, for ye are; And thus.

552. 1, of dyuers thynges; iuftyng; 4, My lorde fayd fyr T.;
fyr D.; 5, fyr G. of Orkeney; 6, kyng A.; fyr G.; 7, it was; 8,
fyr D.; [to haue]; 10, fyr L.; 12, he with; 16, moche people;
17, fyr P.; 18, by caufe he; fyr L.; 23, [ryght wel]; 24, other
maters; 26, [hertely]; 27, no reft; 28, fyr G. ꞁ and fyr D.

553. 2, vnto; 4, la beale I.; 6, her ftanding; 12, [alle]; and
than he brake; 13, drewe; 15, fyr P.; 20, with the; 21, drewe;
22, And than; 23, vnto; 25, 27, 29, fyr L.; 28, do here; [this
day] many; 31, ye knowe not; 32, vnto hym; 34, fyr D.; wonders
dedes of.

554. 1, [& worfhip]; 4, gate them; 7, vpon hym ꞁ that; 8, of
Scotlande [with their Knyghtes]; 10, pryfoners; 13, brake it; 15,
with his; 18, [du lake]; 19, hym the hors; 21, fyr L.; 23, gentyll
brother fayd fyr L. [vnto his broder]; 26, vnto; 27, and with a;
29, dedes of; 34, dyd ꞁ and mooft fpecyally; 35, gretely therof.

555. 2, vnto them; 5, to vs; 8, fyr P.; 10, yow well; 12, fyr
D.; 14, And after that fyr; 15, of Scotlande; 19, fyr P.; 25, vnto;
29, voyce vnto; 32, rode vnto; 33, E. de Marys; and quene la;
35, came to hym; 36, & yᵉ kyng of; 37, that rage.

556. 4, were [in]; 6, had fpoken; vnto the gate of; 7, there fyr
P.; all on; 8, fyr D.; is fyr; 9, fayd fyr T. ꞁ wyll; 10, 12, fyr P.;
14, me wrōgfully; as ye dyd; 16, fyr P.; 18, fyr B.; 20, refted
them; 21, dayes; 29, not be mery; 30, And fo at; 34, as [the].

557. 7, la beale I.; 11, I wolde to god; 12, it [is]; 15, as ye
had there; 16, fyr P.; 20, fayd yᵉ; 33, were ryght forowfull; 34,
vnto fyr P.

558. 2, not abyde; 5, a [fayre]; 6, hym whiche; 7, and [ther
with he]; 10, ye not; 11, fyr P.; 15, ye be none; ye; 17, fayd
fyr; 18, ye well that I am fyr P.; 20, [two]; wyte ye; 21, ben
truly; 23, 25, fyr E.; 25, vnto other; 27, fyr P.; 30, fayd fyr;
33, none; 35, fyr P.

559. 1, fyr E.; 3, ye euer; 4, fyr P.; 6, me the fouleft; 8, had
not done; 15, fyr E.; 17, alas the; 18, fayd fyr; 19, as this; two

of his; 21, vpon his; than beynge; 24, toke our reſt by this; 25, here vnto me; 26, this ſame; 28, on horſbacke; 29, ſo ſore; 31, ferre more; 32, ſayd ſyr.

560. 1, vnto an; 2, toke his reſt; 3, for to; vndernethe; 6, aboute a x .; 9, the whiche; 10, [he]; 13, ſayd ſyr; 15, gate vp; 16, drewe out; [and their ſheldes]; 18, [at the laſt]; 22, [and badde hym take his lady]; 23, vpon his fete / for he; 24, ſayd lady; ſyr E.; he had; 25, hym for to gete her ageyne; 27, one that hyght ſyr; 28, ſayd ſhe; 29, lyfe that he hath loſt; 30, ſyr P.; 31, [A]; 34, ſayd ſyr; 35, largely; to haue me at a vauntage; 36, [ſir]; 38, [not].

561. 2, went to; 3, on fote; 7, [durynge]; ſyr P.; 10, is ſyr; 12, ye wel; 19, And than; 20, vnto; 24, ſyr E.; 25, vnto; 29, ſyr P.; for to; 30, ſyr E. horſed and his lady; 31, amblynge hors; 35, wolde ledde them.

562. 3, [thenne]; this may be; 7, downe and; 8, [many]; 9, Fayre felowes; ſyr P.; 14, wente to; 20, wyte thou; 31, [that]; 33, ſyr P.; 34, for to; 36, haue yelded me.

563. 5, whiche; 6, iuſtyce done on hym; 11, ſo ledde; 12, ſyr P.; 13, at the; 18, vnto them; 20, and vnto; 22, [alle]; 24, from his; 25, herde before; 27, As ſyr T.; 33, whiche; 35, toke.

564. 1, come he put on; 2, how ſyr P. was; 3, to [his]; 3, 5, ſyr L.; 6, for to; [foo]; 16, ſayd ſyr; 19, yourſelfe as well; 20, for hym; And than; 22, brake; 23, drewe out; 24, and within; 25, but that they were layde vnto the erth; 28, ſyr P. of his handes; 30, Than was; 31, ryght well; 32, bycauſe that; 37, from the.

565. 3, that ye; 8, ſyr L. du lake; 10, many; 12, and vnto ſyr P.; 19, vnto the; that ye wyll ſporte with me; 22, or els ſoone; 27, had put of his helme; 29, ſyr P.; 30, vpon his.

566. 3, grete ioye; 6, ſyr D,; 9, had grete; as he was wonte to be; 18, that the whiche; [all]; 22, neuer more; 27, yᵗ there; 30, vnto a; 33, of the [that noble]; 34, whiche were meruaylouſly well made / and full; 35, pyteouſly ſayd; 37, vnto; 38, [and troubled].

567. 2, to haue ſlayne hym; 3, But ſyr T.; 5, that he had hymſelfe; 7, herde all thy; 8, all thy; 13, ſyr P.; 15, of the worlde; 16, as it; 18, loued the quene la; 20, or elles; 27, as [to]; 29, ſyr T.; 30, ſyr P.; 36, vnto the; 37, ſyr P.

568. 3, the quene la; 4, daye of batayle; 5, [that we ſhalle doo bataille]; 8, ſyr P.; 9, am feble & lene; 10, of the quene la; reſt me; tyll that; 12, as that daye; 13, to ſyr P.; 14, me ones; 17, where at that; 18, ſayd ſyr; 20, kepte your; 23, [he] rode; 27, a thre; 28, that yᵉ batayle; 30, of his thygh and wounded hym ryght fore / and the; 31, [hurte hym]; 33, ſtreyght; with full; 36, hurte

that he had in his; 37, that myght; 38, vnto hym; euer fyr
Tryſtram.

569. 1, that fyr Palomydes; bycaufe that; 12, and the thyrde;
13, So thus fyr P.; 15, for to; 17, and that fyr T.; 19, fayd fyr;
25, for to; And bycaufe thou; 30, hole and founde; fyr P. that as;
34, fyr T.; am I.

570. 2, by lykelyhode; 4, is now; 7, toke his armure & rode;
9, after fyr P.; 20, [Allas]; 22, fayd fyr L.; 28, euer now & than.

𝕭ook ri.

571. 1, of fyr T.; 6, on; 9, Kynge A.; 14, fyt in that fyege /
is yet; 16, [ther]; 17, whan the; 19, tyl vpon; 20, the brydge;
23, ye are welcome; 28, [and dayes]; 31, G. hathe done.

572. 5, in thofe paynes; called one of; 6, in that; well fyue;
8, tyme that yᵉ; 12, fayd vnto; 13, landynge & prayfynge; 14,
almyghty god; 16, vnto god; and alle; [both]; 17, god / and
fayd; 21, do it; 35, fyr L.; 36, name is fyr Pelles / kynge.

573. 1, nygh cofyn; 2, [And]; 4, at the; in her byll; 6, as
though all; 8, there came; 13, kynge Pelles; 15, ye well; 16,
whiche ye; kynge P.; 17, full fayne; 19, dame E.; 24, came there;
whiche was called; 25, vnto kynge P.; 26, well that; 27, ye muſt
werke; by my; 28, for to lye; doughter E.; 29, O the mooſt fayre
lady; 30, kynge P.; 31, this dame.

574. 1, lady quene Gueneuer; 3, that fame; 4, this dame; 5,
his doughter E.; to that; [vnto the caſtel of Cafe]; 8, vnto hym
femynge; 13, And as foone as; 14, fo madde; 16, that the lady
E.; 17, was the; dame E.; 19, that the; 21, vnto fyxe of the
clocke on the morowe; 27, fayd he; 28, am I.

575. 3, A thou; thou thus; 4, ſhe anfwered & fayd; 8, a wyfe;
9, may·not put this blame to you but to her that; 12, for her; 13,
foo deceyued; 15, yonge lady dame E.; 20, [and]; whiche; 25,
And as foone as her tyme; 29, fonte ſtone; 32, [the] whiche; 34,
that he myght wedde her; 35, vpon a; 37, fayd ſhe.

576. 6, brydge; 7, to you; 13, hors tayle; lyke as an; 18,
vnto the grounde; began for; 22 as a; 26, dame E.; 28, moche
where; 30, ye not; for all this; 32, me fore; the chylde that ſhe
had in; 34, dame E.; 35, vnto god that the childe myght.

577. 1, there came; 2, her byll; 3, And anone there; 4, yᵗ bare
the; 6, and alfo ſhall; 11, vanyffhed awaye; 12, may well be
called; 14, trouth; kynge P.; 15, here come; 17, late ago; 18,
to wete; 28, kynge P.; for to be; 31, whiche was; 34, to bedde

in to ; 35, aboute y^t ; But whan ; 36, he made all the people to
auoyde ; 38, fo [he] layde ; [doune].

578. 1, whiche he ; 2, whiche came ; And fo ; 7, [there] ; all
armed ; 8, drawen in ; 9, fayd to fyr B. ; 10, fayd fyr B. ; 12, fo at ;
13, hym alwayes ; [that] ; to a ; 14, went ; there refted ; 15, refted
hym ; 16, a newe ; 20, and the ; 21, fmote hym fo fore that he fell
downe ; to fyr B. ; 22, fayd that knight ; 24, that at ; for to be ;
25, as [a] pryfoner and ouercomen ; 28, for to refte hȳ ; 30, dores
or ; 31, he had grete meruayle of it ; there fell many.

579. 1, [all] ; 4, of his lorde kynge ; 9, [alle] ; 11, grete adders ;
14, to go ; 17, doue that euer he fawe / with ; 20, all y^e ; 21, four
fayre ; that bare foure tapers ; 23, fame fpere ; 25, vnto fir ; ye
vnto ; 28, that he ; 30, that of ; 32, in thefe.

580. 7, [for] ; 8, wente ; 10, rode vnto ; 13, fyr L. ; 14, fayre
E. ; 15, vnto fyr L. ; 27, for to ; vnto ; 33, befeen than fhe was.

581. 4, was [fene] ; 9, was fore afhamed ; 11, not fe her / nor
yet fpeke ; 14, that fyr L. ; to her ; 16, well that ; dame E. ; 17, her
gentylwoman ; 18, nerehande fleeth me ; 22, dame E. ; 27, nygh
vnto her ; 28, quene had ; 35, fyr L.

582. 2, vnto your ; 7, came vnto ; 8, be ye a flepe ; 12, toke
his ; 13, vnto her ; 14, them in the ; 19, her gentylwomen ; 21, agayne
vnto the ; all how fhe had fpedde ; 22, [fals] ; 29, in his.

583. 9, therwithall ; 11, [alle] ; 18, and vnto ; [fayr] ; 19, [lady]
dame E. ; herd quene G. ; 21, at the ; 26, for to loue ; 27, hym
aboue all other ; all this ; that hath ; 29, and a caufe ; 30, hath ;
33, I warne and charge you dame E. fayd the quene / that whan.

584. 7, fayd [the] ; 9, there abyde ; 11, a grete ; 13, bay
wyndowe extraught out ; 15, Elayne / I can not tell you ; 19, grete
rebuke ; 20, grounde ; 22, forowfulleft grone ; 23, ony man ; 25, ye
may ; vnto ; 26, an hete ; 27, [euer] ; 29, fayd dame E. ; may [do] ;
30, [and wete] ; 31, or as ; a good caufe I haue ; 33, fayd dame E. ;
34, I fere me y^t I fhall neuer fe hym.

585. 6, fhe began to wepe ; as fhe had ben ; Fy vpon ; [de
ganys] ; 10, leder of vs all ; 15, fyr E. ; fyr L. ; 17, groūde ; a
deedly ; 18, was comen to herfelfe agayn ; 19, her handes ; 21, wote
well ; 27, and in wayes ; as well bothe at ; 28, and enquyre.

586. 1, So than at ; 4, be ye goynge ; 5, fyr M. ; 12, was comen
vnto ; 23, he [there] ; 28, whiche ; 30, fayd vnto them ; 34, bothe
her ; fyr A. ; 36, not abyde here.

587. 1, [thenne] fayd fhe ; 2, [thenne] ; 5, manfully ; 8, whiche
of ; 12, As foone as fhe came agayne to her felfe ; 13, ynough for
them ; [foo] ; 22, vnto ye fquyer ; 23, than that he had anfwered ; 24,
fyr A. ; 26, an euyl ; 28, and to flee ; 29, they pulled ; 33, and [they].

588. 7, and lyghtly; 8, fhall ye; 11, quyckly; 12, went; 14, [thow]; his lorde; 16, fyr G.; 18, fyr A.; 19, caufe faid fyr A.; 25, And than they; 26, two wylde; 27, fo within; 30, a lytel; had downe; 31, to the; 34, buryed; 36, but in no wyfe.

589. 4, fyr A.; for thou; 8, not fayd fyr P.; 9, fo they rode tyll; 10, they came; 12, of ftone; 13, bandes; 19, & that I; 20, [euer]; 25, drewe; 27, and went; 29, [one]; 31, [euer]; 36, vndernethe; 38, vpon.

590. 2, [euer]; 3, he myght fynde; 4, in a Toure; 8, yf that; [my]; 10, hym the beft; 11, chere that he coude deuyfe all; 13, how [that]; 15, bydde my brother that he; for tell hym I am; 16, for to; 19, and [to]; truft vnto; 22, daye whan I; telle them that; 23, fee that; 30, is now; 34, ye were; 35, [they] did.

591. 1, of yours; 2, vnlykely; 5, [And]; 10, they mette; 13, [we]; to; 16, with theyr [noble]; 19, [ryghte]; 21, vpon; 23, a well fyghtynge [knyghte]; 26, a lytell; 28, the of gentylnes; 29, fayd the other; neuer before; 30, neuer no maner of; the whiche; woūded and hurte me fo daungeroufly; 31, of the roūde; 35, that haue; 36, for to; 37, [with your handes].

592. 2, vnto a; 5, [that] ye haue flayne me; 6, he wyll; 9, vnnethes I may; 14, god; that was at; 18, who [that]; holy veffell; 19, of that; 20, [al]; were bothe; 21, lymme and hyde; 22, vnto almyghty god ryght deuoutly; 26, is a parte; 32, amended it as.

593. 1, [longe]; haue knowynge. ❡ Here endeth the . xj . booke of this prefent volume . And here after foloweth the . xij . booke.

𝔅ook rij.

593. 4, a lytell of fyr E.; 5, [of]; 7, which; 10, faue his fherte; And thus; 11, in to a; 12, [by]; 14, there lened agaynft a tree; 17, gaue with; 21, bothe the; 23, for helpe; 25, menyuer; 27, good frende; 28, haft; 29, not [to]; nygh me.

594. 5, come [fo]; 6, [Thenne]; vnto hym; 9, groūde; as though; 10, braft out at; [the] nofe / and eres; 12, there he crepte in to; and in that bedde there; 13, and lyghtly fhe; 14, on the; 15, as though; 18, where yᵉ madde man was; 20, is no; 28, fyr B.; 29, thou in all hafte on; 34, and came.

595. 3, vntyll; 7, Thus fyr L. was; 12, was fyr; 15, theyr fwerdes; 23, his cheynes; and from his; 24, hurte fore bothe his; 30, [there].

596. 1, he was fory; that he had bounde hym; 4, halfe a;

5, in a mornynge ; 8, bothe on ; & [fome] on ; 9, And at the laft fyr L. ; 11, bounde to ; 13, vnto ; 15, vnto a ; 17, hym fodeynly and roue ; 18, of fyr L.'s hors ; fyr L. ; 20, the huckle bone ; 21, gate hym on ; 22, drewe out ; 23, and whan he fawe ; 24, came vnto ; 25, [home] ; 28, And than the ; 29, ouertake ; 30, than no ; 32, me ryght ; 35, waye faft / and in his waye he.

597. 5, full grete ; 9, to the ; 13, of [his] ; and wexed ; 15, in to the ; 16, had borne ; 21, [ouer] ; 22, neuer more ; 23, theyr legges / and fome theyr ; 25, for to refcowe ; 28, they all ; 29, vnto his ; 31, there were [but] fewe or none that wolde ; 33, whofe name ; 34, & [fo] he ; kynge his vncle for to.

598. 2, [fyr] C. ; 3, And fo fyr ; 11, for to ; 15, where as ; whan dame E. ; 17, [alle] ; 18, downe to ; 19, [thus] ; 20, went ; 21, vnto her ; 22, hymfelfe ; 26, fporte me ; 27, byleue it ; fayd fhe ; 28, that he fholde be dyftraught ; 29, fayd kynge P. ; 30, vnto hym ; 38, after [the].

599. 1, kynge Pelles ; all the ; 3, all this ; vpon ; 5, where as ; 7, & vncouered ; 8, was all ; 9, [that he] ; 12, & dame E. ; 13, and thus he fayd . O good lorde Iefu ; 15, how [that] ; 16, man / all out ; 17, ye haue ; 18, tyll that ; 19, welle fyde ; 21, fo ye ; 26, kepe it fecrete and ; 29, [for] to ; out of the countree of ; 30, than a ; 31, euer [that] ; 32, Fayre lady E. ; 34, well how ; 35, [that] ; vpon you ; 36, on the morowe ; 37, me [for].

600. 8, & that my ; 13, [alle] ; vnto her ; 19, greteft ; and alfo ye ; 21, of the noble knyght fyr L. ; 27, as moche to faye ; 28, [euer] ; 32, [here] ; 33, ye well ; 35, afked ; [of] mercy ; 36, as longe as.

601. 2, enclofed with ; 12, on a ; as though ; 13, all to breke ; 14, fyxe myle ; 16, loke that thou ; 17, all the knyghtes that ben there / that ; in [the] ; 18, that his ; 19, all knyghtes ; 22, drewe many ; 25, dyd fuche dedes ; 26, frenffhe booke ; 27, [all the] ; yet there ; 31, fo as ; fayre caftel ; 32, in to it ; 33, none fynde ; 34, that other ; vpon her.

602. 1, afked her who ; 2, fayd the lady ; 3, is dame ; 5, well faye now ; 12, the damoyfell / ye ; 14, that fhall ; 16, vnto ; 17, vntyll I knowe ; maner [a] of ; 20, E. de Marys ; [and] here ; 21, fyr P. paffed ; 22, vnto ; fayd to the ; vnto the ; 23, that here ; 25, there ye fhall fynde ; 30, groūde ; And than ; drewe out theyr fwerdes ; 32, two wylde ; 34, [there] ; 36, knyght as ye are ; 38, you as ye are a.

603. 2, whiche ; 5, that are ; rounde table ; 6, felowe in kynge A.'s courte ; 10, [thenne] ; fayd vnto hym ; 12, your ryght name ; fyr L. anfwered & fayd ; 14, Benwycke ; 15, by [the] quene G. ;

17, [yonder]; 18, Now fyr I praye you for; 23, had grete; 24, there fhe; 25, the greteft chere that fhe coude deuyfe; 27, was there.

604. 1, we of; in [the]; 2, fayre lady; 3, we vnto; 4, whiche; 6, fo as they rode thus; of kynge B.; 10, thofe two; 12, morowe after; 15, A.'s courte; 18, hym vnto; 22, within fhorte fpace after theyr departyng they; 24, was fyr; 25, make hym; 27, turne vnto; 29, came vnto; 35, may ryght well; 36, wolde neuer.

605. 5, vnto; 6, vnto the; 18, but he; 26, began to tell of all the aduentures how; al the tyme; 28, mal fet / as moche to faye; 31, fhe wolde; 32, Than afterwarde; grete ioye.

606. 3, haue founde; 4, And fo the kynge helde hym ftyll and fpake; 13, [thus]; 19, yere and more; 21, of the Sancgreall; 23, fayd la beale I.; 26, vnto; 29, la beale I.; 30, ye are.

607. 1, ye whiche; 3, [all] the; 5, his worfhyp; 14, myfelf alone; 18, at his lady la beale I.; 21, had almooft; 26, neuer yet; 27, y^t myght; 30, therwithall; 32, in an; 34, fyr P.

608. 1, his grete; 6, wylte; 8, thy malyce; fyr P.; 10, the difhonour; 12, that I knowe; 14, well thy; 16, afke you; 17, the cafe; 18, at all poyntes; 23, Wyte thou well fyr P.; 25, fyr P.; 29, wylte not; 30, is chryftened [many a daye]; 32, whiche; 34, but one; 35, be chriftened.

609. 2, ony lenger; 3, whiche; 5, fyr P.; 7, on a; 8, he full; 9, that ye wyl tell; fayd he; 10, rounde table; 13, ye fe that; 16, fyr G.; 17, requyre you; 20, brother vnto; 24, or elles I hym; 25, or [euer]; 26, your grete; 28, fyr G.; 32, yet as well as; 38, And than.

610. 1, drewe; 2, [al]; 4, Than they; 5, [to gyders] that one vpon that other; lyke two noble; 6, whiche; but alwaye; 13, [woode]; 14, and than he; 15, groûde; 17, fyr P.; paffynge fore; & alwaye; 22, fyr T. had flayne hym; 23, fyr P.; a full; 24, fyr P.; 25, at a; me a daye; 26, no good; 29, Than fpake fyr P. and fayd vnto fyr T. . As for to; 30, ony more; 31, fyr P.; that I haue done vnto; 32, but and yf it pleafe you we may; 33, Ifoude / kynge Markes wyfe; 34, dare well.

611. 1, her and bycaufe of her I; 3, whiche; 5, greuous & fadde; 6, well fay; no man; of fo grete a myghte and ftrengthe; 7, were the noble knyght; 8, lord fyr T.; 9, [fame]; 10, vnto; I wyll be clene; 11, [now]; we wyll; 12, all togyder; of my lorde kynge A.; fo that we may be; 13, of Pentecoft; 14, ye haue fayd; fhall it be done; your euyll; 16, Suffrygan; whiche; 18, came afore; 19, cõmaunded to fyll a grete; 24, were kepynge a courte ryall of the mooft noble knyghtes of all the worlde; 25, table were there at

that tyme; 27, fyr G.; 28, the noble; 30, towarde Ioyous garde;
¶ . . . . whiche was drawen; here after fhall folowe; is called.

612. therfor vpon all; bleffid lord Iefu haue thou mercy / that
by the vertue of thy bytter paffyon our fynnes may be forgyuen vs .
And at the laft day of our iudgemēt / that we may come to thyne
euerlaftynge kyngdome in heuen . Amen.

Book xiij.

612. 3, they all herde; & than all the tables were couered /
redy to fet theron the meet; 8, And than the kynge fayd; blyffe
you; 9, fhewe; may ye; 10, kynge A.; fyr L.; 12, [on] wᵗ me; 13,
that fhe; 14, what is your wyll; fyr L.; 15, knowe and vnderftande;
16, I fhall; 17, to fadell; his armure; 18, vnto fyr; 26, he fawe;
27, to open the; 31, ware lyenge.

613*. 4, Soo god; 5, hath brought; 6, as they ftode thus; 7,
whiche; 10, fayd the ladyes; 11, for to; 13, behelde yᵗ; 14, fawe
he was; 23, fayleth hym not; 25, of my lorde; 28, vnderne.

614*. 2, that fayd; 4, they all; a full; 11, that none; 18, faye
trouth fayd kynge A.; 20, [fo] that; 23, kyng A.; 25, than fayd
the kynge; 28, as it had ben; 29, and a ryche; 32, he by whome
I; 34, thefe; 35, that ye be.

615. 1, to it; belongeth not; 2, for to; 7, my fayre; 8, ye
ones; fayd he; [good]; 11, therwithall; kynge A. vnto fyr G.;
17, fayd fyr G.; 18, kynge A.; 19, And than he badde fyr P.;
21, therwithall; vpon the; 22, at it; not ones; 23, no moo; 25,
kyng A.; 26, alle the knyghtes; 27, the yonge; 28, no knyghtes;
31, but for all that / the hall; 32, they were all.

616. 2, that knewe; 7, that is of; 9, wherfore; 15, fyne ermynes;
16, olde man; 17, folowe after me; 19, olde man; [thus]; 20, fyr
G. the good knyght; 21, old man; 23, for ye haue; 25, Pechere;
26, vnto them; that I fhall; 33, none but that he were.

617. 1, fyr B.; 4, had greate; 6, that he; 8, vpon kynge;
9, lye [by]; fyr G.; 12, knyghtes of the roūde table; 13, went;
14, fyr G.; 18, [ryght]; hath; 21, vnto the; 27, to; 31, furete.

618. 2, in to yᵉ fcawberde; 4, vnto you; 5, was belongynge
vnto; 9, fyr B.; 11, all the other; 13, and fhe; 14, [that]; 15,
fyr L. anfwered; 16, [with]; [how]; doynges ben; 17, to daye;
mornynge; fyr L.; 19, now [he]; 20, be openly proued a lyer;
one now; 22, fet [to]; 25, fyr L.; 27, yet are; 30, tell you; 32,
And fo the damoyfell toke her leue &; 34, rounde table.

619. 5, longed to; 6, all the meanynge of [for this entent];

7, fyr G. ; 9, they all ; 13, for to take ; 14, And fo he dyd ; 16, in the ; there he began ; 18, and exceded all ; 22, quene Gueneuer ; 23, And whan ; 25, it is no ; 32, well faye that ; 33, of all the ; the eftates ; 34, Camelot mynftre ; And foo after that they wente to fouper.

620. 1, *wholly omitted ;* 4, to ryue ; 9, [afore] ; knyght that ; 11, on other ; dombe ; 19, vnto god ; his [good] ; 20, kynge A. ; ought gretly ; 21, Iefu Chryft ; 26, ony lenger ; 33, & auowed the fame ; 34, *wholly omitted ;* 35, And anone ; 36, gaynfay.

621. 5, for there ; many dye ; 10, in to his eyen & fayd ; 11, fyr G. fyr G. ; 13, more here ; 20, is to me grete ; 22, [ther] y^t no tongue myght ; 26, bycaufe thofe knyghtes fholde departe ; 30, that haue.

622. 1, [and] ; theyr ladyes ; 2, fyr G. ; 4, fyr L. ; 7, [of the world] ; 8, and fo therfore ; 10, Than was ; 11, fayd vnto the quene / Madame in as moche as ye knowe it of a certaynte ; 14, fyr G. ; 16, he refted hym ; daye lyght ; 18, wente he ; fyr G. ; & vnto ; 19, kynge A. ; fayd agayn ; 20, fyr G. fyr G. ; 24, thou wylte ; 29, that there ; 31, to the ; fyr L. ; fyr G. ; 33, were all ; 37, had taken ; ye Sancgreall.

623*. 1, by [the] ; 2, rounde table ; 5, [and helde her] ; 6, fo that ; apperceyue ; 7, went in to the ; 8, O fyr Launcelot ; 9, to [the] ; 10, fayd fyr L. / I praye ; 13, [he] be to you ; 15, vpon ; 20, lord of that caftel ; 26, beft lyked ; 27, fyr G. ; fo he ; 30, to a ; 31, he was ; 32, of two ; rounde table ; 33, and that other was ; 34, vnto hym ; 35, to fouper.

624. 1, fayd they it ; 3, but yf ; or els ; 5, this ftrauge ; 6, 8, fyr G. ; kynge B. ; 8, I agree ; 9, [me] ; 10, 16, kynge B. ; 15, and therfore ; 17, the beft ; 19, fyr G. ; it wyl ; you [to] ; 20, ye knowe ; [that] ; you here ; fyr G. ; 21, [good] ; 22, the whiche fholde brynge ; 23, a two ; in a ; 24, [And] ; a goodly ; 26, in the ; 27, kynge B. ; 29, and threfte hym ; 37, from me.

625. 1, nor [for] ; 5, to no ; vnto fyr ; 6, kynge B. ; afked hym ; 7, I am fore woūded fayd he / & full harde ; 8, to an ; 10, and his wounde was loked vnto ; 14, king B. ; 16, fyr G. ; 17, his armure ; 19, to god ; 20, 23, 25, fyr G. ; 21, that fhall ; 22, fyr V. ; 27, . xxx . yere ; that toke ; 28, [hooly] ; and at ; 30, vnto a ; 31, came vnto.

626. 1, the whiche ; 2, vpon a ; 4, vnto ; that he ; 6, [there] ; 7, vnto the ; 11, Tollome ; kynge E. ; 13, and than anone ; 14, vpon ; 16, fmytten of ; he bare ; 18, & touche ; 22, than was ; 25, or not ; 26, whiche at.

627. 1, deth bedde ; 2, made grete ; 4, thou fhalte [departe] ; 5, [of yours] ; on the ; 6, ryght gladly fayd Iofeph ; the fheelde ;

7, in to yᵉ; 11, but that; 13, no man; 14, fyr G.; 15, fhall haue it; 16, the whiche; 25, fyr G.; befought hym; 26, tyll that; 27, wyll ye; 28, hygh ordre; 29, vpon me; And fo; and than they; 31, full grete; 33, where as was; 34, fayd he I deme.

628. 1, fyr G.; 6, nere me; 7, fyr G.; 8, but quyckly; 9, lepe out therof; 12, voyce that fayd; [enuyronne]; 13, hurte the; 16, curfed body; 20, [in the Tombe]; [for]; 21, hardnes; 26, was but; 27, fyr G.; 28, all that; on the; 33, fyr G.; [that]; 34, vpon you; 37, me [a]; 38, fyr G.; Than fayd fyr M.

629. 2, graunte you fayd fyr G.; 7, vnto a; on that; 9, for to; 10, that thou goo not; 13, not there; 14, fyr M. vnto fyr G.; 17, 19, fyr G.; 18, Nay I pray; 21, fyr M. rode; 30, come; 32, defende.

630. 5, A fyr M.; 7, that other; 8, he fayd . Sir; 10, fyr G.; 13, fyr M.; 16, And fyr; 18, 20, fyr G.; of the leues; 20, [euer]; And than; 22, vnto the grounde; 25, of the; 30, it pleafeth god; 36, the fpace of.

631. 2, fyr G.; 3, in hand; 9, were fo; 11, of a true and good lyuer; 14, of the holy; for to be; 17–18, [and no knyʒtly dedes in worldly werkes]; 18, is the; 19, from fyr; 21, and thefe were; 22, holy knight fyr G.; 23, and the; doth fignyfye; 24, entyerly; fyr M.; withoute ony; 26, fyr G.; betoke; 28, fe you; good helth; fyr G.; 29, he toke; 32, that was; 33, alwayes wonte; or that he.

632. 4, fayd thus; [thow] now; vnto; 5, all the wycked; 7, Whan as; 10, the whiche hyghte; 12, 14, fyr G.; 16, knyght fayd the olde man / to returne; 17, fayd fyr; 18, his armures; 20, that fayd; 22, for to; here ouer this; fayd fyr; 23, And fo he departed; And than he; 24, fayd . Syr knyghte; 25, forbyd you that; 26, Fayre felowe fayd fyr G. I am comen [for]; 27, Syr fayd the fquyer; 28, fyr G.; 31, fawe fyr; 32, fyr G.; 33, they all for; 34, Than fyr.

633. 5, fyr G.; 6, vntyll; 8, the whiche fayd to hym; 10, ftrete; 11, & they fayd; 12, And than; came vnto; 14, here [to]; 15, and wycked cuftome; 16, fyr G.; 17, all thofe; 20, fayd fyr G.; And thā the gentylwoman; 21, rychely bounden; 22, ye this; 23, And whan; 24, there a; vnto fyr; 27, whiche; 29, a ful fayre; 37, vpon a; 38, to me.

634. 4, yere tofore; 9, fyr G.; 10, [thefe]; 12, her yonger; 14, to do; vnto the dukes; 15, on the; 16, one vnto fyr; [that] fyr G.; 17, fyr G. and fyr V.; 18, And than he toke; 19, to god; 20, yᵉ hiftory; after that; was departed; 21, many dyuers; 22, fo at; vnto yᵉ; where as; 23, the very way; 24, for to folowe; vnto; 25, fyr M.; 26, had done; Truly; 27, all the; 32, he is blyffull; 33, ftode thus; 34, grete ioye.

635. 6, came vnto; 8, And than; banyfſhed; 12, one of yᵉ feuen; 20, and fro whens he came; 21, fayd he; 26, called hy̅; 27, fayd the good man; 28, you vnto; 32, ſo euer he gooth; 34, for truly; 36, by your two all alone; 37, yᵗ he.

636. 2, [Ihefu]; 3, whiche; 4, good knyght ſyr G.; 6, thraldome; 13, *wholly omitted;* 15, rounde table; 16, had rydden; 20, and ſpeketh; [we]; of the noble knyght ſyr G.; 22, vnto a; 24, but none of them bothe; vpon his ſone; 26, and ſyr; ſoo harde; 27, bothe hors; 29, and yf the ſwerde had not; 31, Theſe; were; 34, certaynly; ſyr L. and ſyr P.

637. 1, whan ſyr G.; 2, withall with the; 3, frowarde them; ſyr G.; 5, within a; 6, with an; vs aſke; 8, came vnto; 11, vnto a; 14, not well; 17, to a; he put of; 18, he wente vnto; 20, [clene]; 21, [clene]; 23, a greate; 25, came agayne; 26, and his; 30, bothe.

638. 3, And thus a greate; 5, but he coude ſe no; 8, ſyr L.; 9, vp ryght; 11, the holy; to me; 12, this greate maladye; vpon; and vpon; 15, this maladye; 17, agayne with the candelſtycke; ſyr L.; 18, it became; 20, 21, afterwarde; 21, vp ryght; 22, Than anone; 23, Certaynly; 24, ryght hertely / for; haue ryght greate; 25, whiche hath had neyther grace nor; 26, durynge the tyme that this holy veſſell hath ben here preſent; 27, that this ſame knight is defouled with ſome maner of deedly ſynne / wherof; 36, ſo they.

639. 1, hymſelfe vp ryght; 2, there ſeen; 3, he herde; 10, had more; 11, vnto his; 13, that his helme; was taken; 15, wretchedneſſe; 21, and alſo; 24, foules of the ayre; Than was he; 26, he well; 27, a wylde; 28, vnto an hygh mountayne / and there he; 29, to; 30, ſyr L.; vpon bothe his knees; [on]; 31, that he had done; ſyr L.; 32, the heremyte to hym and; his confeſſyon; 34, of the noble; 35, whiche; 36, and gretely magnyfyed . And now it is ſo / my; 37, and caytyfe of the world; Than the; 38, ſo ſore.

640. 6, with your; 9, ought for to gyue vnto god; 10, to you; 11, to god; 12, to drede; 15, and made full heuy chere; 16, tell me trouth; 19, whiche; 22, [and oute of meſure longe] many yeres; 32, the heremyte by his fayth that he wolde no more come in her company . Loke.

641. 1, here tofore; 2, [hand]; meruaylle therof; 3, that a; 7, more harder; 8, neyther by; 11, [of] grace; 13, for to; you [the]; 14, & hath gyuen you; ye haue; 15, all tymes; ye came; 16, you no; ye shall; 17, ye wyll or not; 18, bytterer; 21, I ſhall; 23, lorde Ieſu Chryſt; 25, coude not fynde one in all; 27, in the; 28, with leues; 32, neyther; 33, Certaynly; 37, enioyned.

642. 1, ſo he; prayed hym; ❡ Here leueth the ſtory; and ſo

endeth the . xiij . booke of this prefent volume. ❡ Here after the
. xiiij . booke whiche treateth of·the noble knyght fyr P. ; etc.

Book xiiij.

642. 8, G. his fone; 9, here aboue reherfed; 11, whiche;
12, and anone; 14, fayd he; 15, So whan; 16, made paffynge
grete; gretely fhe loued; 17, all other knyghtes of the worlde; for
fo of ryght fhe; 18, that the; fhold be; 19, fyr P.; 21, vnto.

643. 1, I was fomtyme called; 3, fo moche my; 4, grete pyte;
[that]; 5, fhe was; 6, ye ony; from your; 7, herde not of her in a
grete whyle; haue dremed; 8, Certaynly; 12, our lyfe; 15, fayd his
aunte; [this]; he oughte; 18, handes; 22, reforte vnto; 29, fuche
a; 30, that fholde; 33, do to the achyeuynge of; 37, and of.

644. 1, whiche herde; 3, fyt therin; [al]; 4, whiche; And
than; 6, vpon; 12, that is; 14, folowe after; 17, [there]; 21, And
after; 22, that was well clofed; 24, in to a; 25, full good; there
all; 26, a maffe; 35, were all.

645. 1, how his; 3, vnto our; 4, and fayd on hygh; 5, layde
hym; 6, for to; 8, vnto; 9, receyued it; and he; 16, that hyght;
17, alwayes; 18, vpon a; 20, tyll that; 23, whan; 24, may ones;
27, the knyght; 29, ye fhall openly fe that your; & or than;
31, aboute a thre; 34, [that] ye be; & knyght of.

646. 1, and knewe his; 2, made of hym; 5, that was [dedely];
6, and fayd / of; 8, grounde; 10, groūde; 14, [me]; 17, groūde;
19, for to; 20, or els; 23, fawe fir G.; had grete; 25, [And thēne
he]; 33, me or defyre me; 37, may I not; 38, hym you; ony
other man.

647. 1, in my lyfe fo; 4, ryghte well; 10, rydynge after; 12,
[fir]; 13, why [fyr]; that of me; fayd the yeman / that; hath taken
from; 14, me by; 15, fo euer he; 16, that I fholde do; 19, folowe;
how ye; 20, moūted vpon; 28, forth his.

648. 1, [grete] euyll; 8, yndly; fyr P.; 14, tyll; 15, that rored;
18, paffe ouer it; 19, the fygne; on his; 21, & makyng; 22, to
hym; 23, [the] whiche; 27, fawe he; 28, [the] whiche; 34, as
foone as.

649. 2, the mooft; 3, and there . . . . till; 4, [hym]; 7,
Whan fyr P.; 8, that / he; the whiche; 9, put of; 11, lyke a; 12,
hym with his hande vpon; and gaue thankynges vnto god; 14, hym
vnto the place that he came fro; 15, ftory; 16, he was; the whiche;
18, perfytely in almyghty god our fauyour and redemer Iefu Chryft;
19, more in confyderacyon; 20, the noble knyght fyr P.; 21, that

no; 22, hym nor peruerte hym out; for to endure and perfeuer; 27, there mette with hym two; 29, & that other; 35, who was her; 37, and wyſte not where ſhe became.

650. 3, to me; 4, fayd he; 7, [as he gat his pray]; 8, [Saye me for what cauſe ye ſlewe hym]; 9, well that; 10, a more; 16, faue ſyth; 17, And therfore; place ſomeuer; 20, his viſion; 25, at the border; 28, good man; 29, rounde table; 31, dureſſe and myſerye; neuer am I; 32, ye not; yf ye; 33, hygh ordre of knyghthode; and alſo of; 34, and ſholde be; nor myſtruſt that; ſholde hurte nor fere you.

651. 2, She that; 3, lyon (fayd the good man); 23, lyon that; 24, [and he ſtryked hym vpon the back]; 27, come; 31, was a; 32, was rychely beſeen; 34, in to this.

652. 4, And than; 5, fayd ſyr P.; who tolde; 6, [Now] Damoyſel fayd ſir P.; 10, [knyghte]; 12, ſhall ſommon; 13, [to fulfylle]; 14, [now]; 15, to a; 16, in to that; 18, was his; drowned; 21, lately; truly madame fayd he / I haue eten; 23, good & holy; 29, me this.

653. 4, taken from hym; 8, gete them; 9, And bycauſe I; 11, that is; 12, & yf ſhe; 16, to brynge; 21, meet ynough; 22, [ynough]; table moche meet; 23, And there was ſo grete plente that ſyr P. had grete meruayle therof; 25, as hym; withall; 29, his loue; And than; 30, for bycauſe; 31, [euer]; 32, chafed.

654. 1, ye fayre lady; 3, what ſomeuer ſhall; 4, that I mooſt deſyre; 9, vpon the; 12, on his; 13, withall; 15, cryed out; 16, [ne]; 17, that was nere; 18, in to the; 20, cryenge / that; 21, that all; 26, my good; 27, ſelf [a]; 28, that whiche; 29, whiche is my; 32, oryent come; 33, And than was.

655. 1, how he had done ſyth he departed from hym; 2, that lad me; 3, ſynne / & tolde hym all; 4, ye her not; [Syr] nay fayd he; 9, vpon the.

Book XV.

656. 1, Now whan; 11, fayd he; 12, [good man]; here deed; 14, a relygyous man; 18, & an; 19, ſo hardy; but that he wolde; 26, where as; 31, [the] whiche; 32, ſawe that; 33, vnkel [the].

657. 9, vpon a day; 12, for to haue; 13, no more; 14, preſerued hym; 15, [alle]; 16, man the; 21, in the fyre; 22, and yet was; on the; 24, ſkynne peryſſhed; 26, haue tolde you the trouth; 27, with an horrible; 31, countree fayd the good man; 33, may ye; 35, longe of; were ye.

658. 3, fayd ſyr; 4, on the; 5, Than fayd ſyr; 8, you ſkynne;

and gretely; 10, of the holy; 15, [thenne]; 16, fyr L.; 19, more nerer; 23, good herborowe; eafe you; 27, toke of; 28, to the; 29, he myght neuer agayn; 31, hym that he had a vyfyon . That hym thought there; 32, all be compaffed.

659. 1, [the] heuen; 2, Than fyr L.; 3, to heuen; 4, opened; & that an; 16, his helme; 17, And whan; 21, vnto; 22, had almooft; 24, & toke his hors; 30, fyr L.; 34, at a.

660. 1, Now fyr L.; 2, haue vnderftande; 3, this . After the; 7, a ryght holy; 10, Lyfyas; 12, [there]; 15, 22, [the] whiche; 19, that thou; 22, begate vpon; 24, an erthely fynner; 27, fyr L.; 34, [and to alle] vnto.

661. 1, fyr L.; 4, moche the; 7, praye thou onely vnto god; 10, that it greued; 19, theyr horfes; 20, all vpon; 21, wherof fyr L. meruayled gretly; 23, vnto the worfte; 24, [there]; 26, bothe hors; vnto; 30, doo fuche dedes; 32, to wery; wynne hym.

662. 1, that he; 3, all they; 6, and than; 9, forowe and fayd. Neuer; 10, [neuer]; but that; the better; 13, in defpayre; 15, he there; 17, to pafture; 18, fyr L.; 20, lyghtly turned; 22, he became; Than he armed hym and; 25, fyr L.; 26, bycaufe he; 28, what he wente; 31, he told her; 32, for to tell.

663. 1, fyr L.; 2, meruaylouft; 3, & the; 7, lord Iesu Chryft; 9, for to; 10, the good kynge; 12, clothed in; tell the; On the daye; 22, vnto that; 24, in the; 29, were foo; 31, vnto; 37, with the.

664. 9, vnto god; 12, toke the water; with a; 14, and without ony worde fpekynge; 15, paffed forth; he became.

Book xvi.

664. 23, and all that whyle coude he fynde; vpon a; 24, that fyr G.; 25, of them made; fo that; 26, they two talked vnto the other and.

665. 2, they all; 3, [haue]; 5, fyr P.; 6, nor of; [foure]; 7, no erthly; 9, and yf; four knyghtes; 11, yf [they] thofe knyghtes; 12, remenaunt of vs knyghtes of the rounde table to recouer it; [as] fyr E. and fyr G.; 13, vpon a; 14, was all to wafted and broken; that it femed; 16, & than thofe two knyghtes; and there they were in theyr; 17, And foone after they fet; 18, And fo as fyr E. and fyr G. fpak; 19, of other; 20, full ftraunge & meruaylous aduentures in dremynge . And fyrft of fyr G.; that he; 22, the whiche; 23, [al]; one of the thre; 27, Let vs go hens; 33, fyr G.

666. 1, fyr E.; 3, of one; 4, vnto the; 8, And than; 10, of that; 12, fro whens he came; thus alwaye flepyng fir E. dremed that he and his brother fyr L. rode vnto the tyme they came; 14, where at that tyme was; 15, that fayd; 17, a lytell; fyr G. & fyr E.; 18, out of theyr flepe; And eche of them; 19, fyr E.; 20; fyr L.; 22, the hande was; 23, the fame hande henge; [ryght]; 24, full clere; 25, than it; 26, where it became; there came; 27, fayd vnto them; full of; 29, come vnto; of the holy; 30, fyr G.; fyr E.; 31, haue herde; 33, that we; 34, fquyer that; 35, vpon a; fayre and cur-teyfly; 36, fyr G.; can ye; vnto ony; Here within a lytell; 37, is one fayd the fquyer; 38, on fote.

667. 2, in all this; 3, where as; well armed; 6, none that; [and] Now; 7, fyr E.; fyr G.; 9, eyther of them dreffed to other for to; 11, and theyr mayles; that one; than that; 12, fyr G.; 15, fadelles downe to the grounde; Than anone; 16, fyr G. arofe; vnto his; 18, for to; fyr G.; 21, here by; 22, fyr G.; 24, you the waye; Than fyr G.; 25, And fo fyr G. lepte vpon the fame hors behynde hym for; 26, longe they rode tyll they came vnto; where as; [wel]; 27, and maker; Than this knyght that was wounded to deth prayed fyr G.; 29, fyr G.; what maner knyght he was / and what was his name / as he knewe; 30, Than the hurte knyght anfwered; & haue ben; 31, thou and I were fworne; 32, and wyte ye well that my; 33, fyr V.; whiche; 34–35, and haue laboured in the queft of the Sancgreall / as thyfelfe fyr G. and many other knyghtes haue done . And my deth I praye to god that he wyll for-gyue it the . For now from hens forth it fhall be fayd / that the; etc.

668. 1, fyr G.; is thus; fyr V.; [moche]; 4, vnto; 5, and vnto all thofe of the rounde table; 6, for the; 7, fyr G. began; & in lyke wyfe dyd fyr E.; fyr V.; 9, foule departed; 11, his name to be wryten vpon his tombe; 12, So than; fyr G.; fyr E.; 13, they rode; 14, 15, vnto; 17, there was; where as; 18, he that; 19, he efpyed; 20, and full curteyfly; 21, fayd the heremyte; hath brought; fyr G.; 22, Syrs; 24, for to; 25, fyr G.; 26, whiche he had; fyr E.; 30, that ben; 31, at no tyme; 32, table ordeyned and founden; 34, be vaynquyffhed nor ouercomen; 35, that fhe; And at the.

669. 1, dyd ete; 2, fet and grounded; 3, And all thofe bulles; very proude; 5, grete fynnes and for theyr outragyous wyckedneffe; 6, is for to; 7, excepte; the whiche; 8, whyte bulles; 9, ony fpotte or wemme; 11, euer fythen; 12, all his offence; 13, And wherfore; by theyr; for bycaufe that they; 14, and in; no maner of pryde; 17, of the holy; withoute ony; 18, 19, in to the; 25, the heremyte N.; fyr E.; that fyr; 27, the whiche; 29, whiche is;

30, That is to meane ; 31, fro his ; fayd the heremyte / and hath ; 32, vnto ; [lowde] ; all his ; 33, veftyted and clothed ; 34, the whiche.

670. 3, vpon in ; flepe dremynge ; ❡ And alfo ; 5, that he ; 7, that men ; [hit] to ; 8, nyghe vnto ; 9, hym as he that ; 11, down for to drynke ; 13, And bycaufe he had ferued ; 17, and there fhall he ; 20, where as ; 22, not into ; 24, of our lord I. ; 27, of the holy ; 28, Certaynly ; fyr G. ; that fele I ; 32, [gladly].

671. 2, ye are ; 4, well faye ; 5, fyth that ; neuer flewe ; 6, tyll the tyme he come to ; 8, And were not that he is fo ; 9, lyke to ; fyr G. ; 10, well his ; 11, a full holy ; 13, fyr G. ; 14, wyll nothynge ; 17, thefe wordes ; to god ; 18, agayn fyr G. ; 19, [that] ye ; 22, vnto oure lorde ; 23, fyr G. ; 25, afore & ; 26, Than fyr G. ; 27, fyr E. ; 28, vnto a ; 31, fyr B. ; 32, vpon ; 33, knewe full well that.

672. 1, fyr B. / I am ; 7, [that] ; 8, fyr B. ; 10, bothe in to ; 13, wylte ete ; 14, fayd fyr B. ; 16, I well ; 21, fcarlot ; tyll that ; 24, therof / and felte ; 25, Helyne ; 29, ony leues ; 31, his byll ; 34, fyr B. ; 35, that the ; dyd not aryfe ; 36, and rode forth his ; So aboute ; tyme by.

673. 2, a lufty yonge ; and a fayre ; 4, to his fouper ; 6, of his ; 7, And fo he did as he was bydden ; 13, there came ; 16, Prydan ; 17, made grete ; 22, the whiche ; 23, I am ; 24, toke vnto her ; in kepynge ; 27, chace ; 28, to me ; 33, that fhe wyll haue.

674. 2, fyr P. ; 4, fyr B. ; 5, wolde he ; 8, And than ; 9, Hym thought there ; that one ; 10, as ony ; and that ; 12, Yf thou ; 15, and went awaye / And than ; 19, fhe departed ; 20, vnto a ; 22, lyke to lylyes ; 23, haue taken from the other her ; 24, that the one ; 25, came [oute] ; 28, groūde ; 31, fyr B. awaked ; 34, fyr B. her ; fo they ; 35, And anone.

675. 1, Than fyr B. ; his armure ; 2, for to take ; his refeccyon ; 5, fo departed ; 8, me grete ; 11, fhall withdrawe ; 12, that had ; [that] his ; 13, make all the landes to reioyfe ; 18, grounde ; 19, fet theyr ; 21, ranne downe by theyr ; more greter ; 22, [more] than ; fir P. ; 23, a full good ; 24, this fyr ; 27, backwarde ; 31, or elles ; 33, neuer more ; 34, fhall be towarde her ; fyr B.

676. 1, fyr B. vnto ; [tho] ; 2, that he ; 3, to her ; 7, [wel] ; 10, vnto an ; 11, vnto a ; 12, And on the ; 13, fyr B. ; 15, of [the] two ; 16, fyr L. ; 20, in more ; 21, all blody ; 22, [euer] ; 24, for to ; 25, loked on ; 31, where as ; 32, he came nygh her ; that he was a ; 33, haue had ; 34, to hym ; 35, ye are ; [in] ; 36, to the.

677. 1, whiche as I ; [that] ; you a knyght ; 3, fyr B. ; 4, that he wyft not ; 8, fayd all ; 10, fyr L. ; none of thefe ; 11, for our

ladyes fake ; 12, And fo he dreffed ; 13, ladde the ; to hym . Syr ;
14, leue your ; 15, was all ; 17, 21, fyr B. ; 19, fyr B. bete ; 22, of
hym at ; [fir] ; 24, I fhall gladly do it fayd fyr B. ; 26, there as ;
27, For yf I ; 29, foreft fayd fyr B. ; 30, not with ; 32, [not] ; had
taken from me ; 34, As fhe ftode thus.

678. 1, fyr B. ; made they ; 3, fyr B. ; 5, to god ; 6, So than ;
fyr L. ; 8, man whiche was ; vpon a ; 9, a beer ; 10, fayd fyr B. ;
11, a lytell fpace ago ; fyr B. ; 13, [for] ; 14, in a thycke ; 15, fyr L. ;
16, grounde ; 17, there a ; 19, he that ; 21, [lyghtely] ; 22, of the ;
23, vnto the ; the waye vnto ; 24, fayd the man ; 29, vnto ; & than
wyll we come hyther ; 30, fyr B. ; 31, you fayd fyr B. / that ye wyll
tell ; 33, whiche befell me ; fyr B. began ; 34, [foo moche].

679. 1, fayd the preeft / I fhall ; 4, the as ; 7, for to ; noo fere
ne for noo drede that ; 10, conquere the prayfe and the vaynglorye ;
11, yf thou ; fyr L. ; 15, full eafely ; 18, for to ; 19, he afked ; 22,
declaracyon ; 24, fyr B. ; 36, no more ; neyther for.

680. 1, lady of eftate ; 2, B. fayd they ; we all ; 4, lady whiche ;
6, was all ; 11, fyr B. ; 14, 17, [ryght] ; fir B. ; 19, [that] ; 21, fayd
fyr B. ; of wyfe ; 22, [hym] ; 26, A fayd fyr B. ; 27, vp in to ; 34,
Than fyr B. loked.

681. 3, within hym ; leuer than he had loft his foule / they ;
4, [than he his] ; And fo ; 5, vnto the ; that fodeyne chaunce ; was
ryght fore ; 6, full grete ; And with that ; 7, a full grete ; 10, he
dyd brynge ; 11, to heuen ; 13, forth his ; 16, he was ; 18, yf that ;
22, fyr B. ; 23, that he ; 29, rychely ferued ; 31, fyr B. ; 32, that
he was ; 35, in [the] ; a foule.

682. 6, lorde Iefu Chryft ; 10, it dooth ; ye toke ; 11, ye fhall ;
14, the whiche ; 17, but fhe is ryght fayre and beautefull ; 18, byrde
that ye fawe ; Sathan the feende of hell ; 19, [how] ; 21, in maner
and condycyon the very feruauntes ; 23, full euyll ; And whan ;
32, fyr L.

683. 3, [for] ; 11, vnto a ; 16, on the one ; 17, fyr B. ; 23, tyll
vpon ; 25, grete ioye ; 27, fyr L. ; fyr B. ; 33, ye haue ryght well ;
from henfforth.

684. 3, fyr L. ; 4, but dethe ; 5, [in] ; 7, Syr B. ; 8, for thou
arte ; 11, thou be ; at thyne ; 12, yf thou do fo ; vpon y^e ; as
thou ; 13, on ; 14, thyne ; that fynne ; I not ; 17, 18, fyr L. ; 19,
[fwete] ; 21, [to] fyr L. cared not ; 23, he wold ; Whan fyr L. ; 24,
otherwyfe do ; not ryfe ; 25, fyr B. ; 26, [fo] fore ; 28, fyr L. ; fro
his ; 29, for to ; 32, had he ; 34, fayd he ; vnto fyr ; 35, on me.

685. 2, one of ; 3, condycyoned ; Now fo god helpe me ; fyr
L. ; 5, Certaynly ; 7, fyr L. ; 9, went backward ; 12, [foo] ; that
fyr C. ; a knyghte of ; 13, as it was ; 15, how fyr L. ; 18, fyr B. ;

Syr L.; 20, fyr L.; 27, ony more; 28, fyr L.; he put; 30, Than
fyr; 33, fyr B.; 34, fyr C.; 35, fight; yf that fyr C. flee hȳ;
38, be his.

686. 1, for to haue; 2, on his; [hym]; tyll that; fyr C.; 3,
fyr L.; 4, and had; 5, fo that; fo moche; 10, Certaynly; fyr L.;
12, fyr B.; he arofe &; 16, cryed fyr C.; and fayd; 18, [it]; 19,
[for] to; 20, of his helme . Whan fyr C.; 21, Fayre lord Iefu
Chryft; 24, [here]; 25, fyr L.; 27, fyr C.; 29, goddes fake; 32, on
the; yf I may; 33, [hand] fayd fyr L.; fyr B.; 35, to daye.

687. 2, not gretely; 4, lorde god I befeche the; fome myracle;
6, fyr B.; 7, Than herde; fyr B.; 10, in the; 11, [two]; 12, fo
that; 14, fyr B.; 15, fore that god; 20, agaynft you; 21, [gladly];
25, vnto hym; 26, [in the myddes of]; on his; 28, And he rode;
29, vpon the; 30, there he; 33, was anone fo darke; 34, not fe
nor.

688. 2, [lye]; And than he; 4, was all; and [he]; 5, fyr B.;
do ye not knowe me; 6, Certaynly; 8, And than fyr P.; 9, made
of other; for to here; 10, fyr B.; how that; 12, [hand]; 13, in to;
16, but the good knyght fyr G.

𝕭ook 𝖗𝖛𝖎𝖏.

689. 1, As fayth; fyr G.; 2, fyr P.; 3, he rode; 4, foūde
there; 5, [the] whiche; 7, yᵗ he; 8, [wonder]; 9, within were; 10,
And whan; 12, put forth; 13, fell to; 15, dyd there; 16, meruayled
therof; fyr G.; 20, [the haute prynce]; 21, that wolde; 23, fyr G.;
25, fyr E.; 26, fyr G.; 27, loue bycaufe; 30, fyr G.; 31, that
ther; no man; 32, he became; fyr G.; 33, vnto fyr E. / the wordes
are true; fyr L.; 36, that is in; and certaynly.

690. 1, of a; fyr E.; 2, 3, fyr G.; 4, in to the; 6, fyr G.
and fyr E.; 7, 8, fyr G.; 10, And fo; 11, full glad whan; that
he; So whan; 13, 16, fyr G.; 15, that; 17, whiche; 18, Than
fyr; 19, 22, fyr G.; 25, So the damoyfell; myght gallop; 26,
that was; 27, that was clofed; 28, with [a]; hygh and ftronge; 29,
with fyr; 31, the damoyfell fayd to her lady. Madame; 32, all this
nyght; 33, dyned and flepte a lytel.

691. 1, and he were bothe; 2, fyr G.; fayre fheelde and a; 3,
and rode tyll; 4, fyr B.; fyr P.; 7, fayd the damoyfell; 10, bothe
receyued hym; 12, vnto a; 13, Than fyr G. toke of; 14, fhyppe
came; 16, [hard]; 17, fayd fyr; 19, comen hyther; 21, A fyr;
fir B.; yf that; 23, fholde lacke nothynge; fyr G.

692. 1, that am; 2, yᵗ ye; 4, in yᵉ fhyppe; 5, it wyll; in it;

6, fyr P. knewe ; 10, fyr G. ; 12, within ; they foūde it fo ; 14, fyr
G. ; 16, fcawberd ; 18, in it ; 24, it / fhall ; 28, he fhall ; 30, whiche
he ; 33, fyr P. ; 35, Syr B. ; 36, fyr G. ; as reed as.

693. 1, fcawberde ; 3, vnto the ; fayd fyr ; 4, fcawberd ; 7, vnto
all ; [al] onely vnto ; 30, fcawberde.

694. 1, whiche femed ; 3, poorely to accounte ; 5, He that ; 6,
yf that ; as I ; 10, to be ; 11, a quenes ; 14, fyr P. ; 18, neceffyte ;
I fhall be ; 19, vnto ; 20, fyr P. ; aboute a ; of our lorde ; 21, the
brother ; 22, than foure ; 24, in [to] the ; 25, it befell ; 26, and
therin ; 29, out of that ; 31, man fawe ; 32, 33, for to ; 38, of the
fwerde ; ouer this.

695. 4, was in ; 7, the one of the other ; 8, kynge M. ; 13, the
fcawberde ; 14, vpon the bedde ; 16, yf ye ; 20, O lord ; 25, fyr G. ;
in thefe ; 36, therwithall.

696. 1, [hym] ; 4, fyr G. ; 6, beddes hede ; two fayre ; 8, ony
blode ; 9, [thre] ; 15, that ; 16, And bycaufe ; 17, in to ye groūde ;
20, came vnto ; 23, that was ; whyte became as grene as ony ; 24,
oute ; 33, [and fee] ; that tyme that ; 37, and of ; 38, [dyuerfe].

697. 2, he difpleafed them ; 3, voyce anfwered ; 4, vnto ; 6, vnto
man ; 7, forowe or heuynes ; that fame ; 8, kynge Salomon ; 13, a
pure ; 14, as was ; 20, that fhe ; 26, and the beft ; 27, vnto ; 28, all
other ; 29, and alfo that fhall ; 33, take ye.

698. 3, [dyd] ; 5, for to ; 7, at the beddes fete ; 8, was the
kynge ; 10, fo bygge a ; 13, fhall neuer ; 17, fayd the carpenter ;
19, as the carpenter ; 22, well make ; 26, done full ; 27, they coude
not tell ; 32, [Now fhalle ye here a] ¶ Of the wonderful tale, etc. ;
33, king S. ; with a fmall ; 34, kyng S. was.

699. 4, in the hyltes ; 8, was fore ; 10, in to the ; and it ; 11,
of it ; 13, kynge S. ; 16, were acertayned ; 17, withoute ony ; 19,
they founde ; fyr P. ; 20, a wrytynge ; 21, fro whens ; 22, fyr G. ;
24, fayd fyr P. ; 35, well founde ; for truly ; 36, your techynge ben ;
37, vpon the ; 38, the thre felowes ; ryght name.

700. 3, 4, fcawberde ; 5, vnto fyr ; 8, fyr G. ; 9, that it ; 15,
Fayre damoyfell ; fyr G. ; 17, that other fhyppe ; 19, it happened ;
24, fir G. ; 26, they fpake ; 28, A.'s courte ; 29, ye are euyll
arryued ; 30, cheef fortreffe ; 33, be comen ; 34, fayd they ; 35, [in].

701. 2, fholde they dye ; 3, therwithall ; renne togyder ; 5, vpon
hym ; and in lyke wyfe ; fyr G. ; fyr B. ; 7, had lefte ; 8, they began ;
9, the knyghtes of the ; 10, ftrongeft ; folowed after ; 11, foo they ;
12, right / and ; So whan ; 13, whiche they ; 14, fyr B. ; 17, he
wyll ; 18, 23, fyr G. ; 23, put of ; 25, ben of the courte ; 27, yf ye
myght ; 28, worlde fhall ; ye neuer ; 29, fyr G. ; 32, [that] ; [lord]
the ; [not] ; 36, And bycaufe.

702. 2, to bete; 6, y^t they; 9, that our; 10, fir G.; 13, whiche; fyr G.; 14, had he neuer feen; 15, full tendyrly; 18, fyr G.; 19, it . Sir G.; 22, his helthe the; 23, fyr G.; 24, as he; [Ryght]; 25, fyr P.; 29, vnto a; 30, where as; 31, entred in; 32, vnto.

703. 4, other vnto; 5, thyrde vnto; 6, theyr fiege; where as; 8, that fayd thus; 9, in to the; of the; 10, was not; 11, grounde; 13, themfelfe; 16, ye are; 18, to whome; 19, vnto an; 30, in the; 31, that from; 33, on the; 34, vnto; 35, vnto a; 36, [them].

704. 5, fyr P.; place fo euer; 6, fhe is; oute of the caftell; 8, a gentylwoman; 12, fyr G.; 13, that of; 14, as longe as; fyr P.; 15, my fayth; 19, vnto; 21, came there; well· a; all armed; 22, vpon; 25, are the; doo ye; 27, 29, fyr G.; 30, And fyr G.; 32, whome that; wolde abyde; 33, but that they; 35, helde theyr; 36, there came.

705. 4, we are; 6, accorde therto; 8, fyr G.; 12, the trouth; 13, we haue; 14, other moo; 16, to a; 18, full of the; 20, her helth; 21, therwith; 22, fyr P.; 23, fyr G.; Certaynly; and yf; 26, vnto my; 29, than euer; 30, on the; 31, or not; All that; 34, was brought forth tofore her; [the] whiche.

706. 1, So anone there came one forth to; 3, vnto; 6, fyr G. fyr P. & fyr B. ftart; 7, her blode; 8, Than whan; 9, fyr P.; muft dye; 11, in to a; 13, vnto the; 15, fhall fyr G.; 16, So whan fyr B.; 17, he graūted; 18, voyce fayd; 20, vnto the; 22, hym / the; 29, vnto the; 30, lyghtnynge and reyne; 34, lorde god; 36, aferre; 37, vnto; 38, fyr G.

707. 6, *wholly omitted;* 7, [Now] the ftory faythe; fyr G. and fyr P.; 10, for to wete; betyde of them; 12, but that they ne were; 13, whiche; 19, eueryche of them; 22, fyr P.; fyr G.; 24, toke they; 26, The ftory fayth; fyr L.; 29, toke his; 32, he had; 33, a grete.

708. 2, his armure; 3, [foo]; 4, and oores; 5, mooft fweteft fauour; 7, [fwete]; 9, on the; 10, daye lyght; 12, fyr L. behelde her; 13, a wrytynge; wherin he found all the; 17, in lykewyfe fedde hym; 19, vpon a; 26, fyr L. went towarde hym; 27, Syr ye; 28, him his name; 29, fyr L,; 31, fyr L. / are ye fyr G.; 38, [to] them.

709. 1, And anone as fyr G.; 3, & that; 4, 9, fyr L.; 6, fyr G.; 9, tyll now; 11, fyr L. and fyr G.; 13, where as; 16, bycaufe thofe; 18, [therof]; [of alle tho aduentures]; 21, croffe of ftone; 24, vpon; 25, Syr G.; 26, lepe; 27, ryde where; 28, vnto hym full curteyfly; 29, vnto hym; [fwete]; 30, of our lorde; fyr L.; 31, vnto the; 34, my fone fyr; fyr L.; 35, vnto the father of heuen for to preferue.

710. 1, bothe you and me; fyr G.; 2, fyr G.; fyr L.; 5, vnto god; haue a fyght of the holy; 6, vpon a; 8, that opened; 13, [foo] armed; he went vnto; 14, the two; he fet; 15, came there fodeynly; that; hym vpon; 17, y^t fayd; 18, more in thy; 20, fyr L.; 22, that thou; 28, fyr L.; 32, moche for to; 34, that the.

711. 1, fyr L.; he wyfte; 4, my foule; here; 6, that whiche; 7, and with that there; 8, as though all; 10, vnto hym; fyr L.; 12, & was ryght heuy; one of them; 19, vnto fyr L.; there were; 22, fyr L.; 23, that the; 24, haue falle; 25, grounde; 26, he came; 28, foo he; 30, [hit]; 32, it all to brent; 33, groūde; [that].

712. 2, on; 3, day lyght; fyr L.; 4, [that]; 7, neyther ftande; 15, fyr L.; 16, as many; whiche [euer]; 17, lyke vnto a; 19, was better; 21, the greate; 24, can tell; & yf my fone had not; 27, as many nyghtes; how it was a; 34, of my.

713*. 1, [that]; 6, ye fe more of; 8, fyr L.; 10, achyeue; 14, fyr L.; 16, And thā; 17, whiche had; 18, 24, kynge Pelles; 19, 22, fyr L.; 20, kynge made; 25, on y^e; 28, that was there / and; of theyr; 29, chefe hall; than it was fo that; 35, that a; vnto; 36, knocked myghtyly.

714*. 1, [there]; 4, that hath; 5, Than was he wonders; 8, countree and realme; 9, fyr E.; vnto the noble knyght fyr L.; 10, kynge P.; [of] that; 11, fyr E.; 14, A lorde god; 15, fyr G.; 16, [to] me; 17, his courfer myght ren; 18, And than; 23, vnto god; 24, vnto an abbey; 25, he had grete chere; 28, lettres of gold; 29, ye whiche; 30, he not; 31, fyr L.; 32, yf it had; fyr G.; 34, domage to.

715*. 1, vnto; 2, as fyr G.; 4, to C.; 5, as he; and quene G.; 7, thre of them; that were fyr G. / fyr E. / and fyr L.; 8, other whiche; Than all; 9, And kynge A.; 10, [many]; fyr G.; 11, fyr L.; 13, fyr G. / fyr P. and fyr B.; 15, wolde god; 16, fyr L.; 18, *wholly omitted;* 19, that fyr G.; 20, vnto; 22, on the; 23, fyr G.; 24, [the] whiche; a longe; 25, Sir G.; 26, [fo]; 32, is fo taken; 33, was of deed oldnes; Whā fyr G.; 34, hym in his armes.

716*. 1, fayd kynge M.; 4, 8, fyr G.; 7, that; 14, that fyr L.; 16, But Iofeph of; 17, And there he founde; fyr L.; 20, it is a; 21, to an ende; 22, all the knyghtes; 23, fyr G.; 24, they lad hym; vnto a; 25, vpon a fteyres; 28, that hath; 32, [wynter]; fyfty yeres; for to; 33, 35, fir G.; 36, in to the.

717. 3, fyr P.; 5, vpon a; 7, at a; that rode; 9, eche; 10, other theyr aduentures; fyr B.; 11, there men; 15, them all; was there made; 16, he knewe well; 19, fyr B.; 20, yf [that]; foudred it agayne togyder; 21, 22, fyr P.; to fyr G.; 24, toke he; 28, vnto fir B.; a full.

718. 3, ſyr G. ; hyed fore to be ; 12, waye agayne ; Syr G. ; 14, & anguyſſhe as ye ſe / haue I ; 26, that ſayd ; 34, the droppes.

719. 1, the whiche ; 5, toke he ; 6, a wapher ; in the lykenes ; 11, vnto a ; 12, vnto ſyr G. ; 13, And than ; 14, as he was bydden / ſo he did [anone] ; ſayd he ye ; 26, to ſyr ; 27, ſo after ; 29, he ſayd ; 30, ſayd ſyr G. ; [will].

720. 1, vnto ; 3, where as ; 8, ſir G. ; 11, wyll I ; 14, ſyr G. ; 16, [after] ; bothe his ; 20, vnto a ; 22, that ſayd thus . Myne owne ; 25, lorde ſayd they ; vs ſoo [thy ſynners] ; 26, [wel] ; 30, ſyr G. vnto ; [that] ; 31, that ye wyl ſalewe ; 32, and all the felawſhyp of the ; 33, that yf ; in thoſe partyes ; 34, ſyr G. / ſyr P. and ſyr B.

721. 2, [of] before ; 6, paſſynge glad ; for to ; 8, and ſyr ; 9, vnto ; [that] he myght ; 10, And ſoo ; tyll at the laſt a ; 13, Syr P. ; 14, for to ; 15, ſyr G. ; 18, that whan ; 21, vnto ſyr G. ; 23, than he ; 26, 29, ſyr P. ; ſyr B. ; and ſyr ; 31, ſyt croked ; 32, 34, 37, ſyr G. ; 36, he ranne ; 37, there aroſe.

722. 3, ſyr P. ; 8, [whiche] ; 14, [that] ; 24, ſyr G. ; 25, for to ; 27, that couered ; 29, ſaye theyr deuocyons ; the ſame daye ; 30, after yᵗ ſyr G. ; 31, vnto ; 33, whiche had.

723. 2, ſakerynge of ; ſyr G. ; 3, vnto hym ; 4, that whiche ; 5, ſyr G. began ; ryght ſore ; 8, that whiche ; 9, good lorde ; 11, vnto ſyr ; 12, whome I am ; 14, [the] whiche ; 15, [that] ; 16, reſembled me in two ; One is that ; 17, And the other is in that ; 18, [haue ben and] ; 19, ſyr G. went to ſyr P. ; 25, vnto ; 27, his two ; 31, for to ; 32, ſyr P. and ſir B. ſawe ſyr G.

724. 1, was he ; 3, 8, 9, ſyr B. ; 4, bycauſe he ; 8, ſyr G. 12, by good ; 13, And than ; 14, where kynge A. ; made greate ; 15, demed all ; 17, kyng A. ; 19, ſyr B. ; 20, his two ; 21, was ſyr G. and ſyr P. [and hym ſelf] ; 22, Than ſyr L. ; 24, vnto ; 25, Syr G. ; [owne] ; 29, ſyr G. ; for to ; 30, this vnſtedfaſt ; 31, fall true ; ſyr L. ; 32, Than ſyr ; 35, me redy ; 36, whyle I haue lyfe ; 37, fayle you.

Book xviij.

725. 4, that alle the knyghtes ; 7, And ſpecyally ; 12, as the frenſſhe ; for to ; 15, in his ; 17, vnto god ; 18, vpon the ; 19, had done ; 20, [hand] ; 21, mooſt ſpecially ; 22, So it ; 24, whiche ; 27, alwayes as.

726. 3, to hym thus ; 8, haue in tyme paſt ; ſyr L. ; 11, my deſeruynge ; [that] my ; 15, ſone ſyr G. / ſyr P. / or ſir B. ; 19, that ſpeke ; 20, this place ; 23, and rydde ; 24, where as ; 32, [my pleaſyr] ; 36, ſo ſhe.

727. 2, [wel]; 4, of me; 5, fayd fhe; 7, charge; [this]; 8, wythin this courte; forbydde the; 13, forbydden; 19, whiche fore; 21, whiche fomtime; 22, whofe name; 23, Fayre cofyn fayd; 25, forbydden; 29, fyr L.; 31, I reft; 33, cofyn I; 37, with a; 38, [nor].

728. 1, but all onely; 2, of outwarde forowe; 3, nor yet; 4, the frenffhe; 7, in yͤ cite of; 12, [for]; 16, [fir] La; 18, fyr A.; 19, vnto; 21, [four and twenty]; 23, deynty meetes and deyntes; 29, of all; 34, that a good; 35, fyr P.

729. 1, toke one of the poyfoned apples; 2, [foo]; 7, fyr G.; 9, [wel]; 11, right fore; 15, vnto the vttermeft; And thervpon; 17, none of them; 18, [all]; 19, the dyner; fo fore; 20, *wholly omitted;* 21, fodeyne crye; vnto; 22, And meruayled gretely what it myght be; of theyr; and the fodeyne deth of the good knyghte fyr Patryce; 25, quene G.; 31, of her.

730. 2, whiche; 3, vnto; 7, praye you; 8, for to come vnto this; 14, [almyghty]; 17, a ryghtwyfe; 18, kynge A. I gyue you day this; 19, ye be; 21, may ye; 27, Than anfwered the quene; 28, nor; 32, that fore; 34, that ye go vnto fyr B. and praye hym to do that batayle for your; 36, ryght wel I perceyue fayd kynge A.; 37, thofe twenty; 38, you in felawfhyp togyder; was fo traytourfly flayn.

731. 3, I can not; 5, full foone; 6, on your; 7, kyng A.; who fomeuer hath; on his; 8, on; 19, nor yet; 20, haue ye; 22, [by]; I gretely; me how; 24, as ye; 32, to me; 33, kynge A.; 34, in a certaynte.

732. 3, me of; 12, come; 15, hertely / & fo departed; 17, Brafyas; 18, happely come; 21, fyr M.; yf he be; 23, fyr B.; 25, vnto the; 27, gretely difpleafed; 29, [all]; but that; 35, and the mooft; 36, alwaye.

733. 5, was alwayes; 6, alwaye fhe; 9, a grete; vnto; 13, fhe oughte hym; 14, the . xx . knyghtes; 15, well faye / that it was for good; 18, fome of vs; 20, not pleafed; 25, [for]; 28, do; 29, fayd fyr B.; 32, profytableft; 33, paft forth; 34, [maner of] the; 35, to the.

734. 3, & there was made a grete; 6, nor for; 7, ryghtwyfe; 11, quene G.; vnto; 13, contrary therto; 17, foone preue; 20, the fo; vnto almyghty god my maker; 21, thy malyce; 27, but that; 28, to mounte vpon; 29, M. de la porte; 30, a fpere; 34, where as; out of a; 35, armed at all poyntes.

735. 1, you to; 8, I can not fhewe you fayd; 11, vnto; 13, vnto the; 20, meruayled they; 26, ranne the one agaynft the other; 27, But fyr L.'s; 28, grounde; and had a; 29, and dreffed; 32, lyghtely from; 34, to batayle.

736. 1, many ſadde ; 3, they had bē two ; 4, a full ; 6, groūde ;
7, for to ; 8, therwithall ; 10, ryght fyerſly ; 13, grounde . And ;
14, for to haue ; from his ; 16, as an ouercomen knyght ; 17, [thy] ;
but onely ; 18, no maner of ; 21, clerely I ; 24, where as kynge ;
25, vnto ; other louyngly ; 26, vnto hym ; 27, And than the ; 28,
to reſt ; 30, that he was the noble knyght ; 32, by the hand.

737. 6, or in ; 7, kyng A. ; 8, you of youre ; 9, downe vpon
the ; 10, where as ſhe ; 17, in the ; 18, whiche was called ; 27, ſyr
P. ; 29, of yᵉ feeſt ; to the entent ; 31, to whome ; 33, [was].

738. 3, vpon yᵉ ; 12, forth vntyll ; daye the ; 13, kynge A. ;
24, not goo ; 26, [noble] ; 27, ſyr G. ; 28, vnto ; 30, that the ; 34,
paſſynge heuy and wrothe ; 36, which is.

739. 1, vnto her and thus ſhe ; 3, wyll ſaye ; 6, vnto ſyr ; 8, to
the quene ; 9, [madame] ; 10, as at ; 11, wyll I ; 13, vnto ; 14,
[ageynſte] all ; 15, quene G. ; 17, are many ; 18, for to ; 21, on
the ; 22, after brake ; 23, ſo departed ; ſo longe tyll ; 24, that now
is called ; 25, vnto an ; whiche ; 27, [dyd] walked ; 29, quod kynge ;
to all ; 30, were there ; in yonder ; 31, [now] ; wyll full well ; 32,
towarde whiche we ; 33, many meruaylous dedes of armes.

740. 3, So as ; 4, & in his chambre vnarmynge ; 5, vnto ; hym
reuerence ; 6, maner that he coude ; 9, is to moche ; 12, whiche
were ; 14, the ſame day that ; 16, ſyr L. ; 18, thoſe iuſtes ; wyghty ;
20, I beſeche you ; 23, you hertely ; 25, haue his ; 27, [that tyme]
the ; 29, frenſſhe booke ; 37, for by cauſe.

741. 1, of hers ; 7, neuer or this tyme ; [erſt] ; 8, damoyſell ;
9, it vntyl that ; 11, the fayre ; 13, in the mornynge ; 14, for the ;
17, for to ; 21, whiche now is called W. ; 23, there was ; 26, they
ſoiourned ; day the ; 27, began to blowe ; 31, yf ſyr ; 32, whan ſyr ;
34, of Scotlande ; 35, vpon kyng A.'s ſyde.

742. 4, this one ; 5, mooſt noble ; 10, [faſt] ; 14, Scotlande ;
17, and alſo ; 23, there came ; 26, le cueur ; 31, [thenne].

743. 3, on our ; 8, and ſyr G. ; 19, in the ; 20, wote well who
he ; [as] ; 23, but alway me ; 24, by cauſe he ; 25, yet bere ; 27,
[euer] ; 29, whiche ; 35, to hym.

744. 7, vnto the grounde ; 9, abode ſtyll ; 10, vpon ; 11,
Scotlande ; grounde ; 14, gate hym ; 15, bothe hors ; grounde ; 17,
began to drawe ; 18, [y] hurte ; 20, vpon ; grounde ; 23, ſyr A. ; by
that tyme ; 25, [all] ; 31, maner of wyſe ; 34, there lyenge ; 35,
after ; 37, ony man ; And alwaye ; 38, was with.

745. 1, ſmote [doune] ; 4, rounde table ; 5, vnto king ; 6, [he]
is ; 8, let blowe ; 9, to the knyght ; 22, [al] ; 26, ſayd he ; 28, it
almooſt ; 29, fayne helpe you ; 30, drawe ; 32, [alle] ; [ryght] ;
33, [al].

746. 2, [fo]; 3, I do now; 6, fyr L.; 8, whiche; [fulle]; 10, vnto; and hath; 11, his poſſeſſyons; 13, For alwaye; 18, vnto that; 21, ende of; [faſt]; me in; 24, whiche is; 25, ryght fore; 28, that was; And whan; 38, was fomtyme.

747. 3, where as the mooſt noble knyght fyr L. was; 6, alwaye; 14, hyde ye; 17, fyth that; for Chryſtes; 24, by that; 25, ryght well; and came to hymfelfe agayne; 26, as it is now in thefe; 33, and his; 34, was the.

748. 4, mooſt greteſt; 10, landes I haue; 13, or [knowe]; not wyte; 14, [man]; [good]; 20, he is; 21, without; 22, not beſtyre; 23, ſhall knowe; yf I may; 25, and rode vpon two hackneys; 26, But as he wente fo he; 28, to L.; 30, where as; was lodged; 31, for to take his reſt; 32, to hym; and alfo his fayre; for to; 33, tydynges he knewe; 35, whiche; 38, dare make it good.

749. 1, forty valyaunt; 2, and ryghte; 4, that good; 5, the whiche; man that euer after; 7, [fir]; 10, he came; 19, for to let; 21, yf it wyll pleafe you to; 22, vnto his; 27, a greate.

750. 17, [and]; 25, as ye thynke beſt; 26, ryght fore; 27, [Ryght]; 29, came vnto; 33, hym fayd; 34, to his.

751. 1, fyr L. meruayloufly; but what; 2, after hym for to; kynge A.; all his courte; 3, vnto all; was the noble knight fyr; 6, heuy & a forowfull; 9, for angre and wrath; 11, fayd vnto hym; 15, that he; is but; 16, befeche you; 17, fayd the quene; 19, grete turneymēt; 20, reed fleue; 22, that be of his; 25, Notwithſtand- ynge; 26, fayd fyr B. / faye; 28, quene G.; 29, meruayle it were.

752. 2, that; 5, the fayr mayde; 7, as fayre; 9, vnto hym; vnto her; 10, how fareth; 13, [that]; 14, vnto; 16, vnto the; 21, her to hym; 25, be full; 31, to angre; 34, to grete.

753. 6, came to; 10, warnynge therof; 12, [with whome he was]; 13, curteys knyghte; 16, vnto the; 19, wepte full; 21, vnto hym thus; 29, of all; where as; 33, or [my]; 34, ye are; 35, hertely welcome; ye fay ouermoche to pleafe me.

754. 1, [the] whiche I fought; 2, you eueurychone; 3, nyghe; was through; 5, not ben; 6, and frendſhip; 16, by his; whiche he; 24, whiche by no maner of; [not].

755. 1, that there; 5, ſtyll with; 7, Than they abode there almooſt; 10, vnto the father nor wyfe vnto her; 12, dyſpleafed; 15, for to; 17, at all poyntes; 19, he ſpurred; 22, So that; 23–24, and hym that was vpon hym / the whiche was the nobleſt knyght of the worlde / he ſtered hym vygoroufly / and he ſtyfly and ſtably kepte; 27, for to gete his; 31, helpe me; 32, vnto; 33, vnto the grounde; 34, meafure grete forowe; 35, and dole.

756. 3, bothe falfe; and why; 7, ryght wroth; he fayd to them . Let ; 8, in to the ; 11, of [hym] his body ; 16, for by caufe ; ftronge ynough ; 19, [hit] ; yf I ; 27, And than ; 29, I oughte.

757. 10, there prefent ; 16, of Scotlande ; 20, at the fame tyme fyr B. de G. ; 21, he had fmytten ; 30, maner of.

758. 4, yf that ; were ftrongly ; 5, ony man ; [the] lyfe ; 10, la blaunche ; 11, they were ; 12, fo on ; 14, and her two bretherne fyr T. & fyr L. ; 16, that ye ; 17, [Now] ; 18, for your ; 19, you vnto ; 20, yᵉ mayde E. ; 21, but certaynly ; be maryed ; 22, [man] ; 23, fholde I ; 26, fayr damoyfel ; 28, [yet] ; 34, fayre mayde ; 35, the damoyfell.

759. 4, doune to yᵉ groūde ; gentylwomen ; 5, made euer ; 10, vnto hym thus ; 11, do therto fayd ; 12, 15, me vnto ; 15, nor late ; 19, ryght well ; 22, fythen that ; 25, came to ; 29, And alfo ; 33, whiche made ; 35, And alwaye ; 36, aboute a ; fhe felte ; 37, fhroue.

760. 2, fayd fhe ; 5, is that ; 6, god vnto ; I neuer loued ; 10, for to haue ; 11, whiche I ; be an ; 12, fwete fauyour Iefu Chryft ; 13, [on the] ; 15, out of all ; 19, wolde endyte ; 21, fhe had ; 23, in to ; 27, where as ; 28, put in a ; 35, and all ; 36, put on ; 37, barge to ; 38, ony man.

761. 1, and [the] ; 3, in to the ; barge ; 4, it myght mene ; 6, Go ye ; vnto ; 7, fyr A. ; 8, thre ; 10, bedde that euer they fawe ; 11, ende of the ; 12, thre ; 13, had foūde ; 14, [foo] ; 16, went in ; 17, a fayre gentylwoman lyenge ; 20, the lettre ; 21, told the kynge therof ; it in his hande ; 22, I am ; 23, [So] than ; 24, And the kynge ; certayne men to wayte ; 28, it open ; 29, my lorde fyr L. ; 32, yet for my foule that ye praye ; 35, art a knyght peerles.

762. 1, of the ; 4, vnto hym ; 5, had herde ; 6, that I am ; 8, my wyll ; vnto her ; 15, or elles ; 17, whiche ; 22, kyng A. ; 27, wente ; 28, And on the ; rychely buryed ; 30, the roūde ; 31, And than whā all was done ; 33, for by caufe ; 36, forowe yᵗ I endure ye take ; 37, paffed forth.

763. 2, [foo] ; 3, the rounde table ; 4, vntyll ; [thenne] ; 5, there were ; that who fomeuer ; 8, all the ; 9, mooft was ; 12, [at] ; 13, to hym many of his ; aduyfed them ; 15, vnto ; 18, [and] ; 19, toke a partye ; 20, made [that] of the ; 21, [of the] & the Iuftes ; 22, full glad ; 23, maner that they coude ; 24, and whan he was comen fhe fayd to hȳ in this maner ; 26, For at ; 28, fo there ; 31, cloth of golde ; 34, [haue] ; 35, whofe name.

764. 1, to reft ; 2, eafe yᵗ ; 3, Whan fyr L. ; were redy they departed ; 5, And fo ; vnto ; 11, And alway ; 15, hoūdes ; 16, that this ; 20, for to ; 21, that the ; 23, hynde whan fhe ; 24, to yᵉ foyle ; hounde ; 25, faft after ; [veray] ; 26, there came the ; 27, whiche ;

by her hoūde; [that fhe had]; 30, [foo] by; 31, brode arowe; 33, whiche; 34, than whan; fayd vnto her; 35, bare thou; 36, made the.

765. 2, and our lorde; 5, now haue ye; 6, as well as he; 7, drewe; & the heed abode; 8, [he]; vnto; [more]; 10, fo hurte; 11, nor the heremyte wyft not; 15, fhedde at that tyme; 16, that fyr L.; 18, knyght that; 28, alfo broughte; 35, Scotlande.

766. 1, good knyghtes; 2, kynge Chalaunce; 5, whiche; 7, fet vpon; 8, vnto; 22, full ftronge; 23, of fyr; 27, fyr G.; 32, vnto them.

767. 6, grounde; And in lykewyfe; 11, groūde; 13, [and] fo; 17, where as; 21, kynge A.; 24, G. of Orkeney; 25, be harde; 30, fyr G. / and that anone; [al]; 31, to reft; 35, frenffhe boke; 37, as faft as he myght vnto fyr L.; fayd thus vnto hym.

768. 5, [noble]; 9, brake; 14, lay there; 20, hurled; 27, gretely whan; 32, that he had; 36, on; 38, ftrayte and ryght harde.

769. 2, almooft nyghte; 5, vnto kynge A.; 7, blode ben; me all; that they; 11, worfhypfullyer; 12, me alwaye; vpon payne; 13, is fyr L. hymfelfe; 21, my beft; 22, and yf he; 36, and gate hym a.

770. 2, kynge A.; 3, they anfwered with a; 4, were all; 7, wente; 15, alfo in lyke; 19, for to; 22, me to fe; 26, [more]; 27, for to; 28, in [a]; 30, man fhamed; 32, where as; 33, cowarde wyll; 34, knyght wyll; 35, were made; to kynges; 37, vnto his.

771. 10, in lyke; 13, [a] rafe; 17, & put awaye true; 26, vnto god; 28, feuen dayes; 34, lycorous.

Book rir.

772. 7, lufty May; 9, erly in; 10, the mornynge; 13, [outher in fylke outher in clothe]; 18, [the Senefchal]; 20, [le cure hardy]; [of the foreft faueage]; 21, & fyr P.; 22, [that was called the knyghte of the reed laundes]; 23, [the louer]; thofe; 24, on the morowe; 25, mayenge with yͤ quene; [in woodes and medowes as hit pleafyd hem]; 27, purpofed to haue ben; with the; 28, her pur-pofe at that tyme; 29, the whiche.

773. 3, he had; as yͤ frenffhe; 5, [for] by; 6, yf fyr L.; 8, that the; 12, they neuer; 16, hygh feeft; 18, that [there]; 19, in theyr ftedes that were; 27, [for] to; 28, the beft; 31, [moffes]; 33, well armed; 34, of areeft.

774. 2, thynkeft; [for]; 4, for to; 5, the hygh ordre of; 9, that I haue; 10, many yeres; 11, a vauntage; 12, [all]; [noble]; 13, all with one voyce & fayd; wete ye well; 16, grete auauntage; 17, on vs; 18, as leue; 19, otherwyſe; 20, ſyr M. ſayd; 24, [none]; 25, with theyr; 26, [ſyr Ladynas]; 28, ſyr P. / ſyr Ironſyde & ſyr P.; 30, [ten]; 31, [the boldeſt and]; 33, cryed and ſayd; 36, [not].

775. 1, ſyr M.; 2, my [owne]; 11, [their horſes]; 15, knowlege; 19, come and ſe me; and that he; 20, thou not; 21, And ſo yᵉ; 22, moūted vpon his; 23, from them as faſt as euer his hors myght renne; 24, ſawe the chylde; well that; 27, But the chylde went from; 28, vnto quene G.; ye be; 30, not lyghtly come.

776. 3, [that] in; to flee; 4, not to haue; 8, in her; the frenſſhe; that ſyr; 10, as he; 15, onely that; 20, there was none myght; 22, a poyntement; 23, and went with; 24, that that mooſt; [that]; 28, for to; 31, to me vnto the; where as; 32, yf I am; 34, he full; 35, and on alle.

777. 1, and as the frenſſhe; 3, for to; ouer the ryuer of; Lambeth; 4, [ſame]; where; 5, [noble]; 6, [that] he; trace; 7, vnto a; & therin; 8, to turne; 12, vpon thy fete; 20, ſyr L.; 21, ſayd ſawe; 23, whyle on fote; was he; with his armure / ſheelde and ſpere; 26, [for] to; 27, ryght ſore; 28, by [hym]; the whiche; 30, for to; 34, fayne ſpeke; 37, thought to; 38, and ſayd . Fayre.

778. 2, ſyr M. caſtell; 4, droue forth as faſt as he coude; 6, quene G.; 7, wyndowe waytynge; 10, to; And than the quene; 15, [Ha]; 17, haſt ben; in a cart; 18, lykened hym; 21, to ſuche; 23, vnto the gate of the; 26, thou falſe; 28, I ſhall; with the; 30, ere; brake; 32, was come; 33, to the quene and.

779. 1, ye myght well; 3, is done; 5, in to your; 6, ſyr M.; 7, [alle] in to; 10, and all your knyghtes and ladyes; to W.; 11, in to your; 12, than alway; 13, ſtryfe is made / the more; 15, whiche; for to; 16, he ſayd; forth here; 17, vnto hym; 18, wherfore aſke; 20, dyſpleaſed than; 25, peaſybly; handes; 28, ye are; 30, and full; [A]; 31, yf I; 33, to you; 35, I haue; 37, well that.

780. 1, bereth [the]; 4, [euer]; 6, ſo that ye; 9, to her; 11, knyghtes were; 12, ſo ſore wounded; 13, of his comynge; 16, had ſet; 18, the one vnto the other; 23, vnto our; 26, vnto a; in to a gardyn; 27, [y] barryd; 28, for to; 30, he forthwith; 32, the whiche; 34, let [ye].

781. 1, wounded were; 4, it was ſhewed vnto; [all]; 8, [by her chamber]; 9, they lacked; 15, perſone with me at this tyme; And than; 17, vnto a; where as; 21, of [many]; 22, myght come in vnto her; 26, for the loue of you; 27, [he]; 28, a grete; 30, of ſyr L.'s hande; 32, And ſo to paſſe forth; 33, went to; 34, and ſo he toke.

782. 1, and came to his; 8, And ſo forth; 11, ſyr L.'s hurte hande; And whan; 12, in hymſelf; 13, vnto; 16, it well that it was ; 19, lyege lorde ; 21, & that I wyll ; 23, to them ; 28, fyr M. faye nay with your ; 32, well that ; 34, demed that fholde hyde his ; in this.

783. 1, A ha / what ; 4, the whyles ; 5, fay and make good / that my ; 8, haue ye ; 11, it with ; 12, fyr L. ; 15, alfo what ; 18, batayle that is done ; 19, as vnto that ; 23, is a ; 26, to the ; 27, Vpon what day ; 30, muft do batayle ; I befeche ; 31, ye are ; 32, in the ; 34, of thofe condicyons ; vnto all ; 35, knewe me / I vfed ; [with] ; 36, to be in the ; vfed treafon ; 37, fyr M.

784. 1, ye all may ryde vnto ; 2, And than ; vnto ; 3, fetures ; 6, peryls leeft ; 7, is as ; But alwaye ; that dealeth ; 8, man ofte ; in to ; 9, And as ; 12, [ful of] vpon ; 13, made femblaunt as though he had not wyft ; 17, put out of the waye ; 19, paft forth ; 20, he had ; horfe lytters ; 23, many other ; wente to ; 24, tolde vnto ; fyr M. ; 26, batayle togyder ; 27, aferd that ; 34, Now returne we vnto ; 35, full grete ; 37, by her.

785. 2, come oute ; 4, defende it fayd ; 8, or feke or els in ; 10, [at] ; 11, or els ; 16, fhame (fayd fyr L.) ; 20, to ftronge herted ; 27, where as ; 29, [the] whiche ; 31, was there ; 32, he comaunded ; 33, to god.

786. 1, gallopynge ; 5, And therfore he ; for to ; 6, for to brynge ; [du lake] ; 9, good lord ; may well ; 11, fo that ; 13, now fayd ; 18, quene G. ; 20, but that ; 32, all them that were prefent ; 37, And fo than ; [els].

787. 5, vnto fyr L. ; 8, grounde ; 11, as an ; 15, And than ; 16, towarde ; 17, fholde haue ; 25, and the ; 28, Whan fyr M. herde that / he ; vp on ; 31, vnto his ; 37, were they.

788. 8, hym vpon ; 12, be buryed ; 14, made moche of ; 15, [hand] ; 17, Hungary ; whofe name ; 21, the whiche hyght ; 22, Hungary ; 29, [the] whiche ; 32, tyll that the beft ; 33, And in this maner ; 34, her vaūt.

789. 1, fyr Vrres moder ; 3, whiche was a ; 4, with her ; 8, So at the laft fhe ; 9, [by fortune fhe came nyghe] to the ; 10, at kynge A.'s ; 11, Caerleyll ; 12, how ; 13, that countree for to haue her foone heeled ; 15, countree ; 16, lorde kynge A. ; 17, the whiche ; 21, vnto the tyme that ; 24, coūtree ; 26, a full ; 27, fayd fhe ; 29, kynge A. ; come hyther ; 30, and yf ony ; 37, fyr V.

790. 2, brother by my ; 7, ten knyghtes ; [that tyme] ; 12, in hymfelfe that he had ben a ; 14, out of the ; vpon the grounde ; 15, of cloth of gold ; 16, [noble] ; 17, [for] ; 18, for to fuffre me foftly to handle thy ; 19, fyr V. ; as it fhall pleafe you ; 20, here at ; 22, on ; Than after kyng A. ; 26, Anguyffhe ; 30, Chalaunce ; 33, Gyngayne ; 34, thre were.

791. 4, & fyr G. & his fones fayled ; 6, whiche ; 7, So there ; fyr L. ; 13, fayled euerychone ; 15, whiche ; 18, Sadocke ; 20, there came ; fyr Grumwors fone ; 21, whiche at that tyme ; 22, one of the ftrongeft knyghtes of the worlde ; frenffhe booke ; 23, this fyr S. le breufe and fyr L. ; 26, S. le breufe ; 27, maner of wyfe ; 28, L. du lake ; 29, of them promyfed vnto other ; 32, and fuche other wylde ; whiche ; 34, as of all the ; 35, to knowe ; 37, Than there came in ; and fyr T. whiche ; 38, but this fyr T. was.

792. 1, A. the cowherde had ; begate all thefe knyghtes ; 3, whiche was one of the ; [one] ; 8, whiche ; 13, whiche was ; by the noble knyghte fyr T. ; 15, le blanke whiche ; vnto ; 19, whiche was ; vnto ; 21, falfe traytour ; 22, Marke flewe ; 29, fyr A. Lorphelyn ; 30, [flewe kynge M.] ; 31, the corps ; 35, whiche ; 36, Neroueus.

793. 5, A. le graunte ; 8, whiche ; 13, fyr Robert ; 14, whiche ; 16, by his ; 18, 19, whiche was ; 19, vnto them ; 20, G. of Orkeney ; 26, whiche came ; and anone it was ; 27, kynge therof ; 29, downe from ; vnto ; 31, vnto her.

794. 3, alle thofe that had ; ferched fyr V. ; 12, to that entent ; 15, as ye be ; 16, and yf ye ; 18, countree ; 22, fayenge thus ; 25, and I fhame ; 28, fayenge to hym ; 29, [the] whiche is full fore ; 38, [alle].

795. 1, feuen yere tofore ; 2, thre other ; 10, [in] ; 11, vnto god ; 12, deuyfed ; 14, bygge ; Than kyng A. ; 15, fayd he ; 17, fyr V. ; 19, of an ; 20, fo on ; 22, make fhorte tale ; 24, them bothe ; 29, vnto ; this knyght ; 33, but alwaye ; 34, in the courte ; 35, But euer.

796. 2, [du lake] for to ; 3, ouerfkyppe ; 6, defpyte of thofe knyghtes and ladyes that ; 7, he had ben ; 8, galous ; 10, after [that] ; 12, dyd in thofe ; 13, of Le cheualer ; 15, vnto the deth.

Book II.

797. 1, At the feafon of ye mery moneth of ; 4, and be gladde ; 7, [faft] ; 8, there befel ; [and vnhap] ; the whiche ; 10, longe of ; 11, fyr A. ; 12, thefe two knyghtes ; 14, vnto ; 16, [alle] ; 19, & knowe ; 27, fyr A. ; 28, I byleue ; 31, knowe well ynough ; 33, it vnto ; 34, Ye fhall not do it by ; for yf there ; 35, wrathe.

798. 3, ben a better knyght ; 7, as whā ; 13, hyde it ; 20, ought I ; euylle of ; 21, [al] ; 22, now is the ; 25, kynge A. ; 26, fyr A. ; whiche I ; 28, and [to] ; 31, And we knowe all ; 34, kynge A.

799. 1, for I tell you fyr ; 10, and for his quene ; 20, fyr A.; 22, hym full ; 23, vpon ; 26, vnto them ; 27, and thus were ; 31, Gromore fomor ioure ; 36, with quene G. ; 38, I alway drede me moche.

800. 1, whiche ; for to ; 6, noo doubte ; 12, that I wyll ; 14, fafe and founde ; 15, vndernethe his ; 16, And fo that noble knyght wente forth in his mantell / and put ; 20, fyr L.; 22, therof to make mencyon ; as it is ; 25, and with . . . . fayd thus ; 31, [there]; 32, I praye you hertely let me haue it.

801. 2, many valyaunt ; 4, no refyft ; 7, ftande in ; 8, neuer thus ; 10, alwayes [in one] ; 18, and poore ; to my ; 19, day that ; 23, for to ; 24, owne dere ; 27, fhall haue ; 33, well that ; 38, quene G.

802. 3, lorde Iefu ; 4, therwithall ; 7, daffhed at ; chambre dore ; 8, daffhynge ; open the ; 13, fyr L.; 15, a bygge ; whiche was called fyr C.; 21, And than fyr L.; 25, Let be ; 28, no fuche ; 31, and before ; 32, [outher els ye all that]; 34, knyghte oughte to do ; came vnto ; 35, I wyll ; [hit].

803. 1, myne owne ; falfe traytour ; 3, wyll let fhe to ; that we ; 6, dore wyde open ; 9, he had ; to the cold ; 10, of all ; 11, a buffet ; 14, vnto an ; 17, maner of yll ; and daungers ; 25, to his ; 26, So whan ; 27, was at that tyme ; 28, [why be ye all armed] what may this meane ; 31, were fo dremynge ; 35, nede fomeuer ; 36, ye had ben in ; 38, than euer.

804. 2, I befeche you ; 3, be of a ; 5, we all ; welth ; 8, all whiche ; that ye ; 9, is no ; 10, but that ; 11, no meanes ; 12, thofe that ; 13, [that] ye ; 21, wolde fayne ; 23, do what I may ; 25, you or not ; 26, to hym ; 29, with fyr V.; 31, made knyghtes ; one of them ; 33, fyr H.; 35, whiche ; Lorphelyns fone ; 36, dame A.; [and fhe] ; 37, [and].

805. 3, and anone they ; 4, & on ; 5, and what ; 7, fcore good and valyaunt ; 8, that I ; 9, well wyllynge ; 15, [and treafon] ; 19, is not ; 21, [I wote well as is] as ; 32, it pacyently ; 33, our lorde god.

806. 2, yf ye ; chryftened of ; 3, ony wrong ; 6, otherwyfe ; 10, and the quene dye fo ; 11, O good lord Iefu ; 13, and from ; 14, ye that be of my ; 16, doo yourfelfe ; 19, to be done ; 20, we thynke that the beft ye may do is this / that ; 22, to be fuppofed that yf ye ; 23, or els ; 31, ryght lothe ; 32, for to ; 35, me moche ; 38, fholde refcowe.

807. 2, dyd not he kepe ; 4, your bothe aduyfes ; 6, be that ; 9, vnto ; 11, home agayne ; [and loue and thanke] ; 17, flewe that noble knyght ; 18, a fharpe groūded ; 22, well that ; 26, yf it ; on the ; 29 a lytell ; 31, whiche whan ; 34, rode ftreyght ; and beten.

808. 3, dyd ye take hym; 5, fyr C.; 8, A Iefu; 12, wyll holde; 13, kynge A.; but that; 14, [the] deth; 15, to [the]; 19, be the; 27, [it] is; 31, knyghte alyue; 35, whiche he had.

809. 5, [I dare faye]; 6, ony vylony; 14, A. vnto fyr G.; 15, for trewly; no grete; 17, and alfo he had almooft; 18, . xij . good; 27, of my fones; 32, that ye wyll; 33, beft araye; 35, receyue her.

810. 1, do in my lyfe; 2, that I; 3, lady quene; fuche a; 7, vnto fyr; 10, [the] whiche; fall there; 12, vnto kynge; 22, vnto her; 28, one whiche; 29, her iudgement; 30, quene was; vnto; and alfo that fhe was; 31, warnȳge therof; 35, [ful].

811. 4, whiche were; 7, fyr G.; 15, vnto quene; 17, that the quene; 26, many knyghtes; were fory of; 27, to; 32, he was reuyued he; 33, ony crowne; I haue now.

812. 2, haue I; 4, neuer more; 8, [telle]; 9, nygh go; 11, all erthly men; 15, [that] he; 18, tyll that; 20, fayd the kynge; 23, [fayre]; 25, the kyng; 29, had; 31, kyng A.; 36, in the; And fo for to; 37, yf he had not.

813. 4, the man / your two bretherne; 6, all the good of; 9, fyr L.; 10, [euer]; 11, fyr G.; 13, to haue ben with; 16, the man; 17, is all; 18, downe in a fwoune; 21, ranne vnto; 23, and my; fyr G. alfo; 25, fell downe in a fwoune; reuyued agayne fyr G. fpake & fayd; 28, be buryed; 30, myne owne lord; 32, that ye wyll tell me; 34, neyther of them bothe.

814. 1, [of hem both]; 4, My mooft gracyous lord & myne vncle fayd; 6, that now; the whiche; 9, vnto the; 16, herde; 19, [he fayd]; 22, kynge A.; 23, and in yᵉ; 24, to affemble; 27, all how; 29, where as; 30, many a; 38, bothe within.

815. 1, and fyr G.; 2, [al]; 4, full ftronge; 5, not ryde; 6, wolde fuffre; 9, So it; on a; [tyme]; 10, to; 12, [al] it is; ye laboure at; 14, out my felfe; 16, fyr L.; 17, in the; 20, thou well; 21, wyll be; 22, and the noble; whiche; 25, [lord and]; 26, wyte you.

816. 4, [as ony is lyuyng vnto her lord]; 11, or that; 15, my gracyous; 17, that I had; [grete]; 19, as fhe; 22, in a; 26, that my; 28, it fhall; 31, vpon thy; 33, [and]; 36, with thyne; 38, by Iefu fayd fyr L.

817. 1, vnto; 3, fyr L.; 4, falfe recreaūt; 6, that I; vnto the; 7, me fore; 8, that it; 9, for none; 13, haft deftroyed; 16, as ye my; 17, [ye] haue; 18, and that; 20, but wyte; that I; 21, for it; [on hand]; 24, Than fayd fyr G. vnto fyr L.; 26, at fuche a vaūtage; 28, I fhall haue but; 29, [the noble].

818. 2, vnto them; and fyr S. his brother; 4, & to hym fayd thus; 5, that we; 6, fyr G.; vnto you; we befeche you; 8, [playnly]; 14, loth to do it; 20, is not this; 26, than on the morowe; 32, in [a]; 33, myddle batayle; 35, as valyaunt.

819. 5, vnto the; 6, moo other; [And]; 8, was there; 13, moche domage and hurte; 19, for to; 24, vnto hym thus; 26, vttermeſt; but euer; 29, was agayne; 32, rode forth; 34, for to reſt; 35, deed bodyes.

820. 3, So on; 4, [there]; as grymme; 7, had done hym; 8, all the; 10, furyously; 11, groūde; ioyned togyder; 12, a grete; 15, were bothe; 17, that ye; 19, they doo you; 20, For alwaye; 23, at ony vauntage; 24, told hym; 29, fete lockes; ſlayne on bothe partyes; 30, withdrewe; And ſo dyd kynge A.'s party. And than; 32, and his party entred in to theyr; 33, deed bodyes; ſalue to; 35, not halfe ſo; orgulous or proude; 38, whiche was.

821. 1, mooſt noble; 10, the Bulles; wyſt not; Gladly he wold accorde with; 18, not be reproued; 20, with hym; 22, vnto; 23, vnto kynge A.; 25, ſyr L. for to; 26, as ſhe; 29 [ſayd ſyr L.]; 31, [euer]; 32, this that; ſure for me & myne.

822. 1, that ſhe; 2, for to; 4, for to drede; 5, and my; 6, to were dyſtreſſed; 13, before me; 14, knowlege; 16, [thenne]; ye may ſaye; 17, lorde kyng; for my lady the; 19, for kynge A.'s loue; 22, kyng A.'s; 24, all they; 25, to the; 27, had with her; 29, vpon; 32, and ſet; 33, And quene Gueneuer; 36, vnto; 37, in to; 38, euery man.

823. 3, ſate in his fete; 7, many a; [ther]; 9, kynge A.; 10, not one; 12, ſpake he vnto the mooſt noble kyng A. full knyghtly / and lyke a man of grete honour; 13, that by; 15, vnto you; 16, [that] he; 18, vnto you; 20, grete; 21, the tyme; 23, lorde and kynge; 24, vnto grete; 30, agaynſt . xiiij . knyghtes.

824. 1, kynge A.; 3, lord and kynge; 4, that I; 5, [yow]; 6, done you in diuers; 8, for to; 9, and in; 12, [many]; 13, myne auaunt; 17, T. de Lyones; L. de Galys; 18, to them; 19, was neuer; 21, full glad; 25, full well; 26, pulled you; 28, your face; 31, ſyr T.; 32, of [his]; 37, for to.

825. 4, twayne; 11, fere y^t; 13, all erthely knyghtes; 16, that I ſhold; 18, [noble]; 25, cauſe to make; 26, [that]; 31, is none; 35, [holyer & more]; 36, vnto theyr; than that my; [kyng &].

826. 1, [ſire G.]; all the; 3, had ben; 6, it ſhall pleaſe hym; 7, the my; 10, ſyr L.; 16, for to; 19, warnynge; 21, that thou; comen hyther; 22, yf that; 23, [ſayd ſyre G.]; 24, [owne]; 30, ſayd theſe wordes.

827. 1, varyable; mutable; is no; 6, haue had; 10, [as wel]; 11, with your neuewe ſyr; 12, for to werre; 14, I beſeche you; 20, with you; Ye no; 24, or [that]; 27, quene G.; 28, all the knyghtes; 30, fende me worde; ye be noyed; 31, with ony; let me haue knowlege; 32, yf that; 33, And fo therwith; 34, openly that all they that were there myght here hym; me fe; 37, vnto.

828. 1, but that they all; 2, of theyr wyttes; 3, fo whan; for to; 5, waye to; 6, And afterwarde he; 8, fir L. departed; 9, [holy]; 10, y^t; do as he; 12, fore at my herte; 13, banyffhed man; 16, was banyffhed oute of this realme; 18, departed afonder; 23, countree; is none; ben here; 24, for dyuers; is this; 25, Courte of kynge A.; 26, take parte; 28, [as] well for; 30, I thanke; 31, as to fuche; 32, [for] to.

829. 5, and in; 6, your grete; 11, whiche; vnto his; 16, for to; 17, And well an; 19, departe from hym; 21, where as; 22, for to; 26, his good; 27, vnto; 28, had eftablyffhed; 30, And he made fyr; to be crouned; 32, whiche; 33, whiche was.

830. 1, departed his hauour; 2, thofe of his; 3, And fyrft he made fyr B. duke of; 15, hym erle; 16, the good knyght fyr P.; coūtree of Prouence; 17, Langedocke; 18, gaue hym; 20, Angeo; 25, [to]; 27, [made]; 31, all his; 32, his quene; kyng A.; ouer the fee.

831. 1, thefe tydynges; vnto; 2, & that they; 3, [full]; 4, is grete; 7, whiche was; 8, gyue you; 12, all alyauntes; 13, vnto fyr; 14, and your; 15, hath caufed; ouer ryde our; 17, hyde vs in; the good knyght fyr G. to; 19, they were without ye walles; 20, [lyke]; we are; 25, fpake all with one voyce; 26, ryde out; 28, whiche; 31, yet my lordes (!); we are full; [for]; 32, warryoures that other whyle made kynge C. and my father kynge B. / & myn vncle kyng Bors for to obey; 36, defyrynge hym to take a tratyce.

832. 1, his warre; 3, vnto the; 4, whofe name was fyr L.; [&] that fayd; 6, for to; 7, fyr L.; 9, that are; 10, wold that; 11, vnto kyng A.; 14, kynge A.'s; ryght gladde; 23, by caufe her; 25, vnto; 26, ye fhall faye; 27, to fyr L.; it was but ydle labour / now to fende to myne; 29, y^t now; 31, to god; vnto the ordre of; that I; 34, vnto her; 35, where as.

833. 2, that ftode about hym fayd; 5, in the myddes; lyghtly be; 11, and for euery of vs; 13, as at; on the; 14, as the; 15, fawe how; was befyeged; 17, them wyghtly; 18, armed at all poyntes; 21, that dare; 24, And fo he; 25, And anone fir B.; 26, there came; 27, vnto; for to; 29, ryghte fpytefully; was fo fyers / that he; 32, And thus; [he]; 34, of peple there was; 35, that fyr G.; 36, vpon a grete courfer.

834. 1, dooft thou hyde; 4, kynne euery deale; 5, than his; fayd all; 6, vnto fyr; 13, a recreaunt knyght; cōmaunded to fadell his; 14, [lete]; 17, whiche; that I; 22, you halfe; and haue; 24, moche as; 27, to a bay; 28, fayd vnto fyr L. Syr L.; 30, began to arme; 33, [all]; 37, that there; 38, come nyghe.

835. 4, horfes myght as faft as they; 7, [&] Than; 10, in many; 11, whiche an; 12, gyuen hym; 14, his owne; 17, they fhold; 18, And all this; G.'s fake; 19, yf that; 20, that his; 25, had of hym grete wonder; 30, and his brethe; 31, fadde ftrokes; 33, [that] he; 36, Than whā fyr L.

836. 1, began he to ftretche; hymfelfe; 2, fayd to hym thefe wordes; 3, that ye; 6, vpon the; 7, and than; 8, thou thyfelfe; 10, Syr I fhall; 11, the grace of god fayd fyr L.; wyte you; 13, in to one of; 14, And anone there were leches; [&] whiche ferched his wounde; 15, falued it; 16, ye fhall; 17, brynge out my; 21, warre began; 23, well feen; 27, of kyng; 28, they within; 29, aboute a thre; 33, Benwyck; 34, on hyghe; 38, foule fayenge.

837. 1, wyte you well; 4, thou traytour; [fayd he]; 6, y^t; 10, were at an ende; 18, for to; 20, they ranne; 24, full quyckly auoyded; 27, for though.

838. 3, houres contynually; 4, fyr L. had grete; [for]; hymfelfe; And after that y^e; 5, felte veryly; 6, myght and ftrength; [and that his greate power was done]; 7, haue I well; 22, to the; 27, towarde the towne.

❡ Thus endeth the . xx . boke . And here after foloweth the . xxj . boke / whiche is the laft booke of this prefent volume . In whiche all thofe that dyfpofe them to efchewe ydelneffe whiche is mother of all vyces / redynge hyftoryall maters . Some wyllyng to rede in dcuoute medytacyons / of the humanyte and paffyon of our fauyour Iefu chryft . Some in lyues and paynfull martyrdomes of holy fayntes . Some in moralyfacyon & poetycall ftoryes . And fome in knyghtly and vyɛtoryous dedes of noble prynces conquerours / as of this prefent volume of this noble conqueroure kynge Arthur / fomtyme kynge of Englande may openly knowe the lamentable deth of hym and the nobleft chyualrye of the worlde knyghtes of the rounde table / caufed by fyr Mordred his fone and the fubiectes of this realme.

839. 2, [that]; 6, he was; 8, to W.; toke [the]; 15, maner [of]; 18, [fhe took the toure of London]; [and]; 22, was deceyued; 23, And to make fhorte; 37, [thou]; 38, that I vtterly defye the.

840. 1, that I ought; 2, where as; that my; [&] it is; 3, an abhomynable; 5, heed to be ftryken of; 6, curfe; 8, And whan the byffhop herde that / he fledde; 10, was a relygyous heremyte;

12, fought vpon ; 14 [meanys] ; 15, hym not ; 18, fyege fro fyr ; & that he ; 19, for to be ; 20, to wryte letters vnto ; 21, vnto hym ; 27, hym than ; we all ; 28, [ye not] ; 30, knyghtes & men of worfhyp ; 31, not we Englyffhe men ; holde vs ; [them] ; 34, Alas alas.

841. 2, towarde D. ; 6, fangled ; 9, carakes ; 11, vpon the ; was there ; 20, noble knyght ; 25, there he ; [thenne] whan he came to hyfelfe agayn ; 26, [fyr G.] ; 34, wounde that ; L. du lake ; of the ; 35, yf fyr L. had ; 37, I my felfe am caufer.

842. 1, cankered ; 5, vnto ; a lettre ; 6, [thenne] ; 7, [thenne] fyr G. ; 8, he had ben ; 12, vnto the ; 14, whiche thou ; 16, vnto my ; 20, for to ; 21, that fame ; 28, & vncle kyng A. ; 29, whiche is ; hymfelfe ; he wolde ; 32, yf fhe had ; 33, lorde & vncle.

843. 1, the as thou arte the ; 3, and alfo ; 8, fyr G. betoke his foule in to the handes of our lorde god ; let bury ; 9, caftel of D. ; 11, to kynge A. ; 13, on ; 19, made to bury them ; And thofe that were fore woūded he caufed ; 22, wrongfully ; 23, the noble ; 24, vnto the fee fyde vnto S. ; 27, vpon a ; 29, vpon that traytour fyr M. ; 31, Southery ; 33, and vnto kynge A. ; 34, that loued ; 35, And fo vpon.

844. 1, hym thought he ; 2, vnto a ; 5, and a depe ; 8, that he ; 13, in a flombrynge ; 14, kynge A. thought that there ; hym veryly ; 16, fo whan ; [thenne] ; 18, the alyue ; 20, that ben comen ; 21, the ladyes ; 22, a man ; 23, in a ryghtwyfe ; 25, to you ; 27, bothe ye ; 31, men that ; 32, vnto you ; his mooft ; 34, profre hym ; 36, & fhall refcowe.

845. 2, lyghtly ; 12, grymly ; 15, And after the dayes of kynge A. to haue all Englande to his obeyffaunce ; 17, So than ; 20, And than ; 24, for [I] ; 25, dyd warne ; that yf ; 27, euer ftandeth before ; 28, that my ; vpon.

846. 1, [than] ; 4, rode he ; 6, raffhyng ; 8, But alway ; 10, dyd there ryght nobly ; fholde do ; 11, he neuer ; 14, groūde ; 16, [wode] ; 20, [one] ; the Butler ; 22, kyng A. ; 24, vnto myne ; 25, [were] ; fyr M. is ; whiche ; 28, to fyr L. ; 29, whiche hath wrought all this woo ; 32, on hym ; My good lord ; remembre well your dreme that ye had this nyght ; 36, be god.

847. 1, is done ; 7, vnto hym ; 11, with all the ; 12, vp to the ende ; 13, that he helde ; 15, banne ; therwith ; fell downe ; 17, [de butlere] ; 24, and he was ; 25, went ; 32, by myne aduyfe ; 33, you vnto.

848. 1, aketh fo ; 4, warned me ; 5, vp [the] kynge A. ; on the one ; 7, that lyfte / that fome of his ; 9, kynge A. came to hymfelfe agayne ; 11, 17, 20, kynge A. ; 12, vnto me ; fo to ; 14, than I haue ; 15, for to ; 22, vnto ; 24, thou fhalte fe there ; 26, And foo ; 27, [the] hafte ; 29, in to ; 33, fayd he ; 35, kynge A. ; 36, [ageyn].

849. 1, it fynne ; 4, fayd he ; 7, two tymes ; 8, vnto me ; 12, I cōmaunde the ; And yf ; 17, water as ferre ; 21, vnto ; 22, had feen ; fro hens ; 23, kyng A. ; 31, thofe thre quenes fet them downe.

850. 1, kynge A. ; 3, for to ; 4, euer more ; 13, vpon ; 14, [was] newly ; 15, had banyffhed ; 16, buryed ; My fayre ; 18, whiche brought this deed corps ; 30, your owne ; 31, fyr B. abode ; 32, whiche had ben ; 35, no more wryten in my copy of the certaynte of his deth ; 35, *from* "wryton," *to next page*, 1, "redde," *is omitted.*

851. 2, a barge ; 3, [quene] ; 5, Nymue ; 6, whiche ; fyr P. ; 11, vnto his ; 14, not of a certaynte ; it was ; 16, it playnly ; 17, Some men yet ; 19, Iefu Chryft ; 24, we here ; 26, And fo ; [theyr] ; 28, that her lord kyng A. ; 29, fhe ftale ; 36, that was a.

852. 9, wonders wroth [oute of mefure] ; 10, now I repēt me ; 11, [euer] ; 12, to my ; kynge A. ; [doleful] lettre of fyr G. / that my lorde kynge A. ; 19, wyte ye ; 23, & fyr ; 28, ye go fe ; 33, for to ; 34, fee & arryued at D. ; 36, enquyred of men ; kyng A. was.

853. 4, 5, kyng A. ; 9, tombe of fyr G. ; 10, full hertely ; 12, ale as the myghte ete and drynke ; 13, dealed ; 17, fyr L. offred fyrft ; 19, *from* " & alfo," *to* 20, " pounde," *is omitted ;* 20, to nyght ; 21, vpon his ; And in ; 22, called vnto hym ; 23, thus he fayd ; 28, and grete ; 29, haue herde ; 37, man neyther.

854. 1, weftwarde ; 2, vnto a ; 4, thre tymes ; 7, this chere ; 8, whiche ; 9, to call ; vnto me ; And whan ; vnto her ; 10, [to all the ladyes] ; 11, [hath] all ; 13, wyte ye well fyr L. ; 15, helth ; for to haue ; 16, Iefu chryft ; at the dredefull daye of dome ; 17, fynfull creatures ; 19, vs two ; 20, neuer loke ; And ferthermore I ; 21, behalfe ryghte ftraytly ; and that vnto ; fhortly thou ; 23, the fyr L. ; not ones ; 24, for bothe ; me & the ; 25, go thou vnto ; 26, I befeche you ; 27, lord god ; 29, now returne ; in to my ; 32, you vnto ; 33, pleafe god ; & fpecially to praye for you ; 34, may not ; 35, ye faye well fayd he.

855*. 3, in the queft of ; 4, my lady dame G. ; 5, you vnto ; me vnto ; 6, haue I ; 8, me for to ; realme and countree ; 10, [euer] ; 11, [yf] that ; ony good ; 13, neuer more ; 14, fuche thynges ; And fo they ; 17, as though they ; 27, threwe abrode ; 37, [for].

856*. 3, ryde through all Englond to feke ; 4, vnto ; 8, came vnto ; whan he fawe ; 13, [fir Blamour] ; 14, abode there ftyll ; 15, fawe that ; 20, but that ; 21, dyd lowly ; 24, & in ; 26, fo that ; 27, vnto ; 28, hym towarde A. ; 29, by that tyme ; thou come ; 30,

puruey the ; 31, and brȳge you ; bury it ; 32, thryes vnto fyr L. ;
34, or it was ; 36, this vyfyon ; 37, on fote ; they wente.

857. 5, or fhe dyed ; 7, for to ; 10, And this ; 11, all thefe two ;
vntyll ; 14, Dirige at nyght and the maffe on the morowe ; 17, his
feuen ; [hors] ; 18, holy & deuout ; 20, tyll they came to G. ; 27,
& than fhe ; 28, after in ; put in to ; 29, ftylle vpon the grounde ;
30, ye are ; 32, well myne ; 34, none ende ; 35, and call to mynde
her beaute / her bounte / and her nobleffe ; was as well ; 36, kynge
my lorde A. as with her ; And alfo whan I fawe the corpfes of that
noble kynge and noble quene fo lye togyder in that colde graue
made of erth / that fomtyme were fo hyghly fet in mooft honourable
places / truly ; 38, my wretched ; how I through.

858*. 1, and through my prefumpcyon and pryde ; 2, the whiche ;
euer were ; 3, of theyr ; 4, fanke & impreft ; fo in to ; that all
my naturall ftrengthe fayled me / fo that I ; 7, but cōtynually
morned vntyll he ; And than ; 10, was as than ; fhorter by a cubyte ;
12, but nedefully as nature requyred fomtyme he ; & alwayes he ;
13, vpon ; G.'s tombe ; 15, nothynge.

❡ O ye myghty and pompous lordes fhynynge in the glory
tranfitory of this vnftable lyf / as in regnynge ouer grete realmes
and myghty grete countrees / fortyfyed with ftronge caftels &
toures edifyed with many a ryche Cite . Ye alfo ye fyers and
myghty knyghtes fo valyaunt in aduenturous dedes of armes
Beholde beholde / fe how this myghty conquerour kynge Arthur /
whome in his humayne lyfe all the worlde doubted . Ye alfo this
noble quene Gueneuer whiche fomtyme fate in her chayre a*d*ourned
with golde / perles & precyous ftones / now lye full lowe in obfcure
foffe or pyt couered with cloddes of erth and claye . Beholde alfo
this myghty champyon fyr Launcelot / pereles of knyghthode / fe
now how he lyeth grouelynge vpon the colde moulde / now beynge
fo feble and faynt / that fomtyme was fo terryble / how & in what
maner ought ye to be fo defyrous of worldly honoure fo daungerous .
Therfore me thynketh this prefent boke called la mort darthur is
ryght neceffary often to be radde . For in it fhall ye fynde the
mooft gracyous knyghtly & vertuous warre of yᵉ mooft noble
knyghtes of the worlde / wherby they gate prayfyng cōtynuall .
Alfo me femeth by yᵉ ofte redyng therof / ye fhall gretely defyre to
accuftome your felfe in folowynge of thofe gracyous knyghtly dedes
/ that is to faye / to drede god / and to loue ryghtwyfnes / faythfully & couragyoufly to ferue your fouerayne prynce . And the
more yᵗ god hath gyuen you the tryumphall honoure / the meker
ye ought to be / euer ferynge the vnftablenes of this deceyuable
worlde . And fo I paffe ouer and turne agayn vnto my mater ; 15,

¶ So within ; 19, that ye wyll gyue ; 20, vnto a ; 21, but a ; 24, I wyll now ; 25, I praye you gyue ; 27, vnto ; 29, Bamborow ; 33, all his ; 34, went all ; 35, byffhop that ; 36, on a ; 37, came vnto.

859*. 5, vpon one daye ; 6, towarde heuen ; 18, with the corps ; 19, vnto ; 27, had fought ; 30, E. de Marys ; 32, fynge the feruyce full lamentably ; 33, [wepe].

860*. 3, [that] ; of none ; 9, thou were ; 12, in the refte ; 15, vnto his ; 17, whiche was ; 25, Vyllyers le valyaunt ; 34, was bothe ; 36, that fyr L. ; [for] fo to do ; 38, and turkes ; they dyed ; 39, hole booke.

861*. 8, For tranflacyon of this boke was fynyffhed . [The Colophon see on the Plate facing page 17].

LIST OF NAMES AND PLACES.[1]

---

[1] This is the first complete and critical Index to "Le Morte Darthur" ever compiled. There occur about 850, and, counting all the various spellings, nearly 1000 names in the text. It was a tedious and difficult task, on account of the bad orthography and carelessness with regard to the names of persons. As the geography of the whole book is confused and unintelligible, I have abstained from giving any conjectures. In cases where I felt sure, I have stated my opinion. The numbers refer to the pages. In some cases I have stated in foot-notes the readings of names of persons and places as they occur in the French and English sources respectively, in order to show how little one can depend on them.

[2] Agente may be either Agen, a city in France, capital of the department of Lot and Garonne, a bishop's see, or the Agendicum (afterwards Sens) of the ancient Gaule; perhaps also Araegenus (Argentan).

tells king Arthur about her, 798; advises the king to go hunting and to take the queen by surprise, 799; comes to capture Launcelot, 800; calls him a traitor, 801; is killed by Launcelot, 803; 805; 809; 823

Aguarus, syr, nephew to the dead man whom syr Launcelot finds in a chapel, 656, 657

Agwysaunce, Anguyssaunce, kyng of Irelond, 52; 54; 56; 60; 257; 259, 260

Aladuke, lord, 171

Alardyn of the Ilys, syr, 106

Albons, St., 39

Aleyn, syr, 427

All halowmasse, al halowmas, 49 (the mass or feast of all Saints, 31st of October)

Almayn, 162; 175; Germany

Almesburye,[1] 851; 856*, 857*

Alphegus of spayne, syr, 788

Alps, mountains, 162

Alyduke, Alyduk, syr, a knight of the round table, not identical with the above Aladuke,[2] 196*; 728; 744

Alys la beale pylgrym, 475, 476, 477; becomes wife of Alysaunder le orphelyn

Alysaunder the grete, the myghty Conquerour, 1; 177; 827

Alysaunder le orphelyn, son of kyng Marke's brother prynce Boudwyne, comes with his parents to the court of king Mark, 466; is taken to the Castel Magouns, after his father's death, to be educated, 467; is made knight and receives his father's doublet, 468; is well equipped, 469; Trystram advises him by letter to go to Arthur's court, 470; he does not follow the advice; smites down four knights of Morgan le fay and fights and overcomes Malegryn, 472; is taken to Morgan le fay's castle, where he promises, in order

to get healed, to stay twelve months, 473; a damoysel helps him, 474; he fights against several knights, 475, 476; becomes enamoured of Alys la beale pylgrym and marries her, 477, 478; 744; his death referred to, 792

Alysaundrye (? country or city), 163

Amant, syr, 423, 424; 436

Ambage, country of, 163 (? one of the provinces or towns of the Roman Empire)[3]

Andred, Andret, syr, nephew of kyng Marke, cosyn to syr Trystram, 297; 321; 325, 326; 368; 401, 402, 403, 404; 459

Anglides, Anglydes, wife of Boudwyn and mother to Alysander le Orphelyn, 466, 467, 468, 469

Anguysshe, kyng of Ireland, once mistakingly (161) called kyng of Scottland, sends to king Mark to ask truage for Cornwall, 277; receives the wounded Tramtryst in his country, 285; arranges a great tournament, 286; asks Trystram why he does not fight, 287; allows Trystram to leave his country safely, 290; is summoned by Bleoberys and Blamor to appear before king Arthur, 302; has to send within three days a knight who will fight for him, 304*; gladly accepts Trystram's offer, 305; yields to Trystram's wish to save Blamor's life, 307; takes Trystram to Ireland and tells all the people about his valiant deed, 308; gives his daughter la beale Isoud to Trystram as wife for king Mark, 309; 314; 372; 410, 411; 529; 554; 738; 741, 742; 757; 763; 765; 790

Anguyssaunce. See **Agwysaunce**

Anioye, duke of, 830; Dynas the seneschal is made duke of A. by Launcelot

Annecians, syr, god-son of kyng Bors, 60

---

[1] Almesbury is a town in Wiltshire not far from Salisbury. Originally the name was Ambrosebury, then Ambresbury, and from this has been made the present name.
[2] E. Brock, "Morte Arthur" (Thornton MS.), in his Index, apparently considers Aladuke, Aliduke, and Alidoyke as names belonging to the same person.
[3] "Morte Arthur" (Thornton MS.) reads "Ambyganyc."

---

[1] "Morte Arthur" (Thornton MS.) reads here "Orcage."

Mordred, he orders all children [1] born on May-day to be destroyed; Mordred, however, is preserved, 75; cannot pull out the sword of a damoysel sent by Lylle of Avelion, 76; requests Balyn to remain in his court, 78; hears from the lady of the lake the name of the sword; refuses to grant her the gift she asks; banishes Balyn from his court, 79; orders the lady of the lake, killed by Balyn, to be richly buried, 80; hears from Merlyn that Balyn has defeated and taken prisoner king Ryons; prepares his army to meet Nero, Ryons' brother, 86; overcomes king Lot by Balyn's help, 87; buries king Lot with great honours, and orders a monument to be erected on his tomb, 88; gives Excalibur to the charge of Morgan le fay, his sister, 89; graciously receives Balyn again, and tells him to fetch back a mourning knight, 89; orders this knight, who is killed by Garlon the Invisible, to be richly buried, 90; by Merlyn's advice he overcomes gradually all his enemies; tells Merlyn his wish to marry Gueneuer; after in vain trying to dissuade the king, Merlyn yields to his desire and sends to king Lodegrean, 100; receives Gueneuer and the round table with a hundred knights; tells Merlyn to find out the best knights of the country; grants young Gawayn's desire, 101; grants the wish of Aries the cowherd, 102; makes Tor, Pellinore's son, and Gawayn, his nephew, knights, 103; is wedded with great solemnity to Gueneuer in St. Stephen's Church at Camelot, 104; is displeased with Gawayn for killing a lady, 109; gives armour and a sword to Tor as reward for his valour, 113; receives Pellinore, 117; gives lands and properties to his knights; tells them to be brave and virtuous, and makes them to swear that they would keep his orders and the principles of the round table, 118; is warned by Merlyn to keep his sword, 119; holds a feast at Camelot; returns to Cardoylle; hears that several kings have invaded his country; goes to defend his country; takes Gueneuer with him to the north, 120; is attacked unexpectedly during the night, but is saved by the courage of his knights, 121; defeats his enemies; thanks God for the victory, 122; wishes to replace the knights of the round table killed in the battle, 123; prefers Tor to the son of Bagdemagus, 124; hunts with Vryens and Accolon; they follow a hart; they find a little ship, 125; twelve damoysels receive the king and his companions; they are well entertained and go to rest; the next morning Arthur finds himself in a dark prison, 126; is ready to fight and to deliver all the prisoners, 127; prepares at once to fight; receives by a damoysel a sword like Excalibur, 129; fights with Accolon, who has Excalibur, 130; is nearly overcome, but is saved by the damoysel of the lake; gets Excalibur, 131; recognises the treason; overcomes Accolon; forces him to tell all he knows, 132; pardons Accolon, 133; is healed in an abbey, and sends Accolon's body to Morgan le fay, 135; is robbed of the sheath of Excalibur by Morgan le fay; follows her, 137; refuses, by the advice of the lady of the lake, the cloak of gold and jewels sent by Morgan le fay, 139; receives Gawayn, Vwayn, and Marhaus, 159; sends word to the emperour Lucius, in answer to his demand for truage, that he will make war against him, 160; consults with his lords what to do, 161; sends the ambassadors back

---

[1] This passage is most likely suggested by the well-known Biblical incident of Herod's murder of the children. It is very similarly told in the Huth " Merlin."

finally declares he would kill him if he refuses to throw the sword into the sea; is carried by Bedwere to the shore, and received by four queens in a little boat, 849; declares to Bedwere he wishes to go to the valley of Avylion to heal his wounds; requests him to pray for his soul, 850; 861*

Arundel, castel of, in Southsex,[1] *see* **Magouns,** 467

Arystause, erle, 790

Aryes, the Cowherd, also called **le vayshere,** 102, 103; 430; 791

Astamor, syr, 728; 791

Astlabor, kyng, 558; 561

Astolat, towne, according to Malory it is in " Englysshe called **Gylford**," 738, 739

Astolat, fayre maiden of. *See* Elayne le blank

Asye, 163, Asia

Auffryke, 163, Africa

Avelyon, lady lylle of,[2] 76; 81

Avylyon, yle of, 255, 256; vale of, 850

Babyloyne, country of, 724

Bagdemagus, Basdemagus, kyng of Gore, 89; 124, 125; 188; 190, 191; 192; 212; 254; 260; 479, 480; 483, 484; 486; 493, 494; 623*, 624*, 625; 714*; 716*; 831[3]

Balan, brother of Balyn, syr, 63; 79; 82, 83, 84; 86, 87, 88; 97, 98, 99

Balyn, Balen le Saueage, syr, called the knyght with the two swerdes; as poor knight in Arthur's court, desires to pull out a sword, 77; succeeds; thanks the king for his kindness, 78; strikes the lady of the lake's head off; is banished from the court, 79; tells his squire about his misfortune; resolves to overcome king Ryons, in order to gain Arthur's favour again, 80; fights against Launceor, 81; kills this knight; is sorry for it; meets his brother Balan, 82; tells him his plans, 83; finds Merlyn, 84; recognises him again through his disguise; follows his advice; takes Ryons prisoner, 85; brings him to Arthur's court and gains the king's good grace, 86; helps the king in the battle against Nero, 87; comes to Arthur; is told to fetch back a knight, 89; finds the knight, who is ready to go with him, but is killed by Garlon; goes with the dead knight's lady into a forest, 90; buries the knight; comes to a castle; refuses first to give his lady, but afterwards yields; hears a noise, 91; promises his host to help him; comes to the castle of king Pellam, 92; kills Garlon; fights with king Pellam and gives him the dolorous stroke, 93; is taken up by Merlin, who tells him that they shall never meet again in this world; promises his help to a knight whom he finds in the forest, 94; goes to the castle and finds the knight's lady in the arms of another; fetches him to see his lady, 95; is warned to go no farther; hears a horn; comes to a castle; exchanges his shield; is again cautioned by a damoysel, 96; finds his brother as a red knight; does not recognise him, and is not recognised by his brother on account of the strange shield; fights against his brother, 97; kills him, and receives himself mortal wounds; dies; is buried by Merlyn, 99; 419

---

[1] The identification of Magouns with Arundel in Southsex is of course Malory's idea. The original French MS. does not contain anything of the sort; there is only spoken of " li chastiaus de magance."

[2] Thomas Wright, " Morte Darthur," vol. i., page 59, note 3, suggests that Lady Lylle of Auelyon may be a corruption of "lady de l'yle d'Auelyon," simply meaning the lady of the yle of Auelyon. Wright, without having seen the original version, has conjectured rightly; Huth, "Merlin," i. p. 213, indeed, reads: " la dame apielee la dame de l'isle d'Avalon."

[3] King Bagdemagus dies and is buried on page 714*; Galahad visits his tomb on page 716*; on page 831 he is said to have spoken again to Launcelot. As Malory used different versions, such anachronisms are natural and not infrequent.

Bamborow, 858; one of the names of the place where the body of syr Launcelot was supposed to have been taken to; perhaps another name for Ioyous gard

Ban of Bewwyck, kyng, 47, 48, 49; 51; 53; 56; 58; 60; 64

Bandes, kyng, 488

Baramdoun, 843; Barham Down, near Canterbury

Barflete,[1] in Flanders, 166

Barnard, Bernard, of Astolat, father of Elayn le blank, 739, 740, 741; 748, 749; 758, 759, 760

Basdemagus. *See* Bagdemagus

Bawdewyn, Baudewyn of Bretayn, 43; 44; 46; 164; 746; 756

Bayen, 829; supposed name for Benwyk

Beale valet, castel of, 455

Bearne, 830; Bearn, a former province of France; syr Vyllyars the valyaunt is made erle of Bearne by syr Launcelot

Beaumayns, surname given by syr Kay to Gareth, *meaning* Fair-Hands. *See* Gareth

Beaume, 829; another supposed name for Benwyk

Bedegrayne, batayle of, 53–64; castel of, 51, 52; 62; forest of, 51

Bedewere, Bedyuere, syr, 166; 169, 170; 257; 743; 792; 846, 847, 848, 849, 850, 851; 860*

Belangere, conestable of the castle of Magouns, 467, 468, 469

Bellangere le beuse, son of Alysaunder le orphelyn, 743; 792; 804; 819; 828; 830

Bellangere le orgulous, syr, 792

Bellaus, syr, 60

Belleus, Bellyus, lord, 189; 212

Bellinus,[2] a fictitious kyng of Bretayne, 161

Bellyaunce, Belleaunce le orgulus, syr, 337, 338

Bellyas of Flaundrys, syr, 56 (perhaps identical with syr Bellaus, 60)

Bendelayne, syr, 264, 265

Benoye, country of, 478

Benwyk, by some called bayen, by others Beaume, also spelled Benwyck or barwyk, 48, 49; 51; 63; 119; 829; 833; 836; 842

Berel, Beriel, syr, 170; 172

Berluse, Berluses, Bersyles, and Bersules, syr, 423, 424; 427, 428; 436

Bernard of Astolat. *See* Barnard.

Berraunt le Apres, Baraunt, generally only called the kyng with or of the honderd knyghtes, 44; 52; 54; 56, 57, 58; 60; 388; 390, 391; 394; 491; 517; 530; 738; 748; 757; 765, 766; 768; 790

Bertelot, Bertolet, syr, 595

Black crosse, abbay of, 402

Black knyght, the. *See* Perard

Blamore, Blamor, or Blamour de ganys, syr, 259; 295; 299; 303; 305, 306, 307, 308; 311; 345; 372; 386; 397; 410; 483; 728; 744; 790; 804; 830; 856*; 860*

Bleoberys de ganys, syr, 57; 295, 296, 297, 298, 299, 300, 301; 305; 308; 342; 344; 373; 376; 385; 397; 399; 410; 416; 421, 422; 479; 483; 485; 501, 502, 503, 504; 534; 555; 556; 728; 743; 768; 790; is made duke of poyters, 830; 856*; 860*

Blewe knyght, the. *See* Persaunt of Inde

Bleyse, mayster of Merlyn, 61, 62

Bloyas de la flaundres, syr, 55

Bloyse de la caase, syr, 60

Blysaunt, syr, 594, 595; 603; castel of, 600, 601

Bohart le cure hardy, syr, 793; son of kyng Arthur

Bochas, 2; Boccacio (Caxton's Preface[3])

---

[1] I did not find any town in Flanders that could be possibly supposed to be Barflete. As can be seen from the Thornton MS., Flanders is Malory's addition. Barflete is an old spelling for Barfleur, in the peninsula of Cotentin, Normandy; it is the harbour from which William the Conqueror set out for England in 1066.

[2] "Morte Arthur" (Thornton MS.) reads here "Belyne."

[3] The work referred to by Caxton is a book printed in the year 1475 by Georg Husner in Strassburg (folio). It contains 155 leaves, 55 lines making a full page; it

Boloyn,[1] godefray of, 1 (Caxton's Preface)

Book, the frensshe, the book, booke, or the Romaunce referred to, *i.e.*, Malory's French and English sources, 40; 63; 143; 182, 183; 207; 211; 227; 233; 271; 284; 311; 328; 333; 353; 363; 393; 396; 399; 408; 463; 475; 478; 480; 536; 554; 571; 580; 601; 701; 740, 741; 744; 752; 757; 767, 768; 773; 775, 776, 777; 780; 788, 789; 791; 796; 799, 800; 811; 817; 822; 835; 837; 842; 858

Borre, 62; child of kyng Arthur and the damoysel Lyonors

Bors, Borce de ganys, syr, son of kyng Bors, 143; is sent as messenger to Lucius, 169, 170; 172; is numbered among the noble knights, 232; fights with the red knight, 259; meets Trystram, 373, 374; 386; 390; 397; 410; smites down Bromel; comes to kyng Pelles, 576; is told that the child Galahad is to sit in the peryllous syege; is confessed; he has a child with the daughter of king Brangoris; goes to bed in a room with many doors; declines to unarm himself, 577; sees a great spear that comes straight towards him; the point of the spear burns; it hurts him on the shoulder; a knight comes and asks him to fight with him; they run against each other; he smites the knight down, and orders him to go to Arthur; sees many arrows come through the window; afterwards a hideous lion; he cuts his head off, 578; then he sees suddenly a dragon with a golden inscription on its forehead; when he has killed the dragon, appears an old man, who sings about Ioseph of Arymathye; sees the Holy Grail;

the old man speaks to him, 579; sees a sword hanging over his head; hears a voice which tells him that he is not yet worthy to be in this place; the next morning he leaves the place, and finds Launcelot; tells him all he has seen, 580; when Elayne tells him about Launcelot, he rebukes her; goes to seek Launcelot, 584; goes to Gueneuer and blames her for her behaviour; goes with Ector and Lyonel in search of Launcelot, 585; sends a message to Gueneuer, 586; comes to king Brandegore; finds his son, Helyn le blanck, and takes him with him to Arthur's court, 604; 612, 613*; 669; meets a man of religion on a donkey, and is recognised by him as one of the knights of the Sangreal, 671; is told that the Holy Grail can only be got by sinless people; has to eat bread and drink water, to wear a garment; sees a great bird, who kills himself in order to feed his young ones with his blood, 672; is lodged in a tower; refuses a fine dinner, and asks for bread and water; hears the lady's story, 673; offers to be her champion; has a vision while he sleeps; rises and goes to the chapel, 674; refuses again to eat; fights with Prydam, and overcomes him, 675; gives the land back to the lady who is the right owner of it; meets two knights who lead his brother Lionel bound with them; wishes to deliver his brother; there comes a lady who implores his assistance, 676; he is doubtful what to do; prays for his brother and succours the lady; kills the knight, 677; twelve knights lead him to the lady's father; he refuses to stay with them, and goes to seek his

---

has no title-page and is without pagination and registration. On fol. 1 recto it commences: "Ioannis Bocacii de Cercaldis historiographi prologus in libros incipit." It ends on fol. 155 verso: "Finit liber nonus & ultimus . . . de casibus virorum illustrium." The eighth book contains one chapter entitled "De Arturo britonum rege."

[1] "Godefray of Boloyn" was printed by Caxton in 1481. The book has no title-page, and the pages are not numbered; 142 leaves, and 40 lines to a full page. After a Preface and Table of Contents occupying eight leaves, it begins on fol. 9: "Here begynneth the boke Intituled Eracles, and also of Godefrey of Boloyne," &c.

[1] The Thornton MS. has here the form "Bremyne" (line 277); there is moreover a third king of the name "Bawdewyne" mentioned.

---

[1] The Thornton MS. gives here no name, but speaks of "a paynyme of Perse." Callyburne is the name given to Arthur's sword in this romance. Malory may have profited by this name, as he generally calls that sword "Excalybur."

[2] "La Queste del Saint Graal," ed. F. J. Furnivall (1864) for the Roxburghe Club, reads here, p. 182, "qui conuerse in calidoine."

[3] Camelot is neither situated in Wales as Caxton states, nor is the English Winchester identical with it. Camel, near South Cadbury, Somersets, is the place where the remains of the old city of Camelot are still to be found.—I am indebted to Sir Edward Strachey for submitting to me a lecture delivered by J. A. Bennet, at a public meeting in Somersetshire in 1887, which endeavours to establish the claims of Cadbury and Camelot to be the places referred to in the romance. There is besides an interesting account given of the different quotations of these places in other English writers.

---

[1] This is Caerleon-upon-Usk, the Roman Isca Silurum.

[2] The Thornton MS. reads here "Crete." I am led to think that the copy of the MS. that Malory used was very badly written; this only would explain such blunders.

[3] "La Queste del Saint Graal," ed. F. J. Furnivall (1864), reads here, page 179: "si entrerent en vne forest qui duroit iusc'a la mer, et estoit chele forest apielee chelibe," &c.

[4] This is the Cotentin peninsula, in the North-west of Normandy, supposed to be named after the Emperor Constantine.

---

[1] Geoffrey of Monmouth, "Hist. Brit.," calls him Gorlois dux Cornubiae ; in the Huth "Merlin" and in the ordinary " Merlin" he is called " duc de Tintaguel."

[2] He is called " Auctor" in the Huth " Merlin;" " Antor" in the ordinary " Merlin."

---

[1] Thornton MS. reads here " Elamet."

[2] "La Queste del Saint Graal" reads here, p. 183 : " si conuerse el fiun d'eufrate, et non mie en autre aigue, et chil poissons est appieles orteniaus."

[3] Thornton MS. reads here " Irritayne."

brings him the keys of the castle; he opens the gates; is welcomed by many people; hears from a gentle-woman that the seven knights will return again at night; receives a horn of ivory; blows it; a priest comes to tell him the history of the castle, 633; the knights of the castle do him homage; hears next morning that the seven brothers are slain by Gawayn and Vwayn, 634; meets Launcelot and Percyval, but they do not know him; fights against them; throws Percyual down; a recluse tells him that he is the best knight of the world, 636; Launce-lot and Percyual, on hearing who he is, follow him, but he escapes them, 637; saves Percyual; follows his adversaries, 646; 688; comes into a waste forest and has many adventures; takes his way to the sea; comes to a castle and helps the knight at a tournament; is recognised; smites Gawayn down; leaves secretly the place, 689; comes to the castle of Carboneck; sleeping in an hermitage, he is called away by a lady, who takes him to another castle, 690; from there he proceeds, with the maiden and the lady, to the sea, where they find a ship; Bors and Percy-ual are in it, and welcome him; he enters the ship; it starts; he asks them about the ship; finds another ship, 691; he enters it with the lady and his fellows; finds a bed and a crown of silk and a sword, 692; likes to draw the sword; arrives in Logrys, 693; 696; 699, 700, 701; the dying earl Hernox requests him to go to the maimed king to heal his wound, 702; 704, 705, 706; departs from Percyual, 707; meets Launcelot his father, 708; tells him about his sword, and remains with him half a year in the ship; a white knight comes to tell

him that he has been long enough with his father; they part from each other, 709; comes to king Mordrayns, who kindly receives him, 715*; buries the king; comes to a forest, and finds a well with boiling water; puts his hand into it; the water ceases at once; comes to Bagdemagus' tomb; quenches the fire in an abbey; passes the night in it, 716*; follows Percyual; finds him; they come to Carboneck; Galahad joins the pieces of the sword, 717; nine knights come to salute him, three from Gaul, three from Ireland, three from Denmark; four ladies bring a sick man on a bed to him, who has a golden crown on his head, 718; is kissed by Ioseph of Arimathia; receives the holy sacrament; is told to take some of the blood of the spear with him; heals the maimed king; leaves with Percyual and Bors the other knights, 720; prays long and instantly; comes to Sarras, 721; is made king of the holy city; orders a table and a precious chest to be made for the Holy Grail, 722; sees closely the holy vessel; prays God to take his soul from him; kisses Bors and Percyual; sends greetings to his father Launcelot; dies, 723; is buried, 724

Galahad, Galahalt, Galahault, the noble or the haute prynce, syr Breunor's sone, duke, lord, syr, of the countrey of Surluse, 257; 260; 313, 314; 445; 478; 480-484; 488, 489; 491; 493; 528; 738; 742; 745; 748; 757; 765, 766

Galapas, a giant, 173; killed by kyng Arthur

Galardoun, syr, 416

Galatyn, 176; name of Gawayn's sword

Galfrydus, 2 (Caxton's Preface); Geoffrey of Monmouth [1]

---

[1] The first printed edition is that of I. Cavellati, Paris, 1508, fol.: "Britānie utriusque regū & principū origo et gesta insignia ab Galfrido Monemutensi ex antiquissimis Britannici sermonis monumentis in latinū sermonē traducta; & ab Ascensio cura &

---

impēdio magistri Iuonis Cauellati in lucem edita:" etc. Caxton must refer to a manuscript.

and cuts his body into a hundred pieces, but is much worse wounded, 249; is healed by Lynet, 250, 251, 252, 253; asks Lyonesse not to tell Arthur where he is, but to propose a great tournament to be held at her castle on Assumption Day, 254; is healed and strengthened by Lynet's drugs; hears by the red knight from Arthur, 255, 256; receives a ring from Lyonesse, by which he can appear. in different colours, 257; appears at the tournament; fights bravely and excites general admiration, 258; 260; spares Launcelot, who recognises him, 261; gives his ring to the dwarf; forgets to take it again; comes back to the tournament in his ordinary shape, and is recognised by a herald, 262; he, however, disappears from the field; comes to a castle and asks lodging, 263; is taken in and well treated, and starts the next morning, 264; fights with Bendelayne, and gives him a mortal wound; is attacked by twelve of his knights, but bravely resists them; comes to a castle which is in the power of the brown knight; he overthrows him and kills him, 265; meet the duke de la rouse, and defeats him, 266; is hurt by a knight, who is no other than his brother Gawayn; Lynet appears in time to tell them; he is very happy to find his brother; Lynet dresses their wounds, and rides to fetch Arthur, 267; Arthur and Morgawse and many knights and ladies come to see him, and are highly pleased to have finally found him, 268; tells Arthur that he loves Lyonesse, 269; is wedded at Michelmas, in the castle of Kynkenadon, to Lyonesse, with great solemnity, 270, 271, 272; 510; 512; 517; rides with Trystram, 530, 531, 532; is compared by Arthur to an eager wolf, 533; is thrown down by Ector de Maris, 534; is horsed again by Trystram, 535; 539; 543, 544; 547, 548, 549; 552, 553; 555, 556; 728; does great deeds of arms at a tournament, 757, 758; 766, 767, 768, 769, 770; handles Vrre's wounds, 793; is killed by Launcelot, 811, 812; 816, 817

Garlon the inuysybel, syr, 90; 92

Garlot, country of, 38 (kynge Nentres)

Garnysshe of the mount, syr, 95

Gallie, 2 (Caxton's Preface); lat. gen. for Galliae

Gaule (France), 49; 718; 720

Gaunter, syr, 202, 203

Gautere, Gauter, syr, 256; 259; 792

Gawayn, Gauwayn, Gaweyn, kyng Arthur's nephew, son of kyng Lot of Orkeney; Gauwayn's skull kept in Dover Castle, 2 (Caxton's Preface); comes with his mother and brothers to Arthur's court, 64; comes again with his mother to his father's burial, 88; requests Arthur to make him knight, 101; is made knight, 103; declares he will slay Pellinore, 104; accompanies Vwayne, 140, 141, 142, 143; rides forth with the youngest of the three ladies, 144; finds a knight who is lamenting, 145; is asked to decide who shall have the lady, the knight or the dwarf; leaves the decision to the lady; fights with two knights; his lady is taken from him, 146; he accords with his adversary, and passes the night at his house; hears about Pelleas, 147; meets Pelleas; consoles him, and promises to help him to win Ettard's love, 148; promises to be true and faithful to him; rides to Ettard's castle, 149; forgetting his promise, he falls in love with Ettard and stays with her, 150; Ettard finds out that he has told her an untruth; leaves her, 151; 154; meets Marhaus and Vwayn again, 158; is sent for by Arthur, 159; is sent as messenger to Lucius, 169; kills a knight of Lucius who speaks ill of the "Bretons," 170; is sent with Florence to find provisions, 175; steals away from his fellowship; meets a knight of Tuskany; fights and overcomes the knight, who is called Pryamus,

and sorely wounded, but yet he is not contented, and will fight for a third time as soon as he has recovered; has to return to England, 838; is found half dead in a boat; tells Arthur that the hour of his death has come; acknowledges that he was the cause of the last terrible war, 841; is set up; writes a letter to Launcelot; asks his pardon, and requests him to come to help Arthur, 842; receives his Saviour; dies; is buried in the chapel of Dover Castel, 843; his ghost appears to king Arthur and warns him not to fight the next day, 844, 845; 852; his tomb is visited by Launcelot, 853

Gawdelyn, syr, 588

Gaynus, nyghe cosyn to Lucius, 169

Germanye, 175; germanie, lat. gen. for germaniae, 2 (Caxton's Preface); comp. Almayn

Geryne le grose, or only Geryn, syr, 473; 488

Gherard, a knyght of walys, 180

Gherard de breusse, syr, 220; 233

Glastyngburye,[1] monasterye of, 2; (Caxton's Preface); 851; 856*

Glatysaunt beest, also glastynge. See Questynge beest

Godard, town, garneson of, 178

Godefray of boloyn, 1 (Caxton's Preface)

Godelake, syr, 257

Goneryes, Gonoreys, Gomoryes, syr, 480; 482

Goodewyn, Godewyn, syr, a baroune, 587, 588

Goothe, castel of, 644

Gorre, Gore, land of, 139; 499; 716*; quene of, 187

Gouernayle, seruaunt of syr Trystram, 276; 281, 282; 296, 297; 304; 309; 319; 326, 327, 328; 353; 364; 380; 384; 418; 420

Gracian, Grastian, Grasian, Gracyens le casteleyn, syr, 50, 51; 60; 63

Grece, 163; Greece

Grene knyght, the. See Pertolepe

Gromere Gromorson, grummore gummursum, syr, a knyght of Scotland, 256; 258

Gromore somyr Ioure, syr, 799; probably identical with syr Gromere Gromorson

Gryflet, le fyse de dieu, once mistakingly spelled le fyse the dene, sone of Cardol, 49, 50; 54, 55; 60; 68, 69, 70; 121, 122, 123, 124; 287; 431, 432, 433; 530; 636; 742, 743; 767; 792

Gryngamore, syr, brother of lady Lyonesse, 242, 243, 244, 245, 246; 248, 249, 250; 254, 255; 257, 258; 268, 269

Gryp, erle, 328

Gueneuer,[2] Gweneuer, daughter of kyng Lodegrean of Camyliarde, wyfe of kyng Arthur, 63; 100, 101; 104; 117; 121; 136; 164; 167; 182; 187; 201; 203; 207; 211; 258; 329; 339; 358; 389; 410, 411; 417; 422; 439; 455, 456; 482, 483; 485, 486; 489, 490, 491, 492; 557; 572; 580, 581, 582, 583–586; 606; 622, 623; 725, 726–731; 734; 739; 751; 757; 759; 761; 763; 772, 773, 774, 775; 777, 778; 780, 781; 786; 796, 797; 800; 816; 821; 828; 830; 851, 852, 853, 854; 857*

Gumret le petyte, syr, 287

Guy of Camylyard, syr, 471

Guyart le petyte, syr, 792

Gwenbaus, syr, brother of Ban and Bors, 50

Gwymyart de bloy, syr, 54

Gwynas de bloy, syr, 55, 56; 60; not improbably the same as syr Gwymyart

---

[1] Glastonbury is a town in Somersetshire, said to have been founded by Joseph of Arimathia. The ruins of the famous abbey are still to be seen. About the abbey of Glastonbury, and its signification for the introduction of Christianity into Britain, see W. W. Skeat, "Joseph of Arithmathie," an alliterative romance, A.D. 1350 (from the unique Vernon MS., Bodleian Library, Oxford), E.E.T.S. 1871, Introd. p. xxiii. ff.; also Paul's and Braune's "Beiträge," Halle a.S., vol. iii., p. 304, ff., F. Zarncke, "Zur Geschichte der Gralsage," and A. Nutt, "Studies on the Legend of the Holy Grail," ch. ix.   [2] "Hist. Brit.": Guanhumara.

---

[1] The form Heles occurs in the eighth book several times for Hebes. In the French "Tristan" the name is always spelled "Hebes." This is either a misprint in the Caxton, or a mistake on my part, as it is often very difficult to distinguish le and be, these being in Caxton's type double letters.

[2] The "Morte Arthure" (Thornton MS.) reads here "Ermonye.'

---

[1] Here Geoffrey's "Hist. Brit." has "Iordanus de Tintagol." The Huth "Merlin" reads "Jourdain."

he sees young Launcelot, who is first called Galahad; he prophesies that he will become a man of great worship, 119; 143; suddenly[1] introduced, 171, 172; excels all other knights; is a great favourite of Gueneuer; sets out with his nephew Lyonel to seek adventures; lies down to sleep under an apple-tree, 183, 184, 185; is found asleep by four queens; taken to Morgan le fay's castle; does not know how he came there; hears that he is a prisoner, 186; refuses Morgan le fay and her companions; on condition that he will help her father, king Bagdemagus, in a tourney, a damoysel promises to deliver him, 187; escapes from the castle by the maiden's help; comes to a pavilion, and enters it to repose himself there; the owner of the pavilion finds him, 188; they fight together; Launcelot overcomes the knight; explains to him how he came thither; tells his name; asks the knight to come to Arthur's court, 189; comes to an abbey, where the damoysel expects him; her father is sent for; is well received; he tells Bagdemagus to send him three knights with white shields, 190; comes to the tournament; throws down Mador de la porte and Mordred; fights against Gahalantyne, 191; overcomes him also; returns to Bagdemagus' castle; is much cheered; starts to seek Lyonel; is told by a damoysel that there lives near at hand a strong knight, 192; he beats on a basin; rides along the gates of the manor of this knight, Turquyne; sees Gaherys tied to a horse, and meets Turquyne, 193; fights against him, 194; overcomes him; delivers Gaherys, 195*; tells Gaherys to deliver the other knights out of prison, 196*; fights and defeats Perys de foreyst saueage, 197; tells the damoysel his ideas about love, and leaves her; smites a fellow down who tries to prevent him from passing a bridge; comes to a castle, 198; kills three giants; delivers sixty ladies; the castle is called Tyntygayl; departs from there, 199; is lodged at the house of an old gentlewoman; sees Kay in great distress; jumps out of the window; fights and throws down his persecutors, and compels them to yield themselves to Kay, 200; returns to his lodging; the next morning he takes Kay's armour and shield, and rides forth before Kay awakes, 201; is mistaken for Kay; overcomes three brothers, Gaunter, Raynold, and Gylmere, and bids them go to queen Gueneuer and render themselves to her grace; meets Sagramor, Ector, Gawayn, and Vwayn; is attacked by them, 203; throws them all four out of their saddles, and disappears; comes into a forest; sees a brachet, 204; follows the brachet to a wounded knight; is told that this knight is Gylbert the Bastard, and that he can only be healed by a piece of cloth and a sword which must be fetched out of the Chappel Peryllous, 205; engages himself to go to the Chappel Peryllous; arrives there; enters it in despite of many knights, 206; takes the cloth and sword; comes out; refuses Hellawes the sorceress; heals Gylbert, 207; catches a falcon which has escaped to a tree; is treacherously attacked by its owner, 208; gets with great efforts out of this difficulty, 209; meets a knight and a lady; the knight kills the lady; Launcelot sends him to Gueneuer, who shall punish him for his bad behaviour; comes in Kay's armour to the court, 211; all his valiant deeds are told to Arthur, 212; 214, 215, 216; fights with Gareth, 217; makes him knight, 218; 226; 232, 233; 241; 251; 254, 255, 256; 260, 261, 262; 270; 272; 300; 303*; 305*, 306*, 307, 308; 315, 316; 322, 323, 324; blames

---

[1] Launcelot is here very abruptly introduced; how he came to Arthur's court and how he was made knight, as well as the early part of his life, are entirely omitted.

---

[1] "Hist. Brit.": has "Lot de Loudonesia" (Lot of Lothian). Huth "Merlin" reads "Loth d'Orcanie."

[2] "Hist. Brit.": "Lucius Tiberius." "Morte Arthure" (Thornton MS.) reads either "Lucius" or "Lucius Iberius."

---

[1] Comp. my note to "Arundel," p. ix.—Through the kindness of Lady Milbanke, of Eartham, Chichester, I was enabled, while staying under her hospitable roof, to visit Arundel Castle, the seat of the Duke of Norfolk (February 14, 1890), and to inquire on the spot about the possible identity of "Arundel" and "Magouns"; there is, however, nothing whatever known on this subject at the castle. Arundel is probably mentioned for the first time in the will of Alfred the Great. Some indisputably certain references to "Arundel" are to be found in the Chronicles of Robert of Gloucester, Peter Langtoft, and Robert Manning of Brunne (see the editions of Hearne, Oxford, 1724 and 1725, printed again 1810), on the occasion of the arrival of the Empress Maud in England and her reception at Arundel Castle. (For further particulars see James Dallaway, "A History of the Western Division of the County of Sussex, etc., London, 1819, 4to, vol. ii. pp. 83 and 95 ff.)

from his own sister, kyng Lot's wife, is begotten, 65 ; escapes with his life ; is found by a good man, and nourished till he is fourteen years old ; then he is brought to the court, 75 ; 87 ; shall be one day against his own father, 89 ; 190 ; is thrown down by Launcelot, 191 ; rides with la cote male tayle ; is thrown down by a knight of the castel Orgulous, 342, 343 ; blames the damoysel Maledysaunt for rebuking la cote male tayle, 344 ; seeing Launcelot, he leaves their company, 345 ; gives his shield and armour to Dagonet, 432, 433 ; is smitten down by Breuse saunce pyte, 454, 455 ; tries to lead Alysaunder's horse away, 477 ; 487 ; 512 ; gives Sir Lamorak a mortal wound, 513 ; 532 ; 590, 591 ; tries to find fault with Launcelot, 726 ; 742, 743 ; does not join the knights to receive sir Launcelot on his return, 759 ; 766 ; is thrown down by Launcelot, 768 ; 791 ; declares he will accuse queen Gueneuer, 797 ; tells king Arthur, 798, 799 ; goes with twelve knights to capture Launcelot, 800 ; calls him a traitour, 801 ; is grievously wounded, but escapes, 803 ; comes to Arthur to tell him about Launcelot's deed, 807, 808 ; is made chief ruler of England during Arthur's absence, 830 ; forges letters stating that Arthur is killed in a battle ; assembles the parliament, and is crowned king of England ; asks Gueneuer's hand ; besieges Gueneuer in the Tower of London ; defies the Archbishop of Canterbury, 839 ; hears of his father's return ; excites the barons to make war against Arthur ; finds many followers, 840 ; fights against Arthur at Dover, 841, 842 ; gathers his knights at Baramdown to fight another battle, 844 ; agrees to make peace on condition of receiving Cornwall and Kent, 845 ; fights at the risk of his life ; all his knights

are killed ; is wounded to death ; dying, he kills his father with his sword, 847 ; 850, 851, 852, 853

Morgan le fay, Arthur's sister, wife of king Vryence, of the land of Gore, 38 ; 67 ; 88, 89 ; 123 ; 126, 127, 128, 129 ; 132 ; 139 ; 186, 187 ; 324, 325 ; 332 ; 373 ; 378, 379 ; 407–412 ; 440 ; 457 ; 470, 471 ; 473, 474 ; 572

Morganore, Morganor, sencial of the kynge of the honderd knyghtes, 55 ; 58 ; 302 ; 792 ; once mistakingly called kyng M.

Morgause, Arthur's sister. *See* **Margawse**

Morris, forest of, 402

Mortayse, Mortoyse, water of, 652 ; 707 ; 727

Moryans, of the castel of maydens, syr, 60

Morys de la roche, syr, 54

Morys, syr, 172

Moyses land,[1] marquys of, 180

Mychels, St., 169 ; mounte of, 167

Myles of the laundes, syr, 117

Mylis, syr, 68

Nabon le Noyre, syr, 330 ; 332, 333

Nacyen the heremyte, 618 ; 621 ; 627 ; 660 ; 668, 669 ; 694, 695

Nanowne le petite, syr, 330

Nappus, a holy man, 660

Naram, syr, 75

Nauntys, cyte of, in Brytayne, 64

Nentres,[2] **Nauntres**, kyng of the land of garlot, or garlott, or garloth, 38 ; 52 ; 54 ; 56 ; 60 ; 64 ; 790

Nero, syr, brother of kyng Ryons, 64 ; 86, 87, 88

Nerouens, Neroneus, Neroueus, syr, 346 ; 348 ; 792 ; 804 ; 830

Normandy, duke of, 830 ; this dignity is conferred on syr Clarrus by syr Launcelot

Northfolk, 843 ; Norfolk

Northgalys, Northwalys, kynge of, 188, 189, 190, 191, 192 ; 212 ; 377 ; 383 ; 385, 386 ; 391 ; 534, 535 ; 545 ; 738, 739 ; 742 ; 745 ; 755, 756, 757 ; quene of, 187

---

[1] The Morte Arthure (Thornton MS.) reads here "the maches of Mees" (Metz).
[2] In the ordinary "Merlin" he is called "kyng Nanters of Gerlot."

---

[1] The "Morte Arthure" (Thornton MS.) reads for this form, line 351, "Petyrsande."

[2] Ranulphus Higden's "Polychronicon," printed by William Caxton, 1482, fol., black letter. I have seen the copy in the British Museum.

[3] Of course, St. Paul's Cathedral did not exist in the days of king Arthur, and therefore "some men" were wrong.

---

[1] For an exhaustive account of the literature of "The Holy Grail," see Alfred Nutt's "Studies on the Legend of the Holy Grail," London, 1888, 8vo.

---

[1] The form "Sowdan," the Middle-English soudan, for sultan, seems to have entirely escaped Wright as well as Strachey. The former passes it over in silence; the latter mentions it separately in his Glossary without giving an explanation.

[2] Geoffrey of Monmouth, "Hist. Brit.," calls this castle "castellum Dimilioc." In the ordinary "Merlin" as well as in the Huth "Merlin" in the corresponding passage this castle is only spoken of as "a second castle," and no name is given. The name "Tarabel" occurs, however, in the Huth "Merlin," i. pp. 241, 252-261, where it is the castle in which the army of king Ryons is defeated and where king Lot is killed. Where the place was situated I am utterly unable to ascertain.

[3] The "Morte Arthure" (Thornton MS.) always reads "Pounte" for "port."

[4] There are a considerable number of MSS. in the British Museum which treat of hunting and hawking—e.g., Cotton Vespasian B. xij, "The Mayster of the Hunt"—but none of them bears the title "Syr Trystram's Book," nor can I find any reference in them to the existence of such a book. The earliest printed book on this subject in English is Lady Juliana Berners' "Booke of St. Albans," printed for the first time by the schoolmaster-printer of St. Albans in 1486 (reproduced in facsimile by William Blades,

279; comes to king Mark; is made knight, 280; goes to meet Marhaus; finds him near his ship, 281; fights with him, 282; overcomes him, 283; returns to Mark; is wounded with a poisoned spear; can only be healed in the country where the spear is made, 284; goes to Ireland; gains the king's favour by his harping; calls himself Tramtryst, 285; Isoud, the king's daughter, nurses and heals him; requests him to fight at a tournament, 286; is nearly discovered; appears on a white horse, and with white shield and harness, given to him by Isoud, 287; makes Hebes le renoumes knight; overcomes Palomydes, 288; is discovered through his sword, 289; leaves the court of Anguysshe, 290; takes leave of Isoud, 291, 292; after calling on his father, returns to Mark's court; becomes, as well as king Mark, enamoured of the wife of Segwarydes; meets Mark, and smites him down, 293; is betrayed by the wife of Segwarydes, who fights against him, 294; Trystram throws him down, and rides to Tyntagil, 295; is rebuked by a lady; rides after Bleoberis, 296; meets Sagramor and Dodynas, and smites them both down, 297; joins Bleoberys and the wife of Segwarydes, 298; fights against him, and overcomes him, 299; the lady refuses to go with him, 300; returns to Tyntagyl; is sent to Ireland by king Mark to ask for Isoud's hand for him, 301; is driven to the coast of England; smites down Ector, 302; hears that king Anguysshe is accused of treason; resolves to help him, 303*; comes to the king, 304*; is accepted, and Anguysshe promises to give him

whatever he will ask, 305*; fights against Blamor, 306; overcomes him, but requests the kings to save his life, 307; is joyfully received by Anguysshe, and goes with him to Ireland, 308; asks for Isoud's hand in the name of king Mark; returns with Isoud to Cornwall; on the way takes a love drink with her, 309; fights against Breunor, and rids the castel Pluere of its bad customs, 310, 311, 312, 313, 314, 315, 316, 317, 318, 319, 320; is betrayed by his cousin Andred; king Mark lifts his sword up to kill him, but Trystram puts him to flight, 321; kills two brothers, knights of king Mark, and wounds about thirty other knights; is sent for by the barons, and reconciled with Mark, 322; refuses to do anything that is against his knighthood; fights with Lamorack, 323, 324; goes daily and nightly to Isoud; is taken by Andred and twelve knights; they bind him and intend to kill him; 325; asks his cousin Andred for mercy; breaks his fetters, and escapes; defends himself in a chapel, where his men join him, 326; delivers Isoud; is hurt by a poisoned arrow; goes to Bretayne, to king Howel's daughter, Isoud la blanche maynys, to get healed, 327; becomes enamoured of her, and marries her, 328; hears that Launcelot blames him for his conduct, 329, 330, 331, 332, 333, 334, 335; 344, 345, 346; 348; receives a sorrowful letter from Isoud, Marke's wife; resolves to go to see her; is driven ashore near the Castel peryllous; leaves his fellowship with Kehydius, 353, 354; fights and overcomes Lamorack; is henceforth his friend,

---

1881, 4to), later by Wynkyn de Worde and many others. In this book Trystram is once thus alluded to :—

"Wheresoeuer ye fare by fryth or by fell,
My dere chylde take hede how Tristram dooth you tell."

From some passages in another book, "The Noble Art of Venerie and Hunting," by G. Tuberville, London, 1611, 8vo, it appears, however, that in days past there existed a "Book of Syr Trystram." Comp. p. 40, "Trystram's lore ;" p. 96, "for noble Tristram's sake ;" p. 148, "Yet our Tristram reckoneth the bore for one of the foure beasts of Venerie;" p. 174, "but our old Tristram calleth it hallow."

Galyhodyn, who wants to take Isoud from him; he smites him down, 527; meets Gawayn, Vwayn, Sagramor, and Dodynas, 528, 529; declines to tell Arthur his name, nor which party he belongs to, 530, 531, 532, 533; is brought to the ground by Launcelot; gets the horse of the king of Northgalis, 534; throws Arthur out of the saddle; reappears in red harness; smites down five knights, 535, 536; smites down Ector, 537, 538, 539, 540, 541, 542, 543; fights very bravely, 544; rides secretly out of the field, 545; arrays himself all in black; returns with Dynadan to the tournament; smites down three knights, 546; fights against Palomydes, who has disguised himself; afterwards with Launcelot, who does not recognise him, 547; helps Dynadan; is recognised by Launcelot, 548; gets the degree of the day; returns to his pavilion with Isoud, 549; hears from Isoud about Palomydes' falsehood; pardons him, 550; receives Arthur and Launcelot in his pavilion, 551; tells Arthur why he was against him, 552; meets with Kay, and throws him down from his horse and three other knights as well; surpasses all other knights, 553, 554; returns to king Arthur's party; the prize is given him again, but he refuses it in favour of Launcelot; returns to his pavilion, 555; returns to Ioyous gard to rest himself seven days, 556, 557, 558, 559; 561; rides to the castel Pelownes to save Palomydes, 563; meets Launcelot, 564; requests him to stay with him at Ioyous gard, 565; hears how Palomydes, alone at a well, talks about his love for Isoud, 566; reproaches him for his perfidy, 567; agrees to fight with him, in fifteen days, near Camelot;

returns to Ioyous gard; one day, being out hunting, he is shot in the thigh by an archer, 568; tells Palomydes that he cannot fight at the day fixed, 569; gets great renown by his valiant deeds of arms; the people of Lyonas send him letters and presents, 570; 606; meets, unarmed, Palomydes, yet fights with him, 607, 608; takes Galleron's armour, shield, and sword, and fights again with Palomydes, 609; overcomes him, 610; leads him to Carleil and causes him to be christened, 611; his death referred to, 768; 807

Tryan, syr, 427

Turkes, or myscreantes, 860*

Turkye, 163; Turkey

Turquyne, syr, 185; 193, 194, 195; 197, 198; 211, 212; 256; 261; 824

Turnaunce, yle of, 694

Tursank, erle of, 830; (?) this dignity is conferred on syr Melyas de lyle by syr Launcelot

Tuskane, 175, 176; 181; Tuscany, a grand duchy in Italy

Tyntagil,[1] Tyntigayll, castle of the duke of Cornwayle, 35; 37; 45; 68; 199; 278, 279; 284; 292; 294; 301; 364; 367; 370; 403; 455; 458, 459, 460, 461; 497

Vlbawes, Vlbause, erle of Surluse, 491, 492; 790

Vlfyus,[2] syr, a noble knyght, the confidant of kyng Vtherpendragon, 36, 37; 43; 48, 49; 53, 54, 55; 60; 62; 67, 68

Vlfyn, heremyte, 690; very likely identical with syr Vlfyus

Vrbyne, cyte of, 181

Vrre, syr, 788, 789, 790, 791, 792, 793, 794; 801; 804; 820, 821, 822-830

Vryence,[3] Vryens, kyng of the land of gore, 44; 52; 56; 64; 89; 123, 124, 125, 126; 140; 257; 260; 760; 790

---

[1] Tintagell is a small town in Cornwall on the coast of the Bristol Channel.
[2] "Hist. Brit." has "Vlfinus de Ricaradock;" Huth "Merlin" reads "Ulfin;" the "ordinary Merlyn" (MS. of the University Library, Cambridge) reads "Vlfyn."
[3] "Hist. Brit." reads "Vrianus;" Huth "Merlin" has "Urien."

---

[1] The "Morte Arthure" (Thornton MS.) reads here once "Vale of Viterbe," in another passage "the Viscownte of Valewnce."

[2] According to the Wilkina Saga, he was the son of Wilcinus and the mermaid Wachild. He is often confounded with Tor. (Comp. "Wade": Lettre à M. Henri Ternaux Compans, par Fr. Michel; Paris, 1837.)

[3] This is most likely "Gwentland" in Monmouthshire.

GLOSSARY.[1]

A, i. *prep.*, = in, on; ii. *interj.*, expressing pain or surprise, 303* 24; 860* 1; iii. *prefix*—(1) for *prep. a* and for Icel. *á* = on (**abak**); (2) for O.F. *a-* and Lat. *ad-* (**abated**); (3) for A.F. *a*, O.F. *e-, es-*, Lat. *e-, ex-* (**abasshed**); (4) adding intensity to the notion of a verb, A.S. *á-* for *ar-*, O.H.G. *ar-*, Goth. *us-* (**aboughte**); (4) for *prep. at* and Icel. *at* (**adone**); (5) for *prep. of* (**adrad**); (6) for A.F. *an-*, O.F. *en-* from Lat. *in-* (**apayre**).

abak, *adv.*, 131 30; backwards;—A.S. *on-bœc.*

abasshe, *v.*, to abash, cast down; **abasshed**, *p.p.*, 62 28; 615 32; ashamed, alarmed; **abeysshed**, *p.p.*, 392 26;—O.F. *esbahiss-* from *esbahir.*

abate, *v.*, to beat down, to calm; **abated**, *pt.*, 158 4;—A.F. *abatre.*

a bedde, 800 21; in bed.

abhomynable, *adj.*, 165 34; abominable;—A.F. *abhominable.*

abreide, *v.*, to start up, to draw (a sword), to thrust out, to blame; **abraide**, *pt.*, 389 20; **abrayed**, *pt.*, 239 21;—A.S. *ábregdan.*

abrode, *adv.*, away, 845* 28.

abyde, *v.*, to abide, await, remain, endure; **abode**, *pt.*, 87 33; **aby-**

den, *p.p.*, 691 6; 702 16;—A.S. *á-bídan.*

abye, *v.*, to buy, to pay for; **aboughte**, *pt.*, 238 33;—A.S. *ábycgan.*

abylement, *sb.*, 64 30; dress, clothing;—O.F. *habillement.*

accept, *p.p.*, 3 4; *for* accepted.

accompanye, *v. inf.*, 314 35; to associate with somebody;—O.F. *accompaignier.*

accomplysshe, *v.*, to achieve, to accomplish; **taccomplysshe**, *inf.*, 177 9; **accomplysshed**, *p.p.*, 1 (*see* **complysshe**);—from O.F. *acompliss-*, p.prs. of *acomplir.*

accompte, *v.*, to count, calculate; *prs.*, 410 20; *inf.*, 622 38;—Late Lat. *accomptare.*

accord, *sb.*, agreement, peace, 37 27; —Lat. *ad* and *cord-* from *cor ;*—O.F. *acord.*

achyeue, *v.*, to bring to an end, achieve; *inf.*, 27 4; **achyeued**, *pt.*, 14 36; **acheued**, *pt.*, 570 8; **thachyeuyng**, *pr. prs.*, 861* (Caxton's Colophon). *See also* **en-cheue** ;—O.F. *acheuer.*

acqueyntaunce, *sb.*, 380 22; acquaintance;—*deriv. of* Late Lat. *adcognitare*, O.F. *acointer.*

acquyte, *v.*, to acquit; *prs.*, 176 6; —O.F. *aquiter.*

---

[1] What is said about the List of Names and Places can be repeated here: this Glossary is the first ever compiled to "Le Morte Darthur." As I am preparing a Caxton Dictionary for all the works of England's first printer for which I have accumulated the material in the course of my studies, I have been able to give to this Glossary more the form of a small Etymological Dictionary. Many words, however, owe their acceptance only to their orthography. The numbers refer to pages and lines. In the etymological part A.F. is written for *Anglo-French;* A.S., *Anglo-Saxon;* Goth., *Gothic;* Icel., *Icelandic;* Lat., *Latin;* Late Lat., *post-classical Latin;* M.E., *Middle English;* O.F., *Old French;* O.H.G., *Old High German;* O.Merc., *Old Mercian;* O.North., *Old Northumbrian;* O.S., *Old Saxon;* Sans., *Sanskrit;* W., *Welsh.* I have always given the different spellings of every word that occur in the text.

actually, *adv.,* 146 32; bravely, actively;—Lat. *actualis.*

Adieu, *adv.,* 393 16; to God, farewell;—Fr. *à Dieu.*

admoneste, *v. prs.,* 173 5; to bring to mind, to warn, admonish;— Late Lat. *admonitare,* O.F. *amonester.*

ado, *sb.,* fuss, trouble, difficulty, 443 5; to haue adoo with, 73 26; ado with her, 62 35; had lytyl ado to cause, 36 16; adone, 441 2.

adoubted, *adj.,* afraid, 481 2.

adrad, *p.p.,* frightened, put in dread, 59 19; 435 6; adradde, 654 44; —A.S. *of-drad.*

aduant garde, *sb.,* vanguard, 56 35;—O.F. *avantgarde. Compare* vaward.

aduysyon, *sb.,* vision, apparition, 27 15;—Lat. *ad* and *visionem. Compare* vysyon.

afer, *adv.,* afar, at a far distance, 706 36;—A.S. *of feorr,* O.S. *fer,* Goth. *fairra.*

afere, *v.,* to frighten, terrify; aferd, *p.p.,* 70 23; 187 28; 656 20;—A.S. *á-færan*

affyaunce, *sb.,* faith pledged to, trust, confidence, 841 30;—A.F. *affiaunce.*

afore, *adv., prep.,* before, 97 2; 135 5;—A.S. *on-foran.*

afterdele, *sb.,* disadvantage, 173 33; —A.S. *æft* and *dæl.*

ageynward, *adv.,* against, towards, 550 33.

agon, agone, *p.p.* and *adv.,* gone away, ago, 435 14; 526 25; 634 4; —A.S. *a-gán.*

agreue, *v.,* to bear heavily on, to grieve, to oppress; agreued, *p.p.,* 43 11;—Lat. *aggrauare.*

aknowen, *p.p.,* known, 295 16;— A.S. *a-cnáwen.*

al, *sb., adj., adv.,* all; al dede, 715* 33; alle to hewe hym, 513 9; alle the hole Iustes, 552 1; al to long, 132 2; al only, 882 16; foughten wyth al, 29 14; alle to sheuers, 554 14;—A.S. *eall, all, al.*

alaye, *v.,* to quiet, alleviate; alayed, *p.p.,* 718 16;—A.S. *a-lecgan.*

allygeaunce, *sb.,* the duty of a subject to his lord, but at 760 11 it seems to be synonymous with forgiveness, alleviation.

almery, *sb.,* cupboard, press; almeryes of Salysbury, 724 24; —Lat. *almariolum.*

almesse, *sb.,* alms, charity, 221 26; —A.S. *ælmesse.*

al one, *adj., adv.,* alone, 74 16; allone, 849 38;—A.S. *al, eal,* and *án.*

alowde, *adv.,* aloud, 452 1;—A.S. *on* and *hlúd.*

allwayes, *adv.,* always, 831 37;—A.S. *al* and *weg.*

al ther, *gen. pl.,* of all, 134 2;—A.S. *ealra.*

Alyaunts, *sb. pl.,* aliens, strangers, 831 12;—Lat. *alienus.*

alyghte, *v.,* to alight, to get down from a horse, to descend; to lighten; alyghte, *pt.,* 403 24; 242 31; 267 4; alyght, *pt.,* 184 20; alyghted, *pt.,* 167 5; alyghte, *p.p.,* 266 23;—A.S. *á-lihtan.*

amase, *v.,* to amaze, stupefy; amased, *p.p.,* 844 12.

amble, *v.,* to move at an easy pace; ambelynge paas, 197 11; — hacney, 234 24; — meule, 267 8;—O.F. *ambler,* Lat. *ambulare.*

ambuler, *sb.,* an ambling horse; 561 30;—O.F. *ambleur.*

amendys, *sb. pl.,* amends, reparation, recompense, 107 15;—Lat. *a* and *menda;* O.F. *amende.*

ammonysshement, *sb.,* admonishment, exhortation, 688 11;—O.F. *amonestement.*

amounte, *v.,* to ascend, rise; to amount; amounted, *pt.,* 416 20; —A.F. *amunter,* from Lat. *ad montem.*

amys, *adj.* and *adv.,* amiss, wrong, 731 26;—A.S. *a, missian.*

anger, angre, *sb.,* affliction, sorrow, wrath, pain, 416 24; 539 29; 797 8;—Icel. *angr.*

anguysshe, *sb.,* anguish, 390 28; —O.F. *angoisse,* A.F. *anguisse,* Lat. *angustia.*

anker, *sb.,* anchor, 281 22;—A.S. *ancor,* Lat. *ancora.*

anon, *adv.*, at once, instantly, soon, 43 35;—A.S. *on án.*

anuylde, anuyld, *sb.*, anvil, 40 22, 26;—A.S. *anfilt, onfilt.*

apaye, *v.*, to satisfy, requite, please; **apayed**, *p.p.*, 767 1;—O.F. *apayer*, Lat. *ad, pacare.*

apayre, *v.*, to harm, diminish, impair; **apayre**, *prs.*, 102 13;—O.F. *ampeirer*, Lat. *in peiorare.*

apease, *v.*, to appease, calm; **appeased**, *pt.*, 32 4;—O.F. *apaisier*, Lat. *ad, pacem.*

apeche, *v.*, to hinder, to impeach, to charge with crime, to cite before a court; **apeched**, *pt.*, 6 32; **appeched**, *pt.*, 30 17; **appeche**, *inf.*, 424 23; **apoeche**, *prs.*, 424 28;—corrupt. of *empeche*, O.F. *empecher*, Lat. *impedicare.*

apoynte, *v.*, to agree, arrange, prepare; **apoynted**, *pt.*, 522 30;—O.F. *apointer.*

apparail, *sb.*, apparel, dress, 418 7.

apparaille, apparaylle, *v.*, to make ready, fit up, furnish, dress, attire; **apparaylled**, *p.p.*, 125 27; *pt.*, 447 32;—O.F. *apareiller.*

appele, *v.*, to call to, to bring before one, appeal; **appeled**, *pt.*, 21 29; —Lat. *appellare.*

apperceyue, *v.*, to perceive, to understand, to notice; **apperceuyued**, *pt.*, 247 36;—Late Lat. *appercipēre.*

appertenaunce, *sb.*, appurtenance, that which appertains or belongs to, 39 34; 134 17;—O.F. *apurtenaunse, apartenance.*

apperteyne, *v.*, to appertain, to belong to; **apperteyneth**, *prs.*, 452 5;—O.F. *apertenir.*

appertyce,[1] *sb.*, open display, proof, or evidence of valour; **appertyces**, *pl.*, 173 14.

appoyntement, *sb.*, agreement, appointment; **appoyntementes**, *pl.*, 821 19. *Compare* **poyntement**, 463 11;—O.F. *apointement.*

approuche, *v.*, to approach; **ap-**

prouched, *pt.*, 173 11;—Lat. *appropriare*, O.F. *aprocher.*

apres, le, surname of Brewnor, king of the hundred knights;—Lat.*asper*, O.F. *aspre*, zealous, courageous.

a purpos, 509 29; on purpose, intentionally;—O.F. *a purpos, propos.*

arage, *v.*, to put in a rage, to render furious; **araged**, *p.p.*, 162 32;— Sans. *rabh*, Lat. *rabere*, O.F. *rager.*

a rase, *v.*, to pull up by the roots, to tear off; *inf.*, 771 13;—Lat. *eradicare*, O.F. *esrachier.*

aray, *sb.*, array, dress, 36 15;—O.F. *arei.*

araye, *v.*, to array, to dress; **arayed**, *p.p.*, 7 13;—O.F. *areier*, A.F. *arayer.*

ardant, *adj.*, ardent, 653 31;—O.F. *ardant*, from *arder.*

a reeste, *sb.*, stop, arrest, custody, 773 34;—O.F. *arest.*

arere, *v.*, to draw back, to withdraw; **areryd**, *pt.*, 524 5;—from A.F. *arere*, adv., Lat. *ad retro.*

arette, *v.*, to reckon, count, accuse; **aretted**, *p.p.*, 2 11;—Lat. *reputare*, O.F. *aretter.*

areyse, *v.*, to raise, arouse; **areyeds**, *pt.*, 465 23.

armyuestal,[2] *adj.*, warlike, martial, 138 15;—?

aromatyk, *adj.*, aromatic, sweetscented, 174 22;—from Late Lat. *aroma.*

arraunt, *adj.*, errant, 404 6;—O.F. *errant.*

arryuayl, *sb.*, arrival, 285 10;—Lat. *adripare.*

arson, *sb.*, bow of the saddle, 678 22; 768 9; **arsson**, 191 30;—A.F. *arcon.*

aryse, *v.*, to arise; *inf.*, 473 25; **aroos**, *pt.*, 471 35; **arysen**, *p.p.*, 659 26;—A.S. *á-risan.*

aryue, *v.*, to arrive, to come ashore; **aryuen**, *p.p.*, 700 22;—Lat. *adripare*, O.F. *arriver.*

aske, *v.*, to ask; *inf.*, 462 21 (frequently **axe**); **asked**, *pt.*, 70 4;

---

[1] *Compare* W. Caxton, "Ovid's Metamorph.," book xi. ch. 22 (edition of the Roxburghe Club, 1819): "He was wyse, dyscrete, and full of al appertyse."

[2] Wynkyn de Worde reads "armyuestall." I have not come across this form in any of the great number of texts I have read, nor can I find the word in any dictionary. It probably owes its existence to a misprint.

axed, *pt.*, 7 1; 460 12; **axyd**, *pt.*, 179 15;—A.S. *áscian*, *áxian*.

a sonder, *adv.*, asunder, 725 1;—A.S. *on sundran.*

aspye, *sb.*, spy; **aspyes**, *pl.*, 753 1; —O.F. *espie.*

aspye, *v.*, to look after, to watch, to search; **aspyed**, *pt.*, 82 18;—O.F. *espier.*

assaye, *v.*, to examine, try, attack; *inf.*, 71 17; **assayed**, *pt.*, 25 35; 42 7;—A.F. *assayer.*

assomone, *v.*, to summon, to command to appear in court; *inf.*, 275 17;—Lat. *ad, submonere.*

assote, *v.*, to dote upon somebody, to be deeply enamoured, smitten; **assotted**, *p.p.*, 4 25; **assoted**, *p.p.*, 118 32;—O.F. *asoter.*

assoyle, *v.*, to loosen, to absolve, explain; *inf.*, 855* 30; **assoyled**, *pt.*, 642 1;—Late Lat. *absoluere*, O.F. *assoldre.*

assuraunce, *sb.*, assurance, 462 35.

astonye, *v.*, to stupefy, amaze, astonish; **astonyed**, *p.p.* and *pt.*, 194 5; 511 4; 703 12;—Lat. *extonare*, O.F. *estoner.*

asure, *sb.*, azure, 165 5; 526 19; —Late Lat. *lazur*, O.F. *asur*, *azur.*

atte, contraction of at, *prep.*, and the *def. article* the — **atte bore**, 596 17; **atte ende**, 707 18; **atte last**, 107 11; 713 37, &c.; *but* at **the laste**, 71 30; **att armes**, F. *aux armes!* 53 5; **atte castel**, 83 16; **atte feste**, 8 27; and many others.

atteyne, *v.*, attain; *inf.*, 4 2;—Lat. *attingere*, O.F. *ateindre.*

attones, *adv.*, at once, instantly, 379 13; 646 9

at travers, *adv.*, *prep.*, right through, 717 7;—F. *à travers.*

atwo, in two, 537 5;—A.S. *on, an,* and *twá.*

auke, *adj.*, turned the wrong way, perverse, sinister, 312 17;—Icel. *afugr.*

aulter, *sb.*, altar, 43 34; 580 1;—Lat. *altare*, O.F. *auter, alter.*

auncyent, *adj.*, old, 616 1;—A.F. *auncien.*

auaunce, *v.*, to advance; *inf.*, 103 24;—O.F. *avancer.*

auaunt, *sb.*, boast, vaunt, 683 28; 788 34; 824 13;—O.F. *avant.*

auauntage, *sb.*, advantage, superiority, 240 18; 412 19;—O.F. *avantage.*

auaunte, *v.*, to speak proudly, to boast, commend; **auauntest**, *prs.*, 176 16;—Late Lat. *ad* and *vanitare*, O.F. *avanter.*

auaylle, *v.*, to avail; **auaylleth**, *prs.*, 224 23; **auaylyd**, *p.p.*, 181 6;— Lat. *valere.*

auentre, *v.*, to put the spear along the side, in order to attack one's adversary; also to throw a spear (Spenser); **auentryd**, *pt.*, 97 7; 145 27;—Lat. *ad ventrem.*

auenture, adventure, *sb.*, chance, occurrence, jeopardy, risk, 83 15; **aduentures**, *pl.*, 803 18; **by aduenture** = by chance, 20 2; 36 14; *v.*, to risk, to venture, 69 1;—O.F. *aventure.*

auoutres, auoultres, awoutres, les, the adulterer; epithet of Vwayne, son of king Vryence; —Lat. *adulterum*, O.F. *auoutre*, *aöutre.*

auowe, *sb.*, vow, promise, 154 7; *v.*, to bind with a vow;—Late Lat. *advocare*, O.F. *avoer.*

auyse, *v.*, to advise, to give advice, to observe, to consider; **auysed**, *pt.* and *p.p.*, 35 24; 402 26;—Late Lat. *advisare*, A.F. *aviser.*

aweyward, *adv.*, *adj.*, away, wayward, turned away, 242 23;—A.S. *on weg.*

axe, *v.*, to ask. *See* **aske.**

ayde, *sb.*, aid, help, assistance, 10 38;—O.F. *aider.*

ayene, *prep.*, *adv.*, *conj.*, again, towards, opposite to, in return for, 342 8;—A.S. *ongéan, ongeagn.*

ayenst, ayenste, *prep.*, *conj.*, against, 377 28; 516 19.

babblynge, *sb.*, babbling, 834 29.

bacyn, *sb.*, (1) basin, cymbal; (2) a light kind of helmet, 184 37;—O.F. *bacinet.*

bak, *sb.*, back, 787 36;—A.S. *bæc.*

bande, *sb.*, frontier ; bandes, *pl.*, 789 8 ;—O.F. *bodne, bonde.*

banysshe, *v.*, to banish, put under a ban; banysshed, *pt.*, 402 18;—O.F. *banniss-* from *bannir.*

baptym, *sb.*, baptism, 651 3, 20;—O.F. *baptisme.*

barayne, *adj.*, barren, 764 17; 765 3;—O.F. *baraigne.*

barbe, *sb.*, beard, or anything resembling it; jags or points which stand backward in an arrow, dart, or spear; fishhook; barbys, *pl.*, 764 32;—Lat. *barba.*

barbour, *sb.*, barber; barbours, *pl.*, 176 34;—A.F. *barbeor.*

barbycan, *sb.*, a kind of watchtower, an outwork to defend the gate of a castle, 168 25 ;—O.F. *barbacane.*

bargayn, *sb.*, business, strife, combat, bargain, 581 36;—O.F. *bargaine.*

barge, *sb.*, a bark, boat, 122 15; 849 29;—O.F. *barge.*

barget, *sb.*, bark, boat, 330 29; 760 28 (diminut. of the former).

Baronage, *sb.*, the men, vassals of a feudal chief; assembly of the barons, 461 33;—O.F. *barnage.*

Baronry, *sb.*, an estate representing the property of a baron; a barony of lands, 157 2; 795 29.

Baroune, *sb.*, baron, 587 18; barons, *pl.*, 39 27;—A.F. *barun.*

barre, *sb.*, bar; barrys, *pl.*, 326 25; —O.F. *barre.*

bataill, batayll, *sb.*, (1) the battle, the fight, 61 2; 62 6; 342 5; (2) the army (Lat. *acies*), 57 21; Northern bataylles, 58 7;—O.F. *bataille.*

bate, *v.*, bate, abate, grow less; bated, *pt.*, 131 12;—O.F. *batre.*

batilment, *sb.*, a parapet with embrasures on the top of a building, originally only used on fortifications; battlement, 846 1;—O.F. *bastillement.*

bauowre, *sb.*, beaver; the part of a helmet which is moved up and down, covering the face, and allowing the wearer to drink; the shade over the eyes, 195 17;—O.F. *baviere.*

bawdy, *adj.*, bawdy, dirty, filthy, wanton, 218 36; 224 15;—O.F. *baude.*

bawme, *sb.*, balm, aromatic plant, fig, anything that heals or soothes pain, 174 21;—Lat. *balsamum.*

baye, *v.*, to bark; bayed, *pt.*, 110 29;—O.F. *abaier.*

bayne, *sb.*, bath, 289 22; 755 16;—O.F. *baine.*

beale, *adj.*, beautiful, epithet given to Isoud, and to the castle Beale valet;—Fr. *belle.*

beare, *sb.*, the bear, 651 31;—A.S. *bera.*

beaume, *sb.*, beam, ray of light, 620 5;—A.S. *béam, beamian.*

beaume, *sb.*, trumpet; beamous, *pl.*, 861 1;—A.S. *béme, býme,* O.Merc. *béme.*

beaute, beaulte, *sb.*, beauty, 17 23; 23 29; 857* 35;—O.F. *biaute, bealteit.*

beau viuante = Fr. *beau vivant,* well living, well behaving; epithet of the damoysel Maledysaunt.

beblede, *v.*, to cover with blood; bebled, *pt.*, 294 12; *p.p.*, 782 10; bebledde, *p.p.*, 130 16;—A.S. *beblédan.*

beclose, *v.*, to enclose, surround; beclosed, *p.p.*, 601 2;—A.S. *bi, be,* and A.F. *clos.*

become, *v.*, to become, to come, to befall, suit; become, *p.p.*, 68 16; 366 15;—A.S. *be-cuman.*

bedasshe, *v.*, to cover with dashes of colour or adornment; bedasshed, *p.p.*, 713 21.

bee, *sb.*, a jewel, ring, 269 36;—A.S. *béah.*

beeste, *sb.*, beast, 6 31; beestes, *pl.*, 648 30;—Lat. *bestia,* O.F. *beste.*

befalle, *v.*, to befall, happen; befalleth, *prs.*, 765 19; befelle, *pt.*, 75 35; 772 1; befallen, *p.p.*, 653 2; befalle, *p.p.*, 420 34;—A.S. *befeallan.*

beforne, biforne, *prep.*, before, 221 32; 306* 6; 513 7;—A.S. *biforan.*

beginne, *v.*, to begin; begynneth, *prs.*, 490 11; begonne, *p.p.*, 5 7; 405 9;—A.S. *beginnan.*

begrype, *v.*, to seize, to take hold of; *inf.*, 692 31;—A.S. *begrípan.*

behange, *v.*, to deck, to clothe; behanged, *p.p.*, 125 31;—A.S. *behôn.*

behated, *adj.* or *p.p.,* hated, much hated, 494 19;—from A.S. *be* and *hatian.*

beholde, *v.,* to hold, to behold; *inf.,* 40 31; **beholden,** *p.p.,* 387 36; 762 11; **behelde,** *pt.,* 472 8; 859* 36; **beholdyng,** for beholden, 42 24; 86 22;—A.S. *behealdan.*

behote, *v.,* to promise; *inf.,* 284 33; *prs.,* 92 12; **behyght,** *pt.,* 444 12; 724 30;—A.S. *behátan. Compare* **byheste.**

behoue, *v. impers.;* behoueth, *prs.,* needs, 311 10; 625 5;—A.S. *behófian.*

beke, *v.,* to bake; **bekynge,** *p.prs.,* 167 33; **baken,** *p.p.,* 196* 32.

beleue, *v.,* to leave, to be left, to remain; **belefte,** *pt.,* 234 35;—A.S. *beléfan.*

belle, *sb.,* bell; **bellys,** *pl.,* 856* 21; —A.S. *belle.*

bemone, *v.,* to bemoan, lament, *prs.,* 518 25;—A.S. *bimœnan.*

bende, *sb.,* band, stripe, 431 27;—A.S. *bend.*

bended, bented, *adj.,* having bands of different colour, 441 34; 442 2; 433 5;—deriv. from the substantive.

benime, *v.,* to take from, deprive; **benome,** *p.p.,* 653 4; 674 23;—A.S. *beniman.*

benyghte, *v.,* to be overtaken by night; **benyghted,** *p.p.,* 587 17; 690 10;—A.S. *be* and *neaht.*

berde, *sb.,* beard, 7 8;—A.S. *beard.*

bere, *v.,* to bear; **boren,** *p.p.,* 694 22; **bare,** *pt.,* 67 36; **beren,** *plur. prs.,* 277 7;—A.S. *beran.*

bere, *sb.,* bier, 646 31;—A.S. *bǽr. Compare* O.F. *biere.*

bereue, *v.,* to bereave; **byreue,** *prs.,* 163 14; **berafte,** *pt.,* 578 34; **berafte,** *p.p.,* 814 27; **bereued,** *p.p.,* 44 7;—A.S. *biréafian.*

beryels, *sb. pl.,* burial, tomb, 287 7; —A.S. *byrgels.*

besaunte, *sb.,* a gold coin named from Byzantium; **besauntes,** *pl.,* 155 15;—O.F. *besant.*

beseme, *v.,* to beseem, appear; **besemeth,** *prs.,* 222 14; 551 33; **bisemeth yow not,** 76 19;—A.S. *be* and *séman.*

besette, *v.,* to fill, occupy, surround, beset; **besett,** *p.p.,* 551 33;—A.S. *bisettan.*

beskyfte, *v.,* to remove hastily; *inf.,* 119 37;—A.S. *be* and *sciftan.*

bestad, bestadde, bystad, *p.p.,* hard bestead, sorely imperilled, overcome, 125 21; 179 25; 824 7; —A.S. *be* and *stede.*

besture, *v.,* rouse, instigate, stir; **bestured,** *pt.,* 536 20;—A.S. *be* and *styrian.*

bestyayl, bestyal, *sb.,* cattle, 125 29; 180 20;—O.F. *bestail.*

besuette, *v.,* to sweat, perspire, *p.p.,* 612 6;—A.S. *be* and *swǽtan.*

besynes, *sb.,* business, activity, care, industry, 481 16;—A.S. deriv. of *bysig.*

bete, *v.,* to beat; **bete,** *pt.,* 746 20; **bete,** *p.p.,* 667 8; **betyn,** *p.p.,* 228 3;—A.S. *béatan.*

beteche, *v.,* to entrust, assign, recommend; **betaught,** *pt.,* 631 26; **bytaughte,** *pt.,* 199 35;—A.S. *betǽcan.*

bethynke, *v.,* to think, plan, reflect; **bethouȝte hym,** *pt.,* 132 31; **bethoughte hym,** *pt.,* 239 31; —A.S. *bi-þencan.*

betrapped, *adj.,* adorned, covered, 803 34.

betyde, *v.,* to happen, to betide; **betyde,** *prs.,* 847 1; **betyd,** *pt.,* 370 3; **betyd,** *p.p.,* 267 34;—from A.S. *tíd.*

beuer, *v.,* to tremble, to quiver; **beuerd,** *pt.,* 56 4;—? A.S. *bifian.*

bien pensaunt, surname of the damoysel Maledysaunt;—Fr. *bien pensant,* well thinking.

bifalle, *v.,* to befall; **bifel,** *pt.,* 35 1; **bifelle,** *pt.,* 730 27; **befallen,** *p.p.;* —A.S. *be-feallan.*

biforne. *See* **beforne.**

bisee, *v.,* to look, to arrange, appoint, manage; **bisene, be sene,** **besene,** *p.p.,* equipped, 44 32; 64 37; 73 6;—A.S. *biséon.*

bitake, *v.,* to commit, entrust, recommend; **bitoke,** *pt.,* 472 3; **bitaken,** *p.p.,* 42 18.

blast, *sb.,* a blowing, 96 9;—A.S. *blǽst.*

blaunche maynys, le or la, surname of Isoud and of Vwayne;—Fr. *mains blanches*, white hands.

blede, *v.*, to bleed; *inf.*, 91 21; bledde, *pt.* and *p.p.*, 8 1; 71 25;—A.S. *blédan*.

blee, *sb.*, colour, complexion, 176 32;—A.S. *bléo*.

blesse, *v.*, to bless; *imperat.*, 745 13; blysse, *imperat.*, 753 21;—A.S. *blétsian*.

blosomme, *v.*, to blossom, *prs.*, 771 3;—A.S. *blóstmian*.

blowe, *v.*, to blow; *inf.*, 529 11; 542 33; blewe, *pt.*, 13 16; 109 30; 766 8; blowen, *p.p.*;—A.S. *bláwan*.

blyndefeld, *adj.*, blindfolded, 138 18;—A.S. *blind* and M.E. *fellen*, to strike.

blythe, *adj.*, blithe, cheerful, 281 8;—A.S. *bliðe*.

bobaunce, *sb.*, pride, vanity, splendour, pomp, 523 12; 751 25;—? O.F. *bobant*.

bole, *sb.*, the body or trunk, 209 3;—O.Norse *bolr*.

bondage, *sb.*, captivity, slavery, 408 19, 21;—O.F. *bondage*.

bone, *sb.*, boon; *originally* a prayer, petition; *secondly*, answer to a prayer, a gift, a favour, 276 2; 316 30; 422 21;—Icel. *bón*.

boost, *v.*, to boast; *inf.*, 176 17;—W. *bostio, bostiau*.

boote, *sb.*, boat, 96 28; bote, 706 11;—A.S. *bát*.

boote, bote, *sb.*, remedy, succour, amendment, boot, 209 6; 585 8;—A.S. *bót*.

bord, *sb.*, table, board, 515 22; boordes, *pl.*, 104 25;—A.S. *bord*.

bordoure, *sb.*, border, frontier, 349 13;—O.F. *bordure*.

borowe, *sb.*, pledge, security; borowes, *pl.*, 240 34;—A.S. *borh*.

bote, *sb.*, (1) boat, (2) remedy. *See* boote.

bote, *v.*, to amend, to help; bote, *pt.*, 130 12; boote, *pt.*, 130 18. *Compare* A.S. *bót, bétan*.

bott, *sb.*, butt, the point, handle, button of a sword or of the helmet, 69 18; but, 185 1; butte, 191 31;—O.F. *boter*, to push, butt, thrust.

bottlere, botteler, butlere, *sb.*, the butler; surname of Lucas son of Corneus.

bounde, *sb.*, boundary, limit, frontier; boundys, *pl.*, 47 23. *Compare* bandes.

bounte, *sb.*, bounty, liberality, kindness, 78 33; 539 26;—O.F. *bonteit*.

bounteous, *adj.*, kind, liberal, 733 7.

bourde, *v.*, to sit at table, or to play, to jest; bourded, *pt.*, 410 22;—? O.F. *bourder* or A.S. *bord*.

bourder, *sb.*, glutton, or gambler, 455 6; 508 2.

bowe, *sb.*, bough, branch; lodge of bowes, 629 23;—A.S. *bóg, bóh*.

boystous, *adj.*, boisterous, rough, 491 26; 648 17;—?

brace, *v.*, to embrace; braced, *pt.*, 551 25. *See* embrace.

brachet, *sb.*, a small hunting dog, brach, a bitch pointer, 104 22;—O.F. *brachet*.

bragge, *v.*, originally to crack, to make a noise, to boast, brag; bragge, *prs.*, 169 33;—Icel. *braka*.

braule, *v.*, to make a loud noise, to quarrel noisily; brauled, *pt.*, 405 19;—?

braundysshe, *v.*, to shake or wave, as a brand or weapon, brandish; braundysshyng, *part. pres.*, 427 8;—O.F. *brand*.

braune, *sb.*, brawn, originally flesh of the boar, the fleshy muscular part of the body, the muscular strength, 596 20; 781 30;—O.F. *braon*.

brayde, *sb.*, a quick movement, a start, a while, a moment (W. de Worde has *brethe*), 835 30;—Icel. *bragð*.

breche, *sb.*, breeches, drawers, 593 10 (*sing.*);—A.S. *bréc*, Icel. *brœkr, pl.*

brede, *adj.*, broad. *See* brood.

brede, *v.*, to breed, produce; bredde, *p.p.*, 427 3;—A.S. *brédan*.

brede, *sb.*, breadth, 814 23;—A.S. *brédu*.

breed, *sb.*, bread, 719 6;—O.North. *bréad*.

breke, *v.*, to break; *inf.*, 401 32; brack, brak, brake, *pt.*, 8 7; 48

18; 71 9; **broken,** *p.p.,* 386 14; 590 12;—A.S. *brecan.*

brenne, *v.,* to burn; *inf.,* 88 32; **brente,** *pt.,* 65 11; **brenned,** *pt.,* 666 24; **brent, brente,** *p.p.,* 10 10; 64 6; **brennyng,** *p.prs.,* 711 15; —Icel. *brenna,* Goth. *brinnan.*

brest, *sb.,* breast, 676 17;—A.S. *bréost.*

breste, *v.,* to burst; **braste, brast,** *pt.,* 95 25; 142 11;—A.S. *berstan,* Icel. *bresta.*

brethe, *sb.,* breath, vapour, voice, word, 711 30;—A.S. *brǽd.*

breuse, le, surname of syr Seruause; —?

breue, *v.,* to shorten; *inf.,* 356 1;— Lat. *brevis.*

broche, *sb.,* brooch, spear; **broches,** *pl.,* 167 34;—O.F. *broche.*

broche, *v.,* to pierce through, to spur; **broched,** *pt.,* 58 24;—A.F. *brocher.*

brood, brode, brede, *adj.,* broad, 72 38; 99 15; 578 5;—A.S. *brád.*

browe, *sb.,* broth, soup; **broweys,** *pl.,* 214 28;—from A.S. *bréowan, p.p., browen.*

brunte, *sb.,* the shock of an onset; **bruntes,** *pl.,* 835 31;—? Icel. *bruna,* to advance with the speed of fire.

brutyll, *adj.,* brittle, fragile, 129 36; —A.S. *bruton, pt. pl.* of *bréotan.*

brym, *adj.,* fierce, furious, angry, 820 4 (W. de Worde has *grymme*); —A.S. *bréme.*

brymme, *sb.,* margin, shore, brim, 648 17;—Icel. *brim,* A.S. *brymme.*

bryse, *v.,* to crush, break, to wound seriously; **brysed,** *pt.,* 97 11; 471 33;—A.S. *brýsan,* O.F. *briser.*

brutysshe, *adj.,* British, 2 20.

buffet, *sb.,* buff, heavy blow, 58 24; **buffette,** 204 14; **buffettes,** *pl.,* 335 7;—O.F. *bufe, bufer.*

bur, *sb.,* a broad iron ring just below the grip of a spear to prevent the hand from slipping, 847 12;—?

burbel, *v.,* to bubble; **burbelynge,** *p.prs.,* 415 17; **burbyl,** *inf.,* 764 8.

burgene, *v.,* to bud, blossom; **burgeneth,** *prs.,* 797 2.

burgeis, *sb.,* burgess, 741 24;—O.F. *burgeis.*

buryellys, buryels, *sb. pl.,* the burial, 466 23; 851 11;—A.S. *byrgels. See* **beryels.**

busshement, *sb.,* ambush, 11 9;— O.F. *en-buschement. See* **enbusshement.**

butte, *sb. See* **bott.**

buttom, *sb.,* 755 27; ? bottom, A.S. *botm,* or ? *equal to* " button," scab of a wound, Fr. *bouton.*

but yf, = unless, 52 2; 91 18; 471 15; 514 14.

by cause, *conj.,* because;—A.S. *be* and Lat. *causa.*

by happe, *adv.,* by chance;—A.S. *be* and Icel. *happ.*

byheste, biheste, behest, *sb.,* promise, 1 22; **byhestes,** 361 6; 759 16;—A.S. *behǽs.*

bylde, *v.,* to build; **bylded,** *p.p.,* 169 38;—? A.S. *bold.*

byleue, *v.,* to believe; *inf.,* 3 36;— A.S. *ge-lýfan.*

byleue, *sb.,* belief, 760 4.

by lowe, *prep.,* below, 110 3;—A.S. *be, bi,* and Icel. *lágr.*

bynde, *v.,* to bind; **bond,** *pt.,* 787 36; **bounden,** *p.p.,* 691 18;—A.S. *bindan.*

by nethe, *prep.,* beneath, 614 23;— A.S. *beneoðan.*

byseche, *v.,* beseech, implore, request; *prs.,* 760 10; **bysechynge,** *p.prs.,* 3 24; 78 34;—from A.S. *bi* and *sécan, sécean.*

bysshopryche, *sb.,* bishopric, 860* 21;—A.S. *biscop* and *ríce.*

byte, *v.,* to bite; **bytynge,** *p.prs.,* 125 24; **boot,** *pt.,* 104 25;—A.S. *bítan.*

bywaryd, *p.p.,* = too good, 246 18; *figurative use of* to beware = to spend.

by yonde, *prep.,* beyond, 207 1; **beyonde,** 2 33;—A.S. *be-* and *geond.*

caas, *sb.,* case, chance, circumstance, 374 18; 730 27;—Lat. *casum* (acc.), O.F. *cas.*

caban, *sb.,* small room, closet, cabin, 135 1;—O.F. *cabane.*

cankeryd, *p.p.,* corrupted, 842 1;— O.F. *cancre,* Lat. *cancer.*

canne, *v.,* to know, to be able; **conne,** *inf.,* 176 34; 820 22; **canne,** *first pers. pres.,* 501 1;

canst, *second pers.*, 209 13; ye con, *prs.*, 269 22; **coude** it, *pt.*, 457 36; **couthe,** *pt.*, 279 8; **coude,** *pt.*, 3 5; 377 5;—A.S. *cunnan.*

cantel, *sb.*, piece, bit, edge, 58 20; 71 25;—O.F. *cantel.*

capytayn, *sb.*, captain; **captayn,** 175 32;—O.F. *capitain.*

carre, *sb.*, cart, carriage, 175 7.

carryks, *sb. pl.*, small ships, 841 9 (ed. of 1634 has *caraks*).

carue, *v.*, to carve, to cut; **carf,** *pt.*, 55 10; **carfe,** *pt.*, 58 20;—A.S. *ceorfan.*

causer, causar, *sb.*, author, he who causes something, 209 28; 269 21; 762 7;—Lat. *causa.*

caytyf, *sb. and adj.*, wretch, miserable captive, 753 27;—O.F. *caitif.*

cedle, *sb.*, a small leaf of paper containing some writing, schedule, 842 6; **sedyl,** 842 22;—O.F. *schedule.*

censer, *sb.*, censer, pan in which incense is burned, 573 5; **senser,** 549 18;—Lat. *incensorium.*

cere, *v.*, to cover with wax; *inf.*, 174 22; **cered,** *p.p.*, shrouded in waxed cloth, 174 22; 857* 26;—Lat. *cerare.*

certaynte, *sb.*, certainty, certitude, 750 20; **certeynte,** 511 34; **certente,** 851 1;—O.F. *certainte.*

chaas, chace, *sb.*, hunting, pursuit, hunting-ground, 174 7; 526 32;—O.F. *chace.*

chace, *v.*, to hunt; **chacynge,** *p.prs.*, 210 3;—O.F. *chacer.*

chacer, *sb.*, hunter, 435 11.

chafed, *p.p.*, 653 26. *See* **chauffe.**

chaflet, *sb.*, a small stage, platform, 844 1;—dimin. of O.F. *chafaut.*

chalenge, *v.*, to accuse, claim, charge; **chalengyd,** *pt.*, 401 6;—O.F. *chalenger.*

chambre, *sb.*, chamber, 572 1;—A.F. *chambre.*

champayn, champayne, *sb.* and *adj.*, field, level country, 53 11; 170 6; —A.F. *champaigne.*

chappel, *sb.*, chapel, 495 29;—A.F. *chapele.*

chappytre, chapytre, *sb.*, chapter, 2 15, 16; 4 32, 34;—O.F. *chapitre.*

charbuncle, *sb.*, carbuncle, precious stone, 176 9;—O.F. *carboncle.*

charge, *sb.*, load, responsibility, impressive command, 35 25;—A.F. *charge.*

charyot, *sb.*, chariot, 760 27;—O.F. *chariot.*

charyte, *sb.*, charity, 635 19;—A.F. *charite,* O.F. *caritet.*

chastysement, *sb.*, chastisement, 627 18;—deriv. of O.F. *chastier.*

chastyte, *sb.*, chastity, purity, 663 20;—O.F. *chasteit.*

chaundeler, *sb.*, candlestick, 638 5 (on the same page, line 17, occurs **candelstyk**);—O.F. *chandelier.*

chauffe, *v.*, to heat, to become hot; *inf.*, 174 28; **chauffed,** *p.p.*, 742 33; **chafed,** *p.p.*, 653 26;—O.F. *chaufer.*

chayer, *sb.*, chair, stool, seat, 91 34; 629 24;—O.F. *chaiere.*

chere, *sb.*, face, time, treatment; **what chere,** 108 26; **straunge chere,** 231 16; **good chere,** 143 33; **heuy chere,** 640 15;—A.F. *chere.*

cherete, *sb.*, charity, love, friendship, 518 34; **chyerte,** 621 23; 816 6;—O.F. *cherte. See also* **charyte.**

chese, *v.*, to choose; *imperat.*, 296 5; —A.S. *ceosan.*

cheualer du charyot, the knight of the chariot; **cheualer malfet,** *i.e.*, *le cheualer qui a mal fait*;—surnames of syr Launcelot.

child, *sb.*, child, child of a noble, young knight, page; **childis,** *gen. sing.*, 37 3; 38 11; 775 16; **chyldren,** *pl.*, 1 21;—A.S. *cild.*

chirche, *sb.*, church, 40 19;—A.S. *cyrce.*

chirche, *v.*, to perform with any one the giving of thanks in church; **chirched,** *p.p.*, 575 31;—from A.S. *cyrce.*

chircheyerd, *sb.*, churchyard, 628 16;—Icel. *kirkju-garðr.*

chorle, *sb.*, peasant, ruffian, 62 21; 70 23; 519 8;—A.S. *ceorl.*

chyef, *sb. and adj.*, chief, head, upper part, principal; 1 9; 3 7; 176 9; —A.F. *chief.*

N

chyerte, *sb. See* cherete.

chyualry, *sb.*, chivalry, the knights of Christendom, 47 22; chyualryes, *pl.*, knightly acts, valiant deeds, 3 21, 30;—A.F. *chivalrie.*

clater, *v.*, to make a rattling noise, to clatter; *inf.*, 582 26; clatered, *pt.*, 582 29.—*Compare* A.S. *clatrung.*

cleche, *v.*, to seize, grasp; cley3te, *pt.*, 185 17;—†

clene, *adj.* and *adv.*, clean, entirely; clene armed, 638 35; clene out of his mynde, 585 2; clene of her lyf, 40 15; 611 10;—A.S. *clǽne.*

clennes, *sb.*, purity, cleanness, 672 6;—A.S. *clǽnnes.*

clepe, *v.*, to call; cleped, *p.p.*, 347 19; 722 15;—A.S. *cleopian.*

clerenes, *sb.*, brightness, clearness, 707 33;—A.F. *cler*, with A.S. term. *-nes, -nysse.*

cleue, *v.*, to split asunder, cleave; claue, *pt.*, 93 4; clafe, *pt.*, 107 9; —A.S. *clifian, cleofian.*

close, *v.*, to close, enclose, cover; close, *p.p.*, 417 25;—A.F. *clos.*

cloystre, *sb.*, cloister, convent, monastery, 854 3;—A.F. *cloister*, O.F. *cloistre.*

clubbe, *sb.*, club; clubbes, *pl.*, 155 34; clubbis, *pl.*, 46 38;—Icel. *klubba.*

clyff, *sb.*, cliff, 700 30;—A.S. *clif.*

clymbe, *v.*, to climb; clamme, *pt.*, 208 32;—A.S. *climban.*

clymber, *sb.*, he who climbs, 208 27.

clyppe, *v.*, to clip, to shear; clypped, *pt.*, 366 20;—Icel. *klippa.*

clyppe, *v.*, to embrace; clypped, *p.p.*, 307 21; clyppyng, 150 35; clyppynge, 582 17;—A.S. *clyppan.*

cofre, *sb.*, box, coffer, 290 4;—A.F. *cofre.*

cogges, *sb. pl.*, cockboats, 164 30.

cognoyssaunce, congnyssaunce, cognoissaunce, *sb.*, knowledge, indication, 260 4; 416 32; 529 26;—A.F. *conisaunce.*

cole, *sb.*, coal, charcoal, 694 16; coles, *pt.*, 140 1;—A.S. *col.*

coller, *sb.*, collar, 369 29;—O.F. *coler.*

comberaunce, *sb.*, encumbrance, 76 21;—O.F. *encombrer.*

combred, *p.p.*, embarrassed, 777 24; —O.F. *encombrer.*

come, *v.*, to come; *inf.*, 4 1; come, *pt.* (!), 38 26; 57 34; came, *pt.*, 5 18; 805 9; comyn, *p.p.*, 35 9; comen, *p.p.*, 280 34; came, *pt.*, 3 22; comen, *pl. prs.*, 425 27; 725 9; come, *p.p.*, 706 4; 804 4;—A.S. *cunnan.*

commaundemente, *sb.*, order, commission, 848 36; commaundementes, *pl.*, 306 4; 323 24;—O.F. *comander.*

compte, *v.*, to count; *prs.*, 342 12; —O.F. *compter.*

complisshe, *v.*, complete, accomplish; complisshed, *pp.*, 213 22. *See* accomplysshe.

comyn, *adj.*, common, 727 3;—A.F. *commun.*

comynal, *adj.*, common, 155 9;—Lat. *communalem.*

comyns, *sb. pl.*, the commons, inhabitants, citizens, 41 4; 43 26; 46 38.

comynycacyon, *sb.*, communication, information, news, 13 10; 28 25; 33 23;—Lat. *communicationem.*

conceyte, *sb.*, conceit, 123 23;—Lat. *concipere.*

conduyte, *v.*, to lead, conduct; *inf.*, 465 12;—O.F. *conduire.*

conduyte, *sb.*, conduct, guidance, 108 34; 428 15;—O.F. *conduit.*

conferme, *v.*, to confirm; confermed, *pt.*, 575 30;—Lat. *confirmare.*

conne, *v. See* canne.

connynge, *sb.*, learning, knowledge, skill, 3 13;—A.S. *cunnan.*

conyes, *sb. pl.*, coneys, rabbits, 387 12; —O.F. *conyn, conil*, A.F. *conyng.*

coost, *sb.*, rib, side of the human body, 110 4;—A.F. *coste.*

cop, *sb.*, cup, tankard, 234 9; coupe, 701 21;—A.F. *cupe.*

coper, *sb.*, copper, 184 37;—Late Lat. *cuprum (cyprium).*

corde, *v.*, to accord, agree; cordyng, *p.prs.*, 51 3;—O.F. *acorder.*

coronacyon, *sb.*, coronation, 44 1.

corps, *sb.*, body, corpse, 761 13; cors 857* 16;—A.F. *cors, corps.*

coste, *sb.*, coast, 302 8 ;—O.F. *coste.*

coste, *v.*, (hunting term) to keep in parallel course with the animal ; costed, *pt.*, 764 19—? O.F. *coste.*

coste, *sb.*, cost, expense ; costes, *pl.*, 372 20 ;—A.F. *cust, coust.*

cote, *sb.*, hut, cottage, 167 26 ;—A.S. *cot.*

cote, *sb.*, garment, coat, 338 26 ; 672 21 ;—A.F. *cote*, O.F. *cotte.*

counceille, *v.*, to consult, to deliberate together ; *inf.*, 722 21.

counceyl, counceylle, *sb.*, consultation, deliberation, plan, purpose, advice, 599 26; 600 32 ;—O.F. *conceil.*

counterfete, *v.*, to counterfeit ; *inf.*, 495 34; counterfeet, *p.p.*, 129 36; —from O.F. *countrefet, p.p.* of *contrefeire.*

countray, countrey, countre, *sb.*, the country, 138 26; 139 3 ; 244 23 ;—O.F. *contree.*

coupe, *sb.* *See* cop.

courage, *v.*, to encourage ; *inf.*, 235 26 ;—O.F. *corage, courage.*

coure, *v.*, to sit close together ; *inf.*, 797 6 (W. de Worde has *cover*); 831 16 ; coureth, *prs.*, 607 4 ;— ? W. *cwrian, cwr.*[1]

cours, *sb.*, course, 97 9; 415 31 ;— A.F. *cours.*

courser, *sb.*, a steed, 134 20 ;—A.F. *coursier.*

courtelage, *sb.*, garden, courtyard, 153 11 ; 668 17.

couenaunt, *sb.*, a covenant, 317 22 ; —A.F. *covenant.*

couerte, *sb.*, shelter, defence, 197 9.

couyn, *sb.*, conspiracy, craft, deceit, trickery, 633 29 ;—A.F. *covine.*

cowardyse, *sb.*, cowardice, 429 31 ; O.F. *couardie.*

coyfe, *sb.*, coif, cap, 283 23 ; 689 23 ;—O.F. *coife, coiffe.*

cracke, *sb.*, crag, rock ; crackys, *pl.*, 326 24 ;—W. *craig.*

craft, *sb.*, might, power, craft, deceit, 88 31 ;—A.S. *cræft.*

creast, *sb.*, crest, summit, 167 31 ;— O.F. *creste.*

creatoure, *sb.*, creator, 759 38 ;— O.F. *creatour.*

creature, *sb.*, creature, being, 764 4.

credence, *sb.*, belief, faith, 162 31 ; —O.F. *credence.*

creme, *sb.*, the sacred oil used in anointing, chrism, 403 16 ;—O.F. *cresme.*

crofte, *sb.*, an underground cell or chapel, 716* 18 ;—Lat. *crypta.*

croke, *v.*, to bend, to turn aside ; croked, *p.p.*, 563 10 ;—Icel. *krókr.*

croppe, *sb.*, crupper, hinder part of a horse, 82 12 ; croupe, 298 4 ;— O.F. *crope.*

crowpers, *sb. pl.*, plates covering the horse's crupper, or straps of leather fastened to the saddle and passing under the horse's tail to keep the saddle in its place, 238 2.

cryppyl, *sb.*, cripple, 721 38 ;—deriv. from A.S. *créopan.*

crysten, *adj.* and *sb.*, Christian, 1 9; 1 11 ; 585 11 ; *v.*, to christen ; *inf.*, 39 9; crystend, crystened, *p.p.*, 490 2, 3, 5 ; vncrystned, *p.p.*, 38 26 ;—A.S. *cristnian.*

culpaple, *adj.*, guilty, 784 16 ;—O.F. *culpaple.*

cure hardy, le, surname of a knight Ozanna, meaning *le cœur hardi*, the courageous heart.

currour, *sb.*, runner, courier, 344 6 ; —O.F. *courrier.*

cursydnes, *sb.*, malice, wickedness, 198 11 ;—deriv. from A.S. *cursian.*

curteyn, *sb.*, curtain ; courtayns, *pl.*, 783 6 ;—O.F. *courtine.*

curteys, *adj.*, courteous, 109 14; curtest, *superl.*, 860* 4 ; moost curteyst, 394 29 ;—A.F. *curteis.*

curtoyse, curtosye, *sb.*, courtesy, 3 31; 16 32; curtosy, 831 14; —A.F. *curteisie.*

cusshyn, *sb.*, cushion, 790 15 ;—O.F. *coissin.*

daffysh, *adj.*, shy, modest, foolish, 409 10 ;—?

---

[1] The Welsh word *cwrian* has generally the sense of sitting in a corner through fear, as, *e.g.*, 831 27 ; but 797 6 and 607 4 the sense seems to be that of the Modern French word *roucouler.*

dale, *sb.*, dale, valley; dales, *pl.*, 243 29;—A.S. *dœl.*

moysel, damoisel, *sb.*, damsel, 73 3, 4;—A.F. *damoysele.*

dampne, *v.*, condemn, sentence: dampned, *pt.*, 656 23; *p.p.*, 275 36; 683 5;—O.F. *damner.*

re, *v.*, to dare; dar, *first pers.*, 61 21; darste, *second pers. prs.*, 505 18; durste, *pt.*, 51 27; 278 22; 466 32;—A.S. *dear.*

dastard, *sb.*, a coward, 344 4.—*Compare* Skeat, Dict.

daunynge, *sb.*, dawning, 566 10; 781 35.

dawe, *v.*, to become day; it dawyd, 691 13;—A.S. *dagian.*

dawe, *v.*, to moisten, sprinkle with cold water; dawed, *pt.*, 585 18;—from A.S. *déaw.*

debate, *sb.*, strife, discord, 440 11; 761 30;—A.F. *debat.*

debonair, *adj.*, mild, gentle, 694 18; —O.F. *debonaire.*

deceyuable, *adj.*, deceitful, 519 2.

dede, *sb.*, deed; dedes, *pl.*, 87 31; dedys, *pl.*, 838 13;—A.S. *déd* (*dǣd*).

dede, *adj.*, dead, 82 4; 715* 33; deed, 847 15;—A.S. *déaó.*

defade, *v.* *See* dyffade.

defame, *v.*, to spread about a rumour, to slander; defamed, *p.p.*, 781 34; —A.F. *diffamer.*

deffaulte, deffaute, defaulte, defaute, *sb.*, defect, fault, 108 26; 480 19; 609 2; 785 3, 5;—A.F. *defaute.*

deffende, *v.*, to defend, protect, forbid; deffended, *pt.*, 836 28; defenden, *prs. plural*, 632 25;—A.F. *defendre.*

defowle, *v.*, to tread down, rebuke; defowled, *p.p.*, 141 28; defoyled, *p.p.*, 77 1;—O.F. *defouler.*

defye, *v.*, to defy, mistrust; defyen, *prs. pl.*, 632 24;—A.F. *defier.*

degree, *sb.*, (1) degree, price, distinction, 420 37; 513 3; (2) different classes of a people; degrees, *pl.*, 394 17;—O.F. *degre, degret.*

dele, *sb.*, deal, share, 36 33; 834 4; —A.S. *dǣl.*

dele, *v.*, to deal, share, divide; dalte, *pt.*, 853 13;—A.S. *dǣlan.*

delyte, *sb.*, delight, 726 32; delytes, *pl.*, 247 26;—O.F. *delit.*

demene, *v.*, to manage, to behave; demenyd hym, *pt.*, 23 7;—O.F. *demener.*

demene, *sb.*, power, possession; demenys, *pl.*, 673 28;—O.F. *demeine.*

demure, *adj.*, sober, modest, staid, 613* 14;—O.F. *de murs, meurs.*

departycyon, *sb.*, departure, 397 11; 621 7;—deriv. of O.F. *departir.*

dere, *v.*, to harm; *inf.*, 61 21;—A.S. *derian.*

dere, *adj.*, dear, beloved, 61 16;—A.S. *déore.*

dere, *sb.*, deer, wild animal, 519 16; —A.S. *déor.*

derke, *adj.*, dark, 116 15; 687 33; —A.S. *deorc.*

descryue, *v.*, to describe, relate; *inf.*, 412 1;—O.F. *descrivre.*

desdayne, *sb.*, contempt, disdain, 727 4;—A.F. *dedeigne*, O.F. *desdein.*

desert, *sb.*, merit, 726 11;—A.F. *deserte.*

deserte, *sb.*, desert, waste land, 708 17;—from Lat. *desertus.*

desguyse, *v.*, to disguise; desguysed, *p.p.*, 767 29; dysguysed, *p.p.*, 767 30;—A.F. *degiser*, O.F. *desguiser.*

desmaye, *v.*, to dismay; *imperat.*, 38 12, 22; desmayed, *p.p.*, 132 26; dysmayed, *p.p.*, 388 24;—O.F. *esmaier.*

despoylle, *v.*, to despoil, strip; despoylled, 466 23; dispoylled, 231 20; 657 20;—O.F. *despoiller.*

desteynye, *sb.*, destiny, 846 38;—deriv. from O.F. *destiner.*

dethe, *sb.*, death, 564 15;—A.S. *déaþ.*

deure, *adj.*, hard, 410 25;—O.F. *deure.*

deuoyr, deuoyre, *sb.*, devoir, knightly duty, 251 5; 829 10;—O.F. *devoir.*

deuyse, *v.*, arrange, order, decide; deuysed, *pt.*, 39 1;—A.F. *deviser.*

deye, *v.*, to die; *inf.*, 224 14;—Icel. *deyja*, O.S. *döian.*

deyntee, *sb.*, a delicacy, worth, pleasure, 161 5;—O.F. *daintie, deintet.*

deyse, *sb.*, daïs, platform in a hall, 213 30;—O.F. *deis.*

dictatour, *sb.*, dictator, one invested for a time with absolute authority, 160 8 ;—Lat. *dictator*.

discomforte, *v.*, trouble, discomfort; *imp.*, 804 11 ;—O.F. *desconforter*.

discomforture, *sb.*, 56 38 ;—? for **discomfyture**.

discomfyte, *v.*, to defeat, to put to flight; **discomfyte,** *p.p.*, 57 36; 74 23 ; **discomfyt,** *p.p.*, 626 4; 639 18; **discomfyted,** *p.p.*, 86 3; **discomfyte,** *p.p.*, 766 26 ; 693 15 ; **sconfyte,** *p.p.*, 146 38 ;—O.F. *desconfire*.

discomfyture, *sb. See* **dyscomfyture**.

disparple, *v.*, to scatter, *or* to become scattered; **disparplyd,** *p.p.*, 798 24; **disperplyd,** *p.p.*, 164 3; —O.F. *desparpillier*.

displeasyre, *sb.*, displeasure, anger, cause of irritation, 367 29; 541 34;—O.F. *desplaisir*.

disseuer, *v.*, to separate; **disseuered,** *pt.*, 611 27 ;—A.F. *deseverer*.

distourble, *v.*, to disturb, trouble; **distourbled,** *p.p.*, 566 13;—O.F. *tourbler*.

disworship, *sb.*, shame, disgrace, 105 3 ;—*dis* and A.S. *weorðscipe*.

dobblet, *sb.*, doublet, 467 16; 679 32; **dobblett,** 468 26 ;—O.F. *doublet*.

doctryne, *sb.*, instruction, doctrine, 3 38 ;—Lat. *doctrina*.

dole, *sb.*, charity, dole, share, portion, 853 11 ;—A.S. *dál*.

dole, *sb.*, grief, pain, sorrow, 94 14; 421 23 ;—O.F. *doel, duel*.

domage, *sb.*, damage, loss, 59 5; **dammage,** 59 5; 72 8; **dommagis,** *pl.*, 56 23 ;—O.F. *domage*.

dome, *sb.*, doom; **day of dome,** 709 34 ;—A.S. *dóm*.

domme, *adj.*, dumb, 451 33 ;—A.S. *dumb*.

doon, *v.*, to do, put, make, cause; *inf.*, 3 19; **doth,** *prs.*, 759 20; **doon,** *p.p.*, 11 16; **dyd,** *pt.*, 65 12; 753 31; **done,** *p.p.*, 343 8; **doo,** *imperat.*, 3 33 ;—A.S. *dón*.

dote, *v.*, to dote, to be foolish; **doted,** *p.p.*, 505 26.

dottage, *sb.*, dotage, a doting, ex-

cessive fondness, childishness of old age, 118 26.

doubel, *adj.*, double, 95 34 ;—O.F. *doble, double*.

doughty, *adj.*, brave, valiant, 189 36 ; **doughtely,** *adv.*, 220 28 ;—A.S. *dyhtig*.

douue, *sb.*, the dove, pigeon, 573 4 ; —Icel. *dúfa*, O.S. *dúba*.

dower, *sb.*, dower, 181 14 ;—A.F. *douayre*.

drede, *sb.*, dread, fear, terror, 209 32; 436 9.

drede, *v.*, to dread, to fear; *prs.*, 745 29; **dredde,** *pt.*, 209 33; 670 7; 784 9; **dradde,** *pt.*, 311 37; 687 15; 775 14; **drad,** *pt.*, 492 29 ; 784 4 ;—A.S. *(on-)drédan*.

dredeful, *adj.*, dreadful, 709 34.

drenche, *v.*, to drown; **drenched,** *p.p.*, 652 18 ;—A.S. *drencan*.

dretche, *v.*, (1) to vex, oppress, torment; (2) to dream, to be disturbed by dreams; **dretched,** *p.p.*, 803 31; **dretchyng,** *p.prs.*, 859* 7; —A.S. *dreccan*.

dretenchid, *pt.*, 171 24; ? for **detrenchid,** from **detrenche,** *v.*, to cut to pieces ;—O.F. *detrancher*.

drinke, *v.*, to drink; **drank,** *pt.*, 759 35; **dronke,** *pt.*, 494 28; **dronken,** *pt.*, 15 35; **dronken,** *p.p.*, 574 13 ;—A.S. *drincan*.

dromounde, *sb.*, dromedary, Arabian camel; **dromoundes,** *pl.*, 164 30 ; —O.F. *dromedaire*.

droupe, *v.*, to droop, to be dismal, cast down; *inf.*, 831 19; **droupyng,** *p.prs.*, 354 7 ;—Icel. *drúpa*.

dryue, *v.*, to drive; **dryuend** (imperfect *part. pres.* for **dryuyng**), 223 7 ;—A.S. *drífan*.

dubbe, *v.*, to dub a knight by a stroke with the flat of a sword; *inf.*, 25 31 ; **dubbed,** *p.p.*, 12 32 ; —A.S. *dubban*.

duc, *sb.*, duke, 181 12 ;—O.F. *duc*.

duche, *adj.*, Dutch, 2 35.

dure, to last, to endure, *inf.*, 118 33 ;—A.F. *durer*.

dwarf, dwerf, *sb.*, a dwarf, 110 15, 21 ;—A.S. *dweorg, dweorh*.

dwelle, *v.*, to dwell, to rest, remain; *inf.*, 36 29; **dwelde,** *pt.*, 61 38;

dwellid, *pt.*, 763 35 ; duelled, *pt.*, 337 6 ;—A.S. *dwellan*, Icel. *dvelja.*

dyffade, *v.*, to fade away, to cause to fade ; dyffaded, *p.p.*, 566 15 ; defaded, *p.p.*, 566 13.

dyghte, *v.*, to order, to rule, to prepare, adorn ; dyȝte, *p.p.*, 93 24 ; dyght, *p.p.*, 186 24 ;—A.S. *dihtan.*

dynte, *sb.*, blow, stroke ; dyntes, *pl.*, 593 11 ;—A.S. *dynt.*

dyryge, *sb.*, name of an anthem in the Mass for the Dead, beginning, in Latin, with the words, " Dirige, Dominus meus," 857* 14.

dyscomfyture, *sb.*, defeat, 11 12 ;—A.F. *desconfiture.*

dyshobeye, *v.*, to disobey ; *prs.*, 856* 36 ;—O.F. *desobeir.*

dysplese, *v.*, to displease ; *inf.*, 839 32 ;—O.F. *desplaisir.*

dysport, *sb.*, pleasure, recreation, mirth, 62 30 ; disportes, *pl.*, 800 21 ; disporte, *v. inf.*, to cheer, amuse, 327 9 ;—O.F. *se desporter.*

dysseyue, *v.*, to deceive ; dysseyued, *p.p.*, 838 11 ;—O.F. *decever, decevoir.*

echone, *adj.*, each one, 202 23 ; eche one, 144 20 ; 497 3 ;—A.S. *ǽlc án.*

edder, *sb.*, adder ; edders, *pl.*, 579 11 ;—A.S. *nǽdre.*

edgyd, *p.p.*, edged, having borders, 426 10.—*Compare* A.S. *ecg.*

eere, *sb.*, the ear ; eerys, *pl.*, 192 4 ; erys, *pl.*, 371 5 ;—A.S. *éare.*

efte, *adv.*, again, afterwards, 294 1 ; 479 17 ; 849 2 ;—A.S. *eft.*

egre, egyr, *adj.*, eager, fierce, sharp, 54 33 ; 71 16 ; eygyrlye, *adv.*, 837 25 ;—A.F. *egre*, O.F. *aigre.*

elder, eldar, *adj.*, *comparat.*, older, elder, 105 23 ; elders, *pl.*, ancestors, 135 15 ; elthers, *pl.*, 807 4 ;—*comparat.* of A.S. *eald.*

ellys, *adv.*, otherwise, else, 14 31 ;—A.S. *elles.*

embassatour, *sb.*, ambassador ; embassatours, *pl.*, 160 7 ; 162 7 ;—O.F. *ambassadeur.*

eme, *sb.*, uncle, 280 7 ;—A.S. *éam.*

emeraude, *sb.*, emerald, 696 8 ;—O.F. *esmeraude.*

emonge, *prep.*, among, 1 10 ; 737 4 ;—A.S. *onmang.*

enbatailled, *p.p.*, ranged for battle, 173 2 ;—O.F. *en* and *bataille.*

enbrace, *v.*, to embrace ; embraced, *pt.*, 444 33 ;—O.F. *embracer.*

enbrayde, *v.*, to wake up, to start, to twist, ? to remind ; enbraydest, *prs.*, 817 25 ;—A.S. *bregdan.*

enbroudre, *v.*, to embroider ; enbroudred, *p.p.*, 378 16 ; 747 6 ;—A.F. *enbroyder.*

enbusshed, *p.p.*, taken in an ambush, 65 23 ; 125 20.

enbusshement, *sb.*, ambush, 50 10 : 53 17 ;—O.F. *embuscher.*

enchauffe, *v.*, to make hot, to heat ; *inf.*, 752 7 ; enchauffed, *p.p.*, 653 32 ; *pt.*, 677 30 ; enchafed, *p.p.*, 649 10 ;—O.F. *enchauffer.*

encheue, enchieue, *v.*, to achieve, to perform, fulfil ; *inf.*, 340 15 ; 794 6 ; encheued, *p.p.*, 42 34 ; *pt.*, 99 27. *See also* achieue.

enclyne, *v.*, incline ; enclynest, *prs.*, 663 22 ; enclyned, *p.p.*, 57 12 ;—O.F. *incliner.*

encountre, *v.*, encounter, meet, fight ; *inf.*, 57 17 ; encountred, *pt.*, 342 14 ;—O.F. *encontrer.*

endented, *p.p.*, having teeth, cut like a saw, notched, jagged, marked with inequalities like a row of teeth, 391 7 ; 396 21 ;—A.F. *endenter.*

endlong, endlonge, *adv.* and *prep.*, along, 193 11 ; 524 16 ;—A.S. *and lang.*

ēne, 147 10. ? corruption of *even*, as Wynkyn de Worde reads, which sometimes occurs in A.S., contracted *enm.*

enele, *v.*, to administer extreme unction ; enelyd, *p.p.*, 858* 27 ;—O.F. *en* and *oil.*

enemytee, *sb.*, enmity, 251 20 ;—O.F. *enamistiet.*

enewe, *v.*, to colour ; enewed with whyte, 110 24 ;—A.S. *in* and *heow.*

enfelaushippe, *v.*, to associate with, to become one's fellow ; *inf.*, 315 4. —*Compare* Icel. *félagi.*

enforce, *v.*, to endeavour, to strive ;

enforceth hym self, *prs.*, 574 7;
enforce your self, *imp.*, 756 30;
763 28;—O.F. *enforcer*.

enforme, *v.*, to teach, to inform;
enformed, *p.p.*, 193 33; **mysen-
formed**, *p.p.*, 78 29;—A.F. *en-
fourmer*.

engendre, *v.*, to engender; *inf.*, 572
25;—O.F. *engendrer*.

engyne, engyn, *sb.*, craft, device,
engine, understanding, 440 13;
677 30;—A.F. *engin*.

enherytaunce, *sb.*, inheritance, 467
32;—Lat. *in*, O.F. *heriter*, and term.
-ance.

enherytour, *sb.*, inheritor, person
who inherits or may inherit, heir,
177 16;—Lat. *in*, *heritator*.

enleuen, *numb.*, eleven, 53 7;—A.S.
endlufon, endleofan.

enoynt, *v.*, to anoint; **ennoynted**,
p.p., 403 35; 821 16;—A.F. *enointer*.

enpayre, *v.*, to make worse, injure;
enpayred, *pt.*, 597 12;—O.F.
empeirer.

enpoysonne, *v.*, to poison; *inf.*, 728
33; **enpoysond**, *p.p.*, 728 32;—
O.F. *enpoisoner*.

enprynte, *v.*, to print; *inf.*, 1 8;
temprynte = to **emprynte**, *inf.*, 1
34;—O.F. *empreindre*.

enquere, *v.*, to inquire; *inf.*, 100 30;
—O.F. *enquerre*, Lat. *inquirere*.

enquest, *sb.*, enterprise, adventure,
16 37;—O.F. *enqueste*.

ensample, ensaumple, ensamble,
sb., example, instance, 1 4; 76 32;
160 24;—A.F. *ensample, essample*.

ensiewe, *v.*, to follow; *inf.*, 162
23;—O.F. *ensuire*.

enstraunge, *v.*, to alienate, make
strange; **enstraunged**, 759 30;—
O.F. *estranger*.

ensure, *v.*, to assure, insure; *inf.*,
205 19; 654 1;—O.S. *asseurer*.

entente, *sb.*, intention, heed, purpose,
36 24; 95 30; also, contents, 761
28;—O.F. *entente*.

enterdyte, *v.*, inderdict, excommuni-
cate, to forbid communion; **enter-
dytynge**, *p.prs.*, 821 5;—Lat.
interdicere.

entere, entiere, entyere, *v.*, to inter,
bury; *inf.*, 274 34; 419 28; 495

28; **entered**, *pt.*, 588 34; **enterid**,
p.p., 40 1;—O.F. *enterrer*.

entermete, *v.*, to meet, to come together; *inf.*, 456 32;—A.F. *entre*
and A.S. *métan*, O.S. *môtian*.

enterpryse, enterpryce, *sb.*, enterprise, undertaking, 514 33; 515 4;
enterpryses, *pl.*, 511 24;—O.F.
entreprise.

enterpryse, emprise, enpryse, *v.*,
to undertake, to commence; **en-
prysed**, *p.p.*, 8 15; 4 13; **enter-
prysed**, *pt.*, 14 32; **emprised**, *pt.*,
16 37.

entiere, *v.* *See* **entere**.

entiere, *adj.*, entire, whole, 296 21;
—O.F. *entier*.

entraylles, *sb. pl.*, the entrails, 168
10;—A.F. *entrailles*.

entre, *sb.*, entrance, 683 22; 710 9;
—O.F. *entrer*.

entremedle, *v.*, intermeddle, mingle;
entremedled, *pt.*, 711 31;—O.F.
entremesler.

entrete, *sb.*, treaty, 37 29, 30;—Lat.
in and O.F. *traiter*.

entyerement, *sb.*, burial, interment,
7 33; **enterement**, 88 18;—A.F.
enterrement.

escape, *v.*, to escape; *inf.*, 461 20;
escaped,*p.p.*, 461 37; **scape**, *inf.*,
92 33;—O.F. *escaper, eschaper*.

enuenyme, *v.*, to envenom, poison;
enuenymed, *p.p.*, 284 28; 327
24;—A.F. *envenimer*.

enuyronne aboute, *adv.*, about, 628
12;—O.F. *environ*, A.S. *on-bútan*.

ermyn, *sb.*, skin of ermine, animal of
the weasel tribe, 616 15;—O.F.
ermine.

ermytage, *sb.*, hermitage, 850 9;
heremytage, 90 34.

ermyte, *sb.*, hermit, 72 31; **heremyte**, 334 33;—A.F. *eremite*
(*heremite*).

erst, *adv.*, formerly, first, 442 8;
463 28; 683 21;—A.S. *ǽrest*.

eschewe, *v.*, to avoid, eschew; *inf.*,
726 1;—O.F. *eschever*, A.F. *eschuer*.

establysshe, *v.*, to establish; **estab-
lysshed**,*pt.*,182 14;—O.F.*establiss-
from *establir*. *See* **stablysshe**.

estate, *sb.*, state; **estates**, *pl.*, ranks,
classes, 311 14;—O.F. *estat*.

estures,[1] *sb. pl.* (Caxton reads *eftures*), (1) being, nature; (2) the inner part of a house, chambers (for *estres*), 784 3;—O.F. *estre.*

eure, *sb.,* use, custom, 59 7.

euen, *sb.,* evening, 40 15; 435 17;—A.S. *æfen, éfen.*

eueryche, *adj.,* every one, every, 144 27; 145 4;—A.S. *æfre + ælc.*

euerychone, *adj.,* every one, 186 12;—A.S. *æfre + ælc + án.*

euyn, *adv.,* even, equal, 849 25;—A.S. *efen, efn.*

expense, *sb.,* expense, cost, 518 20; **expencys,** *pl.,* 585 24;—from Lat. *expendere.*

expowne, *v.,* to expound, interpret; **expowned,** *p.p.,* 27 16; *pt.,* 27 35;—Lat. *exponere,* O.F. *expondre.*

eyder, *adj.,* either, 313 21;—A.S. *ægþer.*

eye, *sb.,* eye; **eyen,** *pl.,* 112 9; 435 28;—A.S. *éage.*

eygyrlye, *adv.,* eagerly. *See* **eger.**

eyle, *v.,* to trouble, afflict, hurt; **eyleth,** *prs.,* 407 2; 511 19;—A.S. *eglan.*

facyon, *sb.,* shape, fashion; **facyons,** *pl.,* 692 17;—O.F. *fason, façon.*

fadom, *sb.,* fathom, 847 9;—A.S. *fæðm.*

faille, *v.,* to fail; *inf.,* 42 28; **faylled,** *pt.,* 42 9; **failled,** *pt.,* 57 29;—A.F. *faillir.*

falle, *sb.,* fall; **fallys,** *pl.,* 477 5;—from A.S. *feallan.*

falle, *v.,* to fall; **fell,** *pt.,* 43 3; **falle,** *prs.,* 3 38; **fyl, fylle, felle,** *pt.,* 30 11; 71 16; 93 31; 122 4; 847 15; **falle,** *p.p.,* 93 35; **fallen,** *pl. prs.,* 213 17; **fallen,** *p.p.,* 625 25;—A.S. *feallan.*

fantasye, *sb.,* fancy, imagination, 285 33;—O.F. *fantasie.*

fare, *v.,* to go, fare, behave; **ferd,** *prs.,* 56 12; 536 18; **farne,** *p.p.,* 595 9; **farynge,** *p.prs.,* 289 10; **faren,** *p.p.,* 235 34;—A.S. *faran.*

faucon, *sb.,* falcon, 208 32;—A.F. *faucon.*

faute, *v.,* to fail, to be wanting,

to stammer; **fawte,** *prs.,* 101 5; **fauted,** *pt.,* 388 23;—Lat. *fallere.* *Compare* O.F. *falte.*

faueour, *sb.,* favour, 338 2;—O.F. *faveur.*

fay, *sb.,* fay, fairy, person endowed with supernatural powers (surname of Morgan, king Arthur's sister);—O.F. *faë (fee).*

fayne, *v.,* to feign; **fayned,** *p.p.,* 2 7; 403 31;—A.F. *feindre.*

fayter, *sb.,* impostor, vagabond, pretender, 87 14;—O.F. *faitour.*

feale, *v.,* to feel; **feale,** *prs.,* 360 29; **felte,** *pt.,* 611 6;—A.S. *félan.*

feaute, *sb.,* track, trace, 205 1; 764 26;—? O.F. *feute.*

feaute, *sb.,* fealty, fidelity, the oath sworn by the vassal to be faithful to his feudal lord, 227 26; 437 37; **fealte,** 181 32;—O.F. *fealte.*

feble, *v.,* to become weak, to make weak; **febled,** *pt.,* 142 38; 759 36;—from O.F. *feble, floible.*

fede, *v.,* to feed; **fedde,** *p.p.* and *pt.,* 717 34;—A.S. *fédan.*

feest, *sb.,* feast, festival, 401 4; 417 14; **fest,** 44 24; **feste,** 44 36;—A.F. *feste.*

felaushyppe, *v.,* to associate; **felaushypped,** *pt.,* 352 23;—Icel. *felagi,* A.S. *scipe. Compare* **enfelaushyppe.**

felle, *v.,* to fell; **feld,** *p.p.,* 204 27; **fellyd,** *p.p.,* 97 17, 27; 836 12;—A.S. *fellan.*

felon, *sb.,* traitor, villain, 550 30;—A.F. *felon, feloun.*

felonsly, fellonysly, *adv.,* feloniously, cruelly, disgracefully, 453 10; 455 5; 504 22.

felyshyp, *sb.,* fellowship, company, 840 30;—Icel. *felagi,* A.S. *scipe.*

fende, *sb.,* enemy, fiend, 136 11; 655 7;—A.S. *feónd.*

fer, *adj.* and *adv.,* far, 135 12; 832 23; **ferre,** 308 15; **ferther,** *comparat.,* 273 30;—A.S. *feorr,* O.S. *fer.*

ferdful, *adj.,* frightful, terrible, timid;—A.S. *fær* and *ful.*

fere, *sb.,* fear, 590 3;—A.S. *fær.*

fere, *v.,* to terrify, to frighten, fear;

---

[1] Compare Walter W. Skeat's notes to Chaucer's "Legend of Good Women," p. 175.

fere, *prs.*, 287 30; 409 15; feryd, *pt.*, 400 32;—A.S. *féeran.*

ferhewen, *p.p.* hewn, beaten, 238 29;—A.S. *for* and *heáwan.*

fete, *sb.*, deed, knightly feat; fetys, *pl.*, 641 36; feates, *pl.*, 1 38;—O.F. *fet, fait.*

fette, *v.*, to fetch; fette, *pt.*, 65 22; fette, *p.p.*, 101 4; fetche, *imperat.*, 103 13; fetche, *prs.*, 93 10;—A.S. *fetian.*

feutre, *v.*, to put a spear into its rest; feutryd, *pt.*, 202 20; 433 17.

fewter, *sb.*, the rest for a spear, 185 13;—O.F. *feutre.*

feyster, *v.*, fester, to corrupt or rankle, suppurate, become malignant; *inf.*, 788 31. *See* Skeat, Dict.

feyth, feythe, *sb.*, faith, 63 28 (by the feythe of our bodyes); 519 27;—O.F. *fei, feid.*

feythful, *adj.*, faithful, 149 23.

flacked, *sb.*, flask, bottle, 309 29;—O.F. *flasque.*

flagan, *sb.*, drinking vessel with a narrow neck, flagon; flagans, *pl.*, 234 4;—O.F. *flascon.*

flatlynge, *adv.*, flat, 321 24; 736 7; —Icel. *flatr* and A.S. *ling.*

flay, *v.*, to skin, to cut off in flags; flayne, *p.p.*, 74 27;—A.S. *fleán.*

flee, *v.*, to fly, flee; fledde, *pt.*, 73 27; flay, *pt.*, 689 13;—A.S. *fléogan, fléon.*

fleme, *v.*, to put to flight; flemyd, *p.p.*, 635 8; 828 13;—A.S. *fléman.*

flesshe, *sb.*, flesh; *but also* meat, 658 10;—A.S. *flǽsc.*

flete, *v.*, to float, swim; fletyng, *p.prs.*, 614 28;—A.S. *fléotan.*

flore, *v.*, to flower, flourish; floreth, *prs.*, 771 20;—O.F. *florir.*

florysshe, *v.*, to flourish, to cause to prosper; *also*, to brandish a weapon; florysshen, *pl. prs.*, 771 4; floryssheth, *prs.*, 771 6;—O.F. *floriss-*, from *florir.*

flynge, *v.*, to send forth, fling, rush; *inf.*, 589 11;—? Swedish *flänga.*

folye, *sb.*, folly, 2 12; foly, 121 36; —A.F. *folie.*

foolysshe, *adj.*, foolish, lustful, silly, 505 6;—O.F. *fol* with A.S. suff. *-lic.*

for, i. *prep.*, for, by, in spite of, for fear of; ii. *conj.*, because, in order that; iii. *prefix*—(1) having the sense of destruction, loss = A.S. *for-*; (2) replacing *before* = A.S. *fore*; (3) replacing the prep. *for*; (4) standing for O.F. *for-*, Lat. *foris.*

forbere, *v.*, to forbear; forborne, *p.p.*, 347 7;—A.S. *for-beran.*

forblede, *v.*, to bleed, to lose blood forbledde, *pt.*, 463 23; forbled, *p.p.*, 350 26;—A.S. *for-* and *blédan.*

force, *sb.*, force, matter, consequence; no force, it matters not, 72 35; I take no force, 79 17; 762 36; 775 6;—A.F. *force.*

fordele, *sb.*, advantage, 173 33.

forder, *v.*, to advance, promote, further; fordered, *pt.*, 229 34;—A.S. *fyrðran.*

fordo, *v.*, to destroy, perish; fordyd, *pt.*, 99 3; fordone, *p.p.*, 334 32;—A.S. *fordón.*

fore cast, *sb.*, that which is contrived beforehand, 805 14;—A.S. *fore*, Icel. *kasta.*

foreye, *v.*, to forage; foreyeng, *p.prs.*, 175 30;—O.F. *forager.*

foreyn, forayn, *adj.*, foreign, strange, 573 1, 22;—O.F. *forain.*

foreyst, forest, *sb.*, forest, wood, 51 15; 60 28;—O.F. *forest.*

forfende, *v.*, to defend, forbid; *prs.*, 727 8; forfendyd, *p.p.*, 727 13; —A.S. *for* and O.F. *(de)fendre.*

forfette, *sb.*, forfeit, crime, 695 22; —O.F. *forfet, forfait.*

forfeture, *sb.*, forfeiture, 39 38; 302 29;—O.F. *forfeture.*

forfighte, *v.*, to tire by fighting, to weaken; forfoughten, *p.p.*, 87 25; 105 35;—A.S. *for* and *feohtan.*

forgete, *v.*, to forget; *inf.*, 381 16; forgeten, *p.p.*, 380 16; 840 34; forgeten, *pl. prs.*, 726 17;—A.S. *forgitan.*

forgiue *v.*, to forgive; forgaf, *pt.*, 43 32;—A.S. *for* and *gifan.* Compare foryeue.

forhede, forheed, *sb.*, forehead, 333 9; 648 19.

foriusted, *p.p.*, unable to fight any longer, exhausted, 323 35; 421 30; —A.S. *for* and O.F. *adjouster.*

forlond, *sb.*, foreland, cape, a point of land running into the sea, 167 4;—Icel. *forlendi*.

forlonge, *sb.*, *adj.*, a furrow long, or the length of a furrow, forty poles, the eighth part of a mile, 166 25; **furlonge**, 354 13;—A.S. *furh*, (the furrow) + *lang*.

formest, *adj. superl.*, first, foremost, 342 31; 347 9;—A.S. *fyrmest*.

forsothe, forsoth, *adv.*, truly, indeed, 531 5; 645 35;—A.S. *for* and *soð*.

forswere, *v.*, to forswear; **forsworne**, *p.p.*, 150 14;—A.S. *forswerian*.

forth, *adv.*, forth, henceforth, throughout; **forth dayes** = far advanced in the day, 804 19;—A.S. *forð*.

forthynke, *v.*, to repent; *inf.*, 711 11; **me forthynketh**, *prs.*, 82 2; 643 12; **forthoughte**, *pt.*, 712 31;—A.S. *forþyncan*.

fortune, *v.*, to happen, to make fortunate; **hit fortuned**, *pt.*, 213 2; 364 21;—from O.F. *fortune*.

forwounded, *p.p.*, desperately wounded, 350 26;—A.S. *for* and *wundian*.

foryeue, *v.*, to forgive; *inf.*, 79 32; **foryaf**, *pt.*, 43 32;—A.S. *forgifan*.

foryeuenes, *sb.*, forgiveness, 251 14; 563 19.

foster, *sb.*, nourishment; **foster broder**, a male child, fostered or brought up with another of different parents, 42 29; *comp.* **nourisshed broder**, 41 10;—A.S. *fóstor*.

foster, *sb.*, forester, one who inhabits a forest, or has the charge of it, 671 28;—O.F. *forestier*.

fostre, *v.*, to foster, support; **fostred**, *p.p.*, 250 23;—A.S. *fóstrian*.

fourde, *sb.*, ford, passage, course, 184 35;—A.S. *ford*.

fourme, *v.*, to form; **fourmed**, *p.p.*, 324 17;—O.F. *former*.

foyle, *v.*, to tread down, to trampel on; **foyled**, *p.p.*, 771 27;—O.F. *fouler, foler*.

foyne, *sb.*, a foin, thrust, prick, 248 7; 847 9; **foynes**, *pl.*, 351 19;—O.F. *fouine*.

foyne, *v.*, to thrust, to beat with a sword; **foynynge**, *p.prs.*, 217 33; O.F. *fouine* (see Littré).

franceis, *sb.*, freedom, liberality, prerogative, 334 35;—A.F. *franchise*.

frende, *sb.*, friend, 274 8;—A.S. *fréond*.

fresshe, freysshe, *adj.*, fresh, new; 350 29; **freyssheyst**, *superl.*, 763 23; **fresshest**, *superl.*, 773 32; **fresshely**, *adv.*, 239 12;—A.S. *fersc*.

fronte, *sb.*, front, forehead, 538 27; **frounte**, 191 1; **frunte**, 87 31;—A.F. *frount, frunt*, O.F. *front*.

fulfeythful, *adj.* (!), faithful, 522 36.

furfare, *v.*, to perish, fare ill, destroy; **fur fared**, *pt.*, 190 30;—A.S. *forféran*.

fyaunce, *sb.*, promise, confidence, trust, 39 2;—O.F. *fiance*.

fyendly, *adv.*, hostile, warlike, adverse, 572 27;—A.S. *féondlíc*.

fyer, fyre, *sb.*, fire, 183 18; 275 38;—A.S. *fýr*.

fyers, *adj.*, fierce, strong, bold, brave, 57 34; **fyerser**, *comp.*, 181 31;—O.F. *fers, fiers*.

fyghte, *v.*, to fight; *inf.*, 127 8; **fyghtynge**,*p.prs.*,426 28; **faughte**, *pt.*, 159 28; **fought**, *pt.*, 71 27; **faughte**, *pt.*, 65 12;—A.S. *feohtan*.

fylle, *sb.*, the amount of anything that a person can stand; **fylle of fyghtynge**, 426 28;—A.S. *ful*.

fylle, *sb.*, colt, filly, young animal, 388 23;—A.S. *fyllo*.

fynde, *v.*, to find; *inf.*, 590 12; **fond**, *pt.*, 205 26; **fonde**, *pt.*, 316 5; 757 32; **found**, *pt.*, 84 5; **fonden**, *p.p.*, 360 24; **founden**, *p.p.*, 246 36; 585 21; **founde**, *p.p.*, 434 34;—A.S. *findan*.

fyse, *sb.*, son;—O.F. *fis, fiz*.

fytloke, *sb.*, fetlock, tuft of hair growing behind the pastern-joint of horses; **fytlokys**,*pl.*, 61 2;—? A.S. *fót* and *locc*.

gad, *sb.*, a wedge of steel, a sharp-pointed instrument, a graver, 657 13;—A.S. *gad*.

gadere, *v.*, to gather, collect, assemble; **gadre**, *inf.*, 51 35; **gad-**

red, *pt.*, 6 20 ; 668 17 ;—A.S. *gade-rian.*

galeye, *sb.*, galley, a long low-built ship with one deck, 164 30; **galeyes**, *pl.*, 841 9 ;—A.F. *galeye.*

galhous, *sb.*, gallows, 796 8 (the 1634 ed. has *gallous*) ;—A.S. *gealga, galga.*

gap, *sb.*, an opening made by rupture or parting, cleft, 403 7 ;—Icel. *gap.*

garderobe, *sb.*, wardrobe, place where dresses are kept, 177 25 ;—O.F. *garderobe.*

gardyne, *sb.*, garden, 583 13; **gar-dyns**, *pl.*, 771 20 ;—A.F. *gardin.*

gare, *v.*, to make, to cause; **garte**,*pt.*, 121 28 ; 185 26 ;—Icel. *göra.*

garet, *sb.*, a look-out on the roof of a house or castle wall, watch-tower, 200 6 ;—O.F. *garite.*

gar-make, 825 25-26 ;—¹ This form is an evident tautology, as *gar* (Icel. *göra*), M.E. "*to ger*," is equal in signification to "*make.*" ¹

garneson, *sb.*, guard, garrison, 178 8 ;—O.F. *garnison.*

garnysshe, *v.*, to supply, to equip, to provide with ; *imperat.*, 35 30 ; *prs.*, 51 8 ; **garnysshed**, *pt.*, 825 33 ;—O.F. *garniss-*, from *garnir.*

gate, *sb.*, gate ; **gatys**, *pl.*, 459 37 ;—A.S. *geat. Compare* **yate**.

gauntelet, *sb.*, a gauntlet, the iron glove of armour, 778 30 ; 780 9 ;—O.F. *gantelet.*

gayn, *adj.*, direct, near, convenient, ready ; **gaynest**, *superlat.*, 243 31 ;—Icel. *gegn.*

gaynsaye, *v.*, to deny, dispute, contradict ; *inf.*, 2 30 ;—A.S. *gean* and *seogan.*

geaunte, *sb.*, giant, 11 5; **gyaunt**, 97 26; **geauntes**, *pl.*, 12 5 ;—A.F. *geant.*

gentyl, **yentyl**, *adj.*, worthy, excellent, noble; **gentylst**, *superl.*, 422 15 ; **yentyllest**, *superl.*, 860* 10 ;—A.F. *gentil.*

genytours, *sb. pl.*, genitals, exterior organs of generation, 168 9 ;—O.F. *genitoirs*, Lat. *genitorium.*

gerfaukon, *sb.*, a kind of falcon, 156 29 ;—Lat. *gyrofalconem. See also* **iarfaucon**.

germayn, *adj.*, closely allied, derived from the same stock, of the first degree, 89 19 ;—Lat. *germanus.*

geste, *sb.*, guest; **gestes**, *pl.*, 310 24; —A.S. *gæst, gest.*

gete, *v.*, to gain, get, to beget ; **gatte**, *pt.*, 297 27 ; **geteth**, *prs.*, 47 33; **gat**,*pt.*, 68 8 ; **gate**, *pt.*, 41 32 ; 763 2 ; **goten**, *p.p.*, 61 28 ; 63 24; **yate**, *pt.*, 39 7 ; 91 9 ;—A.S. *gitan.*

gladde, *adj.*, glad, 401 2 ;—A.S. *glæd.*

glade, *v.*, to make glad, to render merry ; **gladeth**, *prs.*, 180 4; **gladen**, *prs. pl.*, 797 4 ;—A.S. *gladian.*

glastynge, *p.prs.*, making a noise like a dog, barking ; **the glastynge beest**. *Compare* **questyng**.

glatysaunt (*the glatysaunt beest*), barking ;—*p.prs.* of O.F. *glatir, glatisant.*

glayue, *sb.*, sword, 110 26 ; 807 18 ;—O.F. *glaive.*

glemerynge, *p.prs.*, glimmering, 592 19 ;—A.S. *ge-leoman.*

gloton, *sb.*, glutton, 168 6 ;—A.F. *gluttun.*

gnaste, *v.*, to gnash the teeth ; **gnasted**, *pt.*, 206 16 ; — Icel. *gnastan.*

gonne, *sb.*, gun ; **gonnes**, *pl.*, 839 26. *Compare Low Lat.* **gunna**.

gone, *v.*, to go ; **gost**, *prs.*, 70 27 ; **goth**, *prs.*, 733 17 ;—A.S. *gán.*

gomme, *sb.*, gum ; **gommes**, *pl.*, 174 22 ;—O.F. *gomme.*

gouernaunce, *sb.*, government, behaviour, 334 12 ; 405 30 ; 478 26 ;—O.F. *gouvernance.*

Gouernayle, name given to syr Trystram's tutor and servant, meaning rudder, management, leader.

---

¹ I can only explain this strange form (the hyphen is here not inserted in my edition, but is found in the Caxton) by supposing that the compositor, by breaking the word and printing "*gar-*" at the end of one line, forgot what he was to do, and put "*make*" at the beginning of the next. Malory most likely wrote "*gar-nysshe*" as in line 33 of the same page.

Gramercy, *adj. sb.,* grant-mercy, many thanks, 426 30.

gras, *sb.,* grass; **put hem to gras,** 85 1;—A.S. *græs.*

graunte, *adj.,* great, 565 20; **graunte sir,** 696 3; **graunt mercy,** 804 15;—O.F. *grand.*

graunte, *v.,* to grant, give, allow, agree; *inf.,* 762 16; **graunted,** *p.p.,* 12 27; **graunted,** *pt.,* 760 31;—A.F. *graunter.*

graythe, *v.,* to prepare, to dress; **graythed,** *pt.,* 171 34;—Icel. *greiða.*

gree, *sb.,* step, degree, worthiness, price, 447 31; 538 34;—O.F. *gre.*

greece, *sb.,* grease, 219 1; **the hart of greese,** 566 22;—O.F. *graisse.*

Grece, *sb.,* Greece, the country, 163.

grekysshe, *adj.,* Greek, 2 35.

grede, *adj.,* greedy, 179 23;—A.S. *grædig, grédig.*

greese, *sb. See* **greece.**

grette, grete, *adj.;* **gretter,** *comp.,* 38 8; **grettest,** *superl.,* 40 17;—A.S. *gréat.*

grese, *sb.,* step, stair; *pl.,* flight of steps; **gresys,** *pl.,* 716* 25;—O.F. *gre.*

greuaunce, *sb.,* hurt, grievance, 205 17;—O.F. *grevance.*

greue, *sb.,* grove, thicket; **greuys,** *pl.,* 208 35;—A.S. *gráf.*

grone, *v.,* to groan; **gronynge,** *p.prs.,* 283 37;—A.S. *gránian.*

grose, le (surname of Hellyas and Geryne), meaning the great, the stout;—O.F. *gros.*

grutche, *v.,* to grumble, grudge; *inf.,* 177 37;—O.F. *groucher.*

gryef, *sb.,* grief, 342 10;—O.F. *gref.*

grym, grymme, *adj.,* fierce, horrible, heavy, 93 18; 845 12; **grymly,** *adv.,* 206 31;—A.S. *grim.*

gryffon, *sb.,* griffin, 65 10; 176 8;—O.F. *griffon.*

grype, *v.,* to grip, to seize; **grypped,** *pt.,* 193 29; **gryped,** *pt.,* 239 23;—A.S. *gripan.*

grysyly, *adj.,* horrible, dreadful; **grysylyest,** *superl.,* 584 22;—A.S. *grislic.*

guldyssh, *adj.,* gilt, golden, 408 13;—deriv. from A.S. *gyldan.*

guttes, *sb. pl.,* the bowels, 169 9; 778 14;—A.S. *gut, geotan.*

guyse, *sb.,* way, manner, dress, behaviour, 747 26;—O.F. *guise.*

gyfte, *sb.,* gift, present, 69 7; **yeftes,** *pl.,* 453 5;—Icel. *gipt.*

gyue, *v.,* to give; **my herte gyueth me to the,** 214 10; 530 20; 708 29; **gaue,** *pt.,* 101 3; **gaf,** *pt.,* 46 36; 115 3; **yeue,** *inf.,* 38 11; **yeuen,** *p.p.,* 44 9; 61 36; 518 6; **gyuen,** *p.p.,* 15 2;—A.S. *gifan.*

gyle, *sb.,* guile, deceit, fraud, 77 2; 174 2;—O.F. *guile,* A.S. *wil.*

gyrde, *v.,* to gird; **gyrd,** *pt.* and *p.p.,* 76 17, 19;—A.S. *gyrdan.*

gyrdyl, *sb.,* girdle, 849 16;—A.S. *gyrdel.*

gysarme, *sb.,* battle-axe, 248 2; **gysarms,** *pl.,* 155 4;—O.F. *guisarme.*

gyse, *sb.,* guise, manner, wise, 62 17;—A.S. *wise.*

gyse, *sb. pl.,* geese, 62 17;—A.S. *gés.*

haberion, *sb.,* habergeon, a piece of armour to defend the neck and breast, 677 18;—O.F. *hauberjon.*

hackney, *sb.,* small horse, nag, 304 33; **hakeneis,** *pl.,* 50 22; 448 32;—A.F. *hakenai, hakeney.*

haft, *sb.,* handle, 692 20; 848 27;—A.S. *hæft.*

halle, *sb.,* hall, 264 19; **holle,** 264 22;—A.S. *heol,* O.F. *halle.*

hale and how, pull ho! *a cry of sailors,* 236 13.

halse, *v.,* to embrace; **halsed,** *pt.,* 304 37;—A.S. *healsian.*

handed, *adj.,* skilful, strong; **the fayrest and largest handed,** 213 27;—from A.S. *hand, hond.*

handsel, *sb.,* handsel, gift, earnest-money on a purchase, 297 30;—Icel. *handsal.*

hangers, *sb. pl.,* testicles, 474 18;—A.S. *hangian.*

hange, *v.,* to hang; **hangen,** *pl. prs.,* 184 36; **henge,** *pt.,* 193 12; 463 38;—A.S. *hange,* from *hón.*

harneis, *sb.,* armour, 406 14;—O.F. *harnois.*

harnest, *p.p.,* equipped, 324 23; **harnysed,** *p.p.,* 773 33.

hastynes, *sb.,* haste, hurry, 841 33.

hate, v., to be called; heteth, prs., 216 3;—A.S. hatan.

hauberk, sb., a coat of ringed mail, armour protecting the neck, 58 21; 82 11;—O.F. hauberc.

hauke, sb., hawk; v., to hawk, 208 20; hawkynge, 276 33;—A.S. heafoc.

haute prynce, the, the high prince; surname of Galahad son of Launcelot, and of Galahad of Surluse.

haue, v., to have, to take; inf., 756 8; hadde, pt., 489 28;—A.S. habban.

hayre, sb., hair, 657 16; 713* 11; here, 83 22; hayr, 27 27; heyre, 362 19;—A.S. hǽr, hér.

hede, sb., heed, care, 714* 27;—from A.S. hédan.

hede, sb., head, 311 19; heed, 311 20; heede, 311 27; 465 1;—A.S. héafod.

hele, sb., health, soundness, salvation, 705 20; 720 8;—A.S. hǽlu.

helme, sb., helmet, 195 18; helmet, 195* 17; used for "men," 191 10;—A.S. helm.

helpe, v., to help; halp, pt., 91 28; 155 8; holpen, p.p., 125 4;—A.S. helpan.

helthe, sb., health, soundness, salvation, 631 88; 702 22;—A.S. hǽlð.

hem, pron. pl., dat. and acc., them, 37 27; 47 4; 85 21; 631 26;—A.S. him, heom.

heme, v., to make a buzzing sound like bees, hum; hemynge, p.prs., 583 2.—Of imitat. origin.

hens, adv., hence, 267 36;—M.E. hennes, A.S. heonan, hionan.

heraude, sb., herald; heraudes, pl., 533 24;—O.F. heraud, herault.

her, pron., their, 47 2; 101 13; 643 25; 816 11;—A.S. hira, heora.

herberowe, sb., lodging, shelter, 243 35; herberow, 153 11; herburgh, 427 19; herberowes, pl., 263 36;—Icel. herbergi.

herberowe, v., to lodge, to provide shelter; herborowed, pt., 180 19.

here, v., to hear; inf., 850 5; herde, p.p., 703 33;—A.S. héran.

here, sb., hair. See hayre.

hermyte, heremytage. See ermyte, ermytage.

herken, v., to hearken, listen; inf., 366 13; herke, imperat., 703 36; herkened, pt., 447 3;—A.S. hyrcnian.

herte, sb., heart, 393 2; hert, 457 24;—A.S. heorte.

herte, sb., hart, 566 22; hert, 65 17;—A.S. heorot, heort.

heruest, sb., harvest, 815 9;—A.S. haerfest.

herytage, sb., heritage, 652 38;—O.F. heritage.

hete, sb., a hit, 584 26;—from Icel. hitta.

hethe, sb., heath, 845 31;—A.S. hǽð.

hethen, adj., heathen, 2 31; 643 22;—A.S. hǽðen.

heue, v., heave, raise; prs., 72 12; 847 18;—A.S. hebban.

hewe, sb., hue, colour, 165 9;—A.S. hiw.

hewe, v., to hew, to knock; hewe, pt., 463 18; hewen, p.p., 27 26; 97 38;—A.S. héawan.

heyer, sb., heir, successor, 164 27.

hey3te, sb., height, 165 19;—A.S. heáhðu, héhðu.

hit, hyt, pron., it, 61 5; 131 37; 148 6;—A.S. hit.

ho, interj., stop! hold on! 61 9.

hole, adj., whole, entire, 722 24;—A.S. hál.

holsome, adj., wholesome, 100 26.—Compare Icel. heilsamr.

holte, sb., a wood, holt, a wooded hill, grove; holtys, pl., 175 34;—A.S. holt.

honger, sb., hunger, 652 27; hongre, 651 35;—A.S. hungor.

holde, v., to hold, observe, keep; hylde, pt., 48 19; holydyn, p.p., 44 22; helde, pt., 59 20.

houe, v., remain, hover, wait about; houed, pt., 145 15; houynge, p.prs., 99 28.

hool, adj., whole, sound, 36 12; holer, comp., 72 19;—A.S. hál.

hoolly, sb., holly, 155 34;—A.S. holen, holegn.

hoost, hooste, sb., host, army, 36 4; 61 3;—A.F. ost, host.

hore, adj., hoar, hairy, white or grayish-white, aged, 96 5; holtes hore, 853 9;—A.S. hár.

hors lytter, *sb.*, a vehicle containing a bed, drawn by horses, 399 14; hors lyttar, 39 20;—A.S. *hors* and O.F. *litiere.*

horsbere, *sb.*, horse-bier, carriage or frame of wood for bearing the dead to the grave, hearse, 135 23.

hostage, *sb.*, preparation for battle or war, 463 6;—A.F. *hostage.*

hostry, *sb.*, inn, 80 5.

houghbone, *sb.*, the bone at the joint on the hind-leg of a quadruped; the back part of the knee-joint, 596 20;—A.S. *hoh* and *bán.*

hous, hows, *sb.*, the house, 100 16; 143 12;—A.S. *hus.*

housel, *v.*, to housel, to administer the Eucharist; houseld, *p.p.*, 452 7; 702 4; howselyd, *p.p.*, 858* 25;—from A.S. *húsel.*

how be it, *adj.*, howbeit, notwithstanding, 317 10.

hurte, *v.*, to hurt; hurte, *p.p.*, 134 36; 703 10; 764 32; hurte, *pt.*, 20 14;—O.F. *hurter, heurter. Compare* A.S. *hyrt,* wounded.

hurtle, *v.*, to rush, to dash against, to throw down; hurtled, *pt.*, 71 29; 195* 7; hurlynge, *p.prs.*, 226 36; hurled, *pt.*, 764 32.

husbondman, *sb.*, working farmer, husbandman, 166 7;—Icel. *húsbondi,* A.S. *man.*

hyde, *v.*, to hide; hyd, *p.p.*, 62 24; 77 37; hydde, *pt.*, 719 23; 849 2;—A.S. *hýdan.*

hyder, *adv.*, hither, 110 34; 521 25; hyther, 215 5; hydder, 761 23; —A.S. *hider, hiðer.*

hyderto, *adv.*, hitherto, 846 35.

hyhenes, *sb.*, highness, 487 36;— A.S. *héah, heh,* and *nysse.*

hyhe, *adj.*, high, 670 27;—A.S. *héah.*

hye, hyhe, *v.*, to hie, hasten; hyhe, *imperat.*, 465 7; hyhe me, 80 13; hye yow, 37 10;—A.S. *higian, higan.*

hylle, *sb.*, hill, 714* 15; hyllys, *pl.*, 175 34;—A.S. *hyll.*

hylte, *sb.*, hilt, handle; hyltys, *pl.*, 95 36;—A.S. *hilt.*

hynde, *sb.*, hind, female of a stag, 764 17;—A.S. *hind.*

hyr, *pron.*, her, 109 4;—A.S. *hire.*

hystoryal, *adj.*, historical, 1 3;— Lat. *historia.*

hyther, *adv. See* hyder.

hyt, *pron. See* hit.

hytte, *v.*, to hit; hyt, *pt.*, 71 15; hitte, *pt.*, 412 23;—Icel. *hitta.*

incontynent, *adj., adv.*, incontinent, immediately, at once, 162 21;— Lat. *incontinent-,* from *incontinens.*

incoronation, *sb.*, coronation, 44 24.

indignacyon, *sb.*, indignation, 43 14; —Lat. *indignationem.*

infydeles, *sb. pl.*, the infidels, heathen, 163 38; myscreantes, *pl.*, 860 38;—Lat. *infidelis.*

intronysacyon, *sb.*, enthronement, coronation, 182 11.

ire, *sb.*, anger, 313 23;—Lat. *ira. See also* yre.

ialous, *adj.*, jealous, 203 9; 407 32; —O.F. *jalous.*

ialousye, *sb.*, jealousy, 293 3; (ialousnes, 407 32);—O.F. *jalousie.*

iape, *sb.*, joke, jest, mockery, 113 11; —from O.F. *japper.*

iaper, *sb.*, jester, buffoon, 335 35.

iarfaucon, *sb.*, a kind of falcon, 254 31; ierfaucon, 601 21;—Lat. *gyrofalconem. See also* gerfaucon.

iay, *sb.*, jay, bird of the crow family with gay plumage, 582 30;—O.F. *geai.*

ieopardy, *sb.*, jeopardy, hazard, danger, 108 15.

ieoparde, *v.*, jeopard, jeopardise; *inf.*, 74 15; 471 30;—from O.F. *jeu parti.*

iesseraunte, *sb.*, a short cuirass of fine mail; iesseraunce, 619 11;— O.F. *jazerant, iaseran.*

iocounde, *adj.*, joyous, pleasant, 249 6.

iuge, *v.*, to judge; *prs.*, 134 14; iuged, *pt.*, 109 12; *p.p.*, 564 15;— O.F. *juger.*

iugement, *sb.*, judgement, 152 30;— A.F. *jugement.*

iuste, *v.*, to joust, encounter, approach; ioustyng, *p.prs.*, 41 16;— A.F. *jouster.*

iuster, *sb.*, champion, 71 10; iustar, 441 29.

iustes, *sb. pl.*, tournaments, 41 12;— A.F. *joustes.*

kay, *sb.*, key; kayes, *pl.*, 633 9;—
—A.S. *cæg, cæge.*

kechen,*sb.*, kitchen, 214 27; kechyn,
215 17;—A.S. *cycene, cicen.*

kele, *v.*, to cool; *inf.*, 421 1; keleth,
prs., 771 31;—A.S. *célan.*

kempe, *sb.*, warrior, champion; kem-
pys, *pl.*, 223 31;—A.S. *cempa.*

kepar, *sb.*, keeper, 139 29.

kepe, *sb.*, heed; 294 10; 629 29.

kepe, *v.*, to keep, observe, regard;
inf., 831 35; kepe, *imperat.*, 364
14; 407 12; kepest, *prs.*, 472 21;
kepte, *pt.*, 326 20; kepte, *p.p.*, 42
25; 406 15;—A.S. *cépan.*

kertyl, *sb.*, kirtle, short gown, or
tunic, 168 8;—A.S. *cyrtel.*

kerue, *v.*, to carve; keruyng, *p.prs.*,
693 28;—A.S. *ceorfan.*

ketche, *v.*, to catch; *inf.*, 229 12;
caughte, *pt.*, 58 34;—O.F. *cacher.*

keuer, *v.*, to cover; keuerd, *p.p.*,
416 32;—A.F. *covrir.*

keuerchyef,*sb.*,a square piece of cloth,
172 10;—O.F.*covre-chef, couvre-chef.*

keueryng, *sb.*, the covering (of a
shield), 663 35; keuerynge, 448 7.

knaue, *sb.*, knave, servant, 177 31;
knauys, *pl.*, 177 32;—A.S. *cnafa.*

knowlege, *sb.*, knowledge, 31 4;
knouleche, 749 11.

knowleche, *v.*, to acknowledge, to
learn, to tell; *inf.*, 162 21; know-
leched, *pt.*, 14 19;—from A.S.
cnawan, with the Icel. suff. *-leikr.*

knowlechynge, *sb.*, the acknowledg-
ment, acknowledging, 822 14; 773
13.

knowe, *v.*, to know; *inf.*, 182 1; 216
5; knowen,*prs.pl.*,379 17; 729 8;
kno (!), *p.p.*, 1 18; knowen, *p.p.*,
549 30; knewe,*pt.*;—A.S. *cnáwan.*

knyghthode, *sb.*, knighthood, 354
24; 767 33;—A.S. *cnihthád.*

knylle, *v.*, to knell; *inf.*, 856* 6;—
A.S. *cnyll*, a knell.

knytte, *v.*, to knit, bind, join; knyt,
p.p., 450 1;—A.S. *cnyttan.*

kutte, *v.*, to cut; kytte, *pt.*, 781 29.

kybbet, *sb.*, cubit, a measure employed by the ancients equal to the
length of the arm from the elbow
to the tip of the middle-finger,
858* 10;—Lat. *cubitus.*

kyen, *sb. pl.*, cows, 103 16;—A.S.
cý, from sing. *cú.*

kylle, *v.*, to strike, kill; *inf.*, 764 13;
kyld, *p.p.*, 65 38; kylled, *pt.*,
327 13; kylled, *p.p.*, 326 19.

kynde, *sb.*, kind, nature, race, 582
28; 708 36;—A.S. *cynde, gecynd.*

kynne, *sb.*, kin, kind, generation, 83
31; 513 19;—A.S. *cynn.*

kynreed, *sb.*, kindred, 243 5;
kynred, 243 11;—A.S. *cynn* and
ræden.

kysse, *v.*, to kiss; kyst, *pt.*, 78 38;
68 20; kyssed, *pt.*, 82 36;—A.S.
cyssan.

laddre, *sb.*, ladder; laddres, *pl.*,
180 37;—A.S. *hlæder.*

ladyl, *sb.*, ladle, a large spoon
for ladling or dipping out liquid
from a vessel, 219 6;—A.S. *hlædel.*

lady les, *adj.*, ladyless, without a lady,
312 19.

langage, *sb.*, language, 405 19;—
A.F. *langage.*

langaged, *adj.*, having a way of
speaking, 272 11.

langer, *v.*, loiter, saunter about;
langerynge, *p.prs.*, 369 21.

lande, *sb.*, land, country; landes, *pl.*,
830 34; lendes, *pl.*, 831 31.

lappe, *v.*, to wrap; lapped, *pt.*,
274 18; 737 2; lapped, *p.p.*, 205
35. *See* Skeat, Dict.

largesse, *sb.*, bounty, largess, 539 26;
your largenesse, 134 23;—A.F.
largesse.

lasshe,*v.*, to dash against; lasshyed,
pt., 203 4; lasshed, *pt.*, 403 38;
472 33.

late, *adj.*, *adv.*, slow, late, lately, 652
21;—A.S. *lœt.*

laton, *sb.*, brass, bronze, 88 25;
latoen, 184 37;—O.F. *laton.*

laughe, *v.*, to laugh; laugh, *prs.*,
99 8; lough, *pt.*, 45 29; 99 8;—
A.S. *hlehhan.*

laules, *adj.*, lawless, 64 6.

launde, *sb.*, a wild, bushy plain, a
waste field, 145 14, 23;—A.F.
launde.

lawde, *sb.*, praise, 747 35;—Lat.
laudem.

lawe, *sb.*, law; lawes, *pl.*, 760 14.

layne, *v.*, to hide (in Old Norse the verb has this meaning, whereas in A.S. *lígnian* means to deny); *inf.*, 798 14; *prs.*, 747 14.

laye, *v.*, to lay; *inf.*, 837 7; **laydest**, *second p.prs.*, 837 8; **leye**, *imperat.*, 206 32; **layde**, *p.p.*, 126 14; **laid**, *pt.*, 188 34; **layen**, *p.p.*, 29 22; **laide**, *p.p.*, 760 27; **leyd**, *pt.*, 658 30;—A.S. *lecgan*.

layte, *sb.*, lightning, 706 30.

lazarcote, *sb.*, hut or cottage for lepers, 16 21; 376 35;—Church Lat. *lazari* and A.S. *cot.*

leare, *sb.*, cheek, face; **learys**, *pl.*, 371 4;—A.S. *lira.*

leche, *sb.*, physician; **leches**, *pl.*, 371 4;—A.S. *láce.*

lecheoure, *sb.*, glutton, dissolute person, 727 3;—A.F. *lecheur.*

lechery, *sb.*, lewdness, 641 33;—A.F. *lecherie.*

lede, *v.*, to lead, carry; *inf.*, 378 12; **lede**, *prs.*, 621 32; **lad**, *pt*, 54 4; **ladde**, *pt.*, 9 5; **ledde**, *pt.*, 11 29; 531 28; **ledde**, *p.p.*, 549 15; **ladde**, *p.p.*, 54 38; 319 7;—A.S. *lǽdan.*

leder, *sb.*, leader, guide, 387 35; 753 26.

leder, *sb.*, leather, 448 4;—A.S. *leþer.*

leed, *sb.*, lead, 174 23;—A.S. *léad.*

leef, lyef, *adj.*, dear, beloved, glad, 101 16; 849 8; **leuer**, *comp.*, 71 36; 745 21; **moost leuest**, *superl.*, 144 35;—A.S. *léof.*

legacyon, *sb.*, legation, the person or persons sent as legatees or ambassadors; but here the word means their patent as such, 175 10;—O.F. *legation.*

lege, *sb.*, a league; **leges**, *pl.*, 428 35; **leghes**, *pl.*, 601 14;—O.F. *legue.*

legeaunce, *sb.*, allegiance, 177 17;—O.F. *ligeance.*

lene, *v.*, to lend, grant; *imperat.*, 740 8; *inf.*, 96 25; 374 5;—A.S. *lǽnan.*

lene, *adj.*, lean, 102 3;—A.S. *hlǽne.*

lemman, *sb.*, lover, sweetheart, 11 31;—A.S. *léofman.*

lepe, *v.*, to leap; **lepte**, *pt.*, 104 26;—A.S. *hléapan.*

lepe, *sb.*, a leap, jump, 104 26.

lerne, *v.*, to learn, teach; *inf.*, 197 10;—A.S. *leornian.*

lese, *v.*, to lose; *inf.*, 450 13; **lose**, *inf.*, 312 3; **lese**, *prs.*, 59 37;—A.S. *léosan.*

lesses les aler, cry of the heralds at a tournament to start the knights, *laissez les aller !* let them (horses) run, 786 28.

leste, *superl.*, least, 145 30;—A.S. *lǽst.*

lete, *v.*, to let, cause, leave; **late**, *imperat.*, 168 24; 846 30; **lete**, *imper.*, 754 10;—A.S. *lǽtan.*

lette, *v.*, to hinder, to make late; *inf.*, 453 37; 841 10; **letted**, *p.p.*, 11 11;—A.S. *lettan.*

leued, *adj.*, covered with leaves, 191 6;—from A.S. *léaf.*

lewde, *adj.*, unlearned, ignorant; **lewdest**, *superl.*, 74 32;—A.S. *lǽwed.*

leyser, *sb.*, leisure, 126 10; 667 23; **leysers**, *pl.*, 474 35;—A.F. *leisir.*

lieutenaunt, *sb.*, lieutenant, 427 23;—A.F. *lieutenant.*

londage, *sb.*, landing, coming ashore, 841 10.

long, *adj.* and *adv.*, tall, long, 36 29; not longer, *comp.*, 82 33; **lengest**, *superl.*, 757 23;—A.S. *lang.*

longe, *adv.*, dependent on, or owing to, 657 35; generally in M.E. *i-long*;—A.S. *gelang.*

longe, *v.*, to belong; **longyng vnto vow**, 59 28; **longed**, *pt.*, 43 1.

lose, *v.*, to set free; **lose**, *imperat.*, 589 13; **losed**, *pt.*, 24 28; **loused**, 564 27;—A.S. *lésan, lósian.*

lothe, loth, *adj.*, hostile, hateful, grievous, unpleasant, unwilling, 151 33;—A.S. *lád.*

lotles, *adj.*, without harm, uninjured, 419 7.

lordes, *sb. pl.*, the aristocracy, contrary to the "comyns," the people, 41 4; 43 26;—A.S. *hláford.*

lous, loos, *adj.*, free, loose, 366 27; 389 21;—A.S. *leás.*

lough, *pt.* of **laughe**.

lune, *sb.*, a leash, a thong of leather by which a falconer holds his hawk; **lunys**, *pl.*, 208 13;—M.H.G. *line.*

luske, *sb.*, a lazy, idle, good-for-nothing person, 219 6.

lyar, lyer, *sb.*, lier, 84 38; 823 19, 28;—A.S. *léogere.*

lybard, *sb.*, leopard, 355 31; 533 15; 572 23; 579 5;—O.F. *libbard.*

lyberte, *sb.*, liberty, 3 37; 821 33; —O.F. *liberteit.*

lyckly, *adv.*, likely, 205 19;—A.S. *liclic.*

lycours, *adj.*, lecherous, dainty, 771 34;—deriv. from O.F. *lecher.*

lyef, *adj. See* leef.

lyft, *adj.*, left, 387 2. *See* Skeat, Dict.

lyfte, *v.*, to lift, 125 5;—Icel. *lypta.*

lygement, *sb.*, 686 24 (W. de Worde has *alegement;* Sir E. Strachey reads *aligement*); ? ligament, bandage, or alleviation.[1]

lygge, *v.*, to lie; *inf.*, 181 26; lyggest, *prs.*, 841 26; lyggynge, *p.prs.*, 150 31; leyne, *p.p.*, 715* 21; layne, *p.p.*, 188 34; 581 11; lay, *pt.*, 717 11; lyen, *p.p.*, 35 12; lyenge, *p.prs.*, 761 10;—A.S. *licgan.*

lygnage, *sb.*, lineage, descent, parentage, 177 16; 451 14;—A.F. *linage.*

lygne, *sb.*, line, 177 15;—A.S. *line*, Lat. *linea.*

lyke, *v.*, to please; *impers.*, hit lyketh the, 222 10; how lyketh yow, 215 26;—A.S. *lician (lican).*

lymme, *sb.*, limb, 844 9;—A.S. *lim.*

lyste, *sb.*, mind, desire, lust, 376 14.

lyste, *v. impers.*, to desire; me lyst, 71 34; ye lyst, 61 20;—A.S. *lystan.*

lyste, *v.*, to listen; lystned, *pt.*, 708 21; 710 23; lest, *pt.*, 435 37;— ? A.S. *hlystan, ge-hlystan.*

lystes, *sb. pl.*, the lists, the enclosed field for the tournament, 306 27; —A.F. *listes.*

lytel, *adj.*, small, little, 714* 31; lytil, 59 15;—A.S. *lytel.*

lythe, *sb.*, joint, limb, member, 116 10;—A.S. *lið.*

lyttyer, *sb.*, a vehicle containing a bed, 784 20; lyttar, 39 20; lytter, 399 14;—O.F. *litiere.*

mageste, *sb.*, majesty, 721 20;—Lat. *majestatem*, O.F. *majestet.*

make, *v.*, to make; maade, *pt.*, 759 26; maad, *pt.*, 7 23; maad, *p.p.*, 2 6; made, *pt.*, 17 15; made, *pt.*, 23 34;—A.S. *macian.*

makeles, *adj.*, matchless, 322 15; 540 26.

maker, *sb.*, maker, writer, author, 562 32; makers, *pl.*, 860* 31.

Maledysaunt, name given to a damsel going with syr Breunor; = *mal disant*, ill speaking.

male ease, *sb.*, sickness, indisposition, uneasiness, 338 2;—O.F. *malaise.*

male engyne, *sb.*, evil disposition, malice, wickedness, wicked trick, 733 5 (*compare* Spenser's "Faery Queene," *Malengin*);—A.F. *malengin.*

male fortune, *sb.*, misfortune, accident, 356 8; 392 21;—O.F. *malfortune.*

male tayle, la cote, surname of syr Breunor; *la cote mal tayllée*, the badly shaped coat.

malyce, *sb.*, evil, malice, 734 31;— A.F. *malice.*

manoyre, *sb.*, manor, house, castel, 193 14; manoir, 134 17; manayr, 195 35; manore, 196 12;—A.F. *manere.*

marbyl, *sb.*, marbel, 188 3;—O.F. *marbre.*

marche, *sb.*, district, province, border of a territory, border lands; marches, *pl.*, 297 22; — A.F. *marche.*

mare, *sb.*, mare, female of a horse; mares sone, 779 22; marys sone, 887 27;—A.S. *mere.*

mareyse, *sb.*, marsh, tract of low wet land, a morass, swamp, 205 5; mareis, 413 17; maryse, marys, 208 8;—O.F. *marois.*

maronner, maryner, *sb.*, sailor; maronners, *pl.*, 514 10; 518 2; maryners, *pl.*, 236 13.

marre, *v.*, to injure by cutting off a part, to mar, disfigure; marred, *p.p.*, 584 3;—A.S. *ámyrran.*

---

[1] As the passage in the text runs "be to me a lygement of penaunce vnto my foules helthe," it is very probable that the prefix *a-* is dropped after the indefinite article.

martre, *v.*, to torment; **martred**, *p.p.*, 707 18;—A.F. *martirer.*

masse peny, *sb.*, offering at the altar, 762 29.

matchecold, *adj.*, having holes within the parapets of the walls for pouring stones or molten lead through, machicolated, 226 8.

matere, mater, *sb.*, matter, material, stuff, subject, 425 34; **maters**, *pl.*, 727 18;—O.F. *matere.*

matyns, *sb.*, morning prayer or service, 40 19;—O.F. *matins.*

maugre, *sb.*, ill-will, 405 28; 807 12.

maulgre, magre, *prep.*, in spite of, 714 21; 70 35; **maulgre her (thy) (your) hede**, 418 19; 437 32; 701 36;—O.F. *maugre.*

may, *prs.*, may, can, 4 2; 35 26; **maye**, 759 23; **maiste**, *second pers. prs.*, 343 24; **maxste**, 131 14; **mayst**, 472 30; **maist**, 405 24; **my₃t**, *pt.*, 111 35; **myght**, *pt.*, 2 11; **myghte**, *pt.*, 754 4;—A.S. *mæg, meahte, mihte*, inf. *mugan.*

maye, *v.*, to go maying; **mayeng**, *p.prs.*, 772 10.

maylle, *sb.*, mail, defensive armour for the body, formed of steel rings or network;—O.F. *maille.*

mayme, *sb.*, bruise, injury, lameness, the deprivation of any essential part; **maymes**, *pl.*, 57 10;—O.F. *mehaing.*

mayme, *v.*, to render lame, defective, paralyse; **maymed**, *pt.*, 87 2; *p.p.*, 108 20.

mayneal, *adj.*, homely (generally in M.E. *meyneal*), 430 35.

mayntene, *v.*, to support; *inf.*, 657 1; *prs.*, 291 20;—A.F. *meyntener.*

mayntene, *sb.*, royal household, means of support, maintenance, 163 4;—O.F. *meyntien.*

mayster, *sb.*, master, governor, 151 38;—O.F. *maistre.*

maystresse, *sb.*, mistress, 538 3;—O.F. *maistresse.*

maystrye, *sb.*, mastery, 42 6; **maystry**, 467 36; **maystryes**, *pl.* 215 24; 542 9;—O.F. *maistrie.*

medle, *sb.*, medley, fight, combat, 56 6;—O.F. *medle.*

medowe, *sb.*, meadow; **medowes**, *pl.*, 202 3.—Compare A.S. *mǽdwe.*

megre, *adj.*, meagre, lean, 568 9;—O.F. *maigre.*

mekely, *adv.*, meekly, 122 33;—from Icel. *mjúkr.*

mencyon, mensyon, *sb.*, commemorative inscription, mention, 571 17; 788 12;—O.F. *mention.*

mene, *v.*, mean, signify, intent; **ment**, *pt.*, 296 20;—A.S. *mǽnan.*

merueyllous, *adj.*, marvellous, 614 5; **meruayllous**, 5 2; **merueilloust**, *superl.*, 278 35;—O.F. *merveillos.*

merueylle, *sb.*, marvel, wonder, 236 7; **meruayl**, 3 1; **merueill**, 235 10; 241 18; **merueyles**, *pl.*, 723 17;—O.F. *merveille.*

merueylle, *v.*, to wonder, to be astonished; **meruelle**, *imperat.*, 576 29; **merueyled**, *pt.*;—O.F. *merveiller.*

mery, *adj.*, merry, pleasant, bright, 404 28;—A.S. *merg.*

meschyef, *sb.*, mischief, ill-fortune, 210 7; 651 35; *vb.*, to come to mischief, to be destroyed or injured;—O.F. *meschief.*

mescreaunt, *adj.* and *sb.*, miscreant, not believing, infidel; **mescreaunts, Sarasyns**, 135 30; **myscreantes**, *pl.*, 465 30; 860 38; **mescreaunts**, *pl.*, 406 11;—O.F. *mescreant.*

mesel, *sb.*, leper (here probably leprosy is meant), 705 16;—A.F. *mesel.*

messager, messagyer, *sb.*, messenger, 254 40; 277 27; *pl.*, 423 16;—A.F. *messager.*

mete, *sb.*, meat, food, meal, feast, 551 11;—A.S. *mete.*

mete, *adj.*, fitting, suitable, meet, 290 9.—Compare A.S. *mǽte.*

mete, *v.*, to meet, encounter; *inf.*, 94 15; **metten**, *pl. prs.*, 10 33; **mette**, *pt.*, 11 36; **mette**, *p.p.*, 355 1; **met**, *p.p.*, 83 19;—A.S. *métan.*

meuable, *adj.*, movable, 827 1.

meue, *v.*, to move, suggest; *inf.*, 40 33; 321 29; **meued**, *pt.*, 37 35; 384 8; **moeued**, *p.p.*, 779 18;—A.F. *movoir*, Lat. *mouēre.*

meule, *sb.*, mule, 267 35; **mules**, *pl.*, 186 7;—O.F. *meule*.

meyny, *sb.*, household, retinue, company, 430 35; 525 7; **meyne**, 165 14;—O.F. *meisnee*.

moche, *adj.* and *adv.*, great, much, 35 37; 36 7; a moche man, 802 16.

mocke, *v.*, to mock; **mocqued**, *pt.*, 12 24; **mocked**, *pt.*, 19 35; **mocked**, *p.p.*, 87 15;—O.F. *mocquer*.

moeued, *p.p.* *See* meue.

molle, *sb.*, a mole, 239 1;—from A.S. *molde-warp*.

mone, *sb.*, the moon, 403 13;—A.S. *môna*.

montayne, *sb.*, mountain, 264 36; **mountayne**, 266 11; 662 15;—O.F. *montagne*.

monstre, *sb.*, monster, 704 34;—O.F. *monstre*.

moost, *adj. superl.*, greatest, principal, chief, 46 5; 502 12; 695 8; 840 29;—A.S. *mǽst*.

mordre, *sb.*, murder, 118 15;—A.S. *morðer*.

more, *adj.* and *adv.*; *comp.*, more, greater, 218 23; 425 26; **moo**, 45 26; 415 28; 443 5;—A.S. *mára*, *mâ*.

morne, *sb.*, morning; on the morne, 39 11; to morne, 39 10 (but also to morrowe, 70 16, 17);—A.S. *morgen*.

morne, *v.*, to mourn; **morneth**, *prs.*, 117 8; **mornyng**, *p.prs.*, 146 27; 406 1;—A.S. *murnan*.

morsel, *sb.*, morsel, 675 3;—A.F. *morsel*.

mortalyte, *sb.*, mortality, 459 24;—O.F. *mortalite*.

mote, *sb.*, note on the huntsman's horn; **motys**, *pl.*, 223 20;—O.F. *mot*.

mote, *first pers. sing.*, may, must, 67 9;—A.S. *môt*.

mountenaunce, *sb.*, amount, duration, 218 1; 444 10; 463 22;—A.F. *mountance*.

mowe, *v.*, to be able; *inf.*, 122 26;—? A.S. **mugan* (*compare* Sievers' Gram.).

mowth, *sb.*, mouth, face, 848 10;—A.S. *mûð*.

moyane, *sb.*, means; by the moyane, by means of, 6 4; 21 19; **moyan**, 10 23; **moyne**, 16 11; **meane**, 11 30; **menes**, 394 35; **meanys**, *pl.*, 840 14;—A.F. *mene*, O.F. *meiain*, F. *moyen*.

muffle, *v.*, to wrap up as with a muff, to blindfold; **muffeld**, *p.p.*, 311 17;—O.F. *mofle*, *moufle*.

multyplyer, *sb.*, one who multiplies or increases, 652 25.

murdre, *v.*, to murder; *inf.*, 152 15.

murtherer, *sb.*, murderer, 251 10; 428 32.—*Compare* A.S. *morðor*.

muse, *v.*, to ponder, wonder; **musyd**, *pt.*, 457 1;—O.F. *muser*.

musyke, *sb.*, music, 276 31; 422 19;—Lat. *musica*.

myddel, *adj.* and *sb.*, middle, waist, 72 1;—A.S. *middel*.

myghty, *adj.*, mighty, 621 1; **myghtyest**, *superl.*, 438 34;—A.S. *mihtig*, *meahtig*.

mykel, *adj.* and *adv.*, great, much, 37 3; 371 22; 434 2;—A.S. *micel*.

myle, *sb.*, mile, 430 25;—O.F. *mile*.

myn, *pron. poss.*, my, 686 34;—A.S. *min*.

myneuer, *sb.*, meniver, white fur with black specks, ermine, 593 24;—O.F. *menu ver*, *menu vair*.

mynster, *sb.*, minster, monastery, 613 29; 620 1;—A.S. *mynster*.

myre, *sb.*, mire, dirt, 112 11; 140 26.—*Compare* Icel. *myri*.

myrthe, *sb.*, *sing.*, mirth, joy, 37 37; **myrthes**, *pl.*, 500 1; 562 21;—A.S. *myrgð*, *myrð*.

mysauenture, *sb.*, misfortune, accident, 134 2;—O.F. *mesauenture*.

mysbyleuers, *sb. pl.*, infidels, 631 12; **mysbeleuyng men**, 178 38; **myscreantes**, 860 38.

myscomforte, *v.*, lose courage, despair; *imperat.*, 460 30.

mys creature, *sb.*, cripple, monster, disfigured creature, 692 8.

mysdede, *sb.*, bad deed, fault, crime, 683 32;—A.S. *misdæd*.

mysdoo, *v.*, to do amiss; *inf.*, 181 7; **mysdoo**, *p.p.*, 686 22.

mysease, *sb.*, uneasiness, 367 27.

mysere, *sb.*, misery, 84 34;—Lat. *miseria*.

myshap, *sb.*, misfortune, accident, 134 2; 472 24.

myssay, *v.*, abuse, rebuke, slander; *inf.*, 342 9; **myssaid**, *pt.*, 341 23; **myssayenge**, *verbal noun*, 229 33; **myssayed**, *pt.*, 229 34.

mysse, *v.*, to lack, miss; *inf.*, 78 38; **myst**, 405 1; **mys**, 731 18;—A.S. *missan*, *myssian*.

myster, *sb.*, need, want; *also* business, art, occupation, trade, 57 18; 59 5; 224 35;—O.F. *mestier*, *mester*.

naturel, *adj.*, natural, 406 3; 649 2; —O.F. *naturel*.

nauel, *sb.*, navel, 199 9; 645 1; **nauyl**, 167 19;—A.S. *nafela*.

ne, *adv.* and *conj.*, not, nor, 109 16; —A.S. *ne*.

nece, *sb.*, niece, 717 36;—A.F. *nece*, *niece*.

neclygence, *sb.*, negligence, 771 12; —O.F. *negligence*.

nemly, *adv.*, nimbly, actively, quickly, 596 17;—A.S. *numol*. *See* **nymel**.

nerre, *adj.* and *adv.*; *comp.*, nearer, 838 14;—A.S. *néarra*.

nether, *adj. comp.*, lower; *adv.*, below, 294 12;—A.S. *neoðera*, *neoðra*.

newe fangle, *adj.*, new fangled, marked by the affectation of novelty, desiring new things, 841 5.—*See* Skeat, Dict.

next, *adj.*, = nearest, 760 35.

neyder, *neg. pron.* and *conj.* *See* **nother**.

neye, neyhe, *v.*, to neigh (horse); **neye**, *inf.*, 186 1; **neyhed**, *pt.*, 415 20;—A.S. *hnǽgan*.

neysshe, *adj.*, tender, soft, 641 8;— A.S. *hnesce*.

noblesse, *sb.*, nobility, worthy behaviour, 99 4; 387 29; **nobylnesse**, 585 12;—A.F. *noblesse*.

nobley, *sb.*, splendour, dignity, nobility, assembly of nobles, 316 9; 422 32;—A.F. *noblei*.

nobyl, *adj.*, noble, of noble birth, 849 1;—A.F. *noble*.

nold, *pt.*, s., would not, 705 31. *See* **nylle**.

nombre, nomber, *sb.*, number, 1 26; 601 23; 633 11;—O.F. *nombre*.

nonnerye, *sb.*, nunnery, 854 2;— O.F. *nonnerie*.

noselynge, *adv.*, on the nose, headlong, 695 21;—A.S. *nosu* and *gelang*.

not for thenne, *adv.*, nevertheless, notwithstanding, 680 7.

nother, *neg. pron.* and *adv.*, neither, 214 14; **nouther**, 775 21; **neyder**, 818 18; **neyther**;—A.S. *náhwǽðer*.

notoyrly, *adv.*, notoriously, 1 11;— Late Lat. *notorius*.

not withstandynge, *adv.*, notwithstanding, 453 1.

nourisshe, *v.*, to feed, nourish; *inf.*, 37 2; *prs.*, 38 35; **nourisshynge**, *p.prs.*, 38 27, 34; **nourysshed**, *p.p.*, 39 10;—O.F. *noriss-*, *p.prs.* of *norir*.

now and now, *adv.*, now and then, 211 33.

noughte, *neg. pron.* and *adv.*, nothing, not, 684 14; 831 16;—A.S. *náwiht*.

noyous, *adj.*, hurtful, annoying, 701 2.

noyre le, the black, surname of syr Breunor, probably wearing black armour.

nouryture, *sb.*, food, nourishment, 6 6; **nurture**, 276 24;—O.F. *nouriture*.

nygromancye, *sb.*, magic, sorcery, necromancy, 38 5;—O.F. *nigromance*.

nylle, *first* and *third pers. sing.*, will not, 45 27; **nyl**, 81 32; 297 32; **nylt**, 641 17;—A.S. *nyllan*.

nymel, *adj.*, quick, nimble, active, 312 27;—A.S. *numol.*—*Compare* **nemly**.

nys, *third pers. sing.*, is not, 39 28; 804 9; *etc.*

nyst, *third pers. sing.* and *pl.*, knew not, 190 22; 677 3; 729 12; 784 13; 821 10;—A.S. *nytan*.

obeyssaunce, *sb.*, obedience, 45 25; —A.F. *obeisaunce*.

ofte, *adv.*, often; **oftsydes**, oftentimes, 173 32; **ofte**, 686 16, seems to be misprinted for **efte**, = again; —A.S. *oft*.

oke, *sb.*, oak, 203 28 ;—A.S. *āc, āc.*

oldenes, *sb.*, age, old age, 715* 33 ;—A.S. *ealdnysse.*

olyfante, *sb.*, elephant; olyfantes, 236 15 ;—O.F. *olifant.*

on, *prep.*, on, at, in, among; on lowde, 564 35 ; on lyue, 100 20; on slepe, 380 12 ; on hyghe, 149 27 ; on parte (separately), 56 27 ;—A.S. *an, on.*

onles, onlesse, *adv.*, unless, 47 22 ; 446 6.—*See* Skeat, Dict.

ony, *pron. neg.*, any, 292 18 ; 415 28 ; —A.S. *ǣnig.*

oost, *sb.*, host, inn-keeper, 200 6 ;— O.F. *oste, hoste.*

or, *prep.; conj., adv.*, before, ere, 237 19 ;—? A.S. *ǣr.*

ordenaunce, *sb.*, order, command, array, provision, 51 24 ;—A.F. *ordinance.*

ore, *sb.*, oar, 708 4 ;—A.S. *ár.*

orgule, *sb.*, pride, 858* 1 ;—O.F. *orguel (compare* A.S. *orgel).*

orgulous, *adj.*, proud, 827 19 ; moost orgulist, *superl.*, 840 6 ;—O.F. *orgueilleus.*

orgulyte, *sb.*, pride, 413 9 ; 523 33.

ornemente, *sb.*, ornament; ornementys, *pl.*, 711 16 ;—O.F. *ornement.*

orphelyn, *sb.*, orphan; surname of Alysaunder ;—O.F. *orpheline.*

oryent, *sb.*, the East, 654 32 ;—A.F. *orient.*

oryson, *sb.*, prayer, orison, 645 6 ;— A.F. *oreison.*

oth, *sb.*, oath, 52 1 ;—A.S. *áð.*

otys, *sb. pl.*, oats, 111 7 ;—A.S. *áte.*

ouche, *sb.*, clasp, socket of a precious stone ; ouches, *pl.*, 822 2 (M.E. generally *nouche*);—O.F. *nouche, nosche, nusche.*

ought, *sb.*, aught, anything ;—A.S. *á-wiht.*

oultraguously, *adv.*, excessively, 444 32.

oute excepte, excepted, 102 11.

outerage, *sb.*, outrage, insult, 472 24 ;—O.F. *oltrage, outrage.*

oute taken, *p.p.*, excepted, 540 26. *Compare* oute cepte, 589 23.

outher, *conj.*, either, 140 4; 470 21; 726 13; 772 13; outher

els = otherwise, 812 26 ;—A.S. *á-hwæðer.*

outragyousyte, *sb.*, outrage, 118 4.

ouer, *prep.* and *adv.*, over, above, beyond ;—A.S. *ofer.*

ouer gouerne, *v.*, to govern over; ouer gouernyd, *p.p.*, 43 2.

ouer hylle, *v.*, to cover ; ouer hylled, *pt.*, 444 16.

ouer hyp, *v.*, pass over, omit; *inf.*, 796 3.

ouer moche, too much, 414 21 ; ouermoche, 193 36.

ouersee, *v.*, observe, survey, despise, overlook; *inf.*, 346 5;—A.S. *oferseón.*

ouerslyp, *v.*, pass over, omit; *inf.*, 295 26.

ouerthwart, *sb.*, adverse circumstance, 239 14.

ouerthwarte, *adj.*, across, over, against, 359 25 ; ouerthwart, 524 25 ; ouerthwartly, *adv.*, 338 25.

owe, *v.*, to have, possess, to have to be obliged to; oughte, *pt.*, 1 10; 44 9; ouзt, *pt.*, 1 37; 188 3 ; me oughte to doo, 418 17 ; 557 12 ;— A.S. *ágan.*

owre, *sb.*, hour; owrys, *pl.*, 190 3 ; houre, 266 24; 463 22;—Lat. *hora.*

oynement, *sb.*, ointment, 255 14; oyntement, 248 31 ; oynementes, *pl.*, 836 15 ;—A.F. *oignement.*

paale, *adj.*, pale, discoloured, 468 25.

paas, *sb.*, pace, step, passage, 81 25 ; a softe trottyng paas, 564 38 ; a grete paas, 563 32 ; more than a paas, 89 37 ; paas peryllous ;— A.F. *pas.*

pacyently, *adv.*, patiently, 13 7.

pagent, *sb.*, a pageant, scene, theatre ; *sing.*, 544 24 ; pagents, *pl.*, 516 16 ; 553 26.

paleys, *sb.*, palace, 722 3 ; palais, 722 31 ; palays, 615 29 ;—O.F. *palais.*

palfray, *sb.*, saddle-horse, palfrey, 303 28 ; palfrey, 104 30; palfroy, 82 18 ;—A.F. *palefrei.*

palour, *sb.*, parlour, conversation-room in a nunnery, 452 21;—O.F. *parloir.*

paltocke, *sb.*, jacket, paletot, a loose garment ; paltockes, *pl.*, 177 27 ;— O.F. *paletocque.*

pappe, *sb.*, breast, 39 11; **pappys**, *pl.*, 148 33;—from the first cries of an infant for food.

par, per, *prep.*, by, with; **par dy,** 401 30; **per dieu,** 492 15; **per de,** 242 19 (par Dieu); **paramour, peramour,** lover, applied to either sex, 92 4; 133 4; 407 30; **peramours,** *adv.*, 679 4; **peraduenture, perauenture, paraventure,** by chance, 81 32; 229 25; 540 34; 808 33.

parage, *sb.*, family, kindred, descent, birth, 220 5;—A.F. *parage.*

parel, *sb.*, word, word of honour, 119 29;—O.F. *parole.*

pareylle, *adj.*, like, similar, 161 25; —O.F. *pareil.*

parfyt, *adj.*, perfect, 592 20; 695 34; **parfytely,** *adv.*, 649 18;—O.F. *parfeit, parfit.*

parlement, *sb.*, parliament, conference, 829 29; **parlemente,** 839 5; —A.F. *parlement.*

parson, person, *sb.*, person, personage, 67 27; 541 35;—Lat. *persona.*

party, *sb.*, part, portion, side, 147 46; **partyes,** *pl.*, 291 26;—A.F. *partie.*

passage, *sb.*, passage, way, narrow path, 53 20; **passaye,** 53 20;— O.F. *passage.*

passe, *v. inf.*, 830 27; to pass, surpass; **paste,** *pt.*, 762 37; **past,** *pt.*, 781 2; **passed,** *pt.*, 830 32;—A.F. *passer.*

passyng, *p.prs.* of to pass, used as *adv.*, surpassing, very, 38 29; sometimes it has the adverbial termination **passyngly,** 53 25; 763 8.

pauyment, *sb.*, pavement, 190 6;— Lat. *pavimentum.*

payement, *sb.*, payment, reward, 197 23;—O.F. *paiement.*

paylet, *sb.*, pallet, paillasse, a small bed, 89 23; 110 27.

payne, *sb.*, pain, penalty; **do his payne,** do his utmost, 820 16;— A.F. *paine.*

paynture, *sb.*, picture, 190 25;— A.F. *painture.*

paynym, *sb., originally* heathendom, paganism, *but incorrectly used in the sense of* a pagan, heathen, 400 27; **paynyms,** *pl.*, 1 13;—A.F. *paienisme.*

paytrelle, *sb.*, breast-plate of a horse in armour; **paytrellys,** *pl.*, 238 2; —A.F. *peitrel.*

pees, *sb.*, peace, silence, 37 25; 386 2; 581 18;—A.F. *pees,* O.F. *pais.*

pelour, *sb.*, pillar, column, 93 27;— A.F. *piler.*

penaunce, *sb.*, punishment, sufferance, penance, repentance, the punishment inflicted by a penitent on himself, 211 18;—O.F. *penance.*

pensel, *sb.*, pennon, little banner, 488 13; **pensell,** 489 19;—O.F. *penoncel.*

perce, *v.*, to pierce; **perced,** *pt.*, 675 15;—A.F. *percer.*

percloos, *sb.*, partition, enclosure; 644 33;—O.F. *parclos (p.p.).*

perdycyon, *sb.*, perdition, destruction, 648 24;—O.F. *perdition.*

pere, *sb.*, pear, 663 33;—A.S. *pera.*

pere, *adj.*, equal, 165 34; 177 20; **pyere,** 664 7;—A.F. *per.*

perfeccyon, perfectyon, *sb.*, perfection, 855* 5;—O.F. *perfection.*

peron, peroun, *sb.*, tombstone, platform, 414 28; 421 14; 568 16;— O.F. *peron.*

perpetuel, *adj.*, perpetual, 160 24;— O.F. *perpetuel.*

persecucyon, *sb.*, persecution; **persecucyons,** *pl.*, 645 14;—from Lat. *persecutus (persequi).*

perteyne, *v.*, to belong, appertain; **perteyneth,** *prs.*, 679 16;—Lat. *pertinere.*

perylle, *sb.*, peril, danger, 415 30; 548 36;—O.F. *peril.*

perysshe, *v.*, to perish; **perysshed,** *p.p.*, 703 10;—O.F. *periss-, p.prs.* of *perir.*

petycyon, *sb.*, petition, 214 5;—Lat. *petitionem.*

petyte, le, surname of syr Guyart; the short, or the small.

philosopher, *sb.*, a wise man, philosopher, 165 25;—Gr. φιλόσοφος.

pierles, *adj.*, without equal, 761 35; 500 2; **pyerles,** 322 15; 435 33; —A.F. *per* and A.S. *lǽs.*

plenour, *adj.*, plenary, full, complete, 213 1 (Wynkyn de Worde reads *plenare*) ;—Low Lat. *plenarius.*

plente, *sb.*, plenty, 586 24 ;—O.F. *plente, plentet.*

plesaunce, *sb.*, kindness, pleasure, 329 27 ;—O.F. *plaisance.*

plesaunt, playsaunt, *adj.*, agreeable, pleasant, 3 29, 35 ;—O.F. *plaisant.*

pleasyr, *sb.*, pleasure, 248 24 ; **plesyr,** 268 32 ;—A.F. *pleisir.*

plompe, *sb.*, knot, tuft, cluster, number joined in a mass, 60 19 ;—?

plonge, *v.*, to plunge ; **plonged,** *pt.*, 243 30 ;—O.F. *plonger.*

plyte, *sb.*, state, condition, 152 5 ;— O.F. *plite.*

plyte, *v.*, to pledge, *inf.*, 148 31 ; **plyghte,** *pt.*, 149 21 ;—A.S. *plihtan.*

pomel, *sb.*, knob, a boss, 99 5 ; **pomell,** 82 22 ;—O.F. *pomel.*

ponting, *p.prs.*, panting, gasping, breathing quickly, 238 20.

portecolys, *sb.*, portcullis, a sliding door of cross timbers pointed with iron hung over a gateway to be let down in a moment to keep out an enemy, 91 9 ;—O.F. *porte coleïce* (Littré).

postel, *sb.*, apostle ; **postels,** *pl.*, 720 10 ;—A.S. *apostol,* A.F. *apostle.*

posterne, *sb.*, postern, back gate, 289 13 ;—O.F. *posterne.*

potestate, *sb.*, ruler, governor, 174 30.

pounte, *sb.*, bridge, 571 20 ;—O.F. *ponte.*

poure, *adj.*, poor, 7 13 ; 8 23 ; 471 30 ;—O.F. *povre.*

pouse, *sb.*, pulse, 712 5 ;—O.F. *pouls, polz.*

pouerte, *sb.*, poverty, meanness, 84 34 ; 746 10 ;—O.F *poverte.*

powdre, *sb.*, powder, 165 22 ;—O.F. *poudre.*

poyntelynge, *p.prs.*, aiming at somebody, 578 2.

poyntement, poyntemente, *sb.*, appointment, agreement, 463 11 ; 845 29 ;—O.F. *apointement.*

poysond, *p.p.*, poisoned, 729 1 ;—from O.F. *poyson,* Lat. *potionem.*

pray, *sb.*, prey, 650 7 ; **praye,** 176 14 ; —O.F. *proie,* A.F. *praie.*

praye (?), *sb.*, prayer ; **prayes,** *pl.*, 859* 22 ;—A.F. *preiere.*

praye, *v.*, to pray ; **praide,** *pt.*, 240 2 ; **praid,** *pt.*, 401 16 ; 767 33 ;— A.F. *preier.*

preche, *v.*, to preach ; *inf.*, 645 13 ; —O.F. *precher.*

prees, *sb.*, a press, throng, 60 37 ; 77 22 ;—A.F. *presse.*

prefyxt, *p.p.*, prefixed, 839 11.

preste, *sb.*, priest ; **preest,** 634 10 ; —A.S. *préost.*

pretende, *v.*, belong to ; **pretendith,** *prs.*, 64 30.

preue, *v.*, to prove, try, test, 66 15 ; 214 34 ; **preued,** *p.p.*, 353 5 ; —O.F. *prover.*

preuy, *adj.*, privy, secret, 53 17 ; **pryuyest,** *superl.*, 51 15 ;—A.F. *prive.*

preyse, *v.*, to praise ; **preysed,** *pt.*, 19 11 ;—from O.F. *preis.*

procurour, *sb.*, procurator, a governor of a province under the Roman emperors, 160 9 ; 162 10.

profecye, *v.*, to prophesy ; **profecyed,** *pt.*, 419 30 ;—O.F. *profecier.*

profer, *sb.*, offer, promise, proffer, 215 14.

proferre, *v.*, to proffer, offer ; *inf.*, 210 37 ; **profryst,** *prs.*, 176 13 ; **proferre,** *inf.*, 134 31, means, evidently, advance, prefer ; **proferd,** *p.p.*, 147 33 ; **profered,** *pt.*, 759 15 ;—Lat. *proferre.*

profetyly, *adj.*, accomplished ; **profetylyest,** *superl.*, 733 22 ;—compound of the substantive *profit* and adverbial suffix *-ly.*

prowesse, *sb.*, prowess ; **prowesses,** *pl.*, 173 14 ;—A.F. *pruesse.*

pryce, *sb.*, price, value, excellence, 555 25 ;—A.F. *pris.*

prycke, *v.*, to prick, hurt, spur, ride fast ; **prycked,** *pt.*, 661 9 ; **pryckynge,** *p.prs.*, 647 10.

pryker, *sb.*, rider, horseman, 178 5.

prysonement, *sb.*, imprisonment, prison, 83 3.

prysonne, *v.*, to put into prison ; *inf.*, 802 27 ;—from O.F. *prison, prisun.*

pryuete, *sb.*, privity, secret counsel, 456 19 ;—A.F. *privete.*

purfyl, *v.*, to embroider on an edge, 7 8 ;—O.F. *pourfiler*.

pursyewe, *v.*, to pursue, to follow after ; **pursyewed**, *pt.*, 7 18 ;— O.F. *porsuir*.

purueye, *v.*, to provide ; *inf.*, 38 26 ; 40 36 ; **purueyed**, *pt.*, 75 17 ; **purueyed**, *p.p.*, 51 23 ; 86 24 ;— A.F. *purveier*.

puyssaunce, *sb.*, might, power, 75 8 ; 413 38 ;—O.F. *puissance*.

pyctour, *sb.*, picture, 340 10 ;—Lat. *pictura*.

pyece, *sb.*, piece ; **pyeces**, *pl.*, 71 32 ;—O.F. *piece*.

pyere, *adj.* *See* **pere**.

pyerles, *adj.* *See* **pierles**.

pyghe, *v.*, to pitch, fix, to pick ; **pyght**, *pt.*, 84 3.

pyke, *v.*, to pick, to steal ; **pyked**, *pt.*, 411 6.

pylgremage, *sb.*, pilgrimage, 166 35 ; —from O.F. *pelerinage*.

pyllar, *sb.*, plunderer ; **pyllars**, *pl.*, 847 26 ;—from O.F. *piller*.

pylle, *v.*, to plunder ; *inf.*, 847 27 ;— O.F. *piller*.

pyller, *sb.*, pillar, 589 11 ; **pelour**, 93 27 ;—A.F. *piler*.

pylowe, *sb.*, pillow ; **pylowes**, *pl.*, 781 8 ;—A.S. *pyle*.

pynt, *sb.*, pinte, 746 1 ;—A.S. *pynt*.

pyte, *sb.*, pity, 711 4 ; 754 32 ;— O.F. *pite*.

pyteous, *adj.*, pitiful, 32 ; 435 7 ; **pyetous**, 5 16 ;—O.F. *piteus*.

pytte, *sb.*, pit, pool, ditch, 98 18 ; 664 2 ;—A.S. *pytt*.

quakynge, *p.prs.*, trembling, 136 7 ; —A.S. *cwacung*.

quere, *sb.*, choir, 859* 22 ; **quyre**, 859 31 ;—O.F. *choeur*.

queste, *sb.*, (1) an inquiry, jury, verdict, 109 1 ; (2) chase, search, enterprise, 109 11 ;—O.F. *enqueste*.

queste, *v.*, to bark, make a noise like a dog ; **quested**, *pt.*, 371 5 ; **questynge**, *p.prs.*, 65 29.

questyon, *v.*, to question, examine,

ask ; **questyoned**, *pt.*, 254 24 ; 418 12 ;—Lat. *quaestionem*, *quaerere*.

quod, **quoth**, *pt. sing.*, said, told, 60 10 ; 61 34 ;—A.S. *cweðan*.

quyete, *sb.*, quietness, 829 2 ;—from Lat. *quietus*.

quylt, *sb.*, quilt, thick coverlet, 95 17 ;—O.F. *cuilte*.

quyte, *adj.*, quit, 455 13 ; 465 7 ;— from O.F. *quiter*.

quyte, *v.*, to requite, repay, settle ; *inf.*, 92 1 ; *pt.*, 159 27 ;—O.F. *quiter*.

race, *v.*, to scrape, to tear off ; **raced**, *pt.*, 72 1 ; **reaced**, *pt.*, 72 4 ; **rassyd**, *pt.*, 524 29 ;—O.F. *raser*.

race, **rase**, *v.*, to run, to race ; **rasynge**, *p.prs.*, 217 33 ; 194 11 ; **rateynge**, ? *p.prs.*, 432 24 ;—A.S. *ræsan*.

rak, *sb.*, rack, the grating above the manger, 668 28 ; 669 1 ; ? **rake**, 665 22 ;—from A.S. *ræcan*.

ramme, *sb.*, ram ; **rammes**, *pl.*, 71 29 ;—A.S. *ram*, *rom*.

rancour, *sb.*, old grudge, spite, violence, 313 24 ;—Lat. *rancor*.

ransake, *v.*, to search ; *inf.*, 171 2 ; 174 11 ; **ransakyd**, *pt.*, 630 34 ;— A.S. *ræsn*. *See* Sievers' Gram.

raumpe, *v.*, ramp, to seize or scratch with the paws, to rage ; **raump-ynge**, *p.prs.*, 339 31 ;—A.F. *raumper*.

raundon, *sb.*, force, violence, impetuosity, 109 37 ; 142 10 ; 675 15 ; —O.F. *randon*.

raunge, *sb.*, range, space occupied by anything moving, 142 2 ; 481 10 ; 492 23 ; 573 34 ;—O.F. *range*.

raunson, *sb.*, ransom, 178 14 ;—A.F. *raunson*.

rauysshe, *v.*, to seize with violence, to be greatly delighted ; **rauysshed**, *p.p.*, 527 4 ;—A.F. *ravir*.

rayment, *sb.*, raiment, clothing, dress, 331 25.

raynes, *sb.*, fine linen, so called from Rheims, 857* 26.

rechate,[1] *sb.*, the calling back of the

---

[1] In the alliterative romance-poem, "Sir Gawayne and the Green Knight" (about 1360 A.D.), edited by Richard Morris for the E.-E. T. S., 1869, from MS. Cotton: Nero. A. x., forms of a verb "recheat" occur—viz., "rechatand" = blowing the recheat, line 1911 ;

hounds, originally the air which the hunters blow on their horns, when the hounds have lost their game to call them back from pursuing a counter-scent; *v.*, to blow the recheat, 500 11 (hunting term). Wynkyn de Worde and ed. 1634 have *rechace*.

reche, *v.*, to reach, attain; **raught**, 385 33; **raughte**, *pt.*, 265 16; **roughte**, *pt.*, 684 22; **retche**, *inf.*, 597 21;—A.S. *ræcan.*

recke, *v.*, to care for, to regard; *prs.*, 221 1; **reke**, *prs.*, 684 14; **retchyd**, *pt.*, 319 17;—A.S. *reccan.*

recluse, **reecluse**, *sb.*, a female anchorite, 642 10, 15;—A.F. *recluse.*

recountre, *sb.*, encounter, fight, meeting, 213 20;—O.F. *rencountre.*

recreaunt, *adj.*, recreant, defeated, 71 37;—A.F. *recreaunt.*

recueylle, *v.*, to recoil; *inf.*, 180 3; —O.F. *reculer.*

rede, *sb.*, advice, 847 32;—A.S. *rǽd.*

rede, *v.*, to give advice, to take counsel, to advise; *prs.*, 70 33; 244 5; 783 4;—A.S. (*ge*)-*rǽdan.*

rede, *v.*, to read; *inf.*, 3 26; 4 9; **redde**, *pt.*, 3 9; 4 8; **redde**, *p.p.*, 762 1;—A.S. (*ge*)-*rǽdan.*

redoubte, *v.*, to fear; **redoubted**, 823 12;—A.F. *redouter.*

redresse, *v.*, restore, repair, to make up again; *inf.*, 398 28; 443 21; —O.F. *redresser.*

redy, *adj.*, ready, 35 31;—A.S. (*ge*)-*rǽde.*

reed, *adj.*, red, 514 1;—A.S. *réad.*

reest, *sb.* *See* **reyste.**

rehersail, *sb.*, rehearsal, 322 25; **rehersal**, 611 34.

reherse, *v.*, to rehearse, enumerate; *inf.*, 45 27; 562 32; **reherceth**, *prs.*, 105 11; it **rehercyth**, *prs.*, 75 27;—A.F. *rehercer.*

reioyse, *v.*, to rejoice; *prs.*, 797 3;—O.F. *resjoir.*

rele, *v.*, to reel, roll about, stagger;

relyd, *pt.*, 238 13;—from A.S. *reol, hreol.*

relece, *v.*, to release; *prs.*, 481 29; **releece**, *prs.*, 461 28;—A.F. *relesser.*

remenaunte, *sb.*, remnant, 9 20; 39 24;—A.F. *remenant.*

remeue, *v.*, to remove; *inf.*, 104 20; —O.F. *remuër.*

remyssyon, *sb.*, remission, forgiveness, 856* 28.

renne, *v.*, to run; **ranne**, *pt.*, 321 25; **ronne**, *pt.*, 368 34; **ronne**, *p.p.*, 407 33; 526 4;—A.S. *rinnan.*

renoume, *sb.*, renown, 57 37; **renommee**, 3 34; **renomme**, 4 2; **renome**, 187 27;—O.F. *renon, renom.*

renoumes, le, the renowned, the famous, surname of Hebes.

repayre, *v.*, to go to; **repayren**, *prs. pl.*, 643 22;—A.F. *repeirer, repairer.*

repreef, *sb.*, reproof, 324 33; 332 8.

repreue, *v.*, to reprove; **repreuyd**, *pt.*, 7 23;—O.F. *reprover.*

resemblaunt, *sb.*, countenance, appearance, 649 6;—from O.F. *resembler.* *See* **semblant.**

resonable, *adj.*, reasonable, 548 14; —A.F. *resonable.*

resorte, *v.*, to go frequently to a place; **resorted**, *pt.*, 725 24; **resortes**, *sb. pl.*, place much frequented, resource, 725 23;—O.F. *ressortir.*

reste, *sb.*, rest, repose, 461 15; 764 2;—A.S. *rest, ræst.*

retraye, *v.*, to retire, to draw back; **retrayed**, *pt.*, 230 29;—O.F. *retraire.*

restraynte, *sb.*, restraint, limitation, 567 6;—O.F. *restraint.*

reuful, *adj.*, piteous, compassionate; **reufullyr**, *comparat.*, 425 16;—A.S *hréow* and *ful.*

reule, *sb.*, rule, behaviour, 387 31;—A.F. *reule.*

"recheated "= blew the recheat, line 1466. The form "rechace," which Wynkyn de Worde has, occurs in "Three English Metrical Romances" edited by John Robson, 1842, for the Camden Society. There, on page 3, in the tenth stanza, we read, "The king blue a rechase."

reule, *v.*, to rule, to govern; **reulyd**,
p.p., 187 24;—A.F. *reuler*.

reuelacyon, *sb.*, revelation, 202 4;
—O.F. *revelacion*.

rewe, *sb.*, row; **by rewe**, 77 6;—
A.S. *ráwe, réwe*.

reygne, *sb.*, rule, kingdom, 861* 8;
—A.F. *regne*.

reygne, *v.*, to reign; **reygned**, *pt.*,
34 28; **reygneth**, *prs.*, 4 5; 83
14; **regne**, *inf.*, 133 8; **regned**,
pt., 35 2;—A.F. *regner*.

reyse, *v.*, to raise; **reysed**, *pt.*, 77
20;—Icel. *reisa*.

reyste, *sb.*, a support for the spear,
564 34; **reystys**, *pl.*, 237 6;
restys, *pl.*, 194 1; **reest**, 430 37;
—? O.F. *rester* or A.S. *rest, ræst*.

rodde, *sb.*, rod, staff, 162 33; **roddes**,
pl., 366 20;—A.S. *ród*.

rok, *sb.*, rock, 330 2; **roche**, 410 25;
—O.F. *roche*.

rome, *sb.*, space, room, 213 30;—A.S.
rúm.

rome, *v.*, to roam, ramble, wander
about; **romed**, *pt.*, 165 13; 289
23.—*Compare* O.H.G. *rámen. See*
Skeat, Dict.

roofe, *sb.*, roof, 93 32;—A.S. *hróf*.

rore, *v.*, to roar; **rorynge**, *p.prs.*,
396 8; **roryd**, *pt.*, 648 15;—A.S.
rárian.

rote, *sb.*, root, 798 4;—Icel. *rót.*
Compare A.S. *wrót*.

rote, *v.*, to rot; *inf.*, 698 13;—A.S.
rotian.

roted, *p.p.*, practised, skilled, expe-
rienced, 472 9;—O.F. *route, rote*.

roten, *adj.*, rotten, 641 20;—Icel.
rotinn.

rownsepyk, rounsepyk, *sb.*, a branch
with others attached to it, 209 18,
23.

roy, *sb.*, king, le fyse roy Vreyne,
epithet of Vwayne.

royal, *adj.*, royal, 401 4; 499 7;
moost royallest, *superl.*, 215 29.
See **ryal**.

royalte, *sb.*, royalty, royal state,
101 9; **ryalte**, 182 13;—O.F. *royalte*.

royame, *sb.*, kingdom, 1 5; 11 2; 72
29; **royalme**, 4 11; **royamme**,
160 15; **reaume**, 45 8; **reame**,

39 34; 40 3, 7; **realme**, 67 5;—
A.F. *realme*, O.F. *reaume*.

rubrysshe, *sb.*, *literally*, red ochre,
red earth for colouring; *later*, the
portions of books in red ink, index,
register, 6 1;—Lat. *rubrica*.

russet, *adj.*, russet, rusty, reddish-
brown, coarse, rustic, 62 17;—A.F.
russet, O.F. *rousset*.

russhe, *v.*, to rush; **russhed**, *pt.*, 60
35; 132 13; **rosshynge**, *p.prs.*, 195
8; **rasshed**, *pt.*, 217 32; 472 3.

ryal, *adj.*, royal, 2 38; 160 2; **ryal-
lest**, *superl.*, 163 5;—A.F. *roial,
reial*.

ryalte, *sb. See* **royalte**.

ryde, *v.*, to ride; **rode**, *pt.*, 106 19;
757 25; **roode**, *pt.*, 105 15; **ryde**,
p.p., 82 16; **ryden**, *p.p.*, 116 15;
151 7;—A.S. *rídan*.

rynde, *sb.*, rind, bark, the skin of
fruit, 671 22;—A.S. *rind*.

ryse, *v.*, to rise; **rasyth**, *prs.*, 202
37; **rysen**, *p.p.*, 49 28;—A.S.
rísan.

ryuage, *sb.*, bank of a river, 721 2;
—O.F. *rivage*.

ryue, *v.*, to rive, to tear; **roofe**, *pt.*,
95 35; **roof**, *pt.*, 27 21; **rafe**, *pt.*,
596 18; **rofe**, *pt.*, 82 28; 654 23;
ryuen, *p.p.*, 75 18;—Icel. *rífa*.

sabel, *sb.*, sable, animal of the weasel
kind, 601 7; (?) **sable**, 176 9;—
O.F. *sable*.

sadel, *sb.*, saddle, 403 18; **sadell**,
471 35;—A.S. *sadol*.

sak, *sb.*, sack, sackcloth, 437 19;—
A.S. *sacc*.

sale, *sb.*, hall, 713 29;—A.S. *sæl*, Icel.
salr, A.S. *sæl*.

salewe, *v.*, to salute; **salewed**, *pt.*,
215 35;—O.F. *saluer*.

samyte, *sb.*, a rich silk stuff, often
interwoven with gold or silver
threads, 73 1; 687 30; 760 30;—
O.F. *samit*.

sarpe, *sb.*, girdle; **sarpys**, *pl.*, 822
30.—*Compare* O.H.G. *scharpe*, O.F.
escharpe.

saterday, *sb.*, Saturday, 665 13;—
A.S. *Sæter-dæg*.

sauf, *adj.*, safe, healed, made whole,
316 31; 584 21; **sauf gard**, *sb.*,

561 28; safe-keeping ;—A.F. *sauf*, O.F. *salf*.

saufte, *sb.*, safety, security, 290 33; 623 13 ;—A.F. *saufte*.

saulter, *sb.*, psalter, musical instrument; **saulters**, *pl.*, 859* 1 ;—O.F. *sautier*.

saunce, *prep.*, without; **saunce pyte**, surname of Breuse, without pity; **saunce velany**, without villany.

saueage, *adj.*, savage, wild, impetuous; Lynet is called the **damoysel saueage**, and Balyn is surnamed **le saueage**.

saueour, *sb.*, the Saviour, 592 3; 706 21 ;—O.F. *saveor, salveor*.

sauour, *sb.*, smell, savour, pleasantness, 592 17 ;—O.F. *saveur*.

sawe, *sb.*, a saw, saying, 519 8; old **sayd sawe**, 754 6 ;—A.S. *sagu*.

saye, *v.*, to say; **sayne**, *third pers. plur. pres.*, 187 30; **saist**, *prs.*, 67 28; **seith**, *prs.*, 138 25; **sayd**, **seid**, said, *pt.*, 41 37; **saiden**, **sayden**, *third pers. plur. pt.*, 40 25; 140 29; 202 10; 422 12 ;—A.S. *secgan*.

scalde, *v.*, to boil, to burn with hot liquid; **scaldynge**, *p.prs.*, 571 28 ;—O.F. *eschalder*.

scape, *v.* *See* **escape**.

scatere, *v.*, to scatter, disperse; **scateryd**, *pt.*, 206 21 ;—A.S. *scateran*.

scathe, *sb.*, hurt, harm; **scathes**, *pl.*, 464 13 ;—A.S. *sceaða*.

scathe, *v.*, to harm; *inf.*, 90 3 ;—A.S. *sceaðan*.

scaubart, *sb.*, scabbard, 73 17; **scauberd**, 89 7; **scaubard**, 135 26 ;—M.E. *scaubert*. *See* Skeat, Dict.

schaffoldes, *sb. pl.*, 834 21. *See* **skaffolde**.

scoffer, *sb.*, mocker, 488 28 ;—cognate with O.Fries. *schof*, a scoff.

scole, *sb.*, school, 38 4 ;—Lat. *schola*.

scomfyte, *v.* *See* **discomfyte**.

scoute, *sb.*, spy, scout; **scoute watche**, 53 5 ;—O.F. *escoute*.

scrypture, *sb.*, Holy Scripture, 721 22 ;—Lat. *scriptura*.

sease, seace, *v.*, to cease, discontinue;

sease, *inf.*, 836 38; **seaced**, *pt.*, 475 10; **seasse, seace**, *imperat.*, 155 3; 179 4 ;—O.F. *cesser*.

seate, *sb.*, seat, 424 4 ;—A.S. *seto, seotu*.

seculer, *adj.*, secular, 724 4 ;—Lat. *secularis*.

sedyl, *sb.* *See* **cedle**.

see, *v.*, to see; *inf.*, 3 26; **seeth**, *prs.*, 60 7; **sawe**, *pt.*, 761 17; **sene**, *p.p.*, 206 13; **seen**, *p.p.*, 3 9; **sawest**, *second p.pt.*, 113 31 ;—A.S. *séon*.

seekne, *v.*, to become sick, to get weak; **seekened**, *pt.*, 858* 7; **sekene**, *inf.*, 34 25 ;—from A.S. *séoc*.

sege, *sb.*—(1) seat, (2) siege, 439 7; **siege**, 422 28; **seges**, *pl.*, 235 19; 532 3; **syegyng**, 237 20; **syege**, 64 14 ;—A.F. *sege*, O.F. *siege*.

seke, *adj.*, sick, 36 8, 11; 493 30 ;—A.S. *séoc*.

sekenesse, *sb.*, sickness, 406 9 ;—A.S. *séocnes*.

selar, *sb.*, ceiling, canopy of a bed, 698 24 (edit. of 1634 has *seeler*); —? deriv. from *ciel*.

semblable, *adj.*, like, 177 20 ;—O.F. *semblable*.

semblaunt, *sb.*, countenance, appearance, 224 25; 710 25 ;—A.F. *semblant*.

semely, *adj.*, seemly, 205 10 ;—A.S. **sémelic*.

senate, *sb.*, senate, assembly of the senators, 174 35; **senatours**, 175 5.

senceall, sencial, *sb.* *See* **seneshall**.

sendale, *sb.*, a fine cloth, 174 23; **sendel**, 202 5; 616 4 ;—O.F. *cendal*.

seneshall, *sb.*, seneschal, steward; **sencyall**, 86 34; **senceall**, 42 30; **sencial**, 55 13; **senescha**, 123 38; —O.F. *seneschal*.

senser, *sb* *See* **censer**.

serche, *v.*, to search; *inf.*, 64 3; 135 19; **sarche**, *inf.*, 351 7; **serched**, *pt.*, 461 17; *p.p.*, 464 15 ;—O.F. *cercher*, Mod.F. *chercher*.

serkelet, *sb.*, a wreath, or band for the head, 144 13; 147 16 ;—O.F. *cerclet*, dim. of *cercle*.

seruage, *sb.*, thraldom, servitude, 372 31; 408 31 ;—O.F. *servage*.

serue, *v.*, to serve; **seruedest**, *prs.*, 671 20;—O.F. *servir*.

seruyse, *sb.*, service, 251 3;—O.F. *servise*.

seruytour, *sb.*, servant, 457 25;— Lat. *servitor*.

seson, *sb.*, season, 858* 33;—A.F. *seson*.

sette, *v.*, to set, place, appoint; **sette**, *pt.*, 62 34; 65 24; **sette**, *p.p.*, 3 19; —A.S. *settan*.

seurte, *sb.*, surety, 241 10; 617 31; 657 6;—A.F. *seürte*.

seueratly, *adv.*, separately, 127 12; —deriv. from *seuer*, to separate;— O.F. *sevrer*.

sewayr, *sb.*, bearer of dishes, 271 3; —A.F. (*as*)*seour*.

sewe, *v.*, to follow, attend on, persecute; *inf.*, 641 38; 647 19; **sewed**, *p.p.*, 630 23;—O.F. *suir* (*porsuir*).

seye, *v.* *See* **saye**.

seynt, *adj.*, saint, holy, 413 11;— O.F. *saint, seint*.

shaftmon, *sb.*, a measure from the top of the extended thumb to the other end of the fist or palm, about six inches, 248 8;—A.S. *sceaft-mund*.

shape, *v.*, to shape, form; **shope**, *pt.*, 138 2; **shapen**, *pl. prs.*, 698 24; **shapen**, *p.p.*, 102 31; 341 10;— A.S. *sceapan*.

shelde, *sb.*, shield, 266 26; **shild**, 98 5; **sheltes**, *pl.*, 687 11; **shylde**, 69 18; **sheld**, 69 20;—A.S. *scyld, scield*.

shelded, *adj.*, provided with a shield, 333 25.

shende, *v.*, to harm, damage; *inf.*, 831 14; **shente**, *pt.*, 235 27; **shente**, *p.p.*, 432 29;—A.S. *scendan*.

shenship, *sb.*, disgrace, hurt, 235 33;—from A.S. *scendan* and *scipe*.

sherte, *sb.*, shirt, 210 38; 452 30; 634 31;—Icel. *skyrta*.

sherthursdaye, *sb.*, the Thursday before Easter, so called from the custom of shearing or shaving the beard on that day, 719 32.

shete, *sb.*, sheet, 200 18;—A.S. *scête, scŷte*.

shethe, *sb.*, sheath, 76 26; 695 13; A.S. *scéað*.

shette, *v.*, to shut; **shitte**, *pt.*, 713 33; **shytte**, *pt.*, 414 8; **shytte**, *p.p.*, 9 15; 443 8; 710 30; **shette**, *p.p.*, 319 13;—A.S. *scyttan*.

sheue, shewe, *v.*, to show; **sheuyng**, *p.prs.*, 666 21; **shewed**, *pt.*, 46 4; 762 12; **shewed**, *p.p.*, 762 12;— A.S. *scéawian*.

sheuere, *v.*, to break into shivers; **sheuered**, 110 2;—? Icel. *skifa*.

shoke, *pt.*, shook, 321 30;—A.S. *scôc*, from *sceacan, scacan*.

sholder, sholdre, *sb.*, shoulder, 176 6; 281 33;—A.S. *soulder, souldor*.

shote, *v.*, to shoot, rush; **shotynge**, *p.prs.*, 102 23; **shote**, *pt.*, 770 13; **shot**, *pt.*, 764 29; **shotte**, *pt.*, 327 12;—A.S. *scéotan*.

shoure, *sb.*, shower, hard attack, 822 3;—A.S. *scúr*.

shoue, *v.*, to shove; **shouen**, 699 10; —A.S. *scofian*.

showte, *v.*, to shout; **showted**, 173 12;—?

shrede, *v.*, to cut; *inf.*, 831 11;— A.S. *scréadian*.

shrewde, *adj.*, wicked, malicious, 365 7.

shryche, *sb.*, a cry, shriek, 745 34.

shryche, *v.*, to shriek, screech; **shryched**, *pt.*, 850 5; **shryked**, *pt.*, 752 14;—? Icel. *skrækja*.

shryue, *v.*, to confess, prescribe penance; **shryuen**, *p.p.*, 26 28, 36; **shryued**, *pl.*, 759 37;—A.S. *scrífan*.

shyne, *v.*, to shine; **shone**, *pt.*, 403 13; 710 10;—A.S. *scínan*.

shyrly, *adv.*, clearly, brightly, 759 3; —A.S. *scírlic*.

sister, *sb.*, the sister, 189 30; **suster**, 101 37;—A.S. *swuster, sweoster*.

sith, *adv.* and *conj.* *See* **sythen**.

skaffolde, *sb.*, stage, an elevated platform, scaffold, engine of war for besieging a town; **skaffoldes**, *pl.*, 766 7; **skaffoldis**, *pl.*, 191 7; **schaffoldes**, *pl.*, 484 21; —O.F. *escafaut*.

skarmusshe, *v.*, to skirmish, to fight slightly and irregularly; **skarmusshed**, *pt.*, 181 21;—O.F. *escarmoucher*.

sklaunder, *sb.*, scandal, slander, 726 1 ; 731 2 ; 779 28 ; **sklaundre**, 321 20 ;—A.F. *esclaundre*.

skumme, *v.*, to skim, to sweep, to examine the position and strength of the enemy; *inf.*, 52 30 ;—from Icel. *skuma*.

skyfte, *sb.*, shift, change, 211 16 ; 499 31.

skyfte, *v.*, to shift, to part asunder, to change, to remove; *inf.*, 405 25 ; **skyfte**, *pt.*, 405 31 ;—A.S. *sciftan*.

skynne, *sb.*, skin, 657 24 ;—A.S. *scinn*, Icel. *skinn*.

slade, *sb.*, a valley, 188 26 ; 203 28 ; —A.S. *slæd*.

slake, *sb.*, a little valley, hollow, gap or pass between two hills, 189 6.

slake, *v.*, to become slack, cease; *inf.*, 726 4 ;—A.S. *slacian*.

slee, *v.*, to slay; *inf.*, 831 21 ; *prs.*, 132 15 ; **slough**, *pt.*, 65 11 ; 165 31 ; **slewe**, *pt.*, 468 29 ; **slayne**, *p.p.*, 754 3 ;—A.S. *sléan*.

sleer, *sb.*, murderer, he who kills somebody, 679 13.

slente, *v.*, to slant, to slope; **slented**, *pt.*, 689 24 ;—Swedish *slinta*, *slenta*.

sleyghte, *sb.*, skill, cunning, trick, falsehood, 788 7 ;—Icel. *slægd*.

slommer, *v.*, to slumber; **slomerynge**, *p.prs.*, 165 2 ; **slommeryd**, *pt.*, 364 23 ;—A.S. *sluma*, the slumber.

slough, *pt. See* slee.

slyde, *v.*, to slide; **slode**, *pt.*, 58 21 ; 365 2 ; 463 33 ;—A.S. *slidan*.

slyppe, *v.*, to slip; *inf.*, 106 26 ; **slypped**, *pt.*, 404 33 ;—A.S. *slipan*.

smyte, *v.*, to smite; **smote**, *pt.*, 757 25 ; **smyten**, *p.p.*, 471 13 ; **clok smyte**, 644 21 ; 681 14 ;—A.S. *smitan*.

sobbe, *v.*, to sigh convulsively, to weep; **sobbed**, *pt.*, 726 36 ;—? A.S. *seofian*.

socoure, *v.*, to come to one's assistance, to help; *inf.*, 413 38 ;—O.F. *sucurre, soscorre*.

soden, sodayne, *adj.*, 83 3 ; **sodenly**, *adv.*, 82 7 ;—A.F. *sodeyne*.

soiourne, *v.*, to stay, sojourn, abide ; **soiourned**, *pt.*, 143 35 ; **sud-**gerned, *pt.*, 182 14 ;—O.F. *sojorner*, *sojourner*.

solace, *sb.*, solace, rest, pleasure, 623 24 ;—A.F. *solas*.

solemnacyon, *sb.*, the act of solemnising, 270 22.

solempnly, *adv.*, solemnly, magnificently, 328 30 ;—A.F. *solempne*.

solempnyte, *sb.*, festivity, 270 18 ; —A.F. *sollempnitee*.

somette, *sb.*, summit, 174 2 ;—O.F. *som* and dim. suff. *-et*, or *sommite*.

somme, *pron.*, some, 323 2 ;—A.S. *sum*.

sonde, *sb.*, a sending, gift, message ; **sondes**, *pl.*, 840 13.

sonder, *adj.*, apart, separate, sonding, 406 36 ; **in sondyr**, 195 19 ; **a sondre**, 199 5 ; **in sonder**, asunder, 116 38 ; 725 1 ;—A.S. *onsundran*.

sonne, *sb.*, sun, 370 30 ;—A.S. *sunne*.

soppe, *sb.*, a sop ; **soppes**, *pl.*, 673 7 ;—Icel. *soppa*.

sorceresse, *sb.* and *adj.*, sorceress, 143 19 ; 207 27 ; **queens sorceresses**, 187 27 ;—O.F. *sorceresse*.

sore, *adj.* and *adv.*, sore, painful, greatly, violently, 38 11 ;—A.S. *sár*.

sorssery, *sb.*, sorcery, 79 34 ;—O.F. *sorcerie*.

sote, *v.*, to be deeply enamoured of somebody ; **soted**, *p.p.*, 508 30. *See* **assote**.

sothe, *sb.* and *adj.*, truth, sooth, true, 712 34 ;—A.S. *sóð*.

soude, *v.*, to pay, strengthen ; **souded**, *p.p.*, 717 20 ;—O.F. *souder*.

souder, *v.*, to solder ; **soudered**, *pt.*, 695 12 ;—O.F. *souder*.

soune, *v.*, to sound ; **souned**, *pt.*, 209 20 ;—A.F. *soner, suner*.

soupe, *v.*, to sup, drink gradually ; **souped**, *pt.*, 126 10 ;—O.F. *souper*.

souper, *sb.*, supper, 126 9 ;—A.F. *soper*, O.F. *souper*.

souse, *v.*, to plunge into the water ; **sowsyd**, *pt.*, 366 28 ; **soused**, *pt.*, 17 33 ;—from O.F. *sause, sauce*.

southard, *adj.*, southward, 153 8.

sowdan, *sb.*, sultan, 174 17 ;—O.F. *souldan, soudan*.

sowle, *sb.*, soul, 681 35;—A.S. *sáwel, sáwle.*

spaynysshe, *adj.*, Spanish, 2 35.

spaynyardys, *sb. pl.*, Spaniards, 163 27.

spede, *v.*, to speed, prosper, succeed; *inf.*, 51 18; 74 34; **spedde**, *p.p.*, 123 5; 466 10; **sped**, *p.p.*, 111 8;—A.S. *spédan.*

spede, *sb.*, success, speed, 289 15;—A.S. *spéd.*

speke, *v.*, to speak; *inf.*, 761 11; **spack**, *pt.*, 20 23; **speken**, *pl. prs.*, 425 27; 726 19; **spak**, *pt.*, 48 35; **spake**, *pt.*, 68 3; 466 20; **spoken**, *p.p.*, 2 33; spoken, *pl. pt.*, 700 26;—A.S. *specan.*

spende, *v.*, to spend, use; **spendynge**, *p.prs.*, 587 13;—A.S. *spendan.*

spere, *sb.*, spear, 585 28;—A.S. *spere.*

sperhauk, *sb.*, a sparrowhawk, 601 34;—A.S. *heafoc* and *spearwa.*

spore, *v.*, to spur; **spored**, *pt.*, 71 7;—A.S. *sporan.*

sprenge, *v.*, to sprinkle, to diffuse; **sprente**, *pt.*, 699 3;—A.S. *sprengan.*

sprynge, *v.*, to spring; **spronge**, *p.p.*, 436 27;—A.S. *springan.*

spyecery, *sb.*, spices, 573 6;—A.F. *spicerie.*

spyrre, *v.*, to inquire, ask; **spyrred**, *pt.*, 852 36;—A.S. *spyrian.*

spyrytueltees, *sb. pl.*, acts independent of the body, pure acts of the soul, things belonging to the church, 724 9;—from Lat. *spiritualis.*

stablysshe, *v.*, to establish; **stablisshed**, *p.p.*, 44 10; **stablysshed**, *pt.*, 118 12; **stablysshed**, *p.p.*, 860* 35;—O.F. *establiss-* (*establissant*), from *establir.*

stabylyte, *sb.*, stability, 829 9;—from Lat. *stabilitatem.*

staf, *sb.*, a staff, stick, 109 23; **stauys**, *pl.*, 47 1;—A.S. *stœf.*

stakker, *v.*, to stagger, to reel from side to side; **stakkerynge**, *p.prs.*, 464 6;—Icel. *stakra.*

stale, *sb.*, stall, state, station, prison, 179 3;—A.S. *steal.*

stale, *pt. See* **stele.**

stande, *v.*, to stand; *inf.*, 44 2; 472 13; **stode**, *pt.*, 381 22; **stondynge**, *prs.*, 58 31; **standeth**, *prs.*, 80 36;—A.S. *standan.*

stark, *adj.* and *adv.*, strong, firm, severe, thoroughly; **stark dede**, 141 26; **a stark coward**, 143 21; **starke deed**, 847 15;—A.S. *stearc.*

staunche, *v.*, to make stagnant, to stop the flowing blood; *inf.*, 176 34; **staunched**, *p.p.*, 177 1; **staunched**, *pt.*, 706 7;—O.F. *estancher.*

stede, *sb.*, place; **in my stede**, 375 10; **stedys**, *pl.*, 230 27;—A.S. *stede.*

stede, *sb.*, steed, horse, 236 35;—A.S. *stéda.*

stele, *v.*, to steal; *inf.*, 137 9; **stale**, *pt.*, 369 11; 457 19;—A.S. *stelan.*

stere, *v.*, to stir, to move; *inf.*, 40 33; 630 3; **stered**, *pt.*, 755 19;—A.S. *styrian.*

stere, *v.*, to steer, lead, direct; *inf.*, 760 29; **stered**, *pt.*, 56 12; **styred**, *pt.*, 760 37;—A.S. *stýran, stéoran.*

sterre, *sb.*, star; **sterres**, *pl.*, 658 32;—A.S. *steorra.*

sterte, *v.*, to start; **sterte**, *pt.*, 66 12; 94 36; **starte**, *pt.*, 168 6; 382 19;—? Icel. *sterta* and A.S. *steortan.*

steuen, *sb.*, voice, command, time of performing an action, 92 35; 858* 19;—A.S. *stefn.*

steyer, *sb.*, stair, ladder, 736 23;—A.S. *stǽger.*

stole, *sb.*, a robe, stole, 656 16;—Lat. *stola.*

stonien, *v.*, to stun, to amaze with a blow; **stonyed**, *pt.*, 58 17; *p.p.*, 107 22; **stoned**, *pt.*, 107 9;—from O.F. *estoner. Compare* **astonye.**

stoupe, *v.*, to stoop; **stouped**, *pt*, 206 26; 391 22;—A.S. *stúpian.*

stoure, *sb.*, conflict, agitation, commotion, 180 15; 675 25;—O.F. *estour.*

strake, *v.*, to give a quick blow, to dash, to hit; *inf.*, 500 11; **straked**, *pt.*, 370 14;—from A.S. *strícan.*

straungenes, *sb.*, strangeness, 242 9;—O.F. *estraunge.*

strayte, *adj.* *See* **streyte**.

streme, *sb.*, stream, river, 144 7;—A.S. *stréam*.

strene, *sb.*, race, progeny, 622 8;—A.S. *stréon*.

stretche, *v.* to stretche; **stratched**, 836 1; **stretched**, *pt.*, 213 26;—A.S. *streccan*.

streyte, **streyghte**, *adj.* and *adv.*, straight, strict, narrow, 79 26; 457 38; **strayte**, 327 18; 435 14;—A.F. *estreit*.

strond, *sb.*, strand, bank, shore, 687 19; **stronde**, 708 3;—A.S. *strand*.

stryde, *sb.*, a long step; **strydes**, *pl.*, 131 30; **strydys**, *pl.*, 238 14;—from A.S. *strídan*.

stryffe, *sb.*, strife, fight, 840 23;—A.F. *estrif*.

stryue, *v.*, to striue; **stroof**, *pt.*, 10 17;—O.F. *estriver*.

stryke, *v.* to strike, rub, to move quickly; *inf.*, 84 32; **strake**, *pt.*, 122 3; **stryken**, *p.p.*, 122 12; 133 34; 607 21; 842 36;—A.S. *strícan*.

stycke, *v.*, to stick; **stycketh**, *prs.*, 93 9; **stack**, *pt.*, 248 33; **stack**, *pt.*, 40 23; 69 29;—A.S. *stician*.

stynge, *v.*, to sting; **stonge**, *pt.*, 845 32; **stongen**, *p.p.*, 845 33;—A.S. *stingan*.

stynte, *sb.*, stint, portion allotted to somebody; **stynte of my land**, 72 18; **stynte of my crowne**, 269 21;—? A.S. *styntan*.

stynte, *v.*, to stint, to cease, pause; **stynteth**, *prs.*, 205 28; **stynte**, *pt.*, 56 13;—A.S. *styntan*.

styrope, *sb.*, stirrup, 304 36; **styropes**, *pl.*, 481 14; **steroppes**, *pl.*, 487 17;—A.S. *stíg-ráp*.

subgette, *sb.*, subject; **subgettys**, *pl.*, 163 17.

subgette, *adj.* or *p.p.*, subject, dependent, 163 25;—Lat. *subjectus*.

substance, *sb.*, substance, contents, 762 1;—Lat. *substantia*.

sudgerne, *v.* *See* **soiourne**.

sufferaunce, *sb.*, patience, endurance, 539 26;—A.F. *suffraunce*.

suffrecan, *sb.*, assistant, deputy of a bishop, 611 16, 19;—Late Lat. *suffraganeus*.

suffycyaunt, *adj.*, sufficient, 828 35;—A.F. *suffisant*.

suppynge, *sb.*, little draughts; **suppynges**, *pl.*, 370 19;—from A.S. *súpan*.

suraunce, *sb.*, assurance, 45 32;—O.F. *seurance*.

surgeon, *sb.*, surgeon, physician, 285 28; **surgens**, *pl.*, 284 32; **surgyens**, *pl.*, 174 14.

surmyse, *v.*, surmise; **surmysed**, *pt.*, 821 34;—from O.F. *p.p. surmise*.

sursengle, *sb.*, girth, belly-band of a saddle, surcingle; **sursenglys**, *pl.*, 238 2;—O.F. *sursangle*.

suspecyon, *sb.*, suspicion, 287 24; 729 18;—O.F. *suspezion, souspeçon*.

sustene, *v.*, to sustain; *inf.*, 667 25;—A.F. *sustener*.

swalowe, *sb.*, a whirlpool, gulf, 691 27;—Icel. *svelgja*.

swappe, *v.*, to strike, to fall suddenly; **swapped**, *pt.*, 210 29.

swerded, *adj.*, having a sword, 333 25.

swere, *v.*, to swear; **sware**, *pt.*, 275 31; **sworne**, *p.p.*, 9 12;—A.S. *swerian*.

swerue, *v.*, to swerve; **swarued**, *pt.*, 636 30;—A.S. *sweorfan*.

sweuen, *sb.*, dream, 53 1; 859* 7;—A.S. *swefen*.

swough, *sb.*, sound of the wind, sighing, swoon, 165 20;—from A.S. *swógan*.

swoun, *sb.*, swoon, 97 10; **swowne**, 93 32; *v.*, to faint, to swoon; **swouned**, *pt.*, 466 21.

syb, *sb.* and *adj.*, peace, relationship; related, 103 11;—A.S. *sibb*.

sydelyng, *adj.*, from the side, sideways, 524 10;—A.S. *síde* and *? gelang*.

syege, *sb.* *See* **sege**.

sygne, *sb.*, sign, 127 36;—A.F. *signe*.

sygnefye, *v.*, to mean, signify, to compare; **sygnefyeth**, *prs.*, 408 17; **sygnefyen**, *pl. prs.*, 631 23; 682 36; **sygnefyed**, 703 19; 715* 30;—A.F. *signefier*.

sygnette, *sb.*, mark, the privy seal, a seal; **sygnettys**, *pl.*;—dimin. of O.F. *signe*.

sygnyfycacion, *sb.*, signification, meaning, 165 25;—O.F. *signification.*

syker, *adj.*, trusty, sure, secure, 240 34; 621 10. *Compare* O.S. *sikor*, O.H.G. *sichor.*

sykernesse, *sb.*, security, 157 28.

synge, *v.*, to sing; songen, *p.p.*, 579 14; songe, *p.p.*, 464 35; songe, *sb.*, the song, 464 35; 465 5;—A.S. *singan.*

synke, *v.*, to sink; sanke, *pt.*, 59 2; 858* 4; synked, *pt.*, 838 18;—A.S. *sincan.*

synne, *sb.*, sin, 711 27; syns, *pl.* 407 6;—A.S. *syn*, *sinn.*

synner, *sb.*, sinner; synnar, 712 22.

syse, *sb.*, size, 173 21; syses, *pl.*, 500 6;—from O.F. (*as*)*sis*, (*as*)*sise.*

sythen, *adv.* and *conj.*, since, afterwards, 69 6; 480 9; 644 2; syn (contracted form), 96 21; 98 10; sith, 715 25; sythe, 1 24;—A.S. *siððan.*

sytte, *v.*, to sit, befit; *inf.*, 103 37; 717 12; sat, *pt.*, 104 27; satte, *pt.*, 65 25; sytten, *p.p.*, 103 31;—A.S. *sittan.*

taccomplysshe, *v.* *See* accomplysshe.

take, *v.*, to take; toke, *pt.*, 69 22; take, *p.p.*, 715* 32; taken, *p.p.*, 78 12;—Icel. *taka.*

tale, *sb.*, account, narration, tale, reckoning, 623 1;—A.S. *talu.*

talent, *sb.*, desire, appetite, inclination, 446 9;—O.F. *talent.*

talowe, *sb.*, tallow, 219 1;—M.E. *talgh.*

tame, *v.*, to conquer, crush, subdue; tamyd, *pt.*, 97 16; 111 23; 657 24;—A.S. *tamian.*

tapre, *sb.*, taper; tapres, *pl.*, 579 21; —A.S. *tapor*, *taper.*

tatche, *sb.*, quality, mark, sign, fault; tatches, *pl.*, 77 36; 103 20;—O.F. *tache.*

taylle, *sb.*, tail, 165 21;—A.S. *tægl.*

taylle, *sb.*, tax, tallage; taylles, *pl.*, 161 25;—O.F. *taille.*

teche, *v.*, to teach; *prs.*, 142 26; *inf.*, 645 13;—A.S. *tæcan.*

tempils, *sb. pl.*, the temples, 55 26;—O.F. *temples.*

temptacyon, *sb.*, temptation, 648 26;—O.F. *temptation.*

tene, *sb.*, grief, vexation, injury, 94 14; 177 3;—A.S. *téona.*

tere, *sb.*, tear; teres, *pl.*, 621 10;—A.S. *téar.*

the, th, *definite article;* thabyte 34 21; thachyeuement, 30 11; thaduenture, 7 17; tharchebysshop, 34 20; thappoynte, ment, 14 20; thassumpcion, 254 27; thavys, 18 3; thadvyse, 377 35; theffecte, 160 26; thembassatours, 162 7; themperour, 4 27; 70 7; thermytage, 34 20; therth, 857* 28; thescape, 16 9; thexcellent, 1 32; thexposycion, 11 4; thold, 91 16; thoryent, 165 10; thother, 177 18; 721 15; thystorye, 1 34, 37; 699 15;—A.S. ðe, earlier form ða.

thenne, *adv.*, then, than, 395 7;—A.S. *þænne.*

theym, *pron.*, *dat.* and *acc.*, them, 8 14;—A.S. *þeim.*

thise, *pron. pl.*, these, 494 5;—from A.S. *þes*, *pl.*, *þás*, *þǽs.*

tho, *pron. dem.* and *def. art. pl.*, those, 49 12; 59 26;—A.S. *þá.*

thonder, *sb.*, thunder, 409 21;—A.S. *þunor.*

threde, *sb.*, thread, 657 18; thredys, *pl.*, 699 28;—A.S. *þrǽd.*

threnge, *v.*, to press; thrange, *pt.*, 479 29;—A.S. *þringan.*

threste, *v.*, to thrust; threst, *third pers. prs. sing.*, 58 15; threstyd, *pt.*, 180 1;—Icel. *þrýsta.*

threte, *sb.*, threat, menace; thretys, *pl.*, 457 31;—A.S. *þréat.*

threte, *v.*, to threaten, to menace; threted, *p.p.*, 520 31;—A.S. *þréatian.*

throte, *sb.*, throat, 482 13; throtes, *pl.*, 151 13;—A.S. *þrote*, *þrotu.*

thrulle, *v.*, to pierce, traverse; thrulled, *pt.*, 343 28;—A.S. *þyrlian.*

thryes, *adv.*, thrice, three times, threefold, 142 34; the thryes myghte, 143 26;—A.S. *þriwa.*

thurgh, *prep.*, through, 59 12

thorugh, 1 12; thorowe, 37 16; thorou, 235 16;—A.S. *þurh*.

thwart, *adv.*, thwart, through, across, 173 37;—Icel. *þvert. Compare* Skeat, Dict.

thyder, *adv.*, thither, 62 33; ~~——~~; thydder, ~~————~~;—A.S. *þider*.

thyghe, *sb.*, thigh, 13 33; thyes, *pl.*, 29 8; 60 33;—A.S. *þeoh, þéo*.

thylk, *adj.*, that, such, 181 29;—A.S. *þylc*.

to, (1) *prep.*, to, at, in, upon, into, against, as, until; temprynte, 1 34; tenprynte, 1 37; 4 13; texersyse, 4 1; tespye, 171 17; (2) *prefix*, asunder, in twain, to pieces;—A.S. *tó, tó-*.

to breste, *v.*, to burst asunder; to brast, *pt.*, 204 20; 482 15;—A.S. *to-berstan*.

to cratche, *v.*, to scratch, to tear to pieces; to cratched, 583 14.

to forne, *adv.* and *prep.*, before, 247 20; 507 33; to fore, 1 11, 14;—A.S. *tó-foran*.

to gyder, to gyders, *adv.*, together, 397 30; 471 33;—A.S. *tó-gœdere, tó-gœdre*.

to hewe, *v.*, to hew in pieces; *inf.*, 513 9; to hewe, *pt.*, 338 31;—A.S. *to-héawan*.

tokenynge, *sb.*, signification, 663 6;—A.S. *tácnung*.

tomble, *v.*, to tumble, leap; tombled, *pt.*, 507 26;—A.S. *tumbian*.

tornoye, *v.*, to make a tournament, 6 18; tornoyeng, *p.prs.*, 10 30; 23 3;—O.F. *tournoier*.

to ryue, *v.*, to tear, to rend to pieces; to rofe, *pt.*, 330 29;—Icel. *rífa*.

to sheuer, *v.*, to smash, to reduce to shivers; to sheuered, *pt.*, 69 27; 71 15; 87 28; *p.p.*, 481 12;—Icel. *skífa*.

tournement, *sb.*, tournament, 22 38; turnement, 494 13; turnementys, *pl.*, 763 25;—O.F. *tornoiement*.

towel, *sb.*, towel, 719 2; tuell, 404 32;—A.F. *towaille*, O.F. *touaile*.

towre, *sb.*, tower, 45 11; toure,

256 17; tour, 46 1; towres, 97 20;—O.F. *tur, tour*.

traine, *sb.*, train, treachery, stratagem, deceit; trainys, *pl.*, 378 22;—O.F. *trahin, train*.

traitourly, *adv.*, treacherously, like a traitor, 402 10;—A.F. *traitur* and A.S. *lic*.

trak, *sb.*, track, trace, 435 15.

trappe, *sb.*, trap, 32 10;—A.S. *treppe*.

trapped, *adj.*, adorned with trappings, 97 3;—from O.F. **trap*, cognate with Mod.F. *drap*.

trappere, *sb.*, trappings, ornaments, 58 22; trappours, *pl.*, 371 16.

trase, trace, *v.*, to trace, to trace one's way, to rush along; tracyd, *pt.*, 463 18; tracynge, *p.prs.*, 217 33; trasynge, *p.prs.*, 194 11;—O.F. *tracer*.

trauaille, *sb.*, work, labour, toil, trouble, 97 12; trauaill, 599 33;—A.F. *travail, travaille*.

trauaille, *v.*, to work, torment, toil; *inf.*, 273 33;—A.F. *travailer*.

trauerse, *adv.*, in twain, across, 526 5;—O.F. *traverse*.

trauerse, *v.*, to run across; trauercyd, *pt.*, 463 18;—O.F. *traverser*.

tray, *sb.*, grief, affliction, 94 14;—A.S. *trega*.

traytour, *sb.* and *adj.*, traitor, 321 28; 849 6; traitour knyght, 289 34;—O.F. *traïtor*.

treason, *sb.*, treason, 729 25; treson, 76 24 (Malory says: "For the custom was such at that time that all maner of shameful death was called treason," 729 26, 27);—A.F. *treson, traïson*.

trecherye, *sb.*, treachery, trickery, 76 24;—A.F. *tricherie*.

trede, *v.*, to tread; trade, *pt.*, 778 13; 784 10;—A.S. *tredan*.

trenchaunt, *adj.*, cutting, 792 23;—O.F. *trencher*.

trespas, *sb.*, trespass, 79 32;—O.F. *trespas*.

trest,[1] *sb.*, ? (hunting term), 764 14: Wynkyn de Worde reads *treste*.

---

[1] I have tried to find the exact meaning of the word "trest;" it seems to be "a station appointed in hunting." Wright says it must be found in some treatise on

tretabyl, *adj.*, treatable, 308 14.

tretyce, tretys, *sb.*, treaty, 153 12; 207 3; 861 36;—A.F. *tretiz.*

troncheon, *sb.*, truncheon, broken piece of a spear-shaft, 69 29; **truncheon**, 93 6;—O.F. *tronçon, tronchon.*

trouthe, *sb.*, truth, 38 13;—A.S. *tréowð.*

trouthplyte, *v.*, to engage seriously, to promise; *inf.*, 247 13;--A.S. *tréowð* and *plihtan.*

trowe, *v.*, to believe; **trowed**, *pt.*, 666 13; **trowe**, *prs.*, 331 38; 432 14;--A.S. *tréowan.*

truage, *sb.*, tribute, 7 1; 70 4;— O.F. *treüage.*

trusse, *v.*, to pack, pack off; **trussed**, *pt.*, 649 16; 829 16;—O.F. *trusser.*

tuell, *sb. See* **towel**.

turnement, *sb. See* **tornement**.

turret, *sb.*, small tower, 140 23; 141 17;—O.F. *tourette.*

tweyne, *num.*, twain, two, 87 20; 166 34; 483 6;—A.S. *twégen.*

twyes, *adv.*, twice, 91 37; 516 9;— A.S. *twíges, twiwa.*

tyde, *v.*, to happen; *prs.*, 847 1;— A.S. *tidan. Compare* **betyde**.

tydynges, *sb. pl.*, tidings, news, 699 36;—from Icel. *tiðindi. Compare* A.S. *tidan.*

tye, *v.*, to tie; **tayed**, *pt.*, 41 20; 73 18; **teyed**, *pt.*, 198 29; 806 9;— A.S. *tígan.*

tyere, *v.*, to tire, exhaust; *inf.*, 661 32;—A.S. *teorian.*

tylle, *conj.* and *prep.*, till, to, against, 690 26; **tyl**, 757 31; **til a tree**, 380 10; 389 18; 610 3; **til a frende**, 385 28;—Icel. *til.*

vbblye, *sb.*, wafer, sacramental bread, 719 6;—M.E. *oblé, ovelète*, O.F. *oublee*, A.S. *oflǽte*, Late Lat. *oblāta.*

vmbecast, *v.*, to cast about, consider, ponder; *pt.*, 764 25.

vmbre, *sb.*, shade, umbrage, 274 18; 281 32;—Lat. *umbra.*

vnbockel, *v.*, to take off, unbuckle; *inf.*, 516 38.

vncoupele, *v.* (hunting term), to uncouple, loose dogs from their couples, set loose, disjoin (*compare* Shakspere, "Tit. Andron." ii. 2); **vncoupelynge**, *p.prs.*, 500 10.

vncouth, *adj.*, strange, unknown, 105 31;—A.S. *un-cúð.*

vncurteis, *adj.*, not polite, rough, unrefined, 151 30; **vncurtois**, 541 7.

vnderne, *sb.*, the time between sunrise and noon, or between noon and sunset, a meal-time, 242 29; **vndern**, 885 18; **vndorn**, 613 28; **vndorne**, 574 21;—A.S. *undern*, O.S. *undorn.*

vndernethe, *prep.*, underneath, below, 362 6; **vnder nethe**, 548 27;— A.S. *under* and *neoð-an.*

vnderstande, *v.*, to understand; **vnderstanden**, *p.p.*, 166 31; **vnderstonde**, *inf.*, 4 16; **vnderstood**, *pt.*, 348 11; **vnderstode**, *pl.*, 461 21;—A.S. *understandan.*

---

hunting; I have not, however, come across it in any of the treatises on the subject (compare my note to "Trystram"). Sir E. Strachey says "trest" is the participle of *trere* (*tirer*).—In "The Story of England," by Robert Manning of Brunne, A.D. 1338, ed., from MSS. in the Lambeth and Inner Temple libraries, by F. J. Furnivall, the word occurs, page 30, line 856, evidently in the same sense: "att a triste to schete, Brutus was set." The Glossary, page 836, explains triste as tryste, trysting-place, appointed station, and quotes as etymons O.Icel. *traust*, O.Fries. *trast, trust*, most likely on Prof. Skeat's authority. In R. Morris's ed. of "Sir Gawayne and the Green Knight," verses 1146, 1170, 1712, tryster, trysteres, the stations allotted to different persons in hunting, occur.—Mr. Henry Bradley has endeavoured to explain the origin of the word "trest." In a letter to the *Academy* of January 18, 1890, he says: "I do not know whether Romanic philologists will entertain the suggestion that *terra* may, in Gaul, have given rise to a derivative of the form **terristrum, *terristra*, with the accent fluctuating between the first and second syllable. If this hypothesis be admissible, it will, I suppose, account for the forms *tristre, terstre, tertre*, and also for the twofold sense in which *tertre* occurs; and the original English meaning of *tristre, tryst*, would be a 'portion of ground' assigned to each person in certain modes of hunting. The wider sense 'rendez-vous,' might easily have been developed from this, and it is very likely that the word would be at an early period confused with *trist = trust.*"

vngladde, *adj.*, unhappy, 499 27.

vnhelmed, *adj.*, without a helmet, 565 27.

vnmaymed, *p.p.*, not wounded, sound, 515 8.

vnmesurably oute of mesure, *tautol. phrase*, greatly out of measure, exceedingly, 640 22.

vnnailled, *p.p.*, broken, unriveted, 97 29.

vnnethe, *adv.*, scarcely, 127 18; vnnethes, 143 1;—A.S. *uneðe*.

vnslayne, *adj.* or *p.p.*, alive, not slain, 515 8.

vnstabylnesse, *sb.*, unstableness, 671 11.

vnsyker, *adj.*, uncertain, 724 30.

vntrouthe, *sb.*, falsehood, lie, untruth, 702 1.

vnwympeled, *p.p.*, unveiled, 476 7.

vp, *prep.* and *adv.*, up; vp so doune, upside down, 206 12; 654 13; 706 32;—A.S. *up, upp.*

vtas, *sb.*, the octave of a festival, 164 8;—A.F. *utaves*, O.F. *oitauves.*

vtteraunce, *sb.*, extremity, the uttermost, 218 9;—O.F. *oultrance.*

vttermest, *adj. superl.*, the extreme, the utmost, 128 2; 567 34;—A.S. *útor, uttor,* and *meste.*

valewe, *sb.*, value, 78 37;—O.F. *valu, valuë.*

valyaunce, *sb. pl.*, valiant deeds, 173 14;—O.F. *valance, vaillance.*

valyaunt, *adj.*, brave, valiant, 297 26; 482 18; valyaunts men, 83 31; valyaunter, *comp.*, 447 17: valyauntest, *superl.*, 454 21;—O.F. *vaillant, valant.*

valyauntnesse, *sb.*, brave behaviour, valour, 608 14.

vanysshe, *v.*, to vanish; vanysshed, *pt.*, 85 1; 627 23;—O.F. **vaniss-,* from **vanir.*

vanytee, *sb.*, vanity; vanytees, *pl.*, 855* 1;—Lat. *vanitatem.*

varlet, *sb.*, servant, squire, young vassal, 187 4; 403 10; varlette, 434 5;—O.F. *varlet, vaslet.*

varyaunt, *adj.*, changeable, fickle, 827 1;—Lat. *variant-,* from *variare.*

vaute, *sb.*, vault; vautes, *pl.*, 2 38;—O.F. *vault, volte, voute.*

vaward, *sb.*, vanguard, 86 31;—A.F. *avaunt garde.*

vayshere, vaysshoure, *sb.*, the cowherd, father of syr Tor;—O.F. *vachere, vachier.*

velowet, *sb.*, velvet, 822 24;—O.F. *velu.*

venery, *sb.*, hunting, 568 27;—O.F. *venerie.*

venetrete,[1] *v., ?*; venetreted, *p.p.*, 604 32;—? Wynkyn de Worde has also *venetreted;* ed. 1634 has *euill intreated;* Sir E. Strachey reads *so entreated.* The meaning is evidently "badly treated."

vengeable, *adj.*, revengeful, full of vengeance, 834 19.

vengeaunce, *sb.*, vengeance, 367 20; 466 34;—O.F. *venjance.*

ventayls, *sb. pl.*, the movable front of a helmet, covering the face, through which the wearer breathes; sometimes it means the whole front of a helmet, 516 15;—M.E. generally *aventayle* (compare Shakspere, "Troilus and Creseide," line 1557);—A.F. *aventaille.*

venym, *sb.*, poison, 285 2;—O.F. *venin.*

veray, *adj.*, true, 4 15; 565 33; 592 15;—A.F. *verai.*

vermyn, *sb.*, a worm, vermin; vermyns, *pl.*, 500 9;—O.F. *vermine.*

vessel, *sb.*, vessel, ship, 284 16; vessaile, 282 1;—O.F. *vaissel, veissel, vessel.*

veyne, *adj.*, vain, 679 10;—Fr. *vain,* Lat. *vanus.*

vouchesaufe, *v.*, to sanction, vouchsafe; *inf.*, 720 25;—O.F. *voucher* and *sauf.*

voyce, *sb.*, voice, 695 21; 707 13; voys, 580 6; 840 22;—O.F. *vois.*

vygyl, *sb.*, vigil, eve of a feast or fast day, 612 1;—Lat. *vigilia.*

---

[1] The form "venetreted" is evidently a misprint, though I cannot explain it. The M.E. verb "entreten" is used for "to treat," in the good as well as in the bad sense; therefore Sir E. Strachey's reading "so entreated" is satisfactory.

vylayn, *adj.* and *sb.*, villain, ugly, detestable ; **vylaynst,** *superl.,* 450 18 ;—O.F. *vilain, vilein.*

vylony, *sb.*, villany, 832 18 ;—O.F. *vilenie.*

vyloynsly, *adv.*, villanously, 503 8.

vyolle, *sb.*, vial, small bottle, 178 27 ; —O.F. *viole,* A.F. *fyole.*

vysaged, *adj.*, having a face, 213 26 ; —from A.F. *visage.*

vyser, *sb.*, visor, the perforated part of the helmet in front of the face, 181 6 ; **vysure,** 289 8 ;—O.F. *visiere.*

vytaille, *sb.*, provision, 64 29 ; **vy-tilled,** *p.p.*, provisioned, 45 13 ;— A.F. *vitaille.*

wade, *v.*, to wade ; **wade,** *pt.*, 156 4 ;—A.S. *wadan.*

wagge, *v.*, to shake to and fro, to nod ; **waggynge,** *p.prs.*, 787 20 ; **wagged,** *pt.*, 787 18.—*Compare* Icel. *vagga,* a cradle.

wallop, wallope, *sb.*, gallop, pace of a horse while lifting the fore and hind feet together, 69 14 ; 114 9.

wallope, *v.*, to gallop, to leap in running, to ride at a galloping pace ; *inf.*, 179 33 ; **wallopped,** *pt.*, 415 30 ; **wallopt,** *pt.*, 202 17 ; **wallopte,** *pt.*, 204 6 ;—O.F. *galoper.*

walowe, *v.*, wallow, to roll about ; **walowynge,** *p.prs.*, 168 16 ; **walowed,** *pt.*, 242 27 ;—A.S. *wealwian.*

walsshe, *adj.* and *sb.*, Welsh, Welsh-man, foreign, foreigner, 3 10 ; **walysshe,** 767 30 ;—A.S. *wælisc.*

wanhope, *sb.*, despair, 678 12.— *Compare* M.Du. *wanhope.*

wanne, *v.*, to wane, to grow less, to ebb ; *inf.*, 849 5 ;—A.S. *wanian.*

wappe, *v.*, to wap, to lap ; *inf.*, 849 5 (probably from the sound of the sea).

ward, *sb.*, care, heed, regard, keeping, 285 27 ;—A.S. *weard.*

ward, *sb.*, ward, one under the care of a guardian, 180 15 ;—A.S. *weard.*

wardeyn, *sb.*, warden, 44 14 ;—A.F. *wardein.*

warison, *sb.*, reward, property, 372 35 ;—O.F. *warison.*

wasshe, *v.*, to wash ; **wesshe,** *pt.*, 178 29 ; **wasshed,** *pt.*, 380 11 ; **wasshen,** *p.p.*, 49 28 ;—A.S. *wascan.*

wast, *sb.*, waist, the middle part of a human body, 589 11 ; **waste,** 295 7 ;—M.E. *wast,* O.H.G. *vahst.*

waxe, *v.*, to wax, grow ; **waxt,** *pt.*, 130 31 ; **waxte,** *pt.*, 463 23 ; **waxed,** *pt.*, 856* 26 ;—A.S. *weaxan.*

wayte, *sb.*, watch, guard, 726 10 ; 761 24 ;—from A.F. *wayter.*

webbe, *sb.*, sheet of thin plate of lead, 857* 27 ;—? A.S. *webb* or *web.*

wede, *sb.*, weed, garment, 702 33 ; **wedys,** *pl.*, 539 11 ;—A.S. *wéde.*

wede, *sb.*, weed, wild herb, 224 1 ;— A.S. *wéod, wíod.*

weder, *sb.*, weather, 587 2 ; **wheder,** 653 15 ; **whether,** 366 25 ;—A.S. *weder.*

wedlok, *sb.*, marriage, 451 4 ;—A.S. *wedlac.*

welde, *v.*, to govern, possess, have power over ; *inf.*, 172 2 ; **weldeth,** *prs.*, 168 2 ; **welde hymself,** 294 1 ;—A.S. *wealdan.*

wele, *sb.*, weal, prosperity, 310 2 ; 804 15 ;—A.S. *wela, weola.*

welthe, *sb.*, wealth, 400 8 ;—from A.S. *wela* with the suff. *-th.*

weltre, *v.*, to welter, to roll about ; **weltred,** *pt.*, 168 14 ; **weltryng,** *p.prs.*, 168 15.—*Compare* A.S. *wealtan.*

wende, *v.*, to go, to turn ; **wente,** *pt.*, 6 19 ; 136 2 ; 761 9 ;—A.S. *wendan.*

wene, *v.*, to ween, suppose ; **wene,** *prs.*, 163 2 ; **weneth,** *prs.*, 81 33 ; **wende,** *pt.*, 40 5 ; 404 21 ;—A.S. *wénan.*

wepen, *sb.*, weapon, 92 24 ;—A.S. *wǽpen.*

wepenles, *adj.*, without arms, 93 20.

werche, *v.*, to work ; **werches,** *prs.*, 848 1 ; **worcheth,** *prs.*, 643 17 ; **wroughte,** *pt.*, 120 3 ; 378 28 ; **worche,** *inf.*, 135 10 ; **worched,** *p.p.*, 199 13 ; **wrou3t,** *p.p.*, 403 31 ; **wyrchynge,** *p.prs.*, 120 2 ;—A.S. *wyrcan, wercan.*

werke, *sb.*, work, 3 27;—A.S. (*ge*)-
weorc, worc.

werre, *sb.*, war; werrys, *pl.*, 198 9;
werres, *pl.*, 659 10;—O.F. *werre.*

werre, *v.*, to make war; *inf.*, 673
20; werrith, *prs.*, 682 13;—A.S.
werrian. Compare O.F. *werreier,
guerroier.*

wers, *adj. comp.*, worse, 46 22;
werse, 47 34; worse, 297 4;—
A.S. *wyrs.*

werst, *adj. superl.*, worst, utmost,
839 37;—A.S. *wyrst.*

werwolf, *sb.*, man-wolf, 793 17;—
A.S. *wer* (man, husband) and *wulf.*

wery, *adj.*, weary, 664 29;—A.S.
wêrig.

wesshe, *pt. See* wasshe.

wete, *v.*, to know, to observe, to keep,
guard; *inf.*, 1 13; 433 26; wiste,
pt., 402 9; wist, *pt.*, 373 14;
wetest, *prs.*, 379 14; wyste, *pt.*,
82 13; 205 14; we wote, *prs.*, 59
30; I wote, *prs.*, 110 19; 422 3;
thou wotest, *prs.*, 72 10;—A.S.
witan.

wey, *sb.*, way, 36 25; 51 15;—A.S.
weg.

weyke, *adj.*, weak; weykely, *adv.*,
794 21; wayke, 857* 2; weykest,
superl., 144 29;—Icel. *veikr*, A.S.
wac.

wheder, *sb. See* weder.

wheder, *adv.*, whither, 297 21;
whyder ward, 438 17; wheder
ward, whitherward, 341 6; whether, 219 15; whyder, 378 10;
whyther, 297 21; whydder, 702
28;—A.S. *hwider.*

whele, *sb.*, wheel, 827 1;—A.S.
hwéol.

whelp, *sb.*, young of a dog and of
beasts of prey, puppy, 694 4;—
A.S. *hwelp.*

whether, *sb. See* weder.

whether, *pron.*, which of the two,
238 28; *conj.*, whether, if, 244 1;
—A.S. *hwœðer.*

whyder, whydder. *See* wheder.

whylest, *adv.* and *conj.*, while, whilst,
725 1;—from A.S. *hwíl.*

withinforth, *adv.*, inwardly, inside,
836 28.

withoutforth, *adv.*, outside, 836 28.

withsay, *v.*, to contradict, to re-
nounce; *inf.*, 615 17;—A.S. *wið*
and *secgan.*

withstande, *v.*, to resist; *inf.*, 760
16; withstand, *p.p.*, 76 6;—A.S.
wið and *standan.*

woful, *adj.*, sorrowful; wofullest,
superl., 407 3;—A.S. *wéa* and *ful.*

wol, *prs. See* wylle.

wolde, *pt. See* wylle.

wonder, *adj.* and *adv.*, fearful, wonderful, 689 8; 837 35. *Compare*
A.S. *wundor, wundrian.*

wonderly, *adv.*, wonderfully, 300 23.

wonne, *pt. See* wynne.

wonte, *adj.*, accustomed, 831 27.

wood, *sb.*, wood, tree, forest, 56 2;
wode, 85 19;—A.S. *wudu, widu.*

wood, woode, *adj.* and *adv.*, mad,
raging, 58 32; 401 8;—A.S. *wód.*

woodenes, *sb.*, madness, 55 36; 396
2;—A.S. *wódnyss.*

worcheth, *prs. See* werche.

worte, *sb.*, plant, herb, vegetable;
wortes, *pl.*, 668 18;—A.S. *wyrt.*

wote, *prs. See* wete.

wowe, *v.*, to woo, to request;
wowed, *pt.*, 784 36;—A.S. *wógian.*

wrake, *sb.*, destruction, misery, mischief, 797 35; 854 22;—A.S.
wracu.

wrathe, *v.*, to become or to make
angry; *inf.*, 374 18;—from A.S.
wráð.

wreke, *v.*, to wreak, to urge, punish,
avenge; wrackyd, *p.p.*, 531 17;
wroken, *p.p.*, 107 5;—A.S. *wrecan.*

wroth, wrothe, *adj.*, wroth, fearful,
angry, 401 8, 14;—A.S. *wráð.*

wrou3t, *p.p. See* werche.

wrynge, *v.*, to wring, press; wryng-
ynge, *p.prs.*, 167 8; wrange, *pt.*,
389 36; wrong, *pt.*, 168 14;—A.S.
wringan.

wrythe, *v.*, to writhe, to twist;
wrythed, *pt.*, 242 27; 582 23;
wrothe, *pt.*, 595 27;—A.S.
wríðan.

wyde where, *adv.*, far and wide,
340 29.

wyght, *adj.*, active, swift, strong,
344 30; 467 34; 799 22;—A.S.

wyle, *sb.*, guile, trick, a sly artifice;
wyles, *pl.*, 424 11;—A.S. *wíl, wíle.*

wyllar, *sb.,* one who wills, or wishes; **well wyllars,** *pl.,* 465 11;—from A.S. *willan.*

wylsome, *adj.,* dreary, doubtful, 247 11.

wyl, wylle, *prs.,* will, 402 12; 719 22; **I wol,** *prs.,* 59 8; **thou wolt,** *prs.,* 38 27; **he wol,** 70 36; **wylt thow,** 102 5; **woll ye,** 42 22; **wold,** *pt.,* 39 28; 402 26; **thou woldest,** 48 28 ;—A.S. *wille, wolde.*

wyly, *adj.,* wily, full of tricks, 135 38; 238 32.

wymmen, *sb. pl.,* women, 83 28; 407 10;—A.S. *wifmen.*

wympeld, *p.p.,* veiled, 531 59.

wyn, *sb.,* wine, 275 22 ;—A.S. *win.*

wynded, *p.p.,* having much breath, 512 8 ;—from A.S. *wind.*

wynne, wyn, *v.,* to win ; *inf.,* 80 15; 148 19; 312 20; **wan,** *pt.,* 44 16; **wonne,** *pt.,* 134 13; **wonne,** *p.p.,* 105 77; 388 27; 513 32;—A.S. *(ge)winnan.*

wyrchynge, *p.prs. See* **werche.**

wyt, *sb.,* wisdom, intelligence, wit, reason, 50 20; **wytte,** 99 3;— A.S. *(ge)witt.*

wyte, *sb.,* blame, 75 24; 88 11.

wyte, *v.,* to blame; *prs.,* 133 32 ; 556 14; *inf.,* 575 9;—A.S. *witan.*

wytted, *adj.* or *p.p.,* clever, having wit, 253 27.

wyttely, *adv.,* cleverly, 472 15.

y, (1) I, *pron. pers.* ; **y gaf,** 46 36;— A.S. *ic;* (2) **y-,** *prefix = ge;* **y barryd,** 780 27 ; **y fonde,** 699 35 ; **ynombred,** 178 7; **y sette,** 822 32 ; **y sought,** 754 1 ;—A.S. *ge-.*

yate, *sb.,* the gate, 39 7; 91 9;— A.S. *geat.*

ye, *adv.,* yes, 100 14; **yis,** 93 16;— A.S. *gese (géa* and *-se).*

yede, *pt.,* went, 97 36; 110 30; 150 33; **yode,** *pt.,* 185 31;—A.S. *ye-éode.*

yefte, *sb.,* gift, 481 24; **yeftes,** *pl.,* 453 5;—A.S. *gift,* Icel. *gipt.*

yelde, *v.,* to pay, yield; *inf.,* 15 31; 24 13; *prs.,* 71 34; **yelded** (hym), *pt.,* 13 23; 16 3; **yelden,** *p.p.,* 13 1; **yolde,** *pt.,* 189 23; **yolden,** *p.p.,* 180 29 ;—A.S. *geldan.*

yelle, *v.,* to yell; **yellynge,** *p.prs.,* 654 20;—A.S. *gellan.*

yeue, *v.,* to give; *inf.,* 38 11; **yeuen,** *p.p.,* 44 9; 61 36; 412 4; 518 6; **foryaf,** *pt.,* 43 32;—A.S. *gifan. Compare* **gyue.**

yland, *sb.,* island, 422 34;—A.S. *igland.*

ylle, *sb.* and *adj.,* bad, ill, 208 27; 648 1;—Icel. *illr.*

ynde, *sb.,* dark-blue colour;—O.F. *inde,* Lat. *India.*

ynowe, *adj.* and *adv.,* enough, 101 1; **ynow,** 71 6;—A.S. *genóh.*

yole, *sb.,* Yule, Christmas, 177 25;— A.S. *geóla.*

yoman, *sb.,* youth, servant, 646 36: **yemen,** *pl.,* 845 2.—*See* Skeat, Dict.

yongthe, *sb.,* youth, 276 31;—from A.S. *géoguð, gióguð.*

yre, *sb.,* anger, spite, 58 28 ; 391 22; 418 22;—Lat. *ira. See* **ire.**

yssue, *sb.,* issue; **yssues,** *pl.,* 36 3; —A.F. *issue.*

yssue, *v.,* to issue; **yssued,** *pt.,* 403 10.

ytalyen, *adj.,* Italian, 2 35.

ʒere, *sb.,* ear, 778 30 (Wynkyn de Worde has *ere;* ed. 1634, *eare;* Sir E. Strachey reads *ear*);—A.S. *éare.*

CPSIA information can be obtained
at www.ICGtesting.com
Printed in the USA
LVHW081200180721
693015LV00004B/135

9 781375 449618